UNSUSTAINABLE EMPIRE

Statehood

15 years today
        since Statehood
and it's raining-

feel like
        crying

UNSUSTAINABLE EMPIRE ALTERNATIVE HISTORIES OF HAWAI'I STATEHOOD

DEAN ITSUJI SARANILLIO

Duke University Press | Durham and London | 2018

© 2018 Duke University Press
All rights reserved
Printed in the United States of America on acid-free paper ∞
Designed by Heather Hensley
Typeset in Warnock Pro by Westchester Publishing Services

Library of Congress Cataloging-in-Publication Data
Names: Saranillio, Dean Itsuji, [date] author.
Title: Unsustainable empire : alternative histories of Hawai'i
statehood / Dean Itsuji Saranillio.
Description: Durham : Duke University Press, 2018. |
Includes bibliographical references and index.
Identifiers: LCCN 2018021934 (print) | LCCN 2018026377 (ebook)
ISBN 9781478002291 (ebook)
ISBN 9781478000624 (hardcover : alk. paper)
ISBN 9781478000839 (pbk. : alk. paper)
Subjects: LCSH: Hawaii—Politics and government—1900–1959. |
Hawaii—Politics and government—1959– | Hawaii—
History—1900–1959. | Hawaii—History—1959– | Statehood
(American politics) | Hawaiians—Political activity.
Classification: LCC DU627.5 (ebook) | LCC DU627.5 .S27 2018
(print) | DDC 996.9/04—dc23
LC record available at https://lccn.loc.gov/2018021934

Frontispiece: "Statehood," by Wayne Kaumualii Westlake
(1974).

Cover art: Banners that read "HAWAIIAN INDEPENDENCE"
with military fighter aircraft. Photo taken from inside the
Hawai'i State Capitol building, March 18, 2009. Photograph
courtesy of Jonathan Shishido.

FOR Heijin, Hyun, and Yuna

Mother Eloise, Father Dick,
Candace, Shelley, and Drew

Tai, Kota, Devan, Sheyne,
Nanami, and Sora

CONTENTS

PREFACE   "Statehood Sucks"

The owner of a popular Facebook group, "We Grew Up on Maui," posted a photo of a rusting green Chevrolet SUV. In keeping with displaying one's place-based relation to a larger island community via their hopes or concerns, the straight-to-the-point bumper sticker read, "STATEHOOD SUCKS." The caption to the photo added: "Just happened to see this bumper sticker today—Statehood Day—while I was eating breakfast in Kahului. #Ironic."

Such irony is heightened under conditions of occupation as most residents of Hawai'i, and U.S. residents generally, view opposition to statehood as contradictory and unexpected. Such dissent is often dismissed as humorous and kolohe, or "mischievous," yet futile because statehood is imagined as not only having been resolved back in 1959 but permanently settled, the highest form of U.S. governance attainable—the pinnacle of settler civilization. Yet, lying quietly just behind this dismissal is a well of discomfort. Such discomfort might serve as a space of learning, as Kanaka 'Ōiwi (Native Hawaiian) history and an ever-growing movement not only questions the very legitimacy of the United States in Hawai'i, but importantly offers culturally rich and historically meaningful alternatives to the current system. As such, "Statehood Day" or Admission Day becomes a state holiday that enables most to grapple with a major historical contradiction for anyone who has even moderately learned about Hawai'i's history.

This contradiction, however, is not limited to Hawai'i. The neat and tidy spatial geographies of fifty U.S. states constrains imaginative space,

Figure P.1 "Statehood Sucks" bumper sticker from the Facebook group "We Grew Up on Maui," August 16, 2013.

normalizing what Chickasaw scholar Jodi A. Byrd calls the "cacophony of colonialism."[1] The spatial and temporal framing of the fifty U.S. states—the fifty stars adorning the U.S. flag—produces a web of colonial and imperial formations that make absent the over 567 federally recognized tribal nations as of 2017. This number is still not an accurate index of the different Native nations navigating encroaching settler governments.[2] The discourse of fifty states further obscures U.S. territories in Guåhan (Guam), American Samoa, Puerto Rico, the U.S. Virgin Islands, and the Commonwealth of the Northern Mariana Islands, and, importantly, the diverse movements for self-determination across these sites. It similarly obscures the estimated eight hundred military bases as of 2015, outside of the United States, that make it the largest militarized empire in world history.[3] Still, this is only a glimpse into how far-reaching the United States is outside of the territorial borders of fifty states, given its use of black sites, drone warfare, and the imperial legacies of overt and covert wars that have led to the overthrow of numerous countries, including Hawai'i.[4]

U.S. states and their organizing power are such an intimate part of everyday life that they are often not considered a site of colonial critique. This is despite having emerged from intense colonial violence. The Native counterclaims to such obfuscating official histories of statehood are typically made public in the years when different states attempt to commemorate their statehood. In November of 2007, for instance, more than five hundred elders, adults, and children from a wide diversity of Native American nations gathered at the Oklahoma State Capitol to oppose the Oklahoma public schools, which as a part of their statehood celebration forced students to reenact the Oklahoma land runs. Taking place in the last decade of the nineteenth century, land runs enabled white settlers to claim Native lands, planting themselves in Indian Territory, which had already been designated by the federal government for different Native nations. Many of these same Native nations had been previously dispossessed and forcefully removed from their traditional territories under genocidal conditions to make way for earlier instances of white settlement. Protestors carried signs that read "THIS LAND IS OUR LAND" and "THE LAND RUN WAS ILLEGAL IMMIGRATION," along with a large banner that read "WHY CELEBRATE 100 YEARS OF THEFT?" The organizer of the Oklahoma Indians Survival Walk and Remembrance Ceremony, Muscogee Creek Nation citizen Brenda Golden, said she wanted to make a statement that the celebrations were "an affront to the true history of how Oklahoma was legislatively stolen from the people to whom it was promised."[5]

The following year, in 2008, Native demonstrations opposed the 150-year anniversary of the state of Minnesota. Carrying thirty-eight nooses—representative of the thirty-eight Dakota who were executed on Abraham Lincoln's orders on December 26, 1862—Native demonstrators highlighted the genocidal violence of state formation, showing how the public executions were the federal government's response to the Dakota War of 1862. The public mass execution of the thirty-eight Dakota is the largest in U.S. history. Dakota scholar-activist Waziyatawin states that while the protestors pushed for Minnesota state officials to use this year for "truth-telling," state leaders "refused and wanted to continue with their birthday celebration and not let truth-telling get in the way."[6] In her book *What Does Justice Look Like?*, Waziyatawin asks, "What does it mean that Dakota extermination and forced removal (as well as Ho-Chunk removal) were the price of Minnesota's statehood? And, what does it mean in the twenty-first century when Minnesotans celebrate the establishment of the state, despite its shameful historical legacy and the harmful consequences to whole nations of Indigenous peoples?"[7] When the state of Minnesota commemorated its sesquicentennial celebration with a Statehood Wagon that was to travel 101 miles to the state capitol, Dakota people blocked the wagon as it passed Fort Snelling. Fort Snelling offered the colonial force necessary for settlers to create Minnesota statehood, and the fort was itself built overlooking the sacred site of creation for the Dakota. It was also at Fort Snelling that the Dakota were held in concentration camps. Indeed, every U.S. state has a statehood story to tell. These improvisational histories are unique and geopolitical, and continue to play out by normalizing a general silence around Native histories. Whether forcing schoolchildren to reenact land theft or using a Statehood Wagon to commemorate scenes of conquest, the theatricality of the settler state aims to produce good citizen-subjects who revisit historical moments of colonial violence to renew and legitimate ongoing forms of settler colonialism.

In this way, the formation of U.S. states is the violent work of replacing one landscape with another, various modes of life with another, various peoples with another, all of which necessitates a discursive regime—underpinned by juridical and military force—that normalizes occupation and makes sense of the genocide that this kind of replacement requires. Thus, while the Northwest Ordinance of 1787—a blueprint for expansion and the formation of U.S. territories and states—is popularly imagined as foundational U.S. national policy, Philip J. Deloria (Dakota) argues that it should instead be understood as U.S. Indian policy.[8] A clear-cut example of how U.S. states are formed via complex processes of settler colonialism, the Northwest Ordinance illustrates how settler state formation lies at a complicated intersection of diaspora and indigeneity, how those deemed settlers are at once both displaced and displacing.[9] The Ordinance states that after achieving a large enough settler population (five thousand "free male inhabitants of age") white settlers could proceed to organize and incorporate themselves as new territories. After proving capable of reaching a population of sixty thousand and drafting a state constitution, these territories could petition Congress to recognize them as newly formed states on equal footing with previous U.S. states. It is through the fictive creation of nation, states, and property that such settlers are able to seize Native wealth.[10]

The colonial discourse of fifty U.S. states, thus contains one's temporal and spatial imagination of the scale of U.S. empire while also denying the violent imperial histories on the very land beneath our feet. While the linear transition from Native territories to U.S. territories and then to statehood is narrated as the recognition of a maturing government—the destiny of incorporated territories—these transitions are underpinned by racial and gendered discourse. In other words, U.S. statehood has meant not only the containment of seemingly primitive Native nations, but settler expansion was often animated by "proslavery imperialists."[11] Statehood thus masks the very settler-colonial makeup of the settler nation wherever it claims territoriality, which then absolves individuals and governments of any wrongdoing even as its continued existence relies on an expansion of racial violence and the ongoing containment of Native political, cultural, and spiritual associations with place.

In Hawai'i, as elsewhere, statehood operates as a knowledge-making spectacle that abates U.S. occupation and settler colonialism by giving the illusion of settler state permanence, yet requires constant recalibration to shore up ongoing processes of dispossession. There is a photograph that graced the front page of the *Honolulu Star-Bulletin* on the fiftieth anniversary of Hawai'i's admission as a U.S. state that visually illustrates these tensions. It was taken from inside the Hawai'i State Capitol, looking up through the open-air rotunda. Flowing red and black banners that read "HAWAIIAN INDEPENDENCE" wave in the wind in the foreground and are juxtaposed with two military fighter jets doing an aerial flyover of the capitol building in the background. The atrium of the state of Hawai'i capitol building frames the fighter aircraft and the independence banners. A similar photograph in the daily paper—which in the decades prior to statehood was firmly committed to shaping public opinion in its favor—colors with unease and ambivalence the front-page headline "50 YEARS OF STATEHOOD."

Figure P.2 Banners that read "HAWAIIAN INDEPENDENCE" with military fighter aircraft. Photo taken from inside the Hawai'i State Capitol building, March 18, 2009. Photograph courtesy of Jonathan Shishido.

March 18, 2009, the day the photograph was taken, commemorated the signing of the Admission Act, and the Hawaiian Independence Action Alliance (HIAA) had organized a demonstration to counter the state's celebration of itself. Throughout 2009, the HIAA organized marches and public art actions; produced television shows, radio shows, and public talks; held film screenings and community events; and provided other spaces for public dialogue about Hawai'i's admission as a U.S. state.[12] The group aimed to create an alternative message by using alternative media forms and, unlike the Statehood Commission, which had a $600,000 budget to commemorate U.S. statehood, the HIAA was a strictly grassroots effort with no financial support. Anticipating such actions, the state of Hawai'i ruled that no signs would be allowed inside the open-air capitol building. The group planned accordingly and each participant wore a black shirt with a single bright-green letter to collectively spell out the phrases "FAKE STATE" and "HISTORY OF THEFT." Longtime organizer and professor of anthropology Lynette Cruz argued to the press: "There was no treaty of annexation. Show me the treaty. There's been an incorrect interpretation of history all these years."[13] Although the

Figure P.3 The Hawaiian Independence Action Alliance (HIAA) demonstration at the Fiftieth Anniversary of Statehood Commemoration at the Hawai'i State Capitol, March 18, 2009. Photograph courtesy of Jonathan Shishido.

local newspapers and news channels limited their coverage of the demonstration to a brief mention, coverage by the Associated Press provided the group with national and international attention. The late Hawaiian activist Richard Pomai Kinney, who was nineteen years old at the time of statehood, is quoted as saying: "Statehood is a fraud. My parents said Hawai'i would become only a place for the wealthy. Look at it today. There's nothing to celebrate."[14]

At the time of the action, I was a graduate student finishing my dissertation on Hawai'i's admission as a U.S. state and actively organizing with the HIAA. As a fourth-generation Filipino and Japanese settler from Kahului, Maui, I was informed by recent scholarship on settler colonialism in Hawai'i which challenged and expanded my working-class worldview. I had been exposed to Kanaka 'Ōiwi histories and struggles as an undergraduate at the University of Hawai'i, but much of this became crystalized while working as a valet in Waikīkī. Wayne Kaumualii Westlake (whose poem "Statehood" is the frontispiece to this book) and his 1973 poem about working as a janitor in Waikīkī, one of which says simply that he "wrote poems to keep from going insane," resonated with me.[15]

At work, I would witness racist and colonial dynamics play out nightly, in unexpected ways, and the violent realities of occupation kept me up at night. This is to say that by the time I was writing the dissertation the stakes of what I was studying felt urgent and I aimed for my scholarship to be accountable and relevant outside of the university. Knowing that the commemoration of U.S. statehood lent itself to conversations between Hawaiians and non-Hawaiians, I planned the completion of my dissertation at the University of Michigan to coincide with the fiftieth anniversary of Hawai'i statehood in 2009. Throughout the year, I was invited to speak at different events and made every effort to make my work publicly accessible through presentations at community centers, bookstores, television and radio talk shows, local television news interviews, national and local newspaper interviews, university talks, conference panels, colloquiums, and various events throughout the islands. I aimed to offer a "history of the present" that placed the commemoration of statehood within a genealogy of settler colonialism and U.S. imperialism, by offering historical evidence of Kanaka 'Ōiwi opposition to statehood and showing how such resistance was targeted for silencing by state agencies.[16]

In the planning of the March 2009 action, Lynette Cruz asked me to carry the banners that read "HAWAIIAN INDEPENDENCE" into the capitol building, saying she would take photos of the moment when security attempted to stop me from entering. As a security guard confronted me, I tried my best to create a useful photo op but, because he was older than me, it felt disrespectful to argue with him and we instead ended up talking story. He eventually let me through and as I looked toward Lynette to see if she had gotten a good photo, she simply laughed. As the action continued, Uncle Kekuni Blaisdell, Auntie Terri Keko'olani, Lorenz Gonschor, Johanna Almiron, and S. Heijin Lee held each other's hands as they moved directly in front of the U.S. Pacific Fleet Band, interrupting their performance of U.S. naval songs to spell the word *theft*. There were numerous similar actions, enough for those celebrating statehood to move behind closed doors into the chambers of the state House of Representatives. The HIAA group moved together to Beretania Street where motorists driving by read the signs and many honked their horns in solidarity. As we moved back into the capitol building, the Uncle who was working security stopped me and spoke softly: "If you like one good picture, put

Figure P.4 Members of the HIAA together spell the word *theft*, March 18, 2009. Photograph courtesy of Jonathan Shishido.

your banners in the rotunda when the jets fly over." He told me what time the flyover was supposed to start and I notified artist and media activist Jonathan Shishido, whose photo of the moment is featured here (figure P.2), as well as the media journalists covering the action.

What is haunting to me about the photograph is that the major players in Hawai'i's contemporary history are represented while in movement. The constraining logics of the settler state frame the photo, while the coercive nature of empire via its military jets are in the background. Hawaiian independence is figured not only, however, in words but also in a particular form that illustrates how this independence endures but also exceeds the political possibilities of the United States. Donna Burns, the prolific Kanaka 'Ōiwi artist who created the banners (most from Hawai'i would be familiar with her design of the Local Motion Hawai'i logo) conceived of the independence banners to look like the symbol of Lono, a major deity of peace, agriculture, rainfall, and fertility. Military fighter jets designed to resolve political issues with warfare are juxtaposed against a notion of political sovereignty expressed in sacred form tied to life, farming, and peace.

Scholar and activist Noelani Goodyear-Ka'ōpua argues against seeing the settler state as the center of political life, and asserts that sovereignty is not something to be recognized or achieved, but instead practiced at both an individual and collective level. Ea—translated as "rising," "life," "breath," "sovereignty," or "autonomy"—is realized in the present via actions and does not require waiting for the United States to leave Hawaiʻi. In her introduction to the anthology *A Nation Rising*, Goodyear-Kaʻōpua argues that Kanaka ʻŌiwi notions of sovereignty precede and exceed Western notions of sovereignty. Ea is first attached to state-based sovereignty in 1843 after British occupation of the Hawaiian Islands ends and King Kauikeaouli consequently declares, "Ua mau ke ea o ka aina i ka pono," roughly translated as "The life or sovereignty of the land is perpetuated by righteousness." Referencing the work of Leilani Basham and Kaleikoa Kaʻeo, Goodyear-Kaʻōpua points out that even in this moment of deoccupation, Kauikeaouli locates sovereignty not in the government but in the land.[17] Such ways of conceptualizing Hawaiian independence are beyond the political imagination of Western and settler sovereignty; instead, they aim for the flourishing of the conditions of life—the very thing that the permanent conditions of warfare, rampant capitalist development, and their progeny, climate crisis, can destroy. As kumu hula Olana Ai is often quoted as saying: "Aloha is the intelligence with which we meet life."[18]

Despite my expectation that the non-Hawaiian security guard at the state capitol was not an ally for Hawaiian independence—and I am sure that I looked out of place to him as well—it is thanks to his astute political and creative imagination that the photograph with the words "HAWAIIAN INDEPENDENCE" appeared on the front page on the fiftieth anniversary of statehood and is thus archived in the official historical record. Although I argue that the histories existent in this book are very much alive in the present, as evidenced by the interactions between the security guard and me they do not overdetermine our present; and we collectively mediate and change such histories with every action and choice we make.

In this way, diverse non-Native communities can remain vigilant in resisting oppressive systems that enhance various vulnerabilities against us, while also working to become aware of the colonial structures ingrained in U.S. nationalism that render invisible the genocidal violence committed against Kānaka ʻŌiwi. More to the point, not taking into account structures of settler colonialism and occupation can unwittingly reproduce the appearance of legitimate sovereignty by the occupying U.S. settler state. While migration in and of itself does not equate to colonialism, migration to a settler-colonial space—where Native lands and resources are under political, ecological, and spiritual contestation—means that the political agency of diverse non-Native communities can bolster a colonial system initiated by white settlers. The inverse, however, is also true. The political agency of various non-Native communities can also play an important role in bolstering Native movements for deoccupation, many of which are organized around the flourishing of the conditions of all life. Settler states have no interest in non-Natives identifying with Native movements as that opens our visual world to an awareness of processes of settler accumulation by Native dispossession, thus opposing a system set by white supremacy that, while *differently*, comes at the expense of *all of us*.

ACKNOWLEDGMENTS

From the start of graduate school, this book has taken fifteen years to complete. In this time, I have been held by a large and growing community of family, friends, and colleagues. I am grateful for this opportunity to express my appreciation and love for the generosity that has shaped me.

I begin by thanking my most recent ancestors, Grandma Masako Inouye, Grandma Mildred Gragas, Grandpa Itsuji Inouye, Grandpa Fred Saranillio, Uncle Fred Jr. Saranillio, Auntie Janet Yamanoi, Patrick Wolfe, Kekuni Blaisdell, Gigi Miranda, Paul Lyons, Teresia Teaiwa, Juan Flores, and Dawn Bohulano Mabalon. I feel the inertia of your life's intentions even after you have each walked on.

If it wasn't for Candace Fujikane's inspiration and encouragement, I would not have written this book or pursued a PhD. I learn from her example not only as my oldest sister but also as a person whose compassion and love for our communities is so strong that she consistently is able to take strong stances without fear of criticism.

After reading her books, articles, and poetry, in my senior year at the University of Hawai'i, I finally felt ready to take a course with Haunani-Kay Trask. I would never be the same after this course. After class, I would work a ten-hour shift as a valet in Waikīkī. Seeing what we discussed in class, the existence of a freshwater spring under the hotel where workers would urinate, the racist and sexist joy that tourists experience being served by someone brown, reading the Blount report in a parking booth— all of it was enough to completely change my view of the world. Her continued mentorship and phone calls while I was in graduate school and our shared meals when I returned home helped me continue studying settler colonialism at a time when it was not academically advisable to do so.

My dissertation committee at the University of Michigan helped me to articulate ideas that often felt unmanageable. I wish to thank Vicente M. Diaz for chairing my dissertation and tightening my writing and thinking on this topic. No other person could quite grasp the stakes of this project like he could. His tenacious and creative intellect helped me to navigate the precariousness of academia. The diverse talents and strengths of my dissertation committee taught me to think from a range of fields and methods. I am grateful to Philip J. Deloria, Penny Von Eschen, Damon Salesa, and Amy K. Stillman, who each planted his or her own seeds of thought that continue to shape my thinking and teaching.

I was fortunate to find a collective of graduate students at the University of Michigan who helped create a noncompetitive atmosphere that was truly about collective learning and sharing. A deep thank you to Brian Chung, Tyler Cornelius, Tina Delisle, Sam Erman, Lorgia García-Peña, Lloyd Grieger, Cynthia Marasigan, Afia Ofori-Mensa, Isa Quintana, Kiri Sailiata, Kelly Sisson, Urmila Venkatesh, and Lee Ann S. Wang. In particular, Kealani Cook, Stephanie Nohelani Teves, and I formed a writing hui across six time zones that was indispensable to every chapter of this book.

In the summer of 2016, my department organized a manuscript workshop inviting two exceptional scholars from Hawai'i, Noenoe K. Silva and Noelani Goodyear-Ka'ōpua. They each generously offered detailed notes, productive criticisms, and generative conceptual thoughts. Each of their ideas is engaged with in these pages. Their friendship and high standards, as well as their own activism and scholarship, has inspired me to ground this book in what is politically relevant. J. Kēhaulani Kauanui has also been a key interlocutor from whom I have learned so much about anarchist critiques of the settler state through paneling and writings. While I was a graduate student she read various conference papers and gave me detailed responses, and as a professor she has written me letters of recommendation in moments when she was already overburdened with work. I have always been in awe of her uncompromising politics and brilliant analyses of settler colonialism, and I am inspired by her generous nurturing of junior scholars.

My colleagues at New York University have been a major support for thinking through this project, understanding its implications, and conceptualizing it in book form. I wish to thank the entire Department of Social and Cultural Analysis (SCA) faculty, staff, and students. Faculty from SCA generously spent their time during precious summer months to read the manuscript and attend the manuscript workshop. My deepest gratitude goes to Cristina Beltrán, Arlene Davila, Gayatri Gopinath, Jennifer L. Morgan, Crystal Parikh, Andrew Ross, John Kuo Wei Tchen, and Nikhil Pal Singh. Nikhil has been a great mentor and friend. He not only read through the manuscript, but has read different drafts of the manuscript. I thank him for his political acumen and critical support. From everything to comments on specific chapters to interesting conversations/discussion at presentations, I am grateful to Awam Amkpa, Jane Anderson, Paula Chakravartty, Carolyn Dinshaw, Lisa Duggan, Luis H. Francia, Mike Funk, Faye Ginsburg, Rebecca Goetz, Monica Kim, Julie Livingston, Agnes "Bing" Magtoto, Cecilia Márquez, Fred Myers, Andrew Needham, Tavia Nyong'o, Michael Ralph, Ann Pellegrini, Renato Rosaldo, María Josefina Saldaña-Portillo, David Samuels, S. S. Sandhu, Pacharee Sudhinaraset, and Thuy Linh Nguyen Tu. I especially wish to thank Mary Louise Pratt for reading the introduction and constant advice, mentorship, and support. At a critical moment in my writing two hires at NYU were instrumental in helping me to further engage Native studies and critiques of settler colonialism. Simón Trujillo was hired in English and I have learned from his deep and imaginative theorizing of settler colonialism in New Mexico and, just as importantly, have enjoyed sharing funny anecdotes and survival stories about our new roles as dads. Elizabeth Ellis was hired in History and her presence has already made the continued growth of Native American and Indigenous Studies at NYU much stronger. My gratitude also to the staff at SCA: Marlene Brito, Betts Brown, Marty Correia, Nou Moua, Krystal Roberts, and Janiene Thiong, as well as the generous staff at the Asian/Pacific/American Institute: Alexandra Chang, Laura Chen-Schultz, Ruby Gómez, and Amita Manghnani.

A larger artist, activist, and intellectual community exists in New York City around issues that are close to my heart. Thank you to the NYC Stands with Standing Rock Collective, Decolonize This Place, and Nā 'Ōiwi NYC for helping me to plug into organizing and activism so far from home. In 2015, the Heyman Center for the Humanities and the Center for Palestine Studies at Columbia University invited me to workshop what has become chapter 5. This included a detailed and generative response from the brilliant Audra Simpson, and thought-provoking discussion with Lila Abu-Lughod, Nadia Abu El-Haj, Mark Rifken, Alyosha Goldstein, Paige West, Robert Nichols, and Neferti Tadiar.

A continuity of conversations across different conferences and over a number of years has been the most generative of spaces for completing this book. Specifically, the American Studies Association (ASA), Association for Asian American Studies (AAAS), and the Native American and Indigenous Studies Association (NAISA) each has been a site for growth and discussion. This is perhaps too long a list, and apologies because each person here deserves specific praise. To the numerous scholars who differently traverse these sites, thank you for your radical scholarship and activism across diverse landscapes of resurgence: Katherine Achacoso, Hokulani Aikau, Dean Alegado, Ibrahim Aoude, Maile Arvin, Cristina Bacchilega, Nerissa S. Balce, Leilani Basham, Moustafa Bayoumi, Michael Lujan Bevacqua, Maylei Blackwell, Marie Alohalani Brown, Jodi A. Byrd, Ellen-Rae Cachola, Keith L. Camacho, Iokepa Casumbal-Salazar, David A. Chang, Kandice Chuh, Kim Compoc, Kathleen Corpuz, Glen Coulthard, Denise Ferreira da Silva, Iyko Day, Jaskiran Dhillon, Evyn Lê Espiritu, May Farrales, Cindy Franklin, Ruth Wilson Gilmore, Mishuana Goeman, Macarena Gomez-Barris, Vernadette Vicuña Gonzalez, William Gow, Sandy Grande, Jack Halberstam, Lisa Kahaleole Hall, Kara Hisatake, Hiʻilei Hobart, kuʻualoha hoʻomanawanui, Yu-Ting Huang, Sam Ikehara, Adria Imada, Bianca Isaki, Ann Iwashita, Kyle Kajihiro, Noel Kent, Jodi Kim, Eiko Kosasa, Karen Kosasa, Bryan Kamaoli Kuwada, Ilima Long, Laura E. Lyons, David Maile, Sam Markwell, Oscar Marquez, Brandy Nalani McDougal, Davianna Pōmaikaʻi McGregor, Susana Morales, Scott Lauria Morgensen, Nadine Naber, Tad Nakamura, Logan Narikawa, Jonathan Okamura, Josephine Faith Ong, Juliana Hu Pegues, Craig Santos Perez, Kristy Hisako Ringor, Dylan Rodríguez, Judy Rohrer, Demiliza Saramosing, Christen Sasaki, Cheryl Geslani Scarton, Sarita Echavez See, Chad Shomura, Leanne Betasamosake Simpson, Laurel Mei Singh, Dean Spade, David Stannard, Erin Suzuki, Sunaura Taylor, Ty P. Kāwika Tengan, Kēhaulani Vaughn, Michael Viola, Julkipli Wadi, Liza Keānuenueokalani Williams, Erin Kahunawaikaʻala Wright, and Aiko Yamashiro.

I am in deep wondrous gratitude to Lynette Cruz for her tireless organizing and leadership. Roderick Labrador, Johanna Almiron, Faye Caronan, and Tracy Lachica Buenavista: thank you for the continued laughter and friendship even across long distances. Diana Yoon and Manu Vimalassery: I am happy that we are able to continually convene enjoyment studies gatherings now that we are all in closer proximity.

I am indebted to Ken Wissoker, who has been an encouraging voice from when this project was in prospectus form. He also generously attended my department's manuscript workshop, offering detailed and concrete suggestions for edits. Thank you to Anitra Grisales and Emma Jacobs for editing suggestions that have helped to streamline the flow of the book. Thank you to the Duke University Press team who worked on this book: Olivia Polk, Susan Albury, Christopher Robinson, Heather Hensley, Mary Hoch, and Chad Royal for helping to calmly guide this book to fruition.

A special thank you to Jonathan Shishido for permission to use his photographs of the 2009 statehood protests, and to Richard Hamasaki and Mei-Li M. Siy for permission to reprint and for going to great lengths to provide images of Wayne Kaumualii Westlake's poem, "Statehood."

I last wish to thank my family. I have witnessed both of my parents work tirelessly and unselfishly in order to lovingly raise their children in ways that I can only hope to emulate. My mother, Eloise Saranillio, is a retired teacher who often held three jobs. She loved her students to the extent that if they were not getting support at home, during the weekends she (and I) would pick her student up and take him or her to the movies. My father, Dick Saranillio, has an uncompromising wit and impatience for injustice that undoubtedly inspired me and this book. He always helped make the road smoother for me and worked to provide everything that he was never given. Shelley Takasato is strong and grounded. Drew Saranillio is smart, kind, and funny. He is the best brother anyone could ever ask for. Tai, Kota, Devan, Sheyne, Nanami, and Sora, Uncle Dean loves his nieces and nephews very much. Ahpa and Oma, Myungho and Songza Lee, hearing our little ones laugh uncontrollably (they are doing so as I write this), fills my heart with joy that allows me to work on this book knowing the kids are exactly where they need to be. Thank you for all you have done for us, but especially for raising Heijin the way you did.

S. Heijin Lee is simply my best friend. She's my partner, our family's rock, and she helps each of us to be better people. Heijin has grace, strength, and practices a form of intelligence that is loving and wise. She also knows as much about settler colonialism in Hawai'i as I do about her research, the geopolitics of beauty in South Korea. In recent years, I have especially loved watching her grow into becoming a mother to our son, Enzo Hyun Saranillio Lee, who came to us in 2015 and our daughter, Eloise Yuna Saranillio Lee, who was born in 2017. I cannot express the pride that their very existence brings to my heart, the joy in being with them both, and the admiration I already have for each of their unique personalities. I hope something at some point in their lives makes them feel the way they both make me feel.

COLLIDING FUTURES OF HAWAI'I STATEHOOD

> Said moneys . . . being illegally expended are used to aid private
> purposes and individuals and are an illegal gift of public moneys
> to the proponents of statehood for Hawaii . . . to the exclusion
> and detriment of citizens and taxpayers of the territory of Hawaii
> opposed to statehood.
>
> —Alice Kamokilaikawai Campbell, plaintiff in *Campbell v. Stainback*
> *et al.* lawsuit filed on January 17, 1948 (anniversary of the U.S.-backed
> overthrow of the Hawaiian Kingdom)

Contrary to the romantic images of Hawai'i as an exotic American paradise, peddled globally by a multibillion-dollar tourism industry, heated
political battles among groups armed with oppositional histories occur
frequently in Hawai'i. On the morning of August 19, 2006, for instance,
State Representative Barbara Marumoto, dressed as the Statue of Lib-
erty, and State Senator Sam Slom, waving a large American flag, led a
group of around fifty people to 'Iolani Palace to celebrate Admission Day.
This group's state-sponsored commemoration, however, was blocked by
Kanaka 'Ōiwi grassroots activists, also estimated at around fifty, who had
previously asked Marumoto and Slom to hold their celebration next door
at the state capitol. This group stated that 'Iolani Palace is sacred ground
and the site of the U.S. overthrow of the Hawaiian nation. It is also where
Queen Lili'uokalani was wrongfully imprisoned.[1] The two groups clashed
when the group celebrating statehood continued with their program and

began to sing "The Star-Spangled Banner," notably without accompaniment from the Kalani High School Band, which decided to leave the event and not get involved. The Hawaiian group countered by using a public address system to interrupt the U.S. national anthem. Verbal arguments and near-physical confrontations followed and continued for more than an hour, until the group celebrating statehood—tired and frustrated—decided to leave. The Hawaiian group formed a circle and prayed. In 2008, again on Admission Day, more than twenty members of another Kanaka 'Ōiwi group from the island of Maui were arrested for occupying 'Iolani Palace in an attempt to reinstate a Hawaiian government.

In 2009, on the fiftieth anniversary of Hawai'i's admission as a U.S. state, similar actions opposing U.S. statehood celebrations (like the action mentioned in the preface) took place in the months leading up to Admission Day. Concerned about protests on Admission Day and the possible impact on tourism, the state of Hawai'i quietly commemorated its golden anniversary by holding a public conference, "New Horizons for the Next 50 Years," to envision Hawai'i's future as a U.S. state. Meanwhile, Hawaiian groups and numerous non-Hawaiian supporters gathered outside to imagine a future world without U.S. imperialist influence. A twelve-foot-tall effigy of Uncle Sam, painted with dollar signs in his eyes and holding two large guns emblazoned with the words GENOCIDE and IMPERIALISM, led a march of more than a thousand people to the Hawai'i Convention Center where the conference was being held. The march was organized by Lynette Cruz, of the Hawaiian Independence Action Alliance (HIAA) also mentioned in the preface, and Poka Laenui, an attorney and expert on Hawai'i's international claims to independence. Two fellow activists and family members, Candace Fujikane and S. Heijin Lee, held up the GENOCIDE and IMPERIALISM guns, while Kealani Cook and myself helped to push the Uncle Sam effigy on a cart made to look like a U.S. military Stryker tank—a direct reference to a broad-based community struggle to oppose the military tanks being housed on the islands and the further contamination of lands used for live-fire training.[2]

Adding historical legibility and broader context to the protest, Uncle Sam's hat was decorated with feathers inscribed with the names of different nations whose sovereignties have been violated by the United States: First Nations, the Philippines, Guam, Puerto Rico, Cuba, and Iraq. In addition, around the Stryker tank were cutouts of bombs with the names of sites in Hawai'i and elsewhere that have been devastated by U.S. war and military training: Kaho'olawe, Mākua, Bikini, Hiroshima, Nagasaki, and Vieques. Through striking protest art and mass mobilization, the march and demonstration disrupted the official histories publicized in the months leading up to Admission Day and expanded on these narrations' deliberate silences—specifically the genocidal history of U.S. territorial expropriation and military occupation, both processes productive of U.S. statehood.[3] Outside the convention center, speakers addressed the consequences of the United States' presence in Hawai'i and its connections to other sites of U.S. empire. The portion of the demonstration that received the most public attention, however, was the cutting out and burning of the fiftieth star from the U.S. flag.[4]

The intensity of the protests on the fiftieth anniversary of U.S. statehood was not simply inspired by competing nationalisms, but shaped by a wide range of ongoing state-sanctioned assaults against Kānaka 'Ōiwi. Catalyzed by the 2008 global financial crisis, then Republican Governor Linda Lingle appealed to the U.S. Supreme Court to reverse a decision by the Hawai'i Supreme Court that had ruled that the state could not sell or transfer so-called ceded lands until claims on these lands by a future Hawaiian government had been resolved. These are Hawaiian crown and government lands that were seized by the United States—never ceded—at the time of alleged annexation, and then turned over to the state of Hawai'i through the 1959 Admission Act. On March 31, 2009, the High Court ruled that the 1993 Apology Resolution regarding U.S. "participation" in the overthrow of the Hawaiian Kingdom, as a congressional "resolution" requiring a simple rather than a two-thirds majority vote in Congress, did not sufficiently constitute a legal stop to the state's titles to the lands in question.[5] The absurdity of such a decision is that the U.S. annexation over all of Hawai'i was based on just such a resolution, the Newlands Resolution, which was passed by Congress in 1898.[6]

Because such acts of settler accumulation by Native dispossession are central to the economic and political governance of the settler state, state-sanctioned assaults against Kānaka 'Ōiwi have been met with a growing and resilient stand for Native resurgence on numerous fronts. These different fronts include continued desecration by corporate, military, state, and residential developments on Hawaiian sacred sites and burials, such as the proposed construction of a Thirty Meter Telescope on Mauna a

Wākea; the poisoning of communities by multinational agricultural corporations' GMO (genetically modified organism) and pesticide testing in the islands; the continued use of Pōhakuloa for live-fire military training; the various iterations of the Native Hawaiian Government Reorganization Act, or Akaka Bill, which aims to federally recognize Kānaka ʻŌiwi as a Native government, but a nation with no land guaranteed, and potentially precludes future claims to autonomy from the United States; and an unaffordable rental and real estate market responsible for a growing diaspora and tent cities filled primarily with "houseless" Hawaiians who line areas that tourists are told not to visit.[7] Although this is far from a comprehensive list of ongoing issues that continue to proliferate, it shows how the circulation of official state histories and exotic images of Hawaiʻi function to distribute a violent economy of occupation—domination through subjugation, profit through desecration, leisure through exploitation, and the articulation of conservative and liberal notions of U.S. civil rights that attempt to render the U.S. occupation of Hawaiʻi a logical impossibility.

Despite being under constant threat by entities whose interests directly conflict with Hawaiian political, ecological, and spiritual associations, Hawaiian protests of these exotic images and official state histories on Admission Day are often dismissed as ahistorical and politically contrived. Those who make charges of ahistoricism argue that Kānaka ʻŌiwi alive during the 1940s and 1950s wholly embraced statehood and played crucial roles in its achievement.[8] Such disavowals from positions of presumed omnipotence, however, are not without their own truths. One of the primary reasons U.S. statehood took nearly sixty years to accomplish was Hawaiʻi's largely nonwhite population. Southern congressmen were said to have passed around photographs of people from Hawaiʻi—Asians and Hawaiians—in order to sway other white congressmen to oppose statehood.[9] White racist exclusion, combined with the rise of imperial Japan in the early half of the twentieth century, created an inflated fear that Japanese communities in Hawaiʻi were scheming to "take over" the islands on behalf of the Japanese Empire. In response to such consistent instances of discrimination against Hawaiʻi's people, many in Hawaiʻi, including many Kānaka ʻŌiwi, did support a state-led movement to gain their civil rights as "first-class American citizens." Such support advanced a liberal and antiracist ideal that U.S. citizenship and democracy should not be limited to haole (foreigners, often specifically whites) only. Often referenced is the June 1959 congressionally mandated plebiscite, which revealed that of the 155,000 registered voters, seventeen to one were in favor of statehood (132,773 to 7,971).[10]

In the decades leading to the 1959 plebiscite, however, statehood proponents monopolized taxpayer monies to finance a protracted opinion campaign targeting a local and national population to support statehood. This campaign's control of public resources, as well as its volume and visibility, aimed to silence the opposition, even actively blocking Kānaka 'Ōiwi who, despite an atmosphere of intimidation, courageously spoke out against statehood. As Mililani Trask—former Pacific representative to the United Nations Permanent Forum on Indigenous Issues—has argued, the 1959 statehood ballot used in the plebiscite was written to limit the vote to either statehood or territorial status, and did not include the United Nations–mandated options for "independence" or other "separate systems of self-government."[11] In 1998, United Nations Rapporteur Miguel Martinez found Hawai'i's admission as a U.S. state to be in violation of international law, and he recommended to the United Nations that Hawai'i be placed back on the list of Non-Self-Governing Territories.[12]

If nations are themselves narrations, as cultural critics argue, then the government-led movement for statehood tells a familiar American story, a narrative of Western settlement and the linear evolution of the old into the new.[13] Yet, Hawai'i's statehood movement also narrates an American tale that is closely related to but distinct from the settlement stories told on the U.S. continent. Hawai'i's narrative tells a story not just of white settlement but of Asian settlement. This narration describes Hawai'i as a place where Asians, who were largely seen as "perpetual foreigners" by the American public, helped to settle an exotic territory in the middle of the Pacific Ocean—a place where the seemingly oppositional cultures of the East and West were reconciled to create what former President Barack Obama, who grew up in Hawai'i, has referred to as a "true melting pot of cultures."[14]

For many in Hawai'i, the history of statehood is an antiracist, civil rights victory preserved in popular memory, simultaneously a tale about a long struggle to oppose haole racist exclusion of Hawai'i's nonwhite communities and an expression of self-determination that was democratically and definitively settled. In this way, statehood is narrated as an important testament to multicultural forms of U.S. citizenship. Cold Warriors argued that such notions of liberal multicultural citizenship—articulated at the historical intersection of the Cold War, anti-Asian immigration and naturalization legislation, the African American civil rights movement, and federal termination of tribal nations—were going to have implications for world peace. Since the history of Hawai'i statehood is understood as a liberal moral allegory about the important inclusion of nonwhite groups into the United States, the idea that the civil liberties achieved through statehood came at the expense of Kānaka 'Ōiwi human rights to self-determination is cause for major contemporary conflict and animosity.[15] Moreover, the idea that statehood actually facilitated the growth of white supremacist power and privilege that was under threat is even more unimaginable to many.

In other words, despite the fact that statehood is primarily remembered as a moment when Hawai'i's nonwhite residents proved themselves American, and thus worthy of U.S. statehood, a deeper look into the propaganda commissions and the cultural politics of statehood reveals that business and state leaders had already determined statehood as their aim. It was congressional representations of Hawai'i as an "Asiatic" territory that served as an obstacle to achieving this; thus, proponents of statehood aimed to Americanize the nonwhite population only insofar as they were no longer seen as obstacles. The general public was not meant to participate in making these decisions; if judged by the criteria of a democratic free exchange of ideas and opinions, which is how statehood is often remembered, then these leaders failed Hawai'i into statehood. Democracy and debate about statehood, commonwealth, independence, or nonstatist forms of decolonization, were viewed as disruptions to the decisions that had already been made by supposedly superior minds, whose energies were spent less on including the voices of Hawai'i's different nonwhite citizenry than on "manufacturing consent" and rendering U.S. statehood immune to disruption.[16] Thus, stories of American egalitarianism, besides silencing Hawaiian opposition, obscure how economic crises and desires for capital expansion largely produced U.S. statehood.

Unsustainable Empire: Alternative Histories of Hawai'i Statehood thus offers a genealogy of the complex interplay between Kānaka 'Ōiwi, different Asian groups, and haole elites in historical flashpoints of interaction shaped by opposing versions of history. Organized around moments of U.S. economic crisis and capital expansion, each chapter examines how state agencies or propaganda commissions framed the rules of discourse for civil society through a range of state-sanctioned opinion campaigns that reveal affective settler statecraft and the extractive economy of the settler state. In thinking about settler statecraft and economic crises together, I defamiliarize the familiar narration of Hawai'i statehood by tracing how this narrative was produced. I present a genealogy of different propaganda commissions and concomitant series of knowledges of history, gender, and race that were deployed often with economic purposes, to materialize the historical domination that produced statehood. This book examines the organization of knowledge that facilitated economic imperatives, which took shape in various forms of accumulation via settler colonialism, labor, and U.S. militarism.

Building on the archive formation of Kanaka 'Ōiwi scholars who write about Kanaka 'Ōiwi resistance against U.S. occupation in the nineteenth century, I offer sources in the twentieth century that reveal Kanaka 'Ōiwi and non-Native opposition to the admission of Hawai'i as a U.S. state and cite this same history of occupation in the process. Instead of a political history examining powerful individuals and repressive institutions, I pursue a discursive approach to the historical study of statehood. I question the ways in which knowledge and power define and limit not only what is considered "sayable" in a given historical moment but also why certain voices achieve wide circulation and publicity, while still other voices are ridiculed, silenced, and censored.[17]

Kānaka 'Ōiwi did not all either embrace or reject statehood uniformly, but rather adopted a range of responses based on astute political assessments of changing conditions and possibilities occurring in Hawai'i at the time. Accordingly, I examine an asymmetrical discourse on statehood that censored or dismissed Hawaiian resistance as irrelevant to the present to reaffirm colonial power in the past, present, and future. Thus, instead of focusing on the usual suspects—canonized men who fought for statehood such as congressional delegates Joseph Farrington and John Burns, labor organizer Jack Hall, and Senator Daniel Inouye, all men who have been written about over and again in the official histories of statehood—I aim to expand our political imagination of this moment by proliferating divergent stories and unexpected individuals who were largely dismissed as deviant: historical revisionists, unruly women, subversives, communists, con men, gays, and criminals.

The lesser-known but no-less-important agents of history include Kathleen Dickenson Mellen, Abigail Kawānanakoa, Alice Kamokila Campbell, Sammy Amalu, George Wright, Koji Ariyoshi, John Reinecke, and others, many of whom were in conversation with each other and acted as a kind of cultural front—artists, politicians, writers, activists, and performers—who make up the kind of "unexpected" historical "anomalies" that may not be anomalous but, instead, representative. By recovering and examining the frequency of these "secret histories" we become better equipped to challenge historical characterizations and ideological assumptions that portray Kānaka ʻŌiwi as passive during the drive for statehood and write complex and transformative histories informed by or in relation to Kānaka ʻŌiwi cultural politics.[18] An engagement with such culturally grounded politics is critical, as many of these individuals went beyond criticizing imperial violence and aimed to preserve, protect, and enact ʻŌiwi alternatives to the settler state.

NORMALIZING U.S. OCCUPATION

Hawaiʻi's territorial period (1900–1959) is often imagined as a moment so thick in American ideology and patriotism that U.S. statehood was discussed without mention of the U.S. overthrow in 1893. This book shows that not only was the 1893 overthrow frequently invoked but it was persistent in shaping, even haunting, different moments in the decades leading to presumed statehood in 1959. As such, settler colonialism is critical to understanding the process by which the U.S. occupation in Hawaiʻi becomes normalized and, just as importantly, how this normalcy allows for forms of incredible violence to operate hidden in plain sight.

Unsustainable Empire thus breaks down the sharp divisions between analyses of occupation and settler colonialism. As the research and legal actions of numerous legal scholars have shown, the Hawaiian nation may have been overthrown, but subjects of the constitutional government had, in fact, never officially relinquished their national sovereignty.[19] The political consequence of this reality is that it places past and present Hawaiʻi under the formal category of "occupation," rather than a "colonized" territory, a status with equally different legal implications. Hawaiʻi's trea-sonous white settler community articulated their interests with that of the United States and, amid Hawaiian national protests, overthrew the government; then they purported to annex Hawaiʻi in 1898.

I contend that "occupation" and "settler colonialism" are not two irrec-oncilable polarizing frameworks; rather, these are actually both pertinent to an understanding of the uniqueness of Hawaiʻi's situation and the multi-ple tactics that the United States has utilized to occupy Hawaiʻi. Thus, the legal framework of occupation, which examines international law, sov-ereignty, and the law of occupation at an international level, provides a cogent understanding of the illegitimacy of the occupying United States, while at the level of power relations, a discussion of settler colonialism can help to describe the form of power that normalized such occupa-tion. This is to say, if occupation answers the "what" question—What is Hawaiʻi's political relationship with the United States?—then settler colo-nialism answers the "how" question—How did the United States normal-ize the U.S. occupation of Hawaiʻi? Hawaiʻi's patterns of settlement and legal and sovereign legacies, and the colonial discourses of dominance that enabled them, share characteristics of both settler colonialism and nation under occupation. Moreover, these forms of power were also used to establish a violent rationale set during the move for U.S. statehood through which Hawaiians are relegated as permanently "unfit for self-government." At the same time, different settlers who cannot be equated and who are contentious with one another are afforded the masculine and intellectual capacity to turn "primitive" Hawaiian lands into "mod-ern" and "democratic" societies.

SETTLER COLONIALISM FAILS FORWARD

In *Unsustainable Empire*, I argue that U.S. imperialist ventures in Hawaiʻi were not the result of a strong nation swallowing a weak and feeble island nation, but rather a result of a weakening U.S. nation whose mode of production—capitalism—was increasingly unsustainable without enact-ing a more aggressive policy of imperialism. If we think of forms of white supremacy, such as settler colonialism and capitalism, as emerging from positions of weakness, not strength, we can gain a more accurate un-derstanding of how the United States came to occupy Hawaiʻi. As such, settler colonialism "fails forward" into its various imperial formations, including what is intimately known as statehood.[20]

This framing highlights how the present failures of capitalism have long been imagined to be resolved through settler futures. Political thinkers in the early nineteenth century imagined that the establishment of white settler colonies, particularly in North America, would resolve the poverty capitalism produced in Europe.[21] Thus, European civil society was neither stable nor sustainable without relying on the external establishment of settler colonies. Karl Marx argued that such actions to resolve the contradictions of capitalism through emigration and settler colonialism only extend these problems globally, to other lands. That is, such forms of poverty will be reproduced, not resolved, in the settler colonies: "Notwithstanding California and Australia, notwithstanding the immense and unprecedented migration, there must even, without any particular accident, in due time arrive a moment when the extension of the markets is unable to keep pace with the extension of British manufactures, and this disproportion must bring about a new crisis, as it has done in the past."[22]

In this way, the failures of capitalism are most apparent from the colonies rather than the imperial metropoles. Such crises, caused by underconsumption and overproduction, reoccurred long after the initial colonization schemes of Europe. At the same time that Frederick Jackson Turner argued that the U.S. frontier was settled in 1890, an economic depression led to mass-scale labor unrest throughout the United States. Thus, Benjamin Harrison's administration initiated a U.S. foreign policy that Walter LaFeber calls "depression diplomacy," targeting colonies for access to markets to alleviate a glut of industrial goods.[23] Again, more land and markets were sought after, which violently incorporated Hawai'i and other island nations into the United States to alleviate such crises.

While the fail-forward pattern of capitalism often relies on colonial and imperial dispossession to resolve economic crises, such acts of state violence have a theatrical and discursive component to them. The state often relies on theatricality and opinion campaigns to legitimize such forms of violence, as the coup d'état necessitates legitimization and must be represented publicly as a means to capture public opinion. In this way, the birth of the economist is said to happen simultaneously with the birth of the publicist, since the economy and public opinion are each triangulated elements that correlate to government.[24]

Opinion campaigns or propaganda as forms of state theatricality are an important element in the affective work of settler statecraft. In other words, the political work of public opinion recruits subjects emotionally so as to achieve the structures of feeling necessary to sustain the conditions of settler colonialism.[25] In *The Question of Palestine*, for instance, Edward W. Said writes that the colonial project of settlers seeks to "cancel and transcend an actual reality . . . by means of a future wish—that the land be empty for development by a more deserving power."[26] That a present population can be designated for replacement by a "future wish" reveals how settler-colonial theft can be achieved through temporal and spatial tactics. Native peoples are continually made to suffer the present consequences of settler futures. In this way, we can understand the galvanizing power of a "future wish" but also simultaneously the dangerous possibilities of future-oriented abstractions that allow for escapism from Indigenous issues in the present.

Using tactics of theatricality and futurity, the settler state both imagines and propagandizes itself as a more deserving power, which seemingly absolves the settler state and its citizens from present accountability. As a more deserved power, bodies of laws, treaties, sovereignties, ethics, histories, ideas, or consistent failures are simply seen as being in the way of achieving this glorious "future wish." Both settler states and markets rely on such future-oriented abstractions. Advertising strategies utilize "abstraction" to produce a place or state of being that escapes from the present toward an imagined future where consumer are promised things that they will have, or lifestyles they can take part in.[27] Thus, non-Native subjectivities, though widely diverse, are often both in a state of incompletion and in transition to one's future self, escaping to a future place seemingly devoid of imperial violence and difficulties. For instance, white settlers in the 1930s came up with a catchphrase that celebrated their settlement of Hawai'i as a simultaneous act of forgetting: "Hawaii . . . ! I forget what I came here to forget."[28]

Hawai'i's U.S. statehood movement functioned in particular as a "future wish," a kind of settler abstraction of what Hawai'i could become if it were a state, and the American lifestyle one would have as a "first-class citizen," all of which positioned Kanaka 'Ōiwi forms of sovereignty, governance, foodways, and relations in Hawai'i as outmoded and a less deserving power than the emerging liberal settler state. To be sure, attempts to resolve the economic crises of the white settler elite in Hawaiʻi actually furnished them with the possibility of insulating and, in fact, expanding their power that had been under constant threat.

While economic reasons should not be seen as overly determining the motivations for annexation and statehood, they offer important context to the official narrations of the settler state. The economic depressions of the 1890s and 1930s motivated settler leaders to form propaganda commissions with the purpose of "incorporating" Hawaiʻi into the United States—in other words, attempting to solidify U.S. occupation—via alleged annexation and statehood. Settler planters saw this as a means to protect their markets for sugar in the United States. The battle over public opinion gained urgency, however, when it came to the possibility of eliminating tariffs through incorporation. As such, the Hawaiian Bureau of Information (1892–93) used "imperial advertisements" at the World's Columbian Exposition in Chicago to shape public opinion around the 1893 overthrow and early attempts at annexation, as I recount in chapter 1. After the Great Depression, another propaganda commission, the Hawaii Equal Rights Commission (1935–47), attempted to regain profitable tariffs by capturing consent for statehood, as we will see in chapter 2. By the end of World War II, Hawaiʻi's economy slowed as military personnel left the islands. By the 1950s, however, business leaders sought to capitalize on a growing tourism industry and national postwar boom thus driving the economic desire for statehood.

Corporate indentures prohibited large U.S. banks and insurance companies from issuing sizable loans as long as Hawaiʻi remained a U.S. territory.[29] This lack of investment capital inhibited businesses from profiting from record numbers of tourists visiting the islands. Consequently, territorial leaders formed the Hawaii Statehood Commission (1947–59) to lead a more aggressive campaign for statehood, as I recount in chapter 3. But, this book does not end in 1959; I resist a settler temporality that would position the 1959 admission of Hawaiʻi as a U.S. state as a moment of apogee. Instead, I pose statehood as a moment of profound economic and cultural transition, one where the institutional workings of the settler state became further streamlined to respond more quickly to the interests and investments of multinational neoliberal capital. Certainly, such fail-forward processes of settler state formation require not only seizing land and resources but also incorporating diverse populations.

WHITE SUPREMACY AND LIBERAL MULTICULTURALISM

In a moment largely defined by the reemergence of white supremacy, Donald Trump's presidency illuminates why, more than ever, we need a politics other than liberalism. Liberal multiculturalism works in tandem with white supremacy, allowing for forms of racism, settler colonialism, and militarism to be insulated from large movements seeking their end. Indeed, the capacity for liberalism to sustain such forms of white supremacy, to insulate them from disruption—especially when the political climate deems white nationalism unpalatable—allows for its future reemergence.

As such, each chapter of this book attempts to navigate an often unwieldy history of statehood by referencing four coordinates: white supremacy, liberal multiculturalism, settler colonialism, and imperialism.[30] White supremacy and liberal multiculturalism, which structure the tensions of our current Trump climate, are often thought of as historical moments that swing in a pendulum-type fashion, transitioning from one historical moment to the next. As a means of tracing and yet complicating the clean transitions between these moments, the first chapter of this project examines the forms of white supremacy evident at the 1893 Columbian Exposition, popularly named the White City, while the last chapter examines the liberal multiculturalism of the Kepaniwai Heritage Gardens built in the 1960s. I bookend my project with these two chapters to show that forms of white supremacy and liberal multiculturalism coexist in earlier and later times, often working in concert, not contradiction. This is not to flatten critical differences between historical moments defined by white supremacy and those defined by liberal multiculturalism. Rather, the seemingly smooth transition from white supremacy to liberal multiculturalism, which is the official narrative of Hawai'i's admission as a U.S. state—from haole-dominated racist territory to racially harmonious fiftieth state—functions to disavow how white supremacists used liberal multiculturalism to their benefit, facilitating the structural necessity for violent extractive projects of settler colonialism, labor exploitation, and militarism to continue at a time when internationalist movements were pursuing labor rights and decolonization.

To make this a bit clearer, we might look to the specific way that Hawai'i's racial diversity was used to the benefit of the United States during the Cold War. For the majority of the first half of the twentieth century, Congress deemed Hawai'i unqualified for statehood because it was considered a largely nonwhite territory. In order to make Hawai'i statehood more attractive in the eyes of Congress, proponents of statehood began to use Hawai'i's diversity, its alterity, in the service of Cold War politics. In the post–World War II moment, when decolonization was transforming an international order, Cold Warrior ideologues realized that Hawai'i's multiracial population had ideological value in winning the "hearts and minds" of newly decolonized nations—an opinion campaign developed by the "father of public relations" Edward L. Bernays.[31] This U.S. liberal multicultural discourse—articulated through a multicultural "nation of immigrants" narration—helped achieve seemingly permanent control of Hawai'i through statehood while creating a multicultural image of the United States that facilitated the establishment and maintenance of U.S. military bases throughout much of Asia and the Pacific.[32] Specifically, U.S. ambitions for global hegemony during the Cold War found a discursive alliance with portrayals of Hawai'i as a racially harmonious U.S. state and selected narrations of Japanese American loyal military service, setting state-led antiracist narratives to public memory through global circulation, entertainment, and publicity, while colonial narratives of Hawai'i's occupation by the United States were designated for historical deletion.

Despite attempts to maintain white settler hegemony, a new political force emerged that gave birth to a new arrangement of racial power in Hawai'i. The emergence of various labor movements of plantation- and dockworkers, changing demographics and their impact on voting, and the disenfranchisement of rights through martial law during World War II all altered Hawai'i's political landscape.[33] Indeed, various and diverse Chinese, Japanese, Okinawan, Filipino, and Korean communities in Hawai'i, most of whom immigrated to work on Hawai'i's plantations, had every reason to agitate as they were violently exploited for their labor and simultaneously excluded from political participation. Many different Asian groups would have to wait for their children to come of voting age to gain political representation. In 1936, University of Hawai'i sociologist and proponent of the "immigration assimilation model" Romanzo Adams predicted that by 1944, two-thirds of Hawai'i's Asian population would be able to vote, consequently increasing the strength of the "non-

Caucasian majority" and leading to a redistribution of power.[34] Realizing that a previously closed window of political opportunity was poised to open, many Asian Americans helped form the Democratic Party to challenge the Republican Party's control over the legislature. Roger Bell explains, "New forces, which ultimately achieved statehood, were identified with the burgeoning Democratic Party. Supported largely by the descendants of Asian immigrants, who had long been denied equality in island life, the Democrats fervently believed that equality as a state in the Union would pave the way for genuine democracy and equality of opportunity at home."[35] By 1952, Congress passed the McCarran-Walter Act, making it possible for the first-generation Japanese to naturalize and vote; by 1954 Japanese Americans were the largest voting bloc in the territory, and the Democratic Party, with the support of the International Longshore and Warehouse Union (ILWU), dislodged the Republican plantation oligarchy from the legislature in what has been termed in Hawai'i the Democratic Revolution.

Indeed, during the territorial period it became evident that white supremacy was no longer capable of governing a heterogeneous nonwhite population, and a liberal multicultural state began to emerge. Ronald Takaki, who grew up in Palolo Valley, notes that Asian American struggles and resistance against the haole oligarchy formed a new consciousness, "a transformation from sojourners to settlers, from Japanese to Japanese Americans."[36] Takaki, in his seminal books *Strangers from a Different Shore* and *Pau Hana*, was one of the first to argue that Asian Americans are "settlers," challenging notions that Asian Americans in the United States are perpetual foreigners akin to "sojourners."[37] Takaki goes on to argue that Asians in Hawai'i, "by their numerical preponderance . . . had greater opportunities [than on the U.S. continent] to weave themselves and their cultures into the very fabric of Hawaii and to seek to transform their adopted land into a society of rich diversity where they and their children would no longer be 'strangers from a different shore.'"[38]

In fact, the opportunities afforded to Asian groups because of their "numerical preponderance" were key to shifting power away from white supremacists, who dominated through coercion by haole racism, to a hegemonic multicultural democracy that was still organized by hierarchical notions of whiteness, Orientalism, and primitivism. This shift, however, was not without other social and political consequences. If

Takaki celebrates a history within which the children of Asian immigrants in Hawai'i were no longer made to feel like *"strangers* from a different shore,"* Roger Bell, historian of Hawai'i's admission as a U.S. state, notes that after U.S. statehood Kānaka 'Ōiwi "had become . . . *strangers*, in their own land, submerged beneath the powerful white minority and a newly assertive Asian majority."[39] In spite of a movement for genuine equality, the counterhegemonic strategies of Asian Americans against haole supremacy challenged, modified, and yet renewed a hegemonic, U.S. settler-colonial system.

While Takaki utilizes the term *settler* to oppose racist characterizations of Asian Americans as "perpetual foreigners," he never considers the implications of the term *settler* in relation to Native people. Scholar, activist, and poet Haunani-Kay Trask's article "Settlers of Color and 'Immigrant' Hegemony: 'Locals' in Hawai'i" has been the starting point for much of the work on settler colonialism in Hawai'i.[40] Arguments that an analysis of settler colonialism emerged, instead, from non-Native scholars are erroneous, at least in the context of Hawai'i.[41] Trask's work has helped many to think of identities or subjectivities as pedagogical, in that they offer bits and pieces of insight into the historical moment within which we find ourselves. At the same time, the subjectivities that one inherits require political mediation that addresses new historical understandings and possibilities for resistance. This calls for us to critique and redefine the terms of identity within which we are born, and it challenges each of us to become literate in other histories and struggles, which then helps to show how our current strategies for resistance can come at the expense of other marginalized groups.

In her essay, Trask gets at the ways that one can be oppressed while simultaneously participating in the oppression of another. An alternative to binary analyses of power where one is either oppressed or oppressive, this kind of relational thinking requires an examination of the processes of settler colonialism that often lead to difficult and uncomfortable questions. In this way, Trask's use of the term *settler of color* is meant to unsettle not only the entrenched identities comfortably used in Hawai'i—Local and American—but the paradigms of colonial thought and structures of feeling that uphold them. Local is not only a geographical marker in Hawai'i but a working-class cultural identity formed in Hawai'i's plantations and set in direct opposition to haole racism. But the limitation of Local as a category for solidarity, which is how it is often invoked, is that it is premised around a shared victimization from haole supremacy, which flattens critical distinctions between Kānaka ʻŌiwi and non-Native groups.[42] Kānaka ʻŌiwi face distinct forms of colonial oppression within which non-Natives are given every opportunity to participate and from which non-Natives can benefit.

While Hawaiʻi's predominant racial binary, haole versus Local, collapses Asians and Kānaka ʻŌiwi together and configures haole as oppressive and Locals as oppressed, the distance between Asians and Kānaka ʻŌiwi in the Local imaginary is quite clearly illuminated in the common saying among Local Asians that it is better to not get involved in "Hawaiian issues" because "it's the haole who overthrew their nation, not us."[43] This illustrates how culpability for Hawaiʻi's occupation by the United States is framed in relation to whites, not Asians. Because of this commonly held belief that it was them and "not us," many cannot get past Trask's use of the term *settler of color* to refer to Asian groups in Hawaiʻi; they argue that she is reinscribing a binarism of Native and settler. Given that Trask does not argue that Asians are white folks, such criticisms of alleged binaries actually serve to replicate binary analyses of power. Trask's use of the term *settlers of color* in Hawaiʻi, in fact, challenges an either/or analysis, in which one is either oppressed or oppressive; in so doing, she reveals how such binaristic framings allow for what Eve Tuck and Wayne Yang critique as an ever-constant "settler move to innocence," since people are imagined as one or the other but never both.[44] Asian groups, particularly East Asian groups in Hawaiʻi, hold political and economic power distinct from most other Asians on the continental United States. This is not to argue that distinct forms of discriminatory power targeting Asian groups do not exist, but that the binarism produced in the Local category often obscures the complex power relations that permeate the islands. Seemingly in opposition to all forms of white supremacy, "Local" serves as an important liberal component in facilitating multicultural forms of settler colonialism in Hawaiʻi while denying the fact that many non-Native peoples in Hawaiʻi benefit from and many times facilitate forms of settler colonialism at the expense of Kānaka ʻŌiwi.

Recent scholarship has generated productive debates around settler colonial critique and its efficacy. Jodi A. Byrd, for instance, argues, "It is all too easy, in critiques of U.S. settler colonialism, to accuse diasporic migrants, queers, and people of color for participating in and benefiting from indigenous loss of lands, cultures, and lives and subsequently to position indigenous otherness as abject and all other Others as part of the problem, as if they could always consent or refuse such positions or consequences of history."[45] In a Hawai'ian context, my sense of the efficacy of the work of Trask and others is not so much in the chiding of groups for the asymmetrical power relations that constrain agency and constitute marginalized positions. Rather, Trask's critique emerges in a moment where certain Asian groups hold political and economic power and enact such power in a manner that actively opposes Hawaiian struggles for self-determination.[46] Trask invites non-Natives to support Native movements and politics, as opposed to only working within an American colonial system. In other words, Trask's theorizing of settler colonialism goes beyond exposing complicity, offering instead new pedagogies—different ways of knowing, being, and responding to—the living force of the colonial past in the present. Pushing beyond binary conceptions of power—oppressor/victim, white/nonwhite, settler/Indigenous, settler/migrant—the intricate *relationality* of power shows how multiple binaries organize and layer differences within the settler state. As Trask has argued: "The color of violence, then, is the color of white over Black, white over brown, white over red, white over yellow. It is the violence of north over south, of continents over archipelagoes, of settlers over natives and slaves. Shaping this color scheme are the labrinths of class and gender, of geography and industry, of metropolises and peripheries, of sexual definitions and confinements. There is not just one binary opposition, but many oppositions."[47]

As one of the first scholars to utilize relational analyses of settler colonialism, Trask's work is not easily reducible to a settler/native binary. In the above quote, Trask does not collapse enslaved peoples with settlers nor deny systems of anti-Asian violence.[48] Instead, she highlights the existence of multiple binary oppositions underpinned by a structure of white heteropatriarchy to show that differential locations relative to white supremacy and its ongoing effects *un*-settles supposedly natural or inevitable alliances between historically oppressed groups.

And while Trask's political style is to both call out and call in, her critique is still more relational than Othering, tracing liberal strategies of past movements against white supremacy and their damaging impact on contemporary Hawaiian politics. Trask argues about the dominant ideology that underpins statehood:

> Ideology weaves a story of success: poor Japanese, Chinese, and Filipino settlers supplied the labor for wealthy, white sugar planters during the long period of the territory (1900–1959). Exploitative plantation conditions thus underpin a master narrative of hard work and the endlessly celebrated triumph over anti-Asian racism. Settler children, ever industrious and deserving, obtain technical and liberal educations, thereby learning the political system through which they agitate for full voting rights as American citizens. Politically, the vehicle for Asian ascendancy is statehood. . . . Because the ideology of the United States as a mosaic of races is reproduced in Hawaiʻi through the celebration of the fact that no single "immigrant group" constitutes a numerical majority, the post-statehood euphoria stigmatizes Hawaiians as a failed indigenous people whose conditions, including out-migration, actually worsen after statehood. Hawaiians are characterized as strangely unsuited, whether because of culture or genetics, to the game of assimilation.[49]

What the history of Hawaiʻi's admission as a U.S. state thus demonstrates is how opposition to white supremacy without an analysis of settler colonialism can often renew and expand a structure of U.S. occupation initiated by white settlers. In the poststatehood moment, the rise of liberal politics green-lights large-scale land development projects, which heightens displacement and desecrations against Kānaka ʻŌiwi as I write about in chapter 4. The Democratic Party, indeed, relies on a master narrative of anti-Asian oppression on the sugar plantations and valiant military service during World War II, which all too often serves as an alibi for continued acts of Native dispossession and marginalization. By reflecting on the failures of liberal strategies for resistance, we can see how settler colonialism often shapes and constrains our political imaginations in ways that allow for movements seeking reprieve from white supremacy to, sometimes unknowingly, collude in Native dispossession.

In thinking through capacious strategies for co-resistance, I look to the work of Grace Lee Boggs, who as a part of the Black radical tradition argued against imagining racialized groups as "oppressed masses" and sought to instead see them as empowered communities capable of making moral choices.[50] Boggs along with her comrades stated that movements require not only resistance, but *reflection* and challenged those concerned with radical transformation to do the hard work of beginning with themselves. Through a notion of dialectical humanism, they aimed at both an individual and a collective level for a way of becoming a "more 'human' human being," primarily so that one's politics and strategies for resistance do not solidify into a trap for oneself or others. Together they created space for growth by being open and vulnerable to challenge, to demand another mode of being than the good citizen-subject defined by the state.

A problem of Asian settler colonialism, however, is that it leaves no political space for people who want nothing to do with the term *settler*.[51] I critically identify as a Filipino and Japanese settler—and doing so pales in comparison to living as a Native person under occupation. Ultimately, though, I believe that one's political identification is one's own personal choice.[52] Current debates around settler colonialism often revolve around positivist questions or arguments: Is this is a settler? Is this an arrivant? Such framings adjudicate these arguments through a kind of moral hierarchy of competing identities that can elide the very structure of settler colonialism, which remains the same regardless of what term one uses. Thus, how is it beneficial to us all, regardless of how you self-identify, to question the political and pedagogical work that relational analyses of settler colonialism do to open one's political imagination to the genocidal consequences of aligning oneself with the settler state? As such, interrogating one's relationship to a system of settler colonialism might have more efficacy by questioning what one is doing, rather than how one identifies.

While non-Natives are engaged in debates about whether we are settlers and what we should or should not be called, Native people's material struggles over land, resources, and governance continue. Trask argues that a preoccupation with identity is most often a concern for non-Native peoples living on seized Native lands, while a Kanaka 'Ōiwi movement is concerned with struggles to regain these lands. As Trask contends, "The distinction here between the personal and the national is critical. Hawaiians are not engaged in identity politics, any more than the Irish of Northern Ireland or the Palestinians of occupied Palestine are engaged in identity politics."[53] Indeed, positivist discussions over who is and is not a "settler" often dissolve into arguments where one cites one's oppression

like a badge of honor to shield oneself from having to contend with settler colonialism. Recent scholarship arguing that Asian Americans are
"arrivants," for example, voices the important differences between Asian
arrivants and white settlers, while remaining oddly silent on the relationship of Asian arrivants to Native peoples. Such forms of escapism often
take us everywhere but ultimately nowhere, sanitizing the critique of
settler colonialism while sidestepping the important questions posed by
scholars such as Trask. This is not to be mistaken for a dismissal of the
term *arrivant*, but rather a challenge to those who invoke this term to
not mistake "arrivant" as an invitation to "innocence."[54] While an arrivant subjectivity has traveled in such circles, the phrasing is tied to what
Byrd theorizes as "arrivant colonialism," a relational component to her
overall argument that remains conveniently absent in most framings.[55]
Regardless of what terms one deploys, forms of affinity and possible kinship might be better grounded in place-based Native histories and struggles, thus foregrounding Native forms of knowledge and governance and
movements toward Indigenous resurgence.

INDIGENOUS RESURGENCE

In this way, *Unsustainable Empire* also means to describe the particular historical moment we find ourselves in today. Not only is capitalism
unsustainable as an economic system but we are currently in a critical
moment where the planet itself can no longer sustain such human-
centered ways of living.[56] Extreme weather patterns, rising sea levels,
the warming of the planet, and nonhuman extinctions all tell us that
the fail-forward pattern of settler colonialism and capitalism has hit a
limit, even as arguments for the colonization of other planets proliferate. This calls for a critical engagement with the past and present as a
means to produce alternative futures to the settler state. It means to
understand economic crises as an abstraction that makes the primacy
of the ecological crisis seemingly secondary. Such alternative futures are
critically important as we are living in a moment when a refusal of settler governance is a refusal of climate change, as Native movements and
Indigenous sovereignty are often at the front lines blocking extractive
industries.[57] The 2016–17 Stand at Standing Rock against the Dakota
Access Pipeline showed us just this.

Settler abstractions, as theorized by Said's "future wish," have long set the ideological conditions for capitalism and its accompanying environmental degradation via ongoing forms of primitive accumulation—divorcing Native peoples from the means of production and the "material conditions of resistance"—and its seemingly permanent structure, a kind of settler accumulation by Native dispossession. As Noenoe K. Silva and Jonathan Goldberg-Hiller point out, a key difference between Western and Indigenous notions of sovereignty is that Indigenous epistemologies describe the human and nonhuman divide not as a binary, but rather as interdependent familial relations.[58] As such, the United States has often sought to make Native peoples vulnerable by disrupting those familial relations through the elimination of one or more sets of human-to-nonhuman relations. This is a tactic of Native dispossession, whether it is targeting kalo (taro) in Hawai'i through water expropriation; the U.S. Army's elimination of the buffalo, numbering fifteen million in 1871 and only thirty-four by 1903; the genetic modification of corn, wild rice, taro, and salmon in the Pacific Northwest; or military tactics that target the elimination of food sources and ecosystems, as was done in the Philippine-American War, the Korean War, and the Vietnam War, the latter two using herbicides such as Agent Orange.

Our present moment *is* the afterlife of this "future wish," which has targeted nonhumans for elimination to make the "material conditions of resistance" impossible, to literally produce so-called domestic dependent nations or underdeveloped nations. In the death of these nonhuman relations is the continual birth and rebirth of capitalism, the particular mode of production that has evolved to set the current environmental conditions of climate crisis. Given this, the renewal and protection of Native relationality to nonhumans and land can move us toward a more sustainable, healthy, and equitable system for all currently vulnerable than can ever be imagined in this current system: Indigenous, immigrants, refugees, racially subjugated communities, incarcerated peoples, the undocumented, people with disabilities, non-gender-conforming and queer peoples.

Many Indigenous movements aim to cultivate noncapitalist relations and plant the seeds for Indigenous economies to reemerge by imagining ways to use settler colonialism against itself. Where Haunani-Kay Trask begins by revealing the forms of knowledge and subjectivities that uphold

Asian settler colonialism in Hawai'i, the work of Noelani Goodyear-Ka'ōpua builds on Trask and marks a turn in this field by offering a plurality of possibilities that might emerge when diverse settler groups work in place-based affinity with Kānaka 'Ōiwi. Goodyear-Ka'ōpua illustrates in her book *The Seeds We Planted* just how Native movements and educational work address current problems. By rebuilding Hawaiian governance, foodways, and economies they create and imagine alternative power relations to settler colonialism: "The marginalization and suppression of Indigenous knowledges has gone hand in hand with the transformation and degradation of Indigenous economic systems and the ecosystems that nourish us. Conversely, settler-colonial relations might be transformed by rebuilding, in new ways, the Indigenous structures that have historically sustained our societies."[59] Goodyear-Ka'ōpua's work aims for nonstatist forms of deoccupation, which help cultivate mutual respect by setting the conditions of possibility to be determined by the land, urgently critical in a moment of ecological crisis.[60] Candace Fujikane, through community and activist work, has theorized the term *settler ally* to be capacious, as opening ways of being in Hawai'i that co-resist settler colonialism and occupation: "The term 'settler' roots us in the settler colonialism that we seek to rearticulate so that we never lose sight of those conditions or our own positionality or the privileges we derive from it. At the same time, however, the term encompasses the imaginative possibilities for our collaborative work on ea and land-based decolonial nation-building. For there is joy, too, in these practices of growing ea: 'Ohohia i ka hana 'ana aku e.' We rejoice in the practice, we move ourselves to the decolonial joy of practicing ea."[61]

As the work of these scholars and activists illuminates, when we recognize that empire relies on imperialist expansion to respond to the failures of capitalism, we can also identify such *problems* as *possibilities* for replacement. Placing Asian diaspora and Native histories together opens new lines of inquiry, allowing for their different historical and geopolitical forms of oppression to be understood as interdependent in ways that produce possibilities outside of the constrained logics of U.S. empire. As ethnic studies scholar Roderick N. Labrador has argued, the subjugation of Kānaka 'Ōiwi and the oppression of Asian immigrants continues to serve as the foundation for U.S. colonialism in Hawai'i.[62] Asian American studies and Native studies thus offer relational ways to analyze an important assemblage of U.S. empire, where diaspora and indigeneity, settler colonialism and U.S. imperialism geopolitically convene. Understanding that power does not simply target historically oppressed communities but also operates through their practices, ambitions, narratives, and silences offers a way to examine other dynamics of power—labor exploitation, anti-immigrant laws and sentiment, and imperialist wars—that have historically shaped Asian groups, without misrecognizing the context for framing an Asian diaspora on Native lands seized by the U.S. settler state. Asian diaspora and Kanaka 'Ōiwi histories have the potential to be transformative when assembled intersectionally, and can be done without diminishing the complexities of each. This signals a need, as articulation theory argues, for an attempt to situate these different histories in complex unity—not flattening difference and assuming these groups are in solidarity, nor falling into the pitfalls of difference and framing them as always in opposition.[63]

In different colonial situations, historical examples of groups liberating themselves from being used as agents in a system of colonial violence help illustrate alternative ways of being under conditions of occupation.[64] During the Philippine-American War, for instance, many Black soldiers of the Twenty-Fourth Infantry Colored Regiment who had been deployed to the Philippines defected from the U.S. military to fight alongside Filipino "insurgents."[65] Critical Filipinx scholar Nerissa S. Balce traces the work of Apolinario Mabini, who lost the use of both legs to polio at the start of the war and was a critical intellectual during the Philippine Revolution against both Spain and the United States. Mabini wrote letters addressed specifically "To the American Colored Soldier" that were dropped in villages that U.S. soldiers were passing through. Mabini, who was eventually captured and exiled to Guåhan, asked Black soldiers to consider fighting on the side of Filipinos: "You must consider your situation and your history, and take charge that the blood of Sam Hose proclaims vengeance." At the time that the Twenty-Fourth Infantry were deployed to the Philippines, Sam Hose had been violently lynched in Georgia in April of 1899. What's more, prior to arriving in the Philippines, members of the Twenty-Fourth Infantry Regiment caused a race riot in Tampa, Florida, after they saved the life of a young Black boy who had been forced to hold a can atop his head as target practice for white soldiers.[66] Critical ethnic studies scholar Dylan Rodríguez argues that through complex political and creative acts, those whose every day is constituted by the genealogies of genocide—"Manifest Destiny, Middle Passage, racial chattel plantation order, Philippine-American War"—are able to reckon and create within this genealogy by embracing the impasse between themselves and a "racially genocidal state."[67] This is to say that under conditions of genocide, liberation is not to reform the state from corruption but, rather, to urgently liberate oneself from the state.

Refusal to participate in such colonial violence is a form of affinity-based politics that creatively orchestrates interdependency. Black soldiers "defected" from service to a genocidal state, turning themselves into "fugitives" and identifying their life chances as better served in affinity with those who were also the targets of a genocidal state. In this way, learning how one is being used and then refusing to be used as such in a system of violence is a form of both radical affinity and self-care. Manu Vimalassery considers such forms of radical affinity by tracing the movement of Harriet Tubman across territorial dispossession and enslavement and theorizing the position of the "fugitive": "Tubman moved against police powers that protected and served the interest of property claims in her flesh. She moved against declarations of independence, efforts to secure slavery and colonialism that operate under the rules of occupation. . . . The fugitive position is itself a crime against property."[68] This tactic of identifying and recognizing other peoples who refuse the terms of property and a national identity that would otherwise bolster the U.S. settler state's permanent conditions of war and occupation informs my current presence as a Filipino and Japanese settler on Native lands, living in the assemblage of multiple genocides and a continued historical moment when Native people in struggle call on others to defect and support their movement to build alternatives to U.S. empire.

NAVIGATING THE BOOK

The first part of this book examines moments where white supremacy resorts to further acts of settler and imperial violence to mediate its failing system. As my starting point, I identify the 1893 U.S. military–backed overthrow, but I broaden my approach to this moment by looking at Hawai'i from Chicago at the World's Columbian Exposition. Such a wide framing allows me to contextualize the overthrow within the major economic crisis and labor unrest that occurred in the United States at this time. The crux of chapter 1, "A Future Wish: Hawai'i at the 1893 Chicago World's Columbian Exposition," questions how a global celebration of white supremacy could exist in a moment when the U.S. economy was on the verge of collapse. I argue that such seemingly contradictory acts were instead concomitant strategies, where settler state theatricality at the White City represented white supremacy as a "more deserving power" over Native nations and economies in order to justify the historic and ongoing seizure of Native lands and resources. With their eyes set on other sites for imperialism, such future-oriented colonial and imperial processes were necessary to keep a capitalist and white supremacist system from collapsing on itself.

Chapter 2, "The Courage to Speak: Disrupting Haole Hegemony at the 1937 Congressional Statehood Hearings," examines the beginnings of a genuine state-led movement for U.S. statehood. This moment is often wrongly described in official histories as a period where Hawai'i was unified in arguing for statehood. As a result of the Great Depression in 1929, the federal government altered Hawai'i sugar tariffs while also protecting the rights of workers to organize unions. As such, settler planters aimed to alleviate such crises by initiating a serious movement for statehood. This chapter asks: How did the settler state make its heterogeneous population knowable? Many of the University of Hawai'i sociologists who produced such racial ideas were first trained at the University of Chicago, on the actual grounds where the 1893 Columbian Exposition stood. Furthermore, scholars rooted in a white supremacist discourse of eugenics were also at the University of Hawai'i. Despite the best efforts of the settler elite and propaganda commissions to engineer consent, the 1937 statehood hearings show how white supremacist forms of governmentality were no longer capable of reproducing white settler hegemony.

While the first half of the book contends with the ways in which white supremacy disqualified Hawai'i from statehood because it was considered a largely "Asiatic" territory, chapters 3 and 4 examine how Hawai'i's racial diversity made it more attractive in the eyes of Congress and in the service of U.S. imperial politics. In his intricate study of Hawai'i statehood, *Last among Equals*, Roger Bell shows how Southern senators blocked Hawai'i's bid for statehood, as they wished to keep congressional control for the Democrats and also felt nervous that new liberal Asian senators might facilitate the passing of civil rights legislation. In *Completing the Union* John S. Whitehead compares the movements for statehood in Hawai'i and Alaska and their particular utility as military posts during the Cold War.[69] It is at the intersection of civil rights and the Cold War that we can gain a more expansive view of Hawai'i statehood.

Chapter 3, "'Something Indefinable Would Be Lost': The Unruly Kamokila and *Go for Broke!*," traces two mutually constitutive but competing projects in the post–World War II period: the racial project combating the exclusion of Japanese Americans from a U.S. national polity deemed "ineligible to citizenship," and another project where Kānaka 'Ōiwi sought to combat their colonial designation as "unfit for self-government." Together, the Office of War Information, the War Relocation Authority, and the MGM film *Go for Broke!* publicized the devastating casualties sustained by Japanese Americans in World War II, which softened white perceptions of them as foreign threats and even rendered opposition to statehood for Hawai'i as a racist affront to the war record of Japanese Americans. Ultimately, such efforts aimed to reconcile the imperial relationships between Japan and the United States. This chapter juxtaposes such projects with the cultural politics of Alice Kamokilaikawai Campbell, who is quoted in the epigraph. I argue that she protested statehood and effectively stalled its passage for decades by strategically playing to the racism of Congress. Kamokila, as she was publicly known, further pushed and investigated other options for Kānaka and Hawai'i besides statehood, particularly in a moment when elites aimed to deliberately contain Hawai'i's political status to statehood.

Chapter 4, "The Propaganda of Occupation: Statehood and the Cold War," first examines the public relations strategy for achieving U.S. statehood in the context of the Cold War. In a moment when criticism of Western imperialism was the dominant international sentiment, the leading public relations expert Edward L. Bernays argued that if Hawai'i were made a U.S. state, its multiculturalism could aid the Cold War by disproving communist charges of U.S. colonialism and demonstrating to Americans that racial harmony was possible.[70] This public relations work was picked up by novelist James Michener and the person most often given credit for achieving statehood, George Lehleitner, a businessman from New Orleans, Louisiana. The chapter then moves to highlight the oppositional movements that invoked the 1893 overthrow—a range of anticapitalist, anticolonial, and antiwar politics—that reveal different vulnerabilities to both a U.S. imperialist and a settler state: first, by those communists (the Hawai'i Seven) accused of using "force and violence" to overthrow the U.S. government, and second, by Kathleen Dickenson Mellen, whose public scholarship narrated the history of the U.S. overthrow of Hawai'i to oppose statehood. I end by examining Sammy Amalu's 1961 multimillion-dollar hoax on the tourism and real estate industries that turned the tragedy of statehood into a comedy. Disguised as a Swiss investor, all the while living destitute on the outskirts of Waikīkī, Amalu offered to buy numerous hotels, ranches, and other properties in culturally significant places. Covered by the national and international media, Amalu widened political possibilities in a moment when Kanaka 'Ōiwi futures were seemingly nonexistent.

Chapter 5, "Alternative Futures beyond the Settler State," traces the afterlife of the aforementioned future wish, but aims to identify and highlight those who work outside of the constrained logics of the settler state. The Kepaniwai Heritage Gardens on the island of Maui, a county park that features recreations of "traditional" Asian, Pacific, and European houses and gardens, narrates Hawai'i as a racially harmonious state. A manifestation of the University of Hawai'i sociologists' "racial melting pot" discourse, the park's design and architecture materializes a form of liberal multiculturalism that is a vestige of the 1893 Columbian Exposition. During the park's planning in the early 1950s, Kānaka 'Ōiwi protested its construction as they explained that the land contains burials of Hawaiian ali'i (royalty) and was also the site of a major battle. In fact, Kepaniwai translates as "damming of the waters" caused by the bodies of slain Maui warriors. The purported racial harmony represented in the gardens was used in the service of both the U.S. occupation of Hawai'i and military expansion during the period of the Cold War. In addition, this valley is a part of Nā Wai 'Ehā (the Four Great Waters) which was once the largest contiguous taro-growing area in all of Hawai'i. Indeed, contemporary appeals by kalo farmers have led to the replenishing of the rivers to promote more sustainable ways of living and a return to an economy organized around Hawaiian notions of value.

Taken as a whole, this book illustrates the complex ways that Hawai'i's admission as a U.S. state—narrated as an official antiracist, liberal, and state-led civil rights project that excluded an analysis of occupation and settler colonialism—has facilitated and normalized projects of empire. Through a discursive approach to U.S. statehood, and a critical reconsideration of the ways that propaganda commissions framed the rules of discourse to normalize the presence of the United States in Hawai'i, we are better able to understand how Hawai'i statehood became expected, how it came to be considered an inevitable outcome of history, and how ideas about history and race were arranged so as to invalidate and silence opposition to statehood.

Hawaiian demonstrations on Admission Day challenge the state's narration of itself, and, in doing so, also illuminate the hidden aspects of the ideological forces underpinning U.S. occupation. The unearthing and retelling of systemically and deliberately buried histories thus reveal how the state's present power was taken historically by illegal force, and at the expense of Hawaiian birthrights to self-determination. What the settler state has done with this power is revealed in the present and possibly future realities of rising sea levels, environmental degradation, increased militarism, and growing social and economic discord. Hawai'i and its diverse people are tied to a long tradition of resistance to all manners of oppression, across many sites of U.S. empire. This book is an incomplete rendering of a small piece of this resistance.

CHAPTER 1
A FUTURE WISH

Hawai'i at the 1893 Chicago World's
Columbian Exposition

Only four months after helping to lead the U.S. military–backed overthrow of the Hawaiian Kingdom, Lorrin A. Thurston was in Chicago at the
1893 World's Columbian Exposition. Thurston, a third-generation settler
descended from some of the first American missionaries to Hawai'i, was
at the world's fair helping to manage his "Cyclorama of Kilauea"—a five-
story-high and four-hundred-foot-wide landscape painting of Kīlauea
crater designed to encircle the viewer and give the impression of standing in the actual volcano. Using the cyclorama as an "imperial advertisement" for annexation, Thurston placed large American flags at the top
of it.[1] Thurston hoped that the cyclorama might help to present another
vision of the American frontier, one that would extend the imagined borders of the United States into the Pacific, to Hawai'i. For annexationists,
Hawai'i needed to be seen not as the internationally recognized nation
that it had been since 1843, with foreign delegates throughout the world,
but as an exotic island frontier zone, a primitive space to be made anew
with the joint help of white settlers in Hawai'i and a newly industrialized
United States.[2]

Lorrin A. Thurston's activities in Chicago were part of a predetermined opinion campaign with two objectives: to shape public perception
of the overthrow of Queen Lili'uokalani's constitutional government, and
to generate U.S. national and international support for the annexation of
Hawai'i to the United States. Described by historians as the "most ardent
and proficient propagandist on behalf of the provisional government,"

Thurston was responsible for forming two groups: the Annexation Club and the Hawaiian Bureau of Information.[3] The Annexation Club, later renamed the Committee of Safety, conspired with the U.S. foreign minister to Hawai'i, John L. Stevens, to secure U.S. military backing and secretly carry out the overthrow. The Hawaiian Bureau of Information acted as a kind of media arm of the campaign, aiming to shape Hawai'i's image through advertising as a means to facilitate both tourism and white settler colonialism. The Hawaiian Bureau of Information advertised for tourist travel specifically to attract a so-called desirable population to settle in Hawai'i and outnumber Kānaka 'Ōiwi. They also used the "Cyclorama of Kilauea" to frame the narration of the January 1893 overthrow of Queen Lili'uokalani in racist and misogynistic terms.[4] If hegemony is hard work, as is often said, then Thurston worked tirelessly, traveling across the country feeding such settler propaganda to journalists.[5]

The cultural work required to normalize white settler control of Hawai'i resonated at the Columbian Exposition. The entire exposition was referred to popularly as the "White City." With more than twenty-seven million people attending, it commemorated the four-hundredth anniversary of Christopher Columbus's so-called discovery of America, along with the fulfillment of this "divine" event through the imagined defeat of Native Americans and the successful settlement of their lands. It was here that Frederick Jackson Turner pronounced his "frontier thesis," declaring the frontier settled and, more explicitly, describing a linear transition from Native governance and economies to U.S. settler territories and states.[6] The significance of the settlement of the frontier in 1893 was bolstered by the 1890 Massacre at Wounded Knee, a mass murder of an estimated three hundred Lakota by the U.S. Seventh Cavalry, imagined by most Americans at the time to be the final military defeat of Native American resistance.[7] As Philip J. Deloria argues, these specific events together informed many of the displays at the 1893 Columbian Exposition, wherein U.S. history was narrated "not as a frontiersman's struggle with wild lands, but as one long Indian war, a violent contest in which Americans were shaped by constant struggle with a dangerous and challenging adversary."[8] As such, these supposed democratic virtues normalized and mythologized settler colonialism and genocide. Such culminating achievements were issued as evidence of white American superiority.

These claims, however, were made during a time when its economic dominance appeared most threatened. By 1893, the United States was in a major economic depression, with five hundred banks closed and fifteen thousand companies out of business.[9] By the middle of 1894 unemployment had reached a record four million. During this time, greedy management practices coupled with poor economic and work conditions produced class conflicts such as the 1887 Haymarket Riot and the 1893 Pullman Strikes in Chicago, as well as some thirty lesser-known strikes that occurred throughout the country at the time of the Columbian Exposition.[10] U.S. foreign policy thus sought larger foreign markets in which to sell a surplus of products created through rapid industrialization. Many white working-class Americans began to link industrial maturity with degenerating labor conditions and began to call for revolution.[11] In 1894, Secretary of State Walter Gresham wrote: "I am not a pessimist, but I think I see danger in existing conditions in this country. What is transpiring in Pennsylvania, Ohio, Indiana, Illinois, and in regions west of there, may fairly be viewed as symptoms of revolution."[12]

U.S. business and government leaders believed that foreign markets, gained through aggressive imperialist policies, were necessary to guard against both populist revolt and economic depression. Historian Walter LaFeber explains that the Harrison administration's support of Lorrin A. Thurston and others plotting the overthrow of the Hawaiian Kingdom was a product of what he calls "depression diplomacy"—where U.S. leaders deemed the securing of overseas markets a necessity in alleviating a glut of industrial goods.[13] Hawai'i's strategic location in the Pacific Ocean benefited the United States militarily, providing economic access to markets in Asia by protecting and enabling trade routes. This economic depression, coupled with a highly organized and politically effective Kanaka 'Ōiwi movement against white settler hegemony in Hawai'i, consequently animated white settlers in Hawai'i to desperately plot and carry out the 1893 overthrow.

The U.S. occupation of Native American and Kanaka 'Ōiwi lands necessitated opinion campaigns to both legitimize and facilitate such settler violence. In the last decade of the nineteenth century, the presumed final pacification of Native Americans—with stakes in the crafting of American ideas of white manhood and civilization—was imagined to signal America's readiness to transition from a continental power to a hemispheric imperial power. Future President Theodore Roosevelt, a political ally and friend of Hawaiʻi propagandist Lorrin A. Thurston, declared in various volumes of *The Winning of the West* that the closing of the continental frontier only meant the opening of a new frontier overseas.[14]

While the narration of the Columbian Exposition centered white American civilization through the settlement of the frontier, the "Cyclorama of Kilauea" portrayed Hawaiian women, specifically through the figure of Pele—described as the "Goddess of Fire"—as dangerous female threats to the presumed natural development of white heteropatriarchal control over Hawaiʻi.[15] Indeed, the planners of the Columbian Exposition found synergy between the story expressed at their fair and the events taking place in Hawaiʻi. In preparation for the opening day of the exposition, the *Chicago Tribune* suggested hoisting the same American flag above the exposition's "Grand Entrance" that had been flown over the Hawaiian Government Building during the overthrow, opining that such a gesture would "*advertise* the cause of annexation and once more bring it home to the minds and hearts of all Americans."[16] Such settler theatrics were deployed to spread information while also emotionally recruiting others in the service of settler colonialism.

The ubiquitous visual evidence of white supremacy at the White City betrays another story or logic that demonstrates a fail-forward pattern of settler colonialism. The economic crisis of the 1890s is critical to understanding both the Columbian Exposition and the overthrow of the Hawaiian Kingdom. This crisis set in motion a body of racial knowledge that animated mutually constitutive discursive formations—primitivism and Orientalism—with distinct geopolitical implications that articulated U.S. formations of settler colonialism with U.S. imperialism. Spectators of the Columbian Exposition were encouraged to view the nonwhite world as an obstruction to white civilizational progress, and thus a potential threat to their well-being, in ways that scientifically and morally rationalized imperial theft and violence. At the same time, however, specific formations of Orientalism allowed for Japan to be seen as a government that could facilitate modernity by opening Asia to capitalism and get the United States out of its economic depression.

The seeming closing of the frontier can also be viewed as the enclosure of a plurality of Native American economies that itself was only accomplished through colonial violence and theft. The transitions from Indigenous land-based economies to settler capitalism are often naturalized, yet thinking through the transitions between such modes of life can be informative, though not deterministic, of particular reads of the Columbian Exposition.[17] By examining the theft and genocide inscribed within Edward Said's "future wish" that animated exhibits at the Columbian Exposition, this chapter examines how settler statecraft allowed for a global celebration of white supremacy, even in a moment when the mode of production underpinning its existence—capitalism—was most under threat. Such celebrations in a moment of economic depression were not contradictory, but rather strategic. I aim to show that white settler society—the White City—had to be represented as a "more deserving power" than Native nations and economies for a capitalist system to even survive.

"DEPRESSION DIPLOMACY"

By the end of the nineteenth century, the existence of the entire sugar industry in Hawai'i was dependent on low and lucrative tariffs set through reciprocity treaties between Hawai'i and the United States. As historian Jonathan Kamakawiwoʻole Osorio has argued in *Dismembering Lāhui: A History of the Hawaiian Nation to 1887*, the Reciprocity Treaty between the United States and the Hawaiian Kingdom, initially signed in 1876, gave Hawai'i's sugar industry a two-cent-per-pound bounty and thus a favored position over other foreign sugars that were competing in the U.S. market. In return, the Hawaiian government was forbidden from leasing or disposing "any port, harbor, or other territory" to any other nation. Such a Reciprocity Treaty was initiated by the United States as a result of the post–Civil War depression, what is sometimes referred to as the Long Depression.[18] Joseph Nāwahī, an ardent Hawaiian nationalist and representative from Hilo and Puna, strongly voiced the opposition of many Kānaka 'Ōiwi to the Reciprocity Treaty, calling it a "nation-snatching treaty" and the "first step of annexation."[19]

Because of the lagging U.S. economy in the 1890s, however, sugar growers in the United States successfully lobbied Congress to pass the 1890 McKinley Tariff. This act would abolish the tariff relations established through the Reciprocity Treaty and diminish Hawai'i's sugar planters' ability to compete in U.S. markets. Hawai'i's sugar planters viewed the Reciprocity Treaty as not only lucrative but largely a necessity for the sugar industry in Hawai'i to remain competitive. Z. S. Spalding, a prominent sugar planter, reminisced, "Before the reciprocity treaty had passed . . . I do not think that there was a single plantation that had not gone into bankruptcy."[20] In fact, four years after the Reciprocity Treaty was established, sugar production doubled, and by 1890, plantations produced ten times more sugar than they had in 1876.[21] This dramatic rise in sugar production led to the accumulation of more capital for sugar planters; the establishment of banks; new technologies in irrigation and processing; a demand for more land, resources, and labor; and, especially, political influence.

Having amassed economic power through the Reciprocity Treaty, white settler planters were willing to use whatever force necessary to maintain profitable tariff relations with the United States. When the Reciprocity Treaty was up for renewal in 1885, the United States offered to do so only in exchange for the use of Pu'uloa, Pearl Harbor, as a naval base. When King Kalākaua (1874–91) refused, white settlers organized rifle clubs and forced the "Bayonet Constitution" upon him. Written in 1887 by Lorrin A. Thurston, the aforementioned propagandist of the annexationists, the Bayonet Constitution would dramatically limit the influence of the monarch while disenfranchising a majority of Hawaiians from voting for the House of Nobles through income and property requirements. Literacy requirements were also designated but did not hinder Kānaka from voting. Importantly, the Bayonet Constitution also restricted all Asians in Hawai'i from both naturalization and voting.[22]

Although the 1887 Bayonet Constitution was imagined as giving white settlers electoral advantages, it also sparked a highly organized and effective movement whose target was the political structure established by the Thurston-created faction. In the aftermath of the Bayonet Constitution, Hawaiians began organizing politically, forming the Hui Kālai'āina in 1887 and the Hui Aloha 'Āina in 1893.[23] By 1890, one year after an unsuccessful coup attempt to remove the Bayonet Constitution, Hawaiians, through the Hui Kālai'āina, joined forces with the Mechanics' and Workingmen's Political Protective Union to run candidates who were friendly to both labor and a new constitution.[24] Many wealthy Chinese who were Hawaiian nationals but unable to vote began to employ hundreds of Kānaka

'Ōiwi so they could meet the income requirements for voting.[25] This new historical bloc of 'Ōiwi, Chinese, and labor won the 1890 elections by a landslide. Two years later, in an election held in October of 1892, this new political group would also win two vacant seats in the House of Nobles.[26] Indeed, they became effective at politically defeating the plantation elite even when the Bayonet Constitution was designed to marginalize them from political influence.

With white settler economic and political power in decline, the passing of the 1890 McKinley Tariff led sugar planters to consider annexation to the United States as a possible strategy to recapture white settler hegemony. Still, by the early 1890s, some sugar planters needed convincing, as they were concerned that annexation might bring American labor laws that would extinguish the contract system that had made the sugar industry so lucrative. Debates were framed between the benefits of remaining an independent nation and maintaining an exploitable Asian labor force versus reestablishing profitable American trade relations through annexation. Paul Isenberg, a prominent leader of the sugar industry, explained that he was strongly opposed to annexation because he felt having a surplus of exploitable labor led to more stability. Isenberg argued that arranging workers' wages so that the "Chinese and Japanese had to *work or be hungry*" made them easier to control.[27]

The large number of "Oriental" laborers required by the sugar plantations also led to anxieties about the possibility of an imperialist plot by the Japanese government to take control of the islands. By 1897, there were 25,000 Japanese out of a total population of 109,020 in Hawai'i,[28] so fears that such a large Japanese population could gain control of Hawai'i were not without merit. In *Between Two Empires*, Eiichiro Azuma asserts that the exodus of laborers from Japan to Hawai'i coincided with a "branch of Japanese imperialist thought" that viewed the Western Hemisphere as Japan's own frontier to be settled.[29] Meiji leaders, he explains, viewed Japanese emigration as part of a Japanese style of manifest destiny, forged out of overseas settlements that were economically and politically tied to Japan. Azuma argues that government leaders assigned "a nationalist meaning to the act of emigration on the premise that the masses shared the same dedication to the state's collective purpose."[30] As such, white sugar planters needed to contend not only with a burgeoning Hawaiian nationalist movement made up of Kānaka ʻŌiwi and Chinese to protect their national sovereignty, but also a large Japanese population whose government had an interest in the Hawaiian Islands.[31]

Aware of Japan's imperialist views, white settler elites used the Bayonet Constitution to cast Asian plantation laborers in Hawaiʻi as foreign threats, outlawing their naturalization and prohibiting them from voting. But in fact, the relationship between Japanese plantation laborers in Hawaiʻi and the Japanese government was often tenuous. According to Azuma, "Most emigrants of rural origin viewed their endeavors from the standpoint of personal interest without much regard to the purported duties of the imperial subject."[32] It was also "personal interest" that motivated Japanese plantation laborers to initiate a petition, on April 9, 1893, less than three months after the 1893 U.S. overthrow, that did not oppose the overthrow of the Hawaiian Kingdom but rather demanded electoral participation in the new settler government. The petition argued that the Japanese were the "physical and intellectual" equals of any of the other foreigners.[33] Likewise in 1894, some Chinese in Hawaiʻi also sent a petition, signed by hundreds, to the Provisional Government seeking their right to vote.[34]

If white settlers were going to protect political and economic power for themselves—the principle rationale for overthrowing the Hawaiian Kingdom—then they would need some kind of assurance that annexation to the United States was even a possibility. Using the Columbian Exposition as a front to travel to the United States in 1892, Thurston went beyond Chicago to Washington, DC, to meet secretly with the Harrison administration, which expressed interest in annexing Hawaiʻi.[35] Through his secretary of the navy, B. F. Tracy, President Harrison stated, "If conditions in Hawaii compel you people to act as you have indicated, and you come to Washington with an annexation proposition, you will find an exceedingly sympathetic administration here."[36] The previously mentioned U.S. minister in Hawaiʻi, John L. Stevens, was a protégé of Secretary of State James Blaine, who had argued as early as 1881: "The decline of the native Hawaiian element in the presence of newer sturdier growths must be accepted as an inevitable fact, in view of the teachings of ethnological history. And as retrogression in the development of the Islands can not [sic] be admitted without serious detriment to American interests in the North Pacific, the problem of a replenishment of the vital forces of Hawaii presents itself for intelligent solution in an American sense—not an Asiatic or a British sense."[37] With "ethnological history" providing a seemingly clear rationale for the work of U.S. nationalism and settler colonialism, Blaine argued that President Harrison should not wait to annex Hawai'i because he thought that Japan or Britain would annex and settle Hawai'i if the United States did not.[38] The attempts to annex Hawai'i were thus a convergence of interests between white settlers from different locales: settler planters in Hawai'i who anxiously guarded their markets in the United States, and settler imperialists who shared President Harrison's consideration of imperial competition and Hawai'i's role in depression diplomacy.

In January of 1893, Queen Lili'uokalani, who had taken over as constitutional monarch, responded to the numerous calls by the Hawaiian people for a new constitution that would replace the Bayonet Constitution and restore the voting rights of Kānaka 'Ōiwi. Thurston and the Annexation Club used her attempt to promulgate a new constitution as an opportunity to seize the Hawaiian Kingdom. Stating that the actions of the Queen were "dangerous to American lives and property," the planter elite read a pronouncement at the courthouse establishing the Provisional Government while eighty U.S. Marines landed and surrounded the government buildings far from the areas where American homes and businesses were located. Thurston and four others then traveled to Washington, DC. Only two weeks after the overthrow, President Harrison tried, without success, to rush a treaty of annexation through Congress.

Unfortunately for the Thurston faction, the shared interests between them and the U.S. government would be broken, as Grover Cleveland would defeat Harrison in the presidential elections. As a friend of Lili'uokalani, and under counsel from Secretary of State Walter Gresham, Cleveland opposed the annexation of Hawai'i. By 1893, American economic interests in Asia may have been nascent, and the Cleveland administration was focused on Latin America instead.[39] And although he opposed Hawai'i's annexation per se, President Cleveland favored maintaining de facto imperial control of Hawai'i. Cleveland wanted to maintain possession of Pearl Harbor, and Assistant Secretary of State Alvey Adee added that Hawai'i was just too multiracial and not capable of maintaining "a voting population sufficient to confer a rightful claim to state-hood."[40]

Upon receiving the annexation treaty and questioning its rush, Cleveland sent a special investigator, Congressman James Blount from Georgia, to "uncover the facts" about the "Hawaiian Revolution," so-called by white settlers in Hawai'i, who had likened the overthrow to the American Revolution. In the Blount Report, the congressman declared that Hawaiians were overwhelmingly opposed to annexation: "They are convinced they have been the victims of a great wrong committed by American officials. They look to Washington for redress. . . . I am satisfied that if the votes of persons claiming allegiance to foreign countries were excluded [annexation] would be defeated by more than five to one."[41] President Cleveland declared U.S. Foreign Minister John Stevens's landing of the U.S. Marines on Hawaiian national shores an "act of war" without which the overthrow of Lili'uokalani would not have been possible. Grover Cleveland refused to annex Hawai'i as long as he remained in office.

Although the 1893 annexation attempt was defeated by the combined efforts of Hawaiian nationalists and the Cleveland administration, the settler-planter class was still able to maintain possession of the government of Hawai'i. President Cleveland did attempt to restore Lili'uokalani but refused to use necessary force. Consequently, the final decision to restore the Hawaiian Kingdom was left to Congress, which in 1894 proceeded to recognize the Provisional Government as the Republic of Hawai'i. In the same year, Congress passed the Wilson-Gorman Tariff, which restored white settler planters to the position of strategic importance they had enjoyed during the Reciprocity Treaty era. In this way, while motivated by a seeming necessity to protect sugar markets, the overthrow of the Hawaiian Kingdom was also motivated by white settler fears of democracy, and their attempts to create a governmental structure that could maintain a haole oligarchy instead.

A WHITED SEPULCHER: ORIENTALISM AND PRIMITIVISM IN A PERIOD OF ECONOMIC CRISIS

With its domestic and global reach—and celebration of linear national narrations of discovery, settlement, and progress—the 1893 Chicago World's Columbian Exposition is instructive of the kinds of temporal and spatial logics that tie U.S. settler state formation with late nineteenth-century U.S. imperialism. Like other nations that hosted previous world's fairs, the United States attempted to project its imperial prowess through

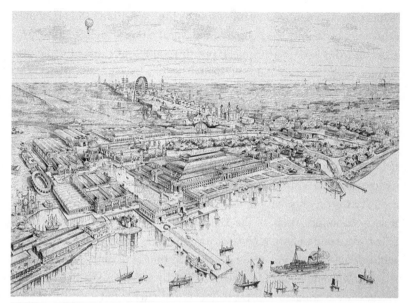

Figure 1.1 "Bird's-Eye View World's Columbian Exposition," *Book of the Fair*, 1893. Photo courtesy of Newberry Library.

displays of its colonial feats and possessions. There was a difference, however. By 1893 the United States had not yet practiced a classical form of imperialism, one that involved governing overseas lands and peoples through administrative functions emanating from a metropole. Instead, the form of colonial power associated with the United States involved practices of settler colonialism, through which the U.S. national land base was itself wholly dependent on settlers seizing and incorporating what were discursively constituted as frontiers filled with savage Indian peoples and seemingly primitive economies. Such settler-colonial practices were celebrated at the exposition as a part of a developmental discourse with simultaneous implications for land and people—replacing Natives with settlers, molding settlers into citizens, and consequently remaking an Indian "wilderness" into U.S. states and territories.

Organizers of the Chicago World's Columbian Exposition sought to illustrate the benefits of white civilization's conquest of the nonwhite world to an international audience. The two foundational sections making up the exposition helped tell that story. The temporal and spatial arrangement of the Midway Plaisance, a two-mile strip leading to the

White City, was deliberately organized by the exposition's Department of Ethnology to classify the people of the world along a smooth linear progression from dark anachronistic primitivism to enlightened white modernity, with the inscrutable "Oriental" somewhere in the middle. This to say, the Midway visually expressed the racist idea that darker races needed to catch up to whiter ones.

Accordingly, groups were racially arranged at the Midway along a "sliding scale of humanity."[42] Their accorded value to global humanity was determined by a pseudoscience that based such hierarchies on a proximity to capitalism. One's mode of life was issued as visual evidence of one's capacity for progress and intelligence. "Savage races," symbolic of land-based economies such as the Dahomey Village and American Indian Show, were said to have made little evolutionary progress, and thus were sequestered on one end of the Midway. At the same time, ethnic whites, the Teutonic and Celtic races represented by two German and two Irish villages, were situated nearest to the White City.[43] Between them were Orientalist representations of the Mohammedan world, West Asia, and East Asia.[44] The location of the "Kilauea Cyclorama" placed Kānaka ʻŌiwi between the "American Indian Show" and the exhibit on "Algeria and Tunisia." By asserting whiteness and capitalism as the pinnacle of all civilizations and cultures, this pyramidal view of the world helped to create space to imagine the formation of an American Empire and, especially, to normalize a contrived racial order where primitives, Orientals, ethnic whites, and whites were seen along a linear march from barbarism to civilization in ascending order. Indeed, when the Samoan delegation arrived in Chicago with short hair and wearing "American garb," organizers forced them to resume "their natural state of barbarism."[45]

The irony of determining a hierarchy of cultures via a proximity to capitalism is that the world's fairs from 1876 to 1916 were organized in response to numerous economic depressions. These cyclical industrial depressions created a "search for order" that required spectacle and theatrics to renew a collective national identity.[46] This identity was predicated on the subordination of nonwhite peoples, which functioned as an excuse for accumulating wealth at the expense of these same peoples. Many ethnologists at the exposition pushed strongly the idea of social evolution—that the way to world peace was for the non-Western world to adopt U.S.-fashioned capitalism and democracy.[47] Social evolution, expressed through competitive capitalism, justified Western rule over non-Western peoples on the basis of "natural" superiority. According to Susan Buck-Morss, one powerful cultural consequence of social evolution is that, "within this pseudo scientific discourse, the claim of social injustice became a logical impossibility."[48] Seizing the lands, resources, and wealth of groups deemed primitive and savage was thus seen as further evidence of white superiority. For instance, the anthropologist Otis T. Mason argued that there were three "modern types of savagery" in the world: the American (Native Americans), the Negroid, and the Malayo-Polynesian.[49] Among these, the latter category "Malayo-Polynesian" was a linguistic collapsing of Malaysians and Polynesians, but more importantly a shift in racial discourse as Polynesians were previously described as akin to Caucasians.[50] This description of savagery undergirded U.S. colonial projects in Hawai'i, Samoa, and Guåhan, as well as a genocidal war in the Philippines in which upward of two million Filipinos lost their lives. As Michael Adas cogently writes about frontier regions throughout the world, "Terms like primitive and savage . . . came to signify sorry pasts and tragic futures that would ultimately end with their cultural, and perhaps biological extinction."[51] People cast as "primitive" were typically regarded as having made no progress toward civilization, their cultures portrayed as "wastelands of non-achievement," which justified seizing their lands and resources.[52]

The American primitivism at the fair operated as a global discourse of both death and dispossession. Peoples racially targeted as such, however, expressed incredible acts of solidarity. In a letter to Queen Lili'uokalani, the "Citizens of the Cherokee Nation" inquired: "How many volunteer Americans would it require to re-establish Your Majesty's Government and displace the oligarchy that usurps your country?"[53] Some Kānaka 'Ōiwi were further aware of the commonality of their struggle with Filipinos against the United States. In 1899, for instance, Robert W. Wilcox, the Hawaiian nationalist who led armed revolts to restore the Hawaiian nation, wrote two letters to Emilio Aguinaldo, the leader of the Philippine war against the United States, to express solidarity with the Filipino fight for independence and to offer his services.[54]

While the Midway Plaisance arranged various nonwhite peoples according to their cultures and economies, it did so in the context of a period of crisis for U.S. capitalism. This is one of the reasons why it was necessary to represent the White City, an ensemble of enormous

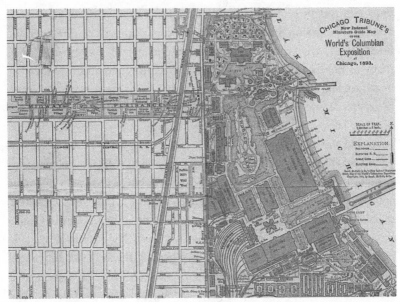

Figure 1.2 "Guide Map and Key to World's Fair Buildings, Grounds and Exhibits," *Rand McNally and Co.*, 1893. Photo courtesy of Newberry Library.

Olympian structures, not in the present but in the future; fairgoers would likely have found a utopic depiction of their present lives laughable. The expositions offered what Robert Rydell calls a "blueprint of future perfection."[55] This "future perfection," akin to Edward Said's "future wish," functioned as an imperial abstraction that produced a state of being not in the present but for one's imagined future self. This required a notion of history where one progressed by looking to the future and turning one's back to the past, a mode of progress that has been described as sustained only through forgetting one's past.[56] Amid populist protests, the future destiny of the United States as figured in the White City was said to be attainable only if the American population remained obedient and practiced what fair organizers defined as "good citizenship."[57] It appears that such demands were rejected by some of those meant to be good citizens; the White City was burned down in July of 1893, allegedly by arsonists who were most likely a part of the white working class involved in the Pullman Strikes of that year.

In Chicago, popularly known as the gateway to the western frontier, the landscape of the Midway and White City acted as a representational

Figure 1.3 The White City at the Columbian Exposition, 1893. Photo courtesy of Library of Congress.

map of the world at the same time that it offered fairgoers a national orientation of the U.S. frontier. Participating U.S. territories and states financed the creation of a building that was representative of the architecture of their state, which served as an advertisement for their industries and resources. William Cronon shows that most out-of-town residents made a point to find their own state exhibition: "The fair reminded people of something not always so obvious back home: the place in which they lived was a hinterland, whose cultural worth would be measured by the metropolitan vision that the White City so clearly exemplified."[58] In much the same way that time is spatially narrated at the fair as progressing from the Midway to the White City, and that racial groups seemingly develop in time into forms of whiteness, the land itself developmentally changes from the chaos of the Midway to the structured order of the White City.

In all of this, U.S. states are offered as the justifiable product of the frontier's replacement of Native American nations. Frederick Jackson Turner's frontier thesis, which speaks about the frontier generally but the admission of U.S. states specifically, declared: "Our Indian policy has

Figure 1.4 The White City after the fire, 1893. Photo courtesy of Chicago History Museum.

been a series of experimentations on successive frontiers. Each tier of new States has found in the older ones material for its constitutions."[59] In Turner's view, it was the destiny of white settlers to venture westward into dangerous frontiers, where they alone possessed both the intellectual capacity as European descendants and the uniquely masculine characteristics as American settlers, to subdue a wilderness and establish proper democratic and safe settlements. The state section of the fair demonstrates the white settler capacity to subdue all forms of primitivism. As such, the specific transition in the settler imagination from Native lands to U.S. states is as much a developmental discourse as it is a white supremacist discourse producing ideas about race and gender that are embedded in imaginings of land.

The state buildings portion of the White City further acted as a point of articulation among differently displaced Europeans. In other words, those identified as white or ethnic whites aiming for inclusion into this category could recognize their interests in both the construction of "whiteness" and the seizure of different Native American lands. The very processes that are productive of U.S. states lie at an obscured intersection of diaspora and indigeneity.[60] Speaking of the seventeenth-century enclosure movements in England, Joanna Brooks argues in her book *Why We Left*, "England colonized its own lands and dislocated its own indigenous peoples before colonizing abroad. . . . We were enclosed and improved out of our own homelands, and then we crossed the ocean to try and make some gain *by doing unto others as had been done unto us*."[61] Land needed to have been made available for such large populations who were fleeing Europe. Patrick Wolfe argues, "A global dimension to the frenzy for native land is reflected in the fact that, as economic immigrants, the rabble were generally drawn from the ranks of Europe's landless."[62] U.S. states are thus produced by settlers most of whom are simultaneously displaced and displacing. The need for more U.S. territories and states demonstrates how settler colonialism fails forward, beginning with the conditions of capitalism that created a massive displacement of people from Europe.

What is not mentioned in this seemingly smooth formation of U.S. territories and states is the genocidal state violence used in the removal or containment of Native nations—frequently, with assistance from the military and territorial militias led by former generals turned territorial governors who were promised land in exchange for governance. The settlement of what would be called the state of Colorado led to the 1864 Sand Creek massacre committed by the Colorado U.S. Volunteer Cavalry against two hundred unarmed Cheyenne and Arapaho. In California, Governor Peter Burnett, the first civilian governor replacing a military bureaucracy, argued to sustain an official policy of genocide in his 1851 message to the California Legislature, arguing that the ongoing wars against California Indians "must continue to be waged between the races until the Indian becomes extinct."[63] And yet, violence against Native people was not the only mode of land acquisition, as the health of the land itself was also named as a strategic target. In 1783, soon after the war with Britain and just prior to the 1787 Northwest Ordinance, Congress requested the opinion of their "Indian experts": Generals George Washington and Philip Schuyler. Washington, also nicknamed "town destroyer" by the Haudenosaunee, argued for the use of military colonies to aggressively push a line of settlement. Schuyler argued that this was expensive and dangerous and proposed a gradual increase of the frontier line so as to avoid alerting Native peoples to settler encroachment and to make federal expansion orderly. As the frontier line marched forward, Schuyler argued, the "supplies of game would be exhausted," which would force Native peoples west of the Mississippi or north to Canada.[64]

U.S. state discourse, as an organizing logic predicated on the removal or containment of Native peoples, also served to shore up another kind of American primitivism in the form of anti-Black politics. In a booklet titled *The Reason Why the Colored American Is Not in the World's Columbian Exposition*, Frederick Douglass, Ida B. Wells, I. Garland Penn, and F. L. Barnett each argues that "State's rights" were used during Reconstruction to build Southern states into a "unit for white supremacy." Given an awareness of the genocide conjured by the cultural work at the exposition, Frederick Douglass referred to the White City as a tomb, a "whited sepulcher": "[That] this World's Columbian Exposition, with its splendid display of wealth and power, its triumphs of art and its multitudinous architectural and other attractions is a fair indication of the elevated liberal sentiment of the American people, and that to the colored people of America, morally speaking, the World's Fair now in progress, is not a *whited sepulcher*. All this, and more, we would gladly say of American laws, manners, customs and Christianity. But unhappily, nothing of all this can be said, without qualification and without flagrant disregard of the truth."[65] Playing on a Christian Bible verse—"For you are like to white washed sepulchers, which indeed appear beautiful outward, but are within full of dead men's bones, and of all uncleanness"— Douglass, along with his peers, worked to expose the Janus-faced nature of white supremacy. Rooted in the antebellum period, a terrorist campaign for state control led by the Ku Klux Klan between 1867 and 1871 was designed by Southern Democrats to prevent Northern Republicans from taking leadership positions. Such acts of terror also aimed to intimidate Black communities away from voting in county, state, and national elections.[66]

Ida B. Wells argues that both the Convict Lease System and lynch laws were the outgrowth of state and county legislation that made Black communities vulnerable to white supremacy.[67] The Convict Lease System allowed for the structure of slavery to continue, as the Thirteenth Amendment abolishing slavery did not do so for convicts. U.S. states leased convicts, the overwhelming majority of whom were Black, to work for "railway contractors, mining companies and those who farm large plantations." Many of these same U.S. states, as Ida B. Wells argued, also practiced "lynch laws." Referencing the continuity of lynchings from Reconstruction to the last decade of the nineteenth century, Wells argues, "The first fifteen years of his freedom he was murdered by masked mobs for trying to vote. Public opinion having made lynching for that cause unpopular, a new reason is given to justify the murders of the past 15 years. . . . He is now charged with assaulting or attempting to assault white women. This charge, as false as it is foul, robs us of the sympathy of the world and is blasting the race's good name."[68]

Between 1882 and 1930 there are 3,320 Black men, women, and children who were murdered by lynch mobs and these numbers were at their peak during the 1890s. Jacqueline Goldsby argues that anti-Black lynchings did not exist in spite of modernity, but were instead the markers and products of such times: "Lynching was not as aberrant a practice as we now think. In the years when anti-black lynchings reached their peak (between 1882 and 1922), the violence was part of a cultural milieu that saw westward expansion and the completion of the transcontinental railroad bring about the Plains Indians Wars of the 1870s and 1880s. Nativist vigilantism against the influx of immigrants from southern and eastern Europe in the Northeast and the entry of the Chinese into the west during the 1890s and 1900s created a lethal synergy with anti-black mob violence."[69] While Black self-representation was deliberately absent at the 1893 Columbian Exposition, the frontier was everywhere present as a dominant organizing logic. But the frontier exists only insofar as it makes Native peoples also absent. In other words, the frontier could only be expressed at the exposition in a manner that positioned Native people in the past, with no present or future claims, and thus as a people whose histories were written like obituaries.

Despite the seemingly incontrovertible narrations at the Columbian Exposition, settler claims to even the city of Chicago, the very land on which the exposition was held, remained very much contested. John Low (Pokagon Band of Potawatomi Indians) traces the savvy work of tribal leader and Chicago celebrity Simon Pokagon at the Columbian Exposition.[70] In a public event covered by the local newspapers, Pokagon publicly reminded the mayor of Chicago, Carter H. Harrison, that the Potawatomi had never been paid for the 994,000 acres of land that the city of Chicago sits on. Pokagon pursued the matter in a letter to the mayor noting that the city should fund a Congress for Native Americans: "The land on which Chicago and the Fair stands still belongs to my people, as it has never been paid for. All we ask from Chicago is that the people help us to come and join our common country. We wish to talk for ourselves. The pottawatomies have a message to deliver to the world."[71] Despite the existence of numerous congresses at the world's fair covering a wide array of international topics, a Native American congress never took place.

The Pokagon Band of Potawatomi, however, were successful in disrupting settler narrations at the exposition. Simon Pokagon's book *Red Man's Greetings*, for instance, was a featured item at the Columbian Exposition. In his book, which was made of birch bark, Pokagon wrote: "On behalf of my people, the American Indians, I hereby declare to you, the pale-faced race that has usurped our lands and homes, that we have no spirit to celebrate with you the great Columbian Fair now being held in this Chicago city, the wonder of the world. No; sooner would we hold the high joy day over the graves of our departed than to celebrate our own funeral, the discovery of America."[72] The building of a birch bark tipi/wigwam along the Midway Plaisance further speaks to both the assertion of a Potawatomi presence and the creative power of Pokagon. Low argues that this was used as a reminder of "the shifting of lifeways and of communities that were forever changed by contact with Euro-Americans." Such a Native presence at the Columbian Exposition served as "monuments to new beginnings," the "potential of Indian peoples in the future of the nation, and to the possibilities that could emerge from their inclusion."[73] As Pokagon's cultural politics demonstrate, representing Native peoples in the future was a highly political act, as it would prevent settlers from asserting themselves as the modern inheritors of Native peoples' lands.

"Orientals," as opposed to "primitives," were not peoples at the beginning of progress; rather, they were seen as symbols of the measure of progress along the spectrum between the "traditional" and "modern" (modern meaning Western).[74] The Japanese government, described as having made greater strides toward "the Western spirit of enterprise and civilization," was given a space for display in the White City at the Wooded Isle, apart from the Midway.[75] Japanese officials stated that they were excited to participate at the exposition in order to further commercial ties with the United States and prove that "Japan is a country worthy of full fellowship in the family of nations."[76]

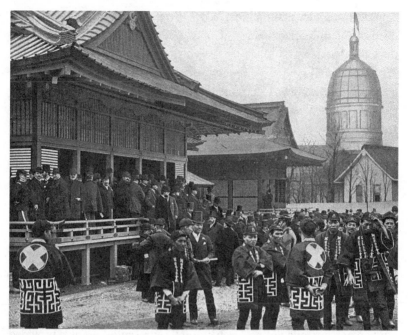

Figure 1.5 Japanese Exhibit at the Columbian Exposition, 1893. Photo courtesy of Chicago History Museum.

The Japanese were imagined as having the ability to open Asia to capitalism, and thus much-needed markets that would help get the United States out of economic depression. Americans consequently referred to the Japanese affectionately as the "Yankees of the East."[77] Azuma explains that the Meiji government understood that in order to be considered a "civilized" nation, Japan would have to "partake in the practice of colonization."[78] Indeed, the Meiji state's colonization of the Ainu people in Hokkaido in 1869 was modeled after the conquest of Native Americans by the United States.[79] Accordingly, Japan would establish its own form of manifest destiny by colonizing Okinawa, Taiwan, South Sakhalin, and Kwantung Province in northern China, and then annexing Korea in 1910. But while Japan was hailed as having a civilizing influence on the otherwise backward Asian continent, it would also need to play the position of subordinate supremacy. As long as Japan remained subordinate to the United States, it could be included in the future utopia that America was creating.[80] By the time of Theodore Roosevelt's presidency, however,

American military and political leaders predicted that the emerging industrial and militarized nation of Japan was destined for future war with the United States.[81]

Orientalist discourse consequently created both a formidable ally and enemy. Japan would be used as a model of a people who had followed the example of the Americans and established itself as a nation worthy of respect. At the same time, however, this respect would also be perceived as a threat to notions of white supremacy. To be sure, fear of the Japanese was often based on an idea that they might, in fact, be a superior people capable of displacing whites. Japan's success in the Russo-Japanese War, for example, was the first time in modern history that a non-European nation defeated a European nation in war. Such instances were used to justify the passing of the 1907 Gentlemen's Agreement. This informal arrangement led to the United States agreeing that it would not block Japanese immigration, so long as Japan did not allow their nationals to settle in the United States. By deeming the Japanese "ineligible to citizenship," further laws would be passed that would block naturalization, land ownership, and voting. Such cultural representations also provided justification for the United States to fortify Hawai'i as a military outpost to defend against Japanese attack in the early twentieth century. Such a military outpost, however, first necessitated occupying Hawai'i by representing Kānaka 'Ōiwi as "unfit for self-government."

"CYCLORAMA OF KILAUEA"

The Hawaiian Bureau of Information's "Cyclorama of Kilauea" functioned as an imperial advertisement for tourism, settlement, and annexation, all of which sought to reaffirm white settler economic and political rule in Hawai'i. Due to the small number of white settlers in Hawai'i, especially when compared with the number of Kānaka 'Ōiwi and Asians, white economic and political leaders saw tourism as an attractive economic alternative to sugar, one that would allow them to increase the white settler population through capital expansion and still be unaffected by American tariffs. In 1891, the *Daily Pacific Commercial Advertiser*, the mouthpiece of the white settler elite that Lorrin A. Thurston would eventually come to own, responded to the effects of the McKinley Tariff:

Figure 1.6 "Cyclorama of Kilauea" at the Chicago World's Columbian Exposition, 1893. Photo courtesy of Chicago History Museum.

> In spite of the blow which the sugar industry has received, there are those who think that we are about to enter upon a period of great expansion and consequent prosperity.... The tourist travel to these Islands is capable of an almost indefinite expansion. It might yield an income of several millions a year. If it comes the country will be opened up by a network of roads which will give to thousands of acres of arable land a ready access to market. With the realization of these conditions the prosperity of the country will be assured and we can laugh at sugar tariffs.[82]

Many believed that tourism would stabilize Hawai'i's economy and increase white settlement in the hopes of eventually outnumbering a Kanaka 'Ōiwi population and giving whites political power at the voting booths.

Numerous articles in the settler newspapers reported the desires of "hundreds and thousands" of whites who would consider moving to Hawai'i only if it were a part of the United States. One such sentiment was expressed in this way: "I would not expatriate myself, but if I could own a little land and have a home in such a climate and stay under the flag it would be a great temptation."[83] Outnumbering the Native population was also seen as fundamental to economic stability and expansion. Thurston wrote in a letter to Secretary of State James Blaine in 1892 that there was an "overwhelming electoral majority in one class [the Natives], and the ownership of practically all the property in another class [white settlers]," consequently creating conflict where settlers "are constantly, more or less openly, threatening revolution and disturbance."[84] Thurston explained that while it might not actually lead to revolution or bloodshed, the "constant possibility" of revolution prevented capital from coming into the country, halting further economic development.[85] Indeed, after facing defeat at the voting polls in 1890, Lorrin A. Thurston became heavily involved in promoting white settlement and tourism to Hawai'i.

Teaming up with Benjamin Dillingham, a well-known owner of the Oahu Railway and Land Company, and William F. Sesser, a railroad advertising agent from Michigan, Thurston used the Hawaiian Bureau of Information to distribute literature throughout the United States that portrayed Hawai'i as a frontier—a place where Hawaiian savagery and white American civilization met. Over one thousand large photographs of the Kīlauea volcano, ten thousand copies of a pamphlet titled *Paradise of the Pacific and Inferno of the World*, and fifty thousand smaller pamphlets titled *Vistas of Hawaii* were distributed nationally.[86] The development of printing technology near the end of the nineteenth century aided the Bureau's campaign tremendously. The opinion campaigns seeking to capture national consent for annexation utilized numerous photographs due to the new low costs of reproducing images of Hawai'i. Thurston himself developed the "specific model" to promote Hawai'i as a tourist destination.[87]

Every person who entered the cyclorama was given the pamphlet *Vistas of Hawaii*. Cristina Bacchilega analyzes the larger pamphlet: "Its photos juxtapose images of powerful steamers to Native canoes, and beautifully landscaped 'private' yards to 'glimpses of the great volcano, Kilauea.' Thurston illustrates the binaries of his subtitle, *Paradise of the Pacific and Inferno of the World*, by displaying Native Hawaiians as part of the 'infernal' scenes—these representing the desolate volcano and that dark world before civilization brought trains and hotels to the islands."[88]

In line with portraying Hawai'i as a frontier zone, white settlement was considered necessary to bring Hawai'i out of its primal and anachronistic space. Through proper white American settlement, the symbols of primitivism and modernity on the farthest margins of the American frontier helped tourists feel a combination of threat from wild, dark savagery, yet safety in knowing that the land had been inhabited and modernized by American settlers. But there was a threshold: if modernity went too far, and extinguished the exoticism associated with the "primitive," Hawai'i's selling power would be lost.

As an advertisement for tourism and annexation, Lorrin Thurston's "Kilauea Cyclorama" represented Hawai'i through frontier logics, a place where American civilization and Native savagery met. Keeping in line with the idea that "primitives" were at the very beginning of human progress, Hawai'i, as represented through Kīlauea volcano, was a geological symbol of the absolute beginning stages of development, a place on earth at its most primitive state. At the same time, this primitive stage of development was represented in what was considered to be one of the most modern forms of Western technological entertainment in existence, the cyclorama. Considered to be "all the rage in America," cycloramas or panoramas were linked to the mobile gaze and new styles of modern visual consumption. With their large panoramic screens that often stood three stories high, cycloramas were also the predecessor to motion picture films.[89] Thurston was certainly very keen on the selling power of visually combining the primitive and the modern.

While the volcano itself helped to create a sense of primitive danger, the evocation of Pele was crucial to providing an explicitly racialized, gendered, and superstitious Native threat. Pele's statue stood above the entrance to Thurston's cyclorama, and, at twenty-five feet, it was said to be the second-largest statue at the Columbian Exposition.[90] An 1893 booklet on the Midway described the statue of Pele this way: "Her hair is blown wildly back and there is a terrible frown upon her beautiful face, as she prepared to annihilate her enemies." Pele's "enemies," as narrated in the superficial Hawaiian stories told in the cyclorama and its advertisements, were always men.

This sense of Native threat was also inscribed upon the spectator in highly visceral and theatrical ways. Frightened initially by the crater's sheer mass and the sinister image of Pele, viewers were then enveloped in

VISTAS OF KILAUEA

Figure 1.7 View from inside the "Cyclorama of Kilauea," 1893. Photo courtesy of Chicago History Museum.

a chant to Pele.[91] In this way, Native "superstition" and the female threat of Pele were pacified by an objective masculine science in the form of enlightened geologists who could measure, categorize, and rationally explain away superstitious Native myth. A write-up of the exhibit speaks to this dynamic: "Language utterly fails to adequately describe the awful grandeur of the vast crater and the terrible fascination of the mighty forces constantly in action within its frowning walls, but a few volcanic facts will give some conception of what the volcano is and its method of action."[92] In the landscape painting of the Kīlauea crater inside the cyclorama, Chicago painter Walter W. Burridge depicts the figure of a geologist walking and studying within the crater. Here, two competing sets of knowledge about one location are seemingly juxtaposed. As a people who were seen as having a more advanced knowledge over the crater, settlers could position themselves as more deserving than Native peoples of that space. The representation of Pele, combined with the science of geology, sought to cancel or trivialize Hawaiian cultural associations with place.

The chant offered at the beginning of the Cyclorama, however, according to Adria L. Imada, was a standard mourning chant for ali'i, whose

VISTAS OF KILAUEA

Figure 1.8 Geologist depicted in landscape painting of Kīlauea crater, 1893. Photo courtesy of Chicago History Museum.

hidden transcript, for those who could understand Hawaiian language, represents resistance to the "symbolic and material control of haole elites."[93] It is thus critical to highlight that the "Cyclorama of Kilauea" is not an actual juxtaposition of two forms of knowledge. This is not "competing epistemologies" so much as two representations set by the same white racist imagination. Thurston's fictive depiction of Hawaiian culture as "antiscience" allows him and other settlers to render themselves as the masculine embodiment of scientific reason. In fact, the initial plans for the Hawai'i exhibit by Kānaka 'Ōiwi themselves at the Columbian Exposition, prior to being usurped by Thurston, were designed with both science and physicality in mind. The Hale Nauā was a royal society that reflected a "new pro-Native national culture"; its national campaign, initiated by Kalākaua, aimed to promote Kānaka 'Ōiwi as masters of their culture while also contributing to an international movement for science. Kealani Cook points out how the Hale Nauā, deeply aware of racist imaginings of Hawaiian people, planned to win the public over at the 1893 Columbian Exposition via sports, culture, and competition. By sending surfers, high-divers, baseball players, sharp shooters, and opera singers,

Cook explains, "the message the Hale Nauā intended to send was clear; Hawai'i, while proudly retaining an explicitly Native culture, was still proficient in the cultural forms of Europe and America."[94]

In stark contrast to the one-dimensional portrayals of Pele in the cyclorama, Kanaka 'Ōiwi scholars describe Pele, and the women associated with her, as powerful female deities. Scholar of Hawaiian literature ku'ualoha ho'omanawanui shows how in the face of such mischaracterizations of Pele, the actual stories of Pele and Hi'iaka are "multiply layered and intertwined" with mana wahine, female empowerment, in direct defiance of the heteropatriarchy undergirding white settler colonialism. The wide publication and readership of this story, ho'omanawanui argues, helped to "resist, counter, disrupt, and overturn the settler colonial discourse that infantilized Kanaka Maoli as inferior beings, mythologized Kanaka Maoli history, and denigrated Kanaka Maoli culture, denying the presence of an intellectual history."[95]

Noenoe K. Silva argues that the figure of Pele also speaks against a heteropatriarchal devaluation of domestic space: "Pele is demanding, jealous, angry, unpredictable, and vengeful. Further, the other women in the epic engage in meaningful and pleasurable activities: they fight off evils, outsmart rapists, chant and dance hula, surf, practice medicine and religion (one and the same at times), and have loves and profound relationships, especially with each other. They are not cooking, cleaning house, or worrying about husbands. They are not domesticated; rather, they are adventurous."[96] Pele's representation in the cyclorama entails the pacification and domestication of an irrational and belligerent Native woman by white masculine science. This links tightly to the narration of the overthrow of Queen Lili'uokalani in January of 1893. Lili'uokalani was one of the world's most politically visible and known women, who was publicly vilified as a direct threat to white settler control over Hawai'i. Not surprisingly, Thurston described Lili'uokalani as a "dangerous woman." As mentioned above, it was Lili'uokalani who sought to promulgate a new constitution to restore a system of checks and balances and full democratic vote to Kānaka 'Ōiwi. This attempt to open political office to vote was characterized as dangerous to "American lives and property," which was taken to justify the landing of U.S. Marines to occupy Hawai'i. The American press also ran numerous stories about

Lili'uokalani's supposed savagery and hot temper. One in particular told of Lili'uokalani's plan to have Thurston and others beheaded for committing treason. Lili'uokalani responded by stating that not only had she never said these words, but beheading was a form of punishment never used in the Hawaiian Islands.[97] In 1895, Lili'uokalani was imprisoned in 'Iolani Palace after a failed armed coup attempted to restore her to the throne. Despite her forced imprisonment, "house arrest" in the domestic space, she was able to utilize such assumptions about her to remain informed about what was happening outside of the palace: "Flowers from home I unwrapped myself, so as to be sure to save these bits of news which I sought opportunity at intervals to read."[98]

The patriarchal tactic of sequestering Lili'uokalani to domestic space has longer ties to the Thurston family, whose missionary anxieties viewed the control and domestic confinement of women as necessary to progress. Lorrin A. Thurston's grandmother, Lucy Thurston, was one of the first Calvinist missionaries from Boston to Hawai'i. She celebrates, in her autobiography, their first successful conversion of a white blacksmith in Hawai'i. After his conversation to Christianity, his first act is to violently sequester his daughter in their home:

> He went into his own shop and made an iron ring in which to in-case her ankle. He then chained her to the post standing in the middle of his thatched house, reaching from the ground to the ridgepole. After being thus confined for three weeks, her ankle became chafed and swollen. She promised fair. He pitied and released her. She immediately left his premises, went straight to a neighboring outhouse, and secreted herself in a barrel. He sought and found her, and, with an unwavering purpose, secured her as before. With a persistence allied to that of Grant's on a broader scale, he now kept her chained to that post three additional months. The battle was won. The daughter had learned to fear, to obey, and to love her father.[99]

Attempts at forcing unruly women into domestic space were a form of primitive accumulation, a way to confine reproductive labor to women so that men could then become wage earners. Such processes were also about containing the power of women, particularly when the needs of capitalism required destroying practices, beliefs, and abilities that were incompatible with the capitalist division of labor.[100]

Figure 1.9 (left) Queen Liliʻuokalani; frontispiece to her autobiography, *Hawaii's Story by Hawaii's Queen*, 1897. Photo courtesy of Newberry Library. Figure 1.10 (right) Pele statue up close, 1893. Photo courtesy of Chicago History Museum.

Thurston and his geologists were entrenched in the gendered and racial discourse of the frontier and spoke of geology as a war between civilization and the destructive female power of Pele. Thomas Jaggar, an early geologist, would eventually title his book *Volcanoes Declare War*, telling of his and Thurston's involvement in the 1935 U.S. Army's dropping of six tons of bombs on a lava flow from Mauna Loa.[101] Interestingly, the lines between a superstitious Native past and rational enlightened present would be blurred, however, when two of the bombers touched wings in

VOL. 26 NO. 644   FEBRUARY 17 1894   PRICE 10 CENTS

LILI TO GROVER.

You listened to my DOLE-ful tale;
You tried your best—'twas no avail.
It's through no fault of yours or mine
That I can't be your VALENTINE.

(The above PENNY VALENTINE was included in the last mail from Hawaii, but through some mistake was not transmitted to the senate.)

Figure 1.11 "Lili to Grover," *Judge*, 1893. Courtesy of the University of Michigan.

midair and burst into flames, an incident that Hawaiians in the area had warned the army about, stating that such bombings were desecrations against Pele.[102] In fact, the ashes of one of the pilots killed in the bombing went missing on their return flight back to the U.S. continent and were never found. Vicente M. Diaz points out that such moments where "men of reason" are thrown for a loop, have the gendered and epistemic effect of calling "into question that particular form of manliness built on reason."[103]

Yet, the portrayals of Pele and Lili'uokalani also show how the aims of colonialism and tourism relied on different representations of Kanaka

'Ōiwi women. Pele's statue was designed by Ellen Rankin of Chicago, whose goal was to portray Pele as a "Venus of the Pacific," the most "beautiful woman that ever lived."[104] In order to lure tourists and settlers to Hawai'i, Pele was sculpted with European features, a beauty aesthetic palatable to a white American audience. Lili'uokalani, on the other hand, was often represented in political cartoons as having "primitive" features, repeatedly described by the missionary elite as both savage and sexually deviant.[105]

In fact, there is also much overlap between the gendered advertising for tourism and annexation. Thurston writes in *Vistas of Hawaii* that it was the wresting of political control from Hawaiians that transformed Hawai'i into a place that could be safely visited by tourists and properly developed by whites. Like most advertisements, the pamphlets and cyclorama produced by the Hawaiian Bureau of Information distracted the viewer from a highly politicized situation, offering in its place a space of fantasy defined by settler desire and colonial imagination. As an imperial advertisement for annexation, the cyclorama sold Hawai'i and Hawaiians as existing in an exotic and primitive past, which thus allowed a future wish for annexation and settlement by a people discursively constructed as more deserving of Hawai'i and more capable of bringing it into the modern world. The "Cyclorama of Kilauea" enjoyed a fairly long run in the world's fair circuits and eventually made its way to the San Francisco Midwinter Fair of 1894–95, a Boston cyclorama theater, and eventually the 1901 Buffalo Exposition.[106] Long capturing the imagination of its viewers, the cyclorama was able to cast the Hawaiian Kingdom, and anything associated with Kānaka 'Ōiwi, as existing in a vanishing past, while presenting a Hawai'i under both American and white settler control as foretelling of a bright future filled with new economic and political possibilities.

A FUTURE WISH FOR HAWAI'I STATEHOOD

Lorrin A. Thurston often obsessively talked about the death of the Hawaiian Kingdom and the birth of a new settler government. He argued that once Hawaiians understood that the monarchy was dead and "this idea penetrates the skulls of the great unwashed electorate," Hawaiians themselves would become annexationists.[107] The state of Hawai'i seal

Figure 1.12 Royal coat of arms of the Hawaiian Kingdom. Photograph by the author.

Figure 1.13 Republic of Hawai'i seal, 1896. Courtesy of Hawai'i State Archives.

used today, adopted in 1896, visually offers us an understanding of this necropolitical logic and Said's "future wish" as it relates to Hawai'i. Viggo Jacobson designed the Hawai'i seal in an 1895 art competition sponsored by the legislature of the Republic of Hawai'i. In a 1979 issue of *Aloha Magazine* the author writes:

> The seal is a modified version of the royal coat of arms of the Hawaiian Kingdom. . . . The rising sun replaces the royal crown and Maltese cross of the original coat of arms, and signifies the birth of a new state. King Kamehameha the Great and Goddess of Liberty holding the Hawaiian flag replace two warriors on the royal coat of arms. Puloulou, or tabu ball and stick, in the second and third quarters was carried before the king and placed before the door of his home, signifying his authority and power. Here, it is a symbol of the authority and power of government. The phoenix as symbol of death and resurrection, symbolizes the change from the monarchy to a freer democratic form of government.[108]

In 1895, three years before Hawai'i was fraudulently made a U.S. territory through joint resolution by the United States, the star at the center of the shield represented "the Star of Hawaii," a "future wish" for statehood, of which Viggo Jacobson wrote, "We hope to see [it] ultimately placed in the banner of the United States."[109] At the same time, however, most Hawaiian nationals had not given up their claims to Hawaiian independence. As Noenoe K. Silva's research has uncovered, Robert Wilcox attempted a failed war in 1895, but in 1897, when talks of annexing the Hawaiian Islands to the United States resumed, the Hui Kālai'āina, Hui Aloha 'Āina, and Hui Aloha 'Āina o Nā Wāhine circulated petitions signed by over 90 percent of the Hawaiian population opposing American citizenship throughout the islands.[110] The Hawaiian nation remained very much alive. White settlers, however, sought to dismiss Hawaiian claims to nationhood by playing to a much more recognizable international threat to white order than that posed by Kānaka 'Ōiwi.

This threat—the Yellow Peril—is also one that Thurston would no doubt learn more about from his experiences at the Columbian Exposition and correspondence with James Blaine. In 1897, Thurston wrote that white settlers in Hawai'i understood their political dilemma as a contest not between Hawaiians and white settlers, but rather between the white and the yellow race, stating: "It is no longer a question whether Hawaii should be controlled by the native Hawaiian, or by some foreign people; but the question is, *What foreign people shall control Hawaii?*"[111] By 1897, the Republic of Hawai'i became anxious of Japan possibly seizing the Hawaiian Islands. The Republic had begun to force ships filled with Japanese laborers to return to Japan in the belief that Japan was participating in a "peaceful invasion" of the islands.[112] This led to talks of war between Japan and the United States. Both the Republic of Hawai'i and U.S. military leaders hoped to exploit these tensions, believing this might force the United States to immediately annex the islands. By the latter part of the 1890s, military leaders wanted to keep Hawai'i away from Japan so that it could never use Hawai'i as a staging point to attack the West Coast.[113]

In 1898, imperialists would again seek annexation. The national press, however, reminded the American public of the 1893 crime upon which annexation stood. The *New York Times* ran an editorial titled "Story of a Crime," stating that before the "Hawaiian crime is actually consummated," the American public should remember the whole story of the January 1893 overthrow.[114] The *San Francisco Call* dubbed the annexation "shameful," because "it made the United States a receiver of goods stolen while we held the owner to be robbed."[115] Unable to get the constitutionally required two-thirds vote from the Senate, Senator Morgan of Nevada, citing the annexation of Texas as a precedent, pushed the annexation through joint resolution, which only required half the vote of Congress. The comparison was, and still is, flawed: Texas was not annexed as a territory but admitted into the union as a "state." Moreover, unlike Texas, neither the white settler elite of Hawai'i nor Washington, DC, sought statehood for Hawai'i. The problem wasn't simply that Hawai'i's majority population was nonwhite. It was that the large numbers of Native peoples could still threaten the political control of the numerically small white settler elites should they gain full voting rights afforded by statehood.

Their inability to achieve annexation legally, neither holding a referendum in Hawai'i which would have failed nor able to win a two-thirds majority in Congress, made state theatricality all the more necessary to give the appearance of legitimate sovereignty. Settler state theatricality thus acted less as ideology than as a productive force that allowed for the illusion of U.S. sovereignty via joint resolution to fail forward to Hawai'i.

A critical retelling of the 1893 Chicago World's Columbian Exposition helps contextualize Hawai'i statehood within the history of the formation of other U.S. states. This political and cultural process was not inevitable; rather, it was a long and violent white supremacist ideology that saw the expropriation of Native peoples' lands and resources as a natural occurrence. Such cultural work, making violent expropriation seem natural, was nearly ubiquitous in the United States, as the very milieu many of these cultural producers worked in was often shaped by the cultural, legal, political, economic, and/or military contestation of the Native land they were literally standing on. The landscape painter and special-effects person, Walter W. Burridge, gained national notoriety after the Columbian Exposition for his three-dimensional lava flows for Thurston's "Cyclorama of Kilauea." Burridge was later hired to design the theatrical set of L. Frank Baum's *The Wizard of Oz* in 1902. Baum himself propagandized the 1890 Massacre at Wounded Knee, arguing in his newspaper, "*The Pioneer* has before declared that our only safety depends upon the total extermination of the Indians. Having wronged them for centuries we had better, in order to protect our civilization, follow it up by one more wrong and wipe these untamed and untamable creatures from the face of the earth."[116] Thurston and Baum both achieved their political aims by propagandizing in newspapers about the inevitable demise of Native peoples and called upon the artistic talents of Burridge to reach a wider audience utilizing settler-colonial theatrics.

In 1927, Lorrin A. Thurston expressed the same general view as many of his peers, relegating Hawai'i statehood to a "future wish" by stating: "Do I object to statehood? Most assuredly not, so long as it remains an ideal, not a reality."[117] A serious movement for statehood did not emerge until 1934, when another major economic depression abolished favorable tariff relations and again motivated Hawai'i's white business and governing elite to secure further colonial control of Hawai'i, this time through statehood. The Hawaiian Bureau of Information, utilized in part to wage an opinion campaign to achieve annexation and regain favorable tariff relations in the 1890s, would be nearly reproduced in 1935 in the form of the so-called Hawaii Equal Rights Commission. This propaganda commission led to another opinion campaign to achieve Hawai'i statehood for economic reasons.

CHAPTER 2

THE COURAGE TO SPEAK

Disrupting Haole Hegemony at the 1937
Congressional Statehood Hearings

The son of propagandist Lorrin A. Thurston, Lorrin P. Thurston, replaced his father as editor of the self-advertised "family paper," the *Honolulu Advertiser*, after the senior Thurston died in 1931. Nine years later, in 1940, Lorrin P. Thurston wrote an editorial seeking a vote on Hawai'i statehood that also aimed to resolve the "great problem" his father's actions had helped to create. In a confessional tone, Lorrin P. Thurston shares information known about his father's involvement in the overthrow and alleged annexation of the Hawaiian Kingdom:

> The question in my mind and many others is, "Shall Hawaii have statehood?" Many people do not know the real facts of the overthrow of the monarchial government and annexation of the Hawaiian Islands; or many people do not want to remember them. . . . As you must surely know the Hawaiian people did not have the opportunity to vote for annexation to the United States and furthermore, the majority of the Hawaiian people did not approve of the overthrow of Queen Liliuokalani and the monarchial government.
>
> It stands by historical facts that Hawaii was overthrown by a few men and not public opinion as has always been thought. . . . We are or should be thankful that the islands were annexed but not under such conditions. . . . It is a known fact that there was no plebiscite of any kind having been taken by the new government. . . . This plebiscite was to state the kind of government the Hawaiians wanted and

whether or not they wanted annexation to the United States or to remain independent. I believe that one solution to this great problem is to have the people of Hawaiian descent given the privilege that was deprived their forefathers from the years 1893 and up to 1898. Let that privilege be to vote for statehood which I believe many members of Congress would be satisfied in knowing that the Hawaiian people would be the rightful heirs to statehood.[1]

Thurston reexamines the "real facts" surrounding the 1893 overthrow and alleged annexation in 1898, arguing that the process by which Hawaiʻi was declared a territory of the United States was emblematic less of democracy than of conquest.[2] Stating that he believes most of his readers do not know about the events that took place between 1893 and 1898, and that others "do not want to remember them," Thurston argues that they have direct bearing on his historical moment, in which a government- and sugar planter–led movement for statehood was in full swing. Indeed, Lorrin P. Thurston simultaneously distances himself from his father, stating that Kānaka ʻŌiwi should be given the privilege to vote that their "forefathers" were denied, at the same time that he is taking up the legacy work of the senior Thurston by attempting to finalize the U.S. occupation of Hawaiʻi, not through annexation, as his father attempted, but through statehood. It is important to note that while Lorrin P. Thurston believes that democracy would resolve past injustices by holding a vote, embedded within the option to vote is his presumption to know better for Kānaka ʻŌiwi. Thurston argues that their "privilege" should be to do as he thinks they should do, which is to vote for statehood. And yet, it is a similar moment of economic and political crisis for an elite haole community that again animates such actions.

The early decades of Hawaiʻi's territorial period saw a rapid growth in both the sugar industry and U.S. military. With nearly 1.8 million acres of Hawaiian Kingdom crown and government lands seized by the new settler government, those who aided in the overthrow of Hawaiʻi further accumulated or gained access to large tracts of land and capital. For instance, between 1910 and 1913, 130,000 acres of land were made available for sugar production and thirteen new plantations were created with $40 million available in new capital investment.[3] Some of these new plantations were built on sacred lands, as was the case in Olaʻa, at the Mountain

View Plantation on the island of Hawai'i.[4] Popularly referred to as the Big Five—Castle and Cooke, Charles Brewer and Company, Alexander and Baldwin, Theophilus H. Davis and Company, and Heinrich Hackfeld and Company (renamed the American Factors during World War I)—these interlocking corporations would come to control forty-one of the forty-seven sugar plantations and over 95 percent of the total sugar production in Hawai'i by 1930.[5] The Big Five, through a system of interlocking directorates, also monopolized the industries that surrounded the plantations, namely banking, insurance, shipping, utilities, and retailing. With their political connections in Washington, DC, they also dominated the territorial positions that appointed key posts in the judiciary, police force, and educational institutions, including the university. Three of these five agencies came under the control of four families (Alexander, Baldwin, Castle, and Cooke), whose patriarchs first traveled to Hawai'i as missionaries.

Economic depression in the 1930s, however, led white settler elites to mount a campaign for U.S. statehood. Beginning with the U.S. stock market crash in 1929, the Great Depression led to over five thousand banks being forced to close in the United States and industrial production falling by 50 percent, a situation that caused an estimated fifteen million people to be unemployed.[6] By December of 1936, nearly one-quarter of Hawai'i's labor force was out of work and the power and prestige held by the Big Five was under extraordinary stress.[7] With a U.S. capitalist system in disarray, Congress passed legislation that again negatively impacted white settler planters' access to U.S. sugar markets. As a part of New Deal agricultural policies, the 1934 Jones-Costigan Sugar Act abolished the tariff relations that had provided the Big Five access to highly lucrative U.S. sugar markets.[8] Unlike in the 1890s, federal policies to combat the Great Depression brought more worries for the Big Five. Congress would also pass the 1935 Wagner Act, empowering Hawai'i's dockworkers to organize themselves into unions without employer interference. In an island society that depended on importing and exporting goods through ports and harbors, Hawai'i stevedores, and eventually agricultural workers who were organized under the same International Longshore and Warehouse Union (ILWU), gained the capacity to oppose the Big Five in unprecedented ways. With the passing of the Wagner Act, the Big Five formed the Industrial Association of Hawaii (IAH) during that same year. Where previously the Big Five had simply fired and blacklisted active union members, the sole purpose of the IAH was to formally oppose the creation of unions. In addition, the Big Five searched for new political means to have a larger voice in Congress, particularly to counter what they called "federal discrimination." They imagined that statehood would provide those means.

The Hawaii Equal Rights Commission (1935–47) was formed by the territorial legislature to oppose "federal discrimination" by capturing statehood. The creation of the Hawaii Equal Rights Commission in 1935 coincided with that of the Hawaii Sugar Planters Association (HSPA), the unincorporated organization made up of plantation owners, with public adoption of statehood as their stated aim. The mid-1930s thus mark the beginning of a genuine government-led movement for U.S. statehood, charging the commission with four responsibilities: to "compile and disseminate information to support equal political rights for Hawaii, prevent discriminatory federal legislation, assist in obtaining amendments to the Organic Act, and make a study of statehood and the advisability of submitting the issue to plebiscite." In this way, the five-member commission—former Governor Lawrence M. Judd, Victor S. K. Houston, James L. Coke, and Louis S. Cain, with the governor as ex-officio chairman—were to "have the people of Hawaii correctly represented before the mainland reading public."[9] The five-member commission organized numerous congressional visits to investigate statehood and sought to frame the rules of discourse within civil society, making it difficult for anyone to oppose statehood without being labeled "misinformed" or "subversive" against both the state and industry.

When thinking about the emerging state-led movement for U.S. statehood in the 1930s, it is important to consider the geopolitical implications of the racial ideas about different Asians and Kānaka ʻŌiwi. The propagation of these ideas, generally through Orientalism and primitivism, allowed Hawaiʻi to be recognized as worthy of statehood by a regime of white supremacy. This is to say that instead of considering only how Native and different Asian voices were often repressed, per critical theory, I question how power operated by growing specific ideas about these groups, creating the proper normative subject, and arranging both the populations and ideas about them in ways that would merit Hawaiʻi's transition from territory to U.S. state.[10]

The "imperial university" thus became a critical U.S. strategic weapon in both U.S. settler-colonial and imperial formations.[11] The establishment of U.S. universities in U.S.-occupied sites (Hawai'i, the Philippines, and Puerto Rico) followed the "imperial acquisitions" at the turn of the century, and thus took part in consolidating U.S. strategic dominance while reshaping the population into specific ideologies that aligned with "producing proper subjects of the empire."[12] Such work aimed to make heterogeneous populations knowable, furnishing white settler leaders in Hawai'i with a racial knowledge to prescribe both the proper policies to govern heterogeneity and the proper conduct that these diverse, nonwhite populations should follow. Here, I utilize settler-colonial critique to discursively analyze how academic and scholarly texts produced in the early half of the twentieth century at the University of Hawai'i at Mānoa—specifically the writings of eugenicist Stanley D. Porteus and the Department of Sociology, which have genealogical ties to the 1893 Columbian Exposition—were theorizing Hawai'i's heterogeneous populations, primarily with the aim of excluding Asian groups and fixing Hawaiians as proper colonial subjects. Thus, across different settler-colonial sites tied to global imperial politics, modern formations of racial power relied on the technology of racial difference, embedded structurally within capitalist and settler state formation.

I juxtapose this work with counterhegemonic sites of resistance and knowledge production, specifically the Japanese community newspaper *Hawaii Hochi* and the weekly *Voice of Labor*. These newspapers produced ideas on behalf of the communities they wrote for and thus the "objects of knowledge" were not the nonwhite population per se, but a system of white supremacy and the Big Five. Given the increased racial and class tensions leading to the 1937 congressional statehood hearings—which included a threat to replace a civil settler government with a military commission—those who were regularly disciplined and surveilled had the opportunity to reverse the imperial gaze and instead appeal to a more powerful white supremacist authority, the U.S. Congress. Those who offered testimony did so at great risk to themselves, yet the courage to speak truth consequently required Congress to demonstrate their own greatness by also accepting being told the truth.[13] This is important because while some history books argue that 1935 marks a moment where public opinion is "strongly united" in favor of statehood, the white supremacy of the 1930s led the majority-nonwhite population to oppose immediate statehood, not endorse it.[14] In this way, white settlers shape and discipline, but have never been able to determine, the actions of Hawai'i's nonwhite population.

TENSIONS BETWEEN SETTLERS AND THE MILITARY: THE MASSIE CASE

The Big Five's desires to maintain access to profitable U.S. sugar markets converged with U.S. federal and military leaders' interests in maintaining the Hawaiian Islands as a military outpost. These converging interests kept their relations amicable. Hawai'i's strategic location in the middle of the Pacific Ocean helped to bolster U.S. economic and military power in Asia and the Pacific. Despite Japan's brief appearance as an almost civilized ally at the Columbian Exposition, by the early part of the twentieth century, the United States had become cautious of Japan, particularly due to its military victory over the Russians in the Russo-Japanese War (1904–5). Success in this war led the U.S. military to fortify both the U.S. Army and Navy in Hawai'i out of fear of an invasion by Japan that could then leave the continental United States vulnerable to attack.[15] Hawai'i's strategic location also provided the U.S. military easy access to conduct operations in "Oriental waters."[16] With military installations in Hawai'i, Samoa, Guåhan, and the Philippines, the United States was in a key position by the early part of the twentieth century to establish itself both economically and militarily as a hemispheric power throughout Asia and the Pacific.

By the 1930s, however, this arrangement came under extraordinary strain. In 1931, Hawai'i's political leaders, and especially a rapidly growing tourism industry, received unwanted national attention after Thalia Massie, a well-connected Washington, DC, aristocrat whose husband was a naval officer, was brutally beaten and allegedly raped by four or five "Hawaiian" men, according to her description. Evidence later confirmed that her accusations of rape were fabricated.[17] In *Honor Killing*, David Stannard describes the atmosphere in Honolulu during the "Massie Affair" as an "ethnically divided powder keg," specifically pointing out Hawai'i's racial diversity challenged the racial norms that naval personnel, who were largely from the U.S. South, brought with them. In 1932 the five accused men, a mix of Hawaiian, Japanese, and Chinese—Joseph

Kahahawai, Ben Ahakuelo, Horace Ida, David Takai, and Henry Chang—were freed on mistrial as the jury could not come to a decision, particularly due to questionable police investigations. Many U.S. congressmen took notice of the ability of men of color in the colonies to be free after "harming" an aristocratic white woman and made attempts to seize governmental control away from the Big Five elite and place Hawaiʻi under a naval form of government.[18] Equally disturbed by what he considered to be the territorial government's incompetence at securing a guilty verdict for those "cutthroats," Admiral Yates Stirling incited violence by suggesting to the press that lynching might be used to restore racial order: "Since the five accused men were as free as air, I half expected, in spite of discipline, to hear any day that one or more had been found swinging from trees by the neck up Nuuanu Valley or at the Pali."[19] Only a few days after Admiral Stirling's comments, one of the accused, Horace Ida, was severely beaten and left for dead at the Pali—a stretch of road that cuts through a generally secluded Koʻolau Mountain. Another of the accused, Joseph Kahahawai, did not survive his attack.

In an attempt to get a confession, Kahahawai had been kidnapped by Thalia Massie's husband, Thomas Massie; her mother, Grace Fortescue; and two enlisted men, Deacon Jones (who was involved in the beating of Horace Ida) and Edward J. Lord. The Massie gang murdered Kahahawai with a gunshot and attempted to place him into a blowhole on the east side of the island, a lava tube that would have dismembered his body. The group, however, was caught en route and apprehended. The already tense relations among Congress, the military, the Big Five, and now especially the nonwhite numerical majority, reached dangerously tense levels after Kahahawai's convicted murderers received a commuted sentence—from ten years hard labor to one hour spent in Governor Lawrence Judd's office. Walter Dillingham, the son of Benjamin Dillingham, whom we met in the first chapter, commented on the dangerous precedent that Governor Judd's decision posed in governing a nonwhite population: "While this may be condoned under conditions which prevail where whites are in the majority, it would be a hazardous thing to give any such recognition of lynch law in our community where it is vital to stress the necessity of abiding by the laws of the country."[20]

Amid several rounds of federal investigations that cited Hawaiʻi settler leaders as incompetent and neglectful, members of Congress again sought to take control of the territorial government by replacing it with a military commission.[21] Southern Representative John E. Rankin, for example, assumed that white settler leadership of the territory was inept at maintaining racial order and control. In 1933, Rankin introduced legislation that aimed to remove Hawai'i's white settler elite from control of the government and allow the president to appoint nonresidents to key positions in the territory. Though the Massie gang had their sentences commuted by Governor Judd, Southern congressmen still believed that a military commission would create the proper conditions, wherein no white person would ever be sentenced to ten years' hard labor for killing someone "Black," especially one who had harmed a white woman.

Hawai'i's occupation by the United States, and the specific forms of settler colonialism there, was thus composed of a complex constellation of federal, territorial, military, Hawaiian, and settler interests. Historians Caroline Elkins and Susan Pedersen explain that settler colonialism in the twentieth century often consisted of a four-sided structure in constant struggle and negotiation: an "*imperial metropole* where sovereignty formally resides, a *local administration* charged with maintaining order and authority, an *indigenous population* significant in size and tenacity to make its presence felt, and an often demanding and well-connected *settler community*."[22] Indeed, these four dimensions of settler colonialism help to name some of the different constituents and institutions involved in the power play surrounding the Massie case, and in the efforts to achieve or defeat statehood: imperial metropole (Washington, DC), local administrations (territorial government and a large military presence), Indigenous population (Native Hawaiians), and settler community (the Big Five). But in Hawai'i there also exists a fifth dimension, what Hawaiian scholar Haunani-Kay Trask calls "Asian settlers." These are the non-Indigenous and nonwhite groups who were exploited for their labor and have their own histories of subjugation by imperialism, yet occupying a kind of liminal space that traces racial difference and instances of cohesion with haole settlers and/or Native peoples. These processes consisted of a delicate arrangement of variously mediated struggles, which were orchestrated by U.S. designs for empire and global imperial politics, labor immigration and protest, economic depression and planter access to U.S. markets, racial tensions and alliances, and struggles for equality in tension with deoccupation.

John P. Rosa argues in his book *Local Story: The Massie-Kahahawai Case and the Culture of History* that the everyday racism of white supremacy led to the emergence of a youth culture that laid the foundations for what is called a Local identity in Hawai'i. Rosa formulates succinctly that "local identity was an identity formed in opposition" and its continued construction relies on the "passing on of unofficial knowledge—knowledge about the past that has often been left out of history books."[23] Rosa cites the work of Jonathan Okamura, who describes this disparity in ethnic, Indigenous, and class terms: "The emergence of local culture and society represents an accommodation of ethnic groups to one another in the context of a social system primarily distinguished by the wide cleavage between the Haole planter and merchant oligarchy on the one hand, and the subordinate Hawaiians and immigrant plantation groups on the other."[24] Not a perfectly plural space, the category "Local" is rife with ethnic tensions and a problematic flattening of Native and non-Native differences. The formation of a Local identity, particularly in the prestatehood moment, however, might be seen as the success of an antiracist cultural politics that lessened nonwhite vulnerability to state or extralegal "premature death."[25] Indeed, only five years prior to Joseph Kahahawai's murderers receiving commuted sentences, Governor Lawrence Judd refused to commute the death sentence of Myles Fukunaga, who had murdered the son of the CEO of the Hawaiian Trust Company. The support for Fukunaga was not a dismissal of his violent crime, but rather empathy for the poverty he lived in after the Hawaiian Trust Company evicted his family from their home, made worse by a violent mandate for cultural genocide, which was said to have led Fukunaga to become "legally insane." Koji Ariyoshi, whom we will meet in chapter 4, wrote about Fukunaga: "The Nisei grew up in the years of U.S. isolationism and an exaggerated popularization of Anglo-Saxon culture. This attempt at cultural genocide of the heritage of the nonwhite minorities was intense, particularly in the public schools."[26]

"Local" thus became a safer space for cultural politics in opposition to the violence of white supremacy, but primarily forged through Pacific forms of kinship. Teresia Teaiwa argues that we often "fail to account for one of the foundational characteristics of kinship in the Pacific—the capacity (and, indeed, in some cases the preference) for assimilating Otherness through a variety of means that have genealogical implications:

adoption, feeding, the exchange of land, titles, gifts, and names."[27] Broad-based resistance in Hawai'i was thus created within the hypocrisy of a settler state that spoke of itself as fostering democracy yet consistently reproduced the violent conditions for white supremacist, heteropatriar-chal violence. The Kanaka 'Ōiwi–created forms of kinship underpinning the category Local, between Asians and Kānaka 'Ōiwi, were also forged in the militant labor movements of Hawai'i's territorial period. Forms of kinship can offer alternative coordinates for unpacking settler colonial-ism that are not trapped within the binary of Native/settler but rather comprised of certain hard-fought-for networks of solidarity.

TRIANGULATIONS

In 1920, Robert Neal argued in *Current History* that the "mass of alien humanity" in Hawai'i, particularly Hawaiians and Asians, must be re-made to American standards. Neal succinctly phrases Hawai'i's white settler elites' problem as a question: "How to get rid of that portion of the population, especially the Oriental element, which cannot be American-ized, and how to make loyal Americans out of that portion which cannot be got rid of [Kānaka 'Ōiwi]?"[28] In this way, the path to Americaniza-tion pivoted around the demands of haole supremacy, set in motion by a need to arrange and order, through distinct but interrelated forms of population management, the exclusion of Asians and the assimilation of Kānaka 'Ōiwi. J. Kēhaulani Kauanui argues that the racialization of Kānaka 'Ōiwi was set by an "on-island triangulation of white-Hawaiian-Asian," presenting itself so frequently as to be a framework for structural relationships. Thus, white settlers obsessively managed Kānaka 'Ōiwi and various Asian settler differences not through a white and nonwhite binary, but through multiple binaries via a kind of entrenched triangula-tion. In the white racist imagination, this is a pyramidal view of the world where everything everywhere is evidence of white supremacy. Kauanui argues that white supremacist projects of colonialism against Kānaka 'Ōiwi worked together with views of Asians as internal and external for-eign threats amounting to "xenophobic anti-immigration sentiments."[29]

Such triangulations structure much of the scholarship on race rela-tions that was intended for use by sugar plantations to pacify labor strikes. Moon-Kie Jung points out that it was after the 1924 Sugar Strike that the

Hawaiian Sugar Planters' Association hired Stanley D. Porteus and Marjorie Babcock to produce an external study of the laboring population for the sugar industry. The 1924 strike is perhaps most remembered for the Hanapēpē massacre, a scene of incredible violence perpetrated by the HSPA, who began to view the "use of force as an instrument of labor relations," leaving sixteen Filipino strikers and four policemen dead on the island of Kauaʻi.[30] The scholarship produced in the HSPA report by Porteus and Babcock became the groundwork for the infamous 1926 book *Temperament and Race*. Stanley D. Porteus, celebrated as "Hawaii's Pioneer Psychologist," was a professor at the University of Hawaiʻi at Mānoa between 1922 and 1948, when he retired and then held the title of emeritus professor of psychology. The University of Hawaiʻi Board of Regents named their social science building Porteus Hall in 1974, but student-led and radical faculty–supported protest in 1997 forced the administration to rename this building.

Much of the information in Porteus and Babcock's *Temperament and Race* concerned the issue of controlling labor dissent primarily by studying racial "temperament" as well as the "educational capabilities" of each community.[31] Porteus and Babcock's method, besides linking intelligence and morality to the different weight and size of these groups' brains, was to gather information about nonwhite groups through interviews with plantation managers, doctors, and educators, who were all white. They also utilized Porteus's self-invented Maze Test in different elementary schools, which was said to determine the capacity for "long-term planning." All of these findings were supposed to help white settler leaders better understand and control Hawaiʻi's nonwhite population.[32]

Porteus and Babcock argued that while haole were considered intellectually superior to all other racial groups, heredity did not automatically guarantee their primacy, especially in places where they were outnumbered. Porteus and Babcock argued that the inborn racial inferiority of nonwhites was evident in Hawaiʻi to a shocking degree, leading inevitably to high rates of "economic waste, poverty and shiftlessness and social dependency."[33] Furthermore, while white economic and political superiority might have been inherited, it was not an inevitable outcome in the face of competition. Porteus and Babcock explained, "It is undoubtedly true that though the word is over-worked, the older civilizations do tend to become 'effete.'"[34] Porteus and Babcock argued that the white settlement of Australia, Canada, and other "new lands" was different from—actually superior to—that of Hawai'i by virtue of maintaining a majority white settler population, which they dubbed a "vanguard of settlement." The more salient issue, however, lay in the threat posed by "Oriental" laborers who were now themselves "clamoring" for equality with whites.[35]

Porteus and Babcock furnished a body of knowledge that highlighted the vulnerability of white settler privilege and power in an effort to impede the different social and political development of nonwhites (Asians and Hawaiians). Accordingly, Porteus and Babcock argued that the "Oriental" groups in Hawai'i, the Japanese and Chinese, were actually gaining in social status and had the potential to surpass whites. This advancement in social status proved to them that "Orientals," though "poorly endowed" when compared with whites, could nonetheless overcome the "handicaps" of color, custom, and language and possibly thrive.[36] In comparing Japanese with Kānaka 'Ōiwi, for instance, they argued that Hawaiians were not driven to succeed because of their "temperamental adaptability," which was owed to the education they received from the American missionaries. The Japanese, on the other hand, lacked Hawaiians' alleged ability to "harmonize" with whites.[37] Indeed, Porteus observed that the Japanese were quick to "turn the white man's own weapons against him" by going out on strike, describing them as "self-assertive and anxious for a larger place in the sun."[38] Such observations became the principal subject and claim of their book, that these "barefooted, horny-handed, ignorant labourers were not poorly endowed, but were rich in an inheritance of temperamental or psychosynergic traits that only needed the opportunity to make their weight felt in inter-racial and social competition."[39] If inherited "temperament" and "psychosynergy" gave "Orientals" the potential to succeed, imperial history furnished the "opportunity," but at an epic risk to white racial power. Porteus and Babcock predicted that Japanese desires for ascendancy amounted to a threat to white society and could result in an "*inevitable* clash of temperaments" if the proper conditions were not prevented.[40] Porteus thus called for the Japanese to be excluded from sites of settler colonialism, which he called "lands that belong to the white race," specifically Canada, the United States, and Australia.[41]

Hailing from Melbourne, Australia, where his Scotch-Irish family settled as pastors after a failed stint in gold mining, Porteus's training and credibility came from work on his first book, *The Psychology of a Primi-*

tive People: A Study of the Australian Aborigine. According to Elizabeth Dole Porteus, biographer and daughter-in-law of Stanley Porteus (perhaps best known as the daughter of the "Pineapple King," James Dole), Porteus's first book examined "the intelligence of the aborigines."[42] His thinking on this topic led him to eventually argue, along with R. J. A. Berry, another eugenicist from Australia, that 15 percent of the Aboriginal population of Australia was of "subnormal mentality," and should be segregated into a colony to be in one way or another eliminated to prevent "economic loss and social disaster" to Australia.[43] Porteus and Berry quote their colleague Henry Goddard, the author of the discredited book *The Kallikak Family*, stating that "the most dangerous group of mental defectives are those who are in no way different from the intelligent man; and not only in outward appearance, but in conversation and bearing, these people often pass for normal."[44] The federal government and various states took Goddard's work seriously enough to limit immigration and force the sterilization of "purportedly feebleminded persons." Porteus replaced Goddard at the Vineland School in New Jersey before returning to the University of Hawai'i as faculty. He thus developed a kind of American primitivism, seemingly legitimated by his work in different settler sites that justified deeming specific populations "unfit for self-government," specifically Australian Aboriginal people, Southern Africans, Filipinos, Puerto Ricans, and Kānaka 'Ōiwi. According to David Stannard, Porteus believed that Filipinos and Puerto Ricans held the "invidious distinction of being last on the list in almost all traits." Near the end of his life, Porteus coined the term *ethnic group retardation*, to describe the presumed intellectual deficiency of Africans, Polynesians, and other dark people as the result of the "extreme speed of the rotational spin" of the Earth as it turned on its axis.[45]

There is no shortage of evidence that Porteus was making things up as he went. What is critical in all of this is the role of disciplinary knowledges in delineating Indigenous sovereignty. Aboriginal scholar Aileen Moreton-Robinson (Geonpul) argues that "white possession, as a mode of rationality, functions within disciplinary knowledges and regulatory mechanisms defining and circumscribing Indigenous sovereignty in particular ways."[46] To label Native peoples' intellectual capacity as "feebleminded," "subnormal," and "lame" is to warrant them as colonial subjects. These terms justify categories that continue today, specifically "wards of the state," where Hawaiian crown and government lands (so-called ceded lands) are held in trust for Kānaka ʻŌiwi. The very terms of occupation are underpinned by constituting Kānaka ʻŌiwi as "unfit," specifically "unfit for self-government," a label that Lorrin A. Thurston used as justification for the 1893 overthrow.[47] Thus, such designations authorized a seemingly more deserving mind to make more superior decisions on behalf of Native people. This points to a major intersection, not often expanded upon, that articulates the concerns of Indigenous studies with disability studies.[48] As Alison Kafer argues in *Feminist, Queer, Crip*, "Eugenic histories certainly bear the mark of reproductive futurity. Even keeping only to the United States, and only to the past one hundred years or so, examples abound of how concerns about the future of the 'race' and the future of the nation (futures often depicted as intertwined) have been wrapped up in fears and anxieties about disability."[49] The work of Stanley Porteus aimed to protect the reproductive futurity of white settlers from degeneracy and disability, supposedly by containing those Asian and Kanaka ʻŌiwi populations who were deemed threats to the project of white civilization. It is no coincidence that white supremacist futures often imagine those with disabilities and Native peoples as not existing in the future.[50] The intertwined projects of white settler colonialism and able-bodied supremacy, as articulated by Porteus, use eugenics to transmit whiteness intergenerationally with a specific mission dedicated to its own self-preservation. This is despite the fact, or perhaps for the very reason, that Stanley Porteus himself had a tenuous claim to whiteness; he was Scotch-Irish, and not Anglo-Saxon. Elizabeth Dole Porteus, whose Anglo-Saxon genealogy included an uncle Sanford B. Dole, the first president and governor after the 1893 white settler–led overthrow, and whose father created the pineapple industry in Hawaiʻi, makes celebratory reference to this: "The life of Stanley David Porteus might serve as proof that an individual need not be a pawn of his heredity and environment."[51] Thus, Porteus and others used the category "feeble-minded," like "Oriental" and "primitive," to enable haole to subjugate and dehumanize any person or group who could be lumped into any of these categories.

For as much academic acrobatics as these scholars needed to do to make their arguments seem credible, Denise Ferreira da Silva offers what she terms the "transparency thesis," which sheds light on a very important function of raciality that boils down the effects of their discourse. Ferreira da Silva argues, "Not the conversion of 'such' peoples' souls, it would turn out, but the cataloguing of their minds, undertaken about three hundred years later, produced the strategies of power governing contemporary global conditions."[52] Emerging from post-Enlightenment Europe, race, via its emergence in scientific reason, functions not only by attaching specific traits to a person's racial body, but by turning one's body into a "signifier of the mind." In this way, those who are white are argued to be the inheritors of post-Enlightenment Europe, what Ferreira da Silva calls the "transparent I," the "kind of mind that is able to know, emulate, and control powers of universal reason."[53] This is argued to be distinct from the "Others of Europe," the "affectable 'I,' the one that emerged in other global regions, the kind of mind subjected to both the exterior determination of the 'laws of nature' and the superior force of European minds."[54] Consider Porteus's laughable argument about the "ethnic group retardation" afflicting those from regions close to the equator. Indeed, Porteus was not considered a rigorous scholar, and he avoided engagement with the scholarship around him that debunked many of his arguments by the 1920s. His ideas circulated largely among white settler elites, namely sugar and pineapple planters. Yet, when examined through the "transparency thesis," the work of sociologists at the University of Hawai'i—who did not imagine Hawai'i to be a space of inevitable clash but rather a "racial melting pot" where culture, not heredity, was the marker of difference—demonstrates how they reproduced Hawai'i's nonwhite population in similar ways.

University of Hawai'i sociologists in the 1920s, particularly Romanzo Adams, planted the seed for describing Hawai'i as racially harmonious, via a liberal multicultural discourse that continues today. These sociologists, as Jonathan Okamura argues, defined Hawai'i as a "racial melting pot" and considered Hawai'i to be, in the words of Robert E. Park, "the most notable instance of a melting pot of the modern world."[55] Where Porteus and Babcock's eugenic proclivities policed the intermarriage between ethnicities and racial groups, the sociologists at the University of Hawai'i both marveled at and encouraged the high rates of intermarriage, deeming it to be evidence of the "unorthodox race doctrine" in Hawai'i. Yet, as Okamura argues, "High rates of intermarriage may indicate an ethnically tolerant society but not necessarily a harmonious or egalitarian one."[56] Indeed, though not entirely, those high rates were a product of

biopolitical attempts to establish Hawai'i as a white settler colony. Plantation managers first recruited Japanese workers and their families in the
hopes that this would create stability. But those workers often left the
plantations to open businesses. The HSPA then began to recruit bach-
elors from the Philippines. The association's hope was that these men
would either return to the Philippines or die without kin. Many, however,
simply married outside of their ethnicity/race. Christine Manganaro, a
historian of science, argues, "Hawai'i's ethnic diversity was engineered,
for the most part, by plantation owners, but social scientists celebrated it
as a human experiment."[57]

The majority of Hawai'i's sociologists were trained at the University
of Chicago, which at this time had intimate links to the propagation and
dissemination of U.S. frontier discourses. The University of Chicago Department of Sociology was built on the site where the Midway Plaisance
of the 1893 Chicago World's Columbian Exposition once stood. Indeed,
the University of Chicago touted itself as taking up the vision of civilization shaped by the 1893 Columbian Exposition.[58] Henry Yu argues that
the Chicago sociologists utilized what he terms "frontier logics" in their
early intellectual iterations under the directorship of Robert E. Park, who
trained sociologists who became professors and/or visiting professors at
the University of Hawai'i's Department of Sociology.[59] Through funding
by John D. Rockefeller, both the University of Chicago and the University
of Hawai'i sociologists produced ideas about race relations in the islands
that combined primitivism and Orientalism, thereby framing Hawai'i as
what they termed a veritable "racial laboratory."[60]

The linear arrangement of the non-Anglo-Saxon world along the Midway Plaisance has similar links to the "race relations cycle," a theoretical
model on the inevitable assimilation of nonwhite communities in the
United States, developed by Robert E. Park. As we saw in the previous
chapter, the two-mile strip of the Midway categorized, exhibited, and arranged peoples of the world according to stages of development in very
specific relationships to a utopic White City, which in turn represented
an American civilizing project over a descending world order of whites,
ethnic whites, Orientals, and primitives. In this imperial demarcation
the assimilation or obliteration of peoples deemed to be weaker than the
West was taken to be an inevitable outcome of civilization. Park saw as-

similation as a linear process, a march of civilization that began in Europe, through which nonwhite groups were either neutralized or incorporated into the always forward-moving project of U.S. civilization.[61] Park offered his "race relations cycle" to explain the inevitable forward march of American (white) cultural supremacy based on the social facts of "conflict and competition," "accommodation," "assimilation," "amalgamation," and "miscegenation."[62] Park thus distinguished between worldly "civilizations" and provincial "cultures." For Park, "cultures" possessed narrow and singular perspectives of the world. "Civilizations," on the other hand, contained perspectives that were global in scope and self-aware of the existence of other cultures' worldviews. The end result was that "cultures" died as they learned that their worldviews were only one of many, while "civilizations" moved on, incorporating and encompassing weaker races.[63] The notion that weaker races would simply assimilate into U.S. society was used in attempts to convince Congress that Hawai'i should not be denied statehood on account of its large nonwhite population.

Henry Yu's *Thinking Orientals* argues that the sociology department at the University of Hawai'i was a place where "Chicago sociology and the theories developed to study the Oriental Problem would dominate as they did nowhere else."[64] Thus, as part of its disciplinary value, sociology was viewed as having the ability to reconcile cultural difference, helping "Oriental" peoples to assimilate properly and gain membership into American modernity. Anthropology, on the other hand, was then used to study and preserve "primitive" cultures, fixing these groups in the past, at the very beginning of an "imagined spectrum of progress" that was produced in opposition to a modern white America.[65] The binary logics inherent in these categories helped to legitimate white settlers' temporal and spatial claims over Hawai'i. For instance, if "Orientals" were "foreigners" from afar, then white Americans could presume to be "natives" here. Similarly, "primitives," defined as cultures preserved permanently in the past, could allow white settlers to imagine themselves to be bearers of modernity and progress to Hawaiians. For instance, future Congressional Delegate Elizabeth Farrington, whose husband was territorial governor and son was a congressional delegate, declared that Kānaka 'Ōiwi had progressed only because of the "education they've gotten from us," and that otherwise they would still be in the Stone Age.[66]

In this way, the work of sociologists at the University of Hawaiʻi, as Christine Manganaro argues, created a "settler rationale" that naturalized cultural and political assimilation as the "next step in Hawaiʻi's emerging history."[67] While different sociologists, as Manganaro explains, had different ethical stances on being used as advocates for statehood, generally their work argued that the recognition of statehood was inevitable and tied to "the rate of cultural assimilation of [Hawaiʻi's] residents."[68] Denise Ferreira da Silva argues that the "race relations cycle" underpinning much of the scholarship coming out of the sociology department at this time, was an effective strategy for producing "the others of Europe as subaltern modern subjects." Ferreira da Silva argues that the physical traits of non-Europeans were read by sociologists as possessing an "inferior" consciousness, whose exclusion and removal to "regions of subalternity" facilitated U.S. modern civilization.[69] Thus, Manganaro and Ferreira da Silva express differing yet complementary arguments about the role of sociology in this moment, if not about the concomitant strategies of the larger U.S. statehood movement. Manganaro describes the University of Hawaiʻi sociologists' view of themselves as improving and Americanizing Hawaiʻi's nonwhite citizenry, thus targeting them as capable of and in the process of becoming their future American selves. Hawaiʻi's nonwhite population had to be deemed assimilable to achieve congressional recognition of Hawaiʻi statehood. Ferreira da Silva, on the other hand, points out that the nonwhite groups were considered "affectable" in a "race relations cycle" that sought to marginalize them, turn them into modern subaltern subjects. Thus nonwhites were targeted for assimilation only to be rendered inconsequential, not participatory American citizens; this, then, positioned them to not be disruptive of the aims of the white subjects in charge of the statehood movement. This is to say that nonwhites were described as capable of assimilating only so they would no longer be obstacles to the political machinery that was dead set on achieving statehood, not for them to be positioned as active citizens who could democratically debate statehood. Such were the aims of the Hawaii Equal Rights Commission, which organized the 1937 congressional hearings on statehood. Manganaro argues that "experts from the continent produced accounts of who Hawaiians and Asian migrants were, but Native Hawaiians, Asian migrants, and mixed race people produced and deployed cultural knowledge and forms of identity that sometimes resisted American experts' framing and at other times contributed to the rearticulation of racial categories."[70] The 1937 congressional hearings exemplify this space of possibility and counterhegemonic knowledge production.

THE 1937 CONGRESSIONAL HEARINGS ON STATEHOOD

In 1937, the popular editorialist and former labor organizer George Wright conveyed in the *Hawaii Hochi* (a Japanese American daily) that he expected the 1937 congressional statehood hearings to be what he called an "engineered affair."[71] Wright believed that the public hearings would be filled with "hand-picked" individuals who "take their orders from the dominant industrial groups."[72] Wright wrote: "There will be a few hardy souls who are willing to come out in the open and oppose the idea of statehood on various grounds, some good and some pretty rotten. But the majority will follow the example of Willie Vocalite at the recent products show and perform their part with robot-like precision just as they have been previously fixed to do it, saying the things that have been transcribed upon the wax records of their mechanical minds."[73] Willie Vocalite was the Hawaiian Electric Company's featured exhibit for the Eighth Annual Hawaiian Products Show. A silver robot hailed for his numerous human-like abilities, Willie "Stands-up—Sits down—Waves flag—Shoots gun—Smokes and Talks."[74] By calling those who voiced the interests of the sugar industry Willie Vocalites, Wright marked just how mechanical and economically subjugated the general populace had become under the Big Five. Indeed, by 1937, there was a general belief that the public either had become so entrenched in the statehood campaign of the Hawaii Equal Rights Commission or had been effectively rendered mute or compliant under the threat of losing jobs that there seemed to be little to no opposing or independent viewpoints.

The Hawaii Equal Rights Commission initiated the dissemination of statehood literature in the daily newspapers in order to shape public opinion in favor of statehood. Beginning in 1934, the *Honolulu Star-Bulletin* had begun to publish numerous articles that supported statehood. As mentioned earlier, statehood was seen as necessary to regain beneficial tariffs for the sugar industry. The Hawaii Equal Rights Commission was quite explicit about the economic motivations for statehood, and since the sugar industry, government, and media publicly declared the virtues

Figure 2.1 Willie Vocalite at the Eighth Annual Hawaiian Products Show, 1937. Photo courtesy of *Honolulu Advertiser*.

and necessity of statehood, any person who opposed it was marked as a detractor, one at odds with Hawaiʻi's powerful elites.

In this climate of fear, and because testimony was heard openly, many people believed that the 1937 joint congressional statehood hearings would be a replay of the 1935 hearings, at which virtually no one spoke out against the repressive tactics of the Big Five. As a matter of fact, in 1937, the Big Five and the Republican Party *paid* the expenses of the congressional visitors.[75] After the sixteen-day hearing was over, however, many would feel differently about the engineered setup of the 1937 congressional hearings. George Wright, for instance, retracted his earlier statements in the *Hawaii Hochi* and wrote that instead of a "triumphant symposium on the incontrovertible right of Hawaii to become the 49th state there was a veritable dog-fight of snarling objectors who came prepared to show the gentlemen from the mainland exactly why Hawaii was unfit for statehood."[76] George Wright himself, and other writers in the alternative papers, played a significant role in agitating such dissent.

In the years and months leading up to the 1937 hearings, an emerging labor movement had shaken the Big Five's hegemony. Dockworkers were successful at getting the federal government to investigate Big Five violations of the Wagner Act of 1935. The Wagner Act, which had also created the National Labor Relations Board (NLRB) to ensure that employers abided by the Act, now provided longshoremen in the islands with the ability to force the Big Five to recognize their unions. Moon-Kie Jung identifies two factors—metropolitan state intervention and de-isolation—that took place in the 1930s that helped to plant the seeds for radical labor movements to come to fruition in the latter part of the 1940s. Metropolitan state intervention, Jung argues, was created with the passing of the Wagner Act and the establishment of the NLRB. De-isolation, in the meantime, had been established when Hawaiian men, like Harry Lehua Kamoku and Levi Kealoha, kept ties with the West Coast maritime workers they met while helping in the 1934 San Francisco Strike and returned to the islands to help organize Hawai'i's longshoremen.[77] Such ties between Hawai'i's longshoremen and those on the West Coast also brought the celebrated labor organizer Jack Hall to the islands.[78]

In March of 1937, with the urging of labor leaders in Hilo, the NLRB agreed to investigate the work conditions of longshoremen. For eighteen days the NLRB heard testimony in Hawai'i, and eventually charged members of the Big Five with unfair labor practices. The NLRB trial examiner also found that Castle and Cooke had specifically violated the Wagner Act and ordered the company to reinstate eleven union members who were unfairly released in a 1936 strike. Thus, by the October 1937 statehood hearings, many believed that the Big Five's power structure was weakened and vulnerable to attack.

In the weeks leading up to the hearings, the *Honolulu Star-Bulletin* and *Honolulu Advertiser* ran articles that posed statehood as a natural and necessary step in the inevitable march toward progress, demanding that Congress treat Hawai'i as an integral part of the United States and not as a foreign country.[79] Alternative papers such as the *Hawaii Hochi* and *Voice of Labor*, however, were critical of the overlap between big business and government, and asked sharp and probing questions about what the Hawaii Equal Rights Commission's organized visit would allow the congressmen to see and hear. For his part, George Wright highlighted Wyoming Senator Joseph C. O'Mahoney's declaration of his intent while in Hawai'i to investigate statehood in relation to "the sugar industry, interlocking control, economic hegemony, political domination by privileged interests, the company store racket, espionage and the blacklist, labor intimidation and the peonage of workers under a medieval system of feudalistic exploitation."[80] Wright capitalized on Senator O'Mahoney's article, in an editorial titled "He Doesn't Know Half of It!," insisting that because of Senator O'Mahoney's "fortunate advertisement" and his general knowledge of the political scene in Hawai'i, there was every possibility that the workers of Hawai'i might be able to "give him the lowdown on the 'system' and introduce him to many new angles that he has never suspected before."[81] In stark contrast to prevailing discourse, these newspapers described those in opposition to the Big Five not as "bad citizens" but as heroes who were capable of independent thinking and speaking truth to power in the face of exorbitant odds.

In addition to running editorials, the *Hawaii Hochi* also ran numerous political cartoons by Bill Moran that further drew the lines, quite literally, of class conflict. Many of the political cartoons that led up to the congressional hearings paid careful attention to the issues of repression and silence, often comparing the Big Five and the territorial government with the repressive fascism of Nazi Germany. The National Labor Relations Board was also making such comparisons as it continued to learn more from workers' testimonies. Indeed, the NLRB went so far as to describe Hawai'i as a "picture of fascism," inasmuch as big business dominated the territorial government and created a general climate of fear that stifled public speech against the interests of the Big Five and government.[82] The political cartoons visually offer an actual "picture of fascism," focusing on the themes of secrecy and transparency, thus exposing Big Five efforts to conceal dirty practices from the view of the visiting congressmen. To be sure, the political cartoons portray the settler elite in a position of visual weakness. There is a reversal of the power of the Big Five, particularly as it is subject to the authoritative gaze of Washington, DC. Members of the nonwhite working class were often used as objects of knowledge,

Figure 2.2 "Getting Ready for Company," *Hawaii Hochi*, 1937.

observed and studied by academics such as Porteus or University of Hawai'i sociologists such as Romanzo Adams, who sought to produce knowledge about them that would maintain white hegemony. But with the congressional committee in Hawai'i, the ability to testify to a higher white authority gave Hawai'i's nonwhite population a powerful opportunity to reverse the gaze and create knowledge about the Big Five and their repression. This momentary reversal that pitted two forms of white masculinity against each other—what might happen if O'Mahoney and the other congressmen could see the corruption, the cover-ups, and the political repression—gave the general public an understanding of Hawai'i's new political possibilities, such as what had been taking place in the labor movement, beyond Big Five hegemony. U.S. congressional oversight on the question of statehood helped cast critical light on the Big Five and settler state power; it offered the general public, and the working class in particular, a louder voice to expose that exploitative power. Since the time of the Massie case, the settler elite had been under surveillance by Congress, and the testimony and observations by the working class in the 1937 hearings had the potential for long-lasting implications for the Big Five power structure.

As was expected, on the first day of public hearings, Senator O'Mahoney began by stating, "In the last two days while in Hawaii it has become apparent to me, and to some of the other members of the committee, that there is a sentiment in the islands which may not find free expression."[83] The question of "free expression" was an issue that came up in much of the testimony and was a major concern of the congressmen. Senator Tom Connally of Texas, for example, was informed that someone in the audience was intimidating witnesses by showing either "approval or disapproval" of their testimony.[84] Indeed, there was a justifiable fear and risk in speaking openly against the interests of the Big Five. Garnett M. Burum, a house manager of the Seamen's Institute and secretary-treasurer for the Hawaiian Island Federation of Labor, testified that while he could not provide examples of Big Five repression at the 1937 statehood hearings, he was himself recently fired from his job for providing testimony before the National Labor Relations Board and also falsely arrested for "conspiring to have a union man beaten up."[85] Such testimony would influence Representative Jack Nichols of Oklahoma, who interrupted the hearings to read into the record this excerpt from an editorial in the October 7 issue of the *Voice of Labor*:

> The Senators and Congressmen ... will be entertained at the Royal Hawaiian, at the Waialae Club, at the homes of the "big shots." They will go on carefully conducted tours to sugar plantations and to pineapple canneries and to model villages. They will hear speeches and they will see the military and naval establishments.
>
> But they will be carefully shepherded away from fields where women or children are working, they will never see the slums of Palama or River Street, they will not see the darkened rooms where aged Chinese live and raise bean sprouts in pans of water in order that they may live. They will hear of the wonderful work Palama Settlement is doing,

but they will not hear how many children are infected with syphilis, how many are illiterate, how many can not speak English, how many have to work to contribute to the support of their families while still of school age.... We don't believe they will know of these things when they leave. But we hope they do.[86]

Representative Nichols reported taking this as a challenge, for the committee, to be wary of what the Hawaii Equal Rights Commission's organized visit would and would not allow them to see, and to be ready "to hear about any condition that is existent in the Territory of Hawaii."[87] Accusations that the Big Five were going to "pull one over" on the visiting congressmen, in fact, made them anxious. The constant repetition, if not obsession, of this challenge seems to have struck at the congressmen personally, thus maneuvering two competing white masculinities (Big Five versus congressmen) against each other. The chairman of the hearings, William King of Utah, however, thought that his fellow congressmen were "making too much of [it]."[88]

Hawaiʻi's largely "Oriental" population, specifically the Japanese, was a major concern for the visiting congressmen and for those testifying against statehood. While many opposed Hawaiʻi statehood based on arguments that the Big Five were using it as a means to maintain control over politics and the economy, the question of Japanese American loyalty and bloc voting was brought up, particularly in light of imperial Japan's invasion of China only a few months earlier. In fact, the very first testimony offered at the hearings was given by an engineer in the navy, who opposed statehood based on a belief that "under statehood we would have a Japanese Governor in three or four sessions," and that such an outcome would, in turn, incite whites to organize "the Ku Klux Klan... for the white man to get justice."[89] Indeed, many opposed statehood, believing that Japanese Americans would remain loyal to Japan because of their dual citizenship. In this way, an Orientalist discourse helped to constitute the Japanese in Hawaiʻi as perpetual foreigners, as ever-looming threats to the safety of the United States in Hawaiʻi. This widespread fear legitimized and naturalized the subsequent military buildup in Hawaiʻi. By 1937, anti–Japanese American racism was at an all-time high, leading Secretary of State Cordell Hull to increase U.S. military personnel in Hawaiʻi. Thomas T. Sakakihara, a territorial House representative and one of four Japanese American legislators, testified that as American citizens by birth, he and many Japanese Americans "bitterly resented" that they were "often pointed out as Japanese," with its inference that they were "alien Japanese."[90] Sakakihara, like many others, asserted that the real obstacle to Hawai'i statehood was not the Japanese but white racism:

> We have the ability, capacity, resources, and power to assume the duty as a State. The greatest obstacles however which are blocking the efforts of the Territory in attaining statehood are those who possess a feeling of superiority complex over citizens of foreign extraction born in Hawaii. They are composed largely of those Caucasian races who have migrated to Hawaii from mainland or some foreign country of Caucasian extraction. They entertain deep, unfounded suspicion as to the loyalty of American citizens of Oriental extraction to the government of their birth which is absolutely ridiculous and unsupported by evidence.[91]

Racism against Japanese communities expressed as a concern over their loyalty remained a major issue both for and against statehood in the coming decades, particularly after the Japanese government's 1941 military attack on Pearl Harbor. During the 1930s, however, many statehood proponents sought to minimize the number of Japanese Americans in Hawai'i.

One such person was University of Hawai'i sociologist Romanzo Adams; he played a key role in downplaying the numbers of Japanese in Hawai'i by forecasting that the population of whites and Kānaka 'Ōiwi would increase, while the "Oriental" population (including Filipinos) was destined to decrease. Adams acknowledged that the president of the University of Hawai'i, D. L. Crawford, asked him to gather specific statistics on the number of Japanese who were born in Hawai'i.[92] Congressional delegate Samuel King, whose Hawaiian mother was a childhood friend of Queen Lili'uokalani and whose haole father was involved in the overthrow and annexation of Hawai'i to the United States, testified that "looking into the future of Hawaii," non-American elements would inevitably be absorbed by feelings of "national loyalty" or die of "natural causes."[93] The driving rationale behind King's statements was the projected demographics Romanzo Adams offered—underpinned by the logics of Park's "race relations cycle"—and the engineering of sugar planters in selecting single male laborers who were expected to emigrate away from Hawaiʻi or die in bachelor camps.[94] Adams was in fact a frequent source of authority for government officials and statehood proponents throughout the hearings.

Finding that the numbers of Kānaka ʻŌiwi were increasing drew a series of anxiety-ridden questions from the congressmen about the theme of Hawaiian "racial mixture." Representative John Rankin of Mississippi continually asked questions about intermarriage and what he called "racial atavism."[95] Rankin specifically asked whether Hawaiians who had married whites would be more "toward the Caucasian or toward the Hawaiian."[96] Though Adams repeatedly answered that this was a question for a biologist, Rankin eventually forced him to concede that the mixed-blood Hawaiian could go either way, but that "they don't like to emphasize their mixed blood. Students in my classes have told me that they always classify themselves as Hawaiians, although they know they have had a little bit of European or Asiatic blood."[97] Delegate Samuel King picked up on this issue. King added that while Adams extolled the increase of Native Hawaiians, everyone born in the islands, regardless of race, was considered Hawaiian. King declared, "All of us of local birth consider ourselves as Hawaiians; and every man who has a drop of Hawaiian blood in his veins or who has lived here for any length of time subscribes to that. . . . In fact, descendants of missionary stock consider themselves as thoroughly Hawaiian as those of Hawaiian blood."[98] King attempted to render "race" a nonissue by stating that birth in the islands automatically made someone Hawaiian. King attempted to avoid racial difference via miscegenation while still upholding the unequal power relations between these groups.[99]

King's views notwithstanding, John Hoʻopale's testimony showed how expressions of indigeneity and opposition to settler colonialism remained relevant to other Hawaiians when he spoke of Kānaka ʻŌiwi in this way: "Now, my people, the original Hawaiians—not these naturalized Hawaiians, or foster Hawaiians—I am speaking about the aboriginal Hawaiians, who want to live on this land without interference from outsiders."[100] Hoʻopale was concerned that statehood might lead to Hawaiians being outnumbered in their own homeland. Hoʻopale argued that more Hawaiians would testify in opposition to statehood, but many were impoverished and employed by the Big Five, making them "afraid" to lose their "bread and butter."[101] By this time, Hawaiians held a large proportion of government jobs and were thus constrained from speaking publicly against statehood.[102] As such, Ho'opale was concerned, since he saw statehood as a question of "the death and life of our country."[103] A former House representative in the legislature, Ho'opale knew intimately the repercussions involved in opposing statehood; indeed, he was never again reelected because of his public stance against statehood.[104] John Ho'opale would again oppose statehood in 1950, asking that Congress "restore the independence of our beloved land."[105]

Being numerically outnumbered in one's ancestral land was, of course, a primary concern for many Kānaka 'Ōiwi. In 1922, Hawaiians comprised 50 percent of the voting population; but by 1936, this percentage decreased to 30 percent.[106] Since the overthrow of their government in 1893, Hawaiians had been unable to control immigration to Hawai'i. In 1932, Princess Abigail Kawānanakoa—the daughter of Abigail Kuaihelani Maipinepine Campbell who helped organize the Kū'ē petitions opposing U.S. annexation—expressed the feeling that Hawaiians were being made strangers in their own homeland: "We [Hawaiians] must live here, we cannot go to China, we cannot go to the Philippines, we cannot go to Japan. . . . I have nothing but admiration for the Chinese and the Japanese and the Filipinos, but this is our home, and everybody is crowding us out of our home. . . . It is a desperate situation."[107] The forms of colonial power with which Kānaka 'Ōiwi were contending in their ancestral homeland thus targeted them for replacement. Another more immediate reason for opposition was that Hawaiians on the neighboring islands viewed statehood as but a precursor to reapportionment, which would give the island of O'ahu a majority of seats in both the House and Senate. Many Kānaka 'Ōiwi residents who lived in the neighbor islands viewed reapportionment as but another step toward the triumph of American values and interests, symbolized by the rapid growth of O'ahu.[108]

Despite the best efforts of the Hawaii Equal Rights Commission and the Big Five to get the congressmen to support statehood, the final congressional report that was released in 1938 did not recommend immediate statehood for Hawai'i. The committee stated: "There is not complete unity on the question of statehood among the people of Hawaii," and recommended a territory-wide plebiscite to ascertain the views of Hawai'i's general public.[109] Moreover, the committee recommended further study and consideration, especially of the growing Japanese population in Hawai'i, which had quadrupled in the preceding eight years, and which the committee identified as a cause of "considerable local discussion" due to the "present disturbed condition of international affairs."[110] At this time, tension between China and Japan had escalated into war, and the same was happening in Europe. In 1935, Germany ceased to recognize the Treaty of Versailles and, by 1938, had annexed Austria and most of Czechoslovakia, with aims to invade Poland the following year. Such events culminated in Japan's military attack on Pearl Harbor in 1941. Porteus's *inevitable* clash of temperaments" between Japan and the United States finally took place.

While only seventeen of the sixty-eight witnesses opposed statehood, such numbers need to be understood within the general climate of fear that existed around publicly opposing the interests of the Big Five. George Wright, in fact, called the 1937 hearings a historical moment within which the "submerged nine-tenths of the population became vocal."[111] Wright criticized the mainstream media for favoring the advocates of statehood as a way to also discredit the opposition. But he also explained that "the crowds that attended the hearings knew what was going on and the news spread like wildfire, bringing others to join in the spectacle."[112] Indeed, the political cartoons coming out of the *Hawaii Hochi* celebrated the vocal opposition against the Big Five. One in particular, titled "Hey! We Got the Wrong Congressmen!," showed a defeated pumpkin head, perhaps King, crying at a desk before which statehood proponents, figured as circus animals, "trained seals," read statements titled "Why I Favor Statehood," and the "monkey press" took sugar cubes out of the "$ugar Bowl," each performing as they have been trained.

While unsuccessful at pulling off the "Statehood Hocus Pocus" in 1937, the Hawaii Equal Rights Commission succeeded with a 1940 plebiscite, a measure that in hindsight was responsible for putting the statehood movement back on track. It accomplished this, however, with effective and purposeful imprecision. The 1940 plebiscite was "deliberately imprecise," and had been intentionally worded in such a way as to avoid the very real possibility that a majority of voters would reject immediate statehood.[113] The plebiscite's original wording, crafted by Joseph Farrington, read, "Are you in favor of immediate statehood for Hawaii?" In the penultimate draft of the ballot, the wording was changed slightly, to em-

Figure 2.3 "Hey! We Got the Wrong Congressmen!,"
Hawaii Hochi, 1937.

ploy a two-step process to ensure numbers: step one would have asked the preliminary question, "Are you in favor of statehood for Hawaii?" Those answering affirmatively would then answer: "Are you in favor of statehood for Hawaii NOW?" The final draft of the plebiscite question, however, was changed to simply read: "Do you favor statehood for Hawaii?" The plebiscite yielded a 67 percent vote in the affirmative, although the question only received 60 percent support on the island of O'ahu, where the statehood campaign had been most active. Because of the ambiguity of the plebiscite question, members of the Equal Rights Commission conceded that the plebiscite had settled very little. Statehood remained, as John Snell (Executive Secretary for the Hawaii Equal Rights Commission) acknowledged, "a hotly debated issue in the territory."[114]

By the mid-1930s, the movement for statehood was clearly seen as an attempt to reconsolidate haole racial power and privilege. The Big Five's prestige and influence were always emboldened by their relations with the federal government, which for its part desired control over Hawai'i as a means to maintain a large military force in the middle of the Pacific. Because of the Great Depression, however, Congress extinguished the profitable tariffs and empowered dockworkers to unionize in ways that would extinguish the mutual interests of the Big Five. Such acts by Congress signaled to the Big Five that they needed to gain full congressional representation in Washington, DC, through statehood in order to counter what they called "federal discrimination." But gaining admission into the United States as a state would be a difficult project given the racist views held by U.S. congressmen against Hawai'i's largely nonwhite population. Indeed, prior and leading up to the initial movement for statehood in 1934, perceptions of Hawai'i's Asian and Kanaka 'Ōiwi population had been largely shaped by frontier logics of assimilation and obliteration developed and advanced by academics such as Stanley Porteus and the sociologists at the University of Hawai'i. After World War II, however, the Japanese were no longer viewed as obstacles to achieving U.S. statehood; rather, they became objects of propaganda that were globally circulated to prove Japanese American loyalty to the United States and reconcile postwar relations between the two countries.

CHAPTER 3

"SOMETHING INDEFINABLE WOULD BE LOST"

The Unruly Kamokila and *Go for Broke!*

> There was a time in the mysterious past of these Islands, when
> the very air was peopled with the spirits of the departed, and
> a thin veil divided the living from the dead, the natural from the
> supernatural.
> —Kamokila Campbell, *Legends of Hawaii*

In 1933, Alice Kamokilaikawai Campbell opened a theater in San Francisco
at what was once 960 Bush Street. There, she "converted" a Methodist
church into a temple and theater for Hawaiian performance. Kamokila,
as she preferred to be called publicly, though sometimes other Hawaiians
referred to her as "Chiefess Kamokila," flipped the linear march of missionary progress on its head with her sacrilegious act, which was highlighted in the newspapers.[1] Using the most advanced lighting available,
Kamokila decorated her theater with "paintings, royal insignia, crimson
and gold drapes, and elaborate decorations fashioned of feathers [kāhili
used by ali'i (royal) families to indicate their lineage]."[2] Kamokila's performances, some of which were of Pele, aimed to expose Americans
to Hawai'i not as a U.S. territory but as a nation with its own forms of
sacredness and modernity distinct from the United States. In a newspaper interview Kamokila recalled childhood memories dancing hula
for Queen Lili'uokalani in 'Iolani Palace and said of Americans, "You in
America smother music, art—smother everything with too many committees. In Hawaii, we are a law unto ourselves. Each person acts according to

what he believes is right, and so long as he profoundly believes that he is right, morally, spiritually or otherwise. The moment doubt enters, he is wrong."[3] Her statement to "you in America" reveals her refusal to include herself in an American national identity, while her description of being a "law unto ourselves" is akin to Hawaiian notions of ea. Noelani Goodyear-Kaʻōpua asserts: "Like breathing, ea cannot be achieved or possessed; it requires constant action day after day, generation after generation."[4] Kamokila embodied the continued practice of ea, expressed tactically by pushing the limits of what was "sayable" under U.S. occupation at this time. She asserted Hawaiian national sovereignty in the decades after U.S. occupation and carried this resistance throughout the territorial period against statehood.

The daughter of Abigail Kuaihelani Maipinepine Campbell, the president of the Hui Aloha ʻĀina who gathered an enormous number of signatures on the petitions successfully opposing U.S. annexation in 1897 (see chapter 1), and the younger sister of Princess Abigail Campbell Kawānanakoa, the heir to the throne of the Hawaiian Kingdom (see chapter 2), Kamokila was also an heir to the Campbell estates, one of the largest landowners in Hawaiʻi—not to be mistaken as a part of the Big Five.[5] Elected in 1942 as the first woman territorial senator from Maui County, Kamokila publicized her campaign by running a radio advertisement that spoke of the overthrow of Queen Liliʻuokalani, promising to bring freedom from oppression to all peoples in the islands. "To that end I shall dedicate my life," she asserted.[6] The Hawaiian genealogist Sammy Amalu (see chapter 4) writes that Kamokila descends from Laakapu, a direct descendant of the goddess "Hina and Ahumaikealakea the First, who was a High Priestess of the Temple of Hina at Paliuli, and Kamokila's own children are direct descendants of the famed Prince Priest Kekuaokalani who died defending his gods."[7] Informed by a long matrilineal genealogy of Hawaiian leadership and resistance, Kamokila thus challenged colonial assumptions that Kānaka ʻŌiwi, particularly ʻŌiwi women, were incapable of self-government. She continued the perpetuation of Hawaiian national claims during the territorial period, as her genealogy and elected political office afforded her the means and responsibility to voice the "silent fears" of Kānaka ʻŌiwi. Kamokila maintained that with the attainment of statehood, "something indefinable would be lost."[8]

Often referred to as an "untamed woman," Kamokila Campbell spoke openly against rampant development and the political marginalization of Kānaka 'Ōiwi through statehood. As a member of the political and economic elite, Kamokila knew that *private* interests were looking to profit from tourism and were using *public* funds to persuade the general public through opinion campaigns to support statehood. With a brief recession between 1946 and 1947, Hawai'i's economy otherwise surged for the next twenty years. Large military spending during and after World War II, a kind of "military Keynesianism," a term that describes the centrality of a military industrial complex and war making in mitigating economic depressions, helped to get the United States out of the economic depression of the 1930s.[9] America's gross national product (GDP) more than doubled in the 1950s and doubled again by the 1960s. Such increased national prosperity, combined with government subsidization of the development of commercial airlines, greatly increased tourist travel to Hawai'i. Malcolm MacNaughton, former president of Castle and Cooke and the Chamber of Commerce of Honolulu, pointed out in 1986 that statehood was about gaining "capital for investment" in tourism.

Despite holding an economic monopoly on Hawai'i, the Big Five were unable to come up with the kind of wealth necessary to take advantage of the growing number of tourists. Thus they looked to giant lending institutions and insurance companies (particularly life insurance) that did have the required sums of capital to invest. These potential investors, however, were unwilling unless Hawai'i became a U.S. state. U.S. territories were considered offshore investments and lending institutions were prevented by their corporate indentures from investing there. MacNaughton reflected: "We couldn't get this money. And air travel was increasing. Tourism was coming. . . . We needed this money. Statehood would get it for us."[10] While prior to World War II it was economic depression that led a settler elite to fight for statehood to regain profitable tariffs for the sugar industry, after the war statehood was seen as necessary to capitalize on the postwar boom and the growing numbers of tourists visiting Hawai'i. Castle and Cooke, for instance, averaged $10 million annually in 1947, but by 1970 they averaged a yearly revenue of half a billion dollars, possessing enough capital to expand internationally.[11] In fact, just prior to the admission of Hawai'i as a U.S. state in 1959, an industrialist and major land developer in

Hawai'i, Henry Kaiser, was aware of the buildup of hotels in Waikīkī after statehood and secured a permit for both a quarry and a cement plant.[12]

Kamokila and MacNaughton viewed the future of Hawai'i in oppositional ways. For MacNaughton a future Hawai'i under statehood meant larger economic prosperity through land development and an economic transition to tourism that would gain Castle and Cooke enough capital to expand their ventures globally. But for Kamokila, statehood meant the continuation of the forms of settler domination that began after the U.S. occupation of Hawai'i, which include a system reliant on the political and economic marginalization of Kānaka 'Ōiwi, coupled with spiritual and environmental desecrations. What made MacNaughton's future come to fruition was not the might of the conservative Right, but rather the emergence of a liberal Left and the new hegemonic bloc formed between these groups on the opposite ends of the political spectrum. Indeed, Japanese Americans after World War II, particularly veterans returning from war, emerged as a political vehicle for both statehood and land development. Differently racialized and gendered settlers—moderate, conservative, and liberal haole backed by labor, and an influential Japanese American voting bloc—forged alliances through a common interest in large economic gains in tourism that would require the achievement of statehood. With this bloc, the white supremacy of the Porteus type went out of fashion, though not extinct, and an assimilative and more inclusive liberal form took its popular place. As Hawai'i's political climate shifted from the conservativism of the Republican Party to the liberalism of the Democratic Party, it still maintained a violent colonial rationale that hardened notions of primitivism against Kānaka 'Ōiwi but mediated the Orientalism constituting Japanese Americans. The logics governing racial knowledge were historically created to respond to this new form of liberal inclusion, organized around fraternal forms of settler-colonial power sharing.

Current memories of the postwar period are saturated by the heroics of the Japanese American soldiers in the 442nd and 100th Battalion, narrated as not just fighting valiantly in World War II but returning to defeat the last vestiges of haole racism in Hawai'i. By tracing two mutually constitutive but colliding projects in the post–World War II period—the state-led project for Hawai'i statehood that required challenging the perception of Japanese Americans as "aliens ineligible for citizenship," and another project that sought to challenge the idea of Kanaka ʻŌiwi as "unfit for self-government"—we can see how U.S. empire targeted these dissimilar groups for different ends. I begin by tracing the shift from Japanese Americans as "Japs"—killable populations who were obstacles to statehood—to "Japanese Americans," who became symbols of an antiracist America that embraced statehood for Hawaiʻi. The 1951 MGM propaganda film *Go for Broke!*, featuring the Japanese American 442nd Regimental Combat Team, stages production of official antiracism; in it we can see the changing relations between haole and Japanese Americans, but also an attempt to reconcile two formidable empires—the United States and Japan.

If Japanese Americans countered a racist notion that they were "ineligible for citizenship," Kānaka ʻŌiwi challenged a primitivist notion that they were "unfit for self-government" by at once organizing against statehood and conjuring the 1893 overthrow. The Hawaii Statehood Commission (1947–59), created by Act 115 of the territorial legislature, took the place of the Hawaii Equal Rights Commission, leading to a more aggressive campaign for capturing hegemony and normalizing public opinion for statehood. Kamokila brought a successful lawsuit against the Hawaii Statehood Commission that was filed on January 17, 1948—the fifty-fifth anniversary of the 1893 overthrow of the Hawaiian Kingdom. In voicing other avenues for self-governance for Kānaka ʻŌiwi, Kamokila faced repeated attempts by the fraternal hegemonic bloc, including Hawaiian elites, to pacify and contain her speech by disqualifying her comments in sexist and racist terms. Similarly to the way in which the subject position "primitive" was used to constitute Kanaka ʻŌiwi sovereignty as "unfit for self-government," with minds that lacked the capacity to make rational decisions, Kamokila was repeatedly discredited as acting according to the whims of her emotion.

What is thus never considered are the political strategies and unexpected tactics Kamokila created to block statehood by aligning herself with white supremacists based on changing conditions and possibilities occurring in different times. Indeed, John Burns, congressional delegate and governor, revealed in a 1960 interview: "The reasons why Hawaii did not achieve statehood, say, ten years ago—and one could without much exaggeration say sixty years ago—lie not in the Congress but in Hawaii. The most effective opposition to statehood was always originated in Hawaii itself. For the most part it has remained under cover and has marched under other banners. Such opposition could not afford to disclose itself, since it was so decidedly against the interests and desires of Hawaii's people generally."[13] Burns's description of resistance to statehood operating "under cover" and marching "under other banners" offers commentary on the forms and limits of resistance to U.S. occupation during the territorial period. In this statement Burns reveals a tactical component of the fight against statehood. Kamokila first marched under the "banner" of anti-Japanese racism, arguing that the large population of Japanese in Hawaiʻi disqualified it from statehood. Just two years earlier, in 1944, Kamokila had, in fact, publicly opposed anti-Japanese racism, arguing that those "whose heart and mind are set against statehood for reasons based on prejudice, rather than ideals, those are the people of Hawaii who should be pitied rather than condemned."[14] In the 1950s, Kamokila switched her strategy as the Cold War took precedence, arguing that there were too many communists in Hawaiʻi for statehood. Here, I do not argue that Kamokila's tactics were excusable. Whether an actual racist or pretending to be one, the material implications for those vulnerable to such a discourse remain the same.

My aim is not to resolve this contradiction, nor to split ambivalence by creating a good-versus-bad dichotomy. Instead, I highlight the particular tactics Kamokila deployed, for better or worse. Much of the historical literature on Kamokila Campbell dismisses her political work based on her anti-Japanese racism, lumping her with the Big Five elite. Histories that determine the value of an individual based on a binary of being either oppressed or oppressive often disregard Kamokila. That Kamokila Campbell is not a well-known political figure in either public memory or academic discourse speaks to the success of the opinion campaigns in shaping the memory of the past and their continued hold on governing how we are allowed to talk about this history in the present.

"THEY'RE NOT JAPS, THEY'RE JAPANESE AMERICANS"

The Japanese American soldiers became part of a grand story, nearly biblical in form, whose premise is that all events in U.S. history have been steps on the road to the realization of a glorious end that was in fact already foretold at the nation's beginning. . . . All the past is then made to contribute to the grand narrative in such a way that every moment between the beginning and the end, including anomalies such as institutional racism, can be reinscribed as minor aberrations on the path to the promised land. The problem with this narrative, of course, is that realization of the promise may be forever deferred or shifted onto different groups.

—Takashi Fujitani, "*Go for Broke*, the Movie"

One of the biggest obstacles facing statehood proponents was that Hawai'i contained a large population of Japanese Americans who were construed by American Orientalism as inscrutable foreign threats. In the decades leading to World War II, and punctuated by the December 7 attack in 1941, U.S. nationalism was formed by what Moon-Kie Jung terms an "anti-Japanese Americanism."[15] Japanese Americans who were linked to a belligerent empire seizing resources and territories throughout Asia were racialized differently from other nonwhite groups in Hawai'i. Jung explains, "Anti-Japanese racism was not based on an assured belief that the Japanese were inferior but on a fear that they were *not*."[16] At the onset of the war, Japanese American men were designated 4C "enemy aliens," a classification that not only made them ineligible for the draft, but also cast further suspicion over their loyalty to the United States.

After World War II, Japan was pacified as a nonthreat and perceived as a new economic ally of the United States. Consequently, key opportunities to transform prevailing perceptions of Japanese Americans as "enemy aliens" soon appeared. Indeed, while the large Japanese population in Hawai'i provided a reason for the congressional committee in 1937 to recommend against statehood for Hawai'i, by the end of World War II, the loyal military sacrifice of Japanese Americans during the war had become vital to a movement for statehood. Japanese American veterans returning from war emerged as a political vehicle for both statehood and land development.

Statehood proponents highlighted Japanese American loyalty by pointing to the military heroism and massive casualties sustained by the 100th Infantry Battalion and 442nd Regimental Combat Team. Nicknamed the "Purple Heart Battalion," the 100th Battalion and 442nd Regimental Combat Team received more than 18,143 decorations but also suffered an unusually high number of casualties at 9,486. Indeed, the high casualty and injury rates show how officers of the U.S. Army viewed

Japanese American soldiers as expendable; even the soldiers themselves believed they were ordered on what they called "suicide missions."[17] The cultural work to convince an American public of the trustworthiness of Japanese Americans was already done for statehood proponents by the U.S. military.

Historian Tom Coffman explains that while Japanese American soldiers faced discrimination in the military, they were key to winning the "hearts and minds" of Japan and Asia. Edwin O. Reischauer, the principal architect of postwar U.S. relations with Japan (and eventual ambassador to Japan under John F. Kennedy), argued in 1942 that the internment of Japanese Americans had "unwittingly contributed" to Japanese propaganda. Such propaganda stated that Japan was fighting a war to stop the United States from spreading white supremacist domination throughout Asia. Reischauer wrote: "We should reverse this situation and make of these American citizens a major asset in our ideological war in Asia. Their sincere and enthusiastic support of the United States at this time would be the best possible proof that this is not a racial war to preserve white supremacy in Asia, but a war to establish a better world order for all, regardless of race."[18] As a result of President Truman's decision to use atomic bombs against Japan, coupled with the United States' later military occupation of the country, Reischauer highlighted the need to celebrate with vigor the wartime heroics of Japanese American veterans.

The MGM film *Go for Broke!* played one such role in combating the idea that Japanese Americans were foreign threats to be permanently excluded from the U.S. national polity. The film first screened at the national Capitol on May 24, 1951. The *New York Times* heralded the film as an expression and demonstration of Japanese American humanity: "Without fuss or feathers or an over-expense of preachy words, is aptly revealed and demonstrated the loyalty and courage of a racial minority group, along with the normal human qualities of decency and humor inherent in these men."[19] *Go for Broke!* challenged sentiments from around the world that the United States remained a white supremacist nation that restrained the civil rights of Japanese Americans. The film was written and directed by Academy Award–winning Robert Pirosh, who also earned an Oscar nomination for the screenplay. The protagonist Lieutenant Michael Grayson was played by Van Johnson, who had also starred in Pirosh's Academy Award–winning film *Battleground*, cel-

ebrated for depicting soldiers as vulnerable and imperfect. The cast of
Go for Broke! included actual veterans from the 442nd Regiment, notably Lane Nakano, George Miki, Akira Fukunaga, Ken Okamoto, Henry
Oyasato, and Henry Hamada. Much like world's fairs, whose authen-
ticity relied on blurring the lines between performance and historical
reenactments, the casting of actual Nisei (second-generation) veterans
aimed to convey legitimacy, as their embodied presence verified the information expressed in the film as both trustworthy and authentic. The
Publicity Department of MGM explained: "It was their own personal
story, a story, with apologies to General Stillwell, they wrote in Italy
and France 'with their blood.'"[20] Major General F. L. Parks, the father
of modern army public affairs, offered an official approval from the Department of the Army. *Go for Broke!* screened nationally and internationally in parts of Europe and Asia, but most prominently, it screened
in Japan on December 7, 1952, the eleventh anniversary of Japan's attack
on Pearl Harbor.

In the film, the heroism and valor of Japanese American soldiers, especially their unwavering loyalty and military sacrifice to the American
nation, are deployed to rid the newly commissioned Second Lieutenant
Michael Grayson of his bigoted views of Japanese Americans. From the
start of the film, anti-Japanese racism is addressed through a series of
pedagogical lessons on liberal racial tolerance. The film begins with a
superimposed text of President Franklin Roosevelt's words over footage
of the marching Nisei soldiers. It reads: "The proposal of the War Department to organize a combat team consisting of loyal American citizens of
Japanese descent has my approval. The principle on which this country
was founded and by which it has always been governed is that Americanism is a matter of the mind and heart; Americanism is not, and never
was, a matter of race or ancestry." The idea that "Americanism" is not
a question of race but one of "heart" provides a sentimental and overly
generous view of U.S. race relations. This myopic view frames the rest
of the film. Tellingly, while the film relies on the valor of the Nisei—for
example, also superimposed on the same scene described above is a table
of their battle record: "7 Major Campaigns in Europe; 9,486 Casualties;
18,143 Individual Decorations; 7 Presidential Unit Citations"—there are
many instances where even in the film's noble narrative, Japanese American
death becomes a backdrop for centering white life.

The issue of white racial tolerance and the project of subduing white anxiety around blurred racial lines are the focus of much of the film. In the service of teaching white Americans how to think differently about Japanese Americans, Lieutenant Michael Grayson takes center stage. Upon arrival at Camp Shelby in Mississippi, a Japanese American soldier drives a visibly disturbed Lieutenant Grayson through the camp. The script describes Grayson's discomfort with what he sees: "The distasteful expression on his rugged, handsome features leaves no doubt as to what *he* thinks of American citizens of Japanese descent. Grayson throws a glance at the jeep driver, then shifts his angular, six-foot frame to get as much space between them as possible."[21] Accordingly, the cameras offer the perspective of what Grayson sees from the jeep, providing the audience with a scene where a white racial order is flipped on its head. Grayson is disturbed and offended to see an American military camp overrun by Japanese, where Japanese American soldiers doing a roll call respond to their "Oriental" names being called: "Kawaguchi!" "Tsukimura!" Grayson is even more bothered by what the script describes as a "Hawaiian war chant" where so-called Kanakas from Hawai'i, played by Japanese actors, perform what appears to be hula, which is as contrived as the song they are dancing to. Such displays of white discomfort with "Oriental" foreignness set the stage for Grayson to be reformed.

In the next sequence, Grayson meets with the sergeant major and immediately asks to be transferred back to the U.S. Thirty-Sixth Infantry, his previous Texas National Guard unit. When asked if his request isn't due to the Japanese American troops, Grayson responds, "Because they're Japs? No, sir, it isn't that at all."[22] The film then moves into its first of many disciplinary lectures on the use of the term *Japs*: "They're not 'Japs,' they're Japanese-Americans—Nisei—or, as they call themselves, boodaheads [*sic*]. All kinds of boodaheads, Lieutenant. From Hawaii, Alaska, California, New York, Colorado—yes, and some from Texas. They're all American citizens and they're all volunteers. Remember that. And another thing. We officers are referred to as 'haoles,'—not white men. Any questions?"

Grayson is uncomfortable because he is outnumbered by Japanese Americans and is racialized as "haole." Indeed, the older white officers at Camp Shelby, ranked higher in the white heteropatriarchal order, lecture Grayson on his racism, demonstrating America's new inclusive position on Japanese Americans. While possessing the necessary qualities of a military officer—white, tall, blonde, and Texan—Grayson is infantilized as a newly commissioned officer. As such, his racism becomes evidence of his lack of maturity, where his superior officers consider racial tolerance of Japanese Americans necessary for masculine and democratic leadership. Such lessons of official antiracism, however, function to maintain the established hierarchy that includes senior white leadership over junior white leadership over subordinate nonwhite (Japanese American) soldiers. In this way, the inclusion of Japanese Americans in the fraternity of soldiers recalls how the 1893 Chicago World's Columbian Exposition included the Japanese in the White City in ways that actually displayed white supremacy. In other words, the take-home point for moviegoers is that the inclusion of Japanese Americans can be tolerated so long as they, too, play the role of subordinate supremacy.

In order to portray the United States as a nation founded on democratic ideals, not white supremacy, the film needed to provide sufficient reasons for why the United States interned 120,000 Japanese Americans into concentration camps. Grayson broaches the topic when he asks the captain if they use live ammunition at the rifle range, stating that all he knew was that the Japanese were placed in "relocation centers" and maybe "the army just had some surplus barbed wire they wanted to use, was that it?"[23] The captain admonishes Lieutenant Grayson by offering another forced lesson in racial tolerance: "The army was facing an emergency at the start of the war—a possible invasion by Japanese troops. So all Japanese-Americans on the West Coast were evacuated as a precautionary measure. There was no loyalty check—no screening—nothing. If there were any spies among them, I can assure you they're not in the four-four-two. Every man in the outfit has been investigated, reinvestigated and re-reinvestigated. (rising) I suggest you start getting acquainted."[24] Upon learning that he will be in charge of an all–Japanese American unit, Grayson takes his frustrations out on his platoon by maintaining strict regulations and orders. The film, and the intensity of the drama, proceeds in a series of juxtapositions of scenes featuring private conversations among the white officers and private conversations of the Japanese American soldiers. In one scene, a soldier named Sam—played by Lane Nakano, who was actually interned with his family at the Heart Mountain Internment Camp—prepares a care package of canned goods. Sam explains to fellow soldier Tommy (Henry Nakamura) that the package isn't being sent to his brother who is serving in the 100th Battalion, but rather to Arizona, where his family is interned in conditions worse than Camp Shelby. Tommy asks Sam why he would volunteer to fight, given the poor treatment of his family. Sam explains that the purpose of fighting is to end discrimination against Japanese Americans. Tommy, whose family were killed in Hawaiʻi during the Japanese attack on Pearl Harbor, responds in pidgin: "We show 'em! We show 'em us boodaheads good soldiers, good Americans!" Sam responds: "All we need now is the casualty lists."[25]

Go for Broke! offers space for a critical assessment of the coercive forms of assimilation seemingly required to end the unfair treatment of Japanese Americans. In the transition from "Japs" to "Japanese Americans" is a delicate play on necropolitics and biopolitics. The term *Jap* was used in wartime propaganda as a quick way to determine that a person was killable: "Let's blast the Jap clean off the map." Or magazine magnate Henry Luce's observation, "Americans had to learn how to hate Germans, but hating Japs comes natural—as natural as fighting Indians once was."[26] The transition from "Jap" to "Japanese American," an approximate relation to whiteness, still necessitated a sacrifice of "Jap" death. A kind of logic of resurrection occurs in the film, reflecting a theological dimension to settler sovereignty.[27] To end discrimination for being a sinful "Jap," one needs to be reborn as a "Japanese American," which requires one's seeming racial sin to be sacrificed on the altar of American war.

After fighting alongside the 442nd in Italy and France, Grayson comes to respect his fellow soldiers. In a pivotal scene, which sets up the climactic rescue of the Texas Battalion by the Nisei soldiers, Grayson stands up for his Japanese American regiment in the presence of his unreformed, racist friend, named Culley, who is also from the Texas Battalion. While drinking at a bar, Grayson explains that the 442nd would be the Texas Battalion's artillery, and the ensuing dialogue between Grayson and Culley provides yet another pedagogical moment for reforming prevailing social conflations of Japanese Americans with enemy "Japs":

CULLEY: They're sending us up without our own artillery? Just the Japs?

GRAYSON: They're a good outfit, Culley. Plenty good.

CULLEY: Practically winning the war single-handed, what I hear. (*contemptuously*) Japs!

Embarrassed as some of the Japanese American soldiers over hear their conversation, Grayson asks Culley to step outside.

GRAYSON: They're not Japs, Culley.
CULLEY: What?
GRAYSON: They're Japanese-Americans—Nisei—or, if you prefer, boodaheads. But not Japs. They don't like it and neither do I.
CULLEY: What are you, a Jap-lover or something?
GRAYSON: I said, they're not Japs. I'm warning you, Culley—

Grayson proceeds to scuffle with Culley, who eventually comes to change his views of Japanese American soldiers, but only after they rescue the Texas Battalion. Popularly referred to as the "Lost Battalion," the 100th Battalion and 442nd Regiment suffered 800 casualties to save 211 of the Texan soldiers.[28] Forty years later, Daniel Inouye, one of the most famous and powerful senators on Capitol Hill personally tied to the military buildup of Hawai'i, would state forcefully, "I am absolutely certain that all of us were well aware that we were being used for the rescue because we were expendable."[29]

While Japanese Americans are shown to have the ability to be included in American culture, Japanese culture is shown to be of particular value to the United States. For example, a Japanese American soldier nicknamed Chick (played by George Miki) constantly complains about racism and the conditions of the camp. Chick explains that while most others were enlisted from internment camps, prior to the war he was in Iowa getting paid $500 a month to determine the sex of chickens. He exhorts, "Chick-sexing is a science. It was developed in Japan and it's one place a boodahead gets a break."[30] In another moment—this one on "dirty tactics" hand-to-hand combat—Grayson has his sergeant, a Japanese American, in a hold for which he says there is no escape. But the sergeant suddenly flips Grayson with a judo maneuver. The idea of combining Japanese knowledge with American know-how provided the cultural groundwork for integrating Japanese American soldiers into the army.

This project of inclusion is also about integrating Asia into American political and economic hegemony at the outset of the Cold War. As

Takashi Fujitani succinctly argues, *"Go for Broke was part of a new pattern of representations and discourses in which values considered to be traditional in Asian societies were celebrated as conducive to Americanism."*[31] The cultural fluidity with which Japanese Americans could be both Japanese and American also justified the disproportionate number of casualties the Nisei suffered. Japan's soldiers were racialized in popular culture as "kamikaze" pilots, posing a luminous foreign threat because they were obedient to the point of death. In the context of war, the motto "go for broke," a Hawaiian reference to gambling until one loses everything, but popularized nationally by the film, continues to essentialize Japanese Americans in self-sacrificial obedience to the U.S. nation. This characterization of Japanese American soldiers (as willing to "go for broke") helped to justify the disproportionately large casualty rates of Japanese American soldiers. In a scene where the exhausted soldiers are sent on yet another suicide mission to rescue the Texas Regiment, Tommy and Sam speak of the need to change the attitudes of white Americans like Lieutenant Grayson toward Japanese Americans. Facing possible death, Tommy tries to encourage a disheartened Sam, "It's rough—it's plenty rough—but we know what's it all about. You bet. More bettuh we 'go for broke,' eh, Sam?" Sam eventually responds with a smile saying, "That's about it, Tommy. More bettuh we 'go for broke!'" Soon after, a shell explodes near two other soldiers, injuring one and killing the other.

Though white racism is often the brunt of many of the jokes, the film actually pivots around a fragile and delicate white masculinity that continually requires reassurance. Japanese Americans are "shot" in the film in ways that highlight both their sacrificial deaths and short physical statures. These shots render them unthreatening to white heteropatriarchal order. In one particular montage, the soldiers are shown training for combat by running through an obstacle course, but they are unable to leap over trenches or climb a wooden wall. Their inability to perform what "normal" soldiers are routinely able to do is a symbolic form of emasculation. The racial order of the United States would symbolically become more inclusive as a multicultural nation, yet still preserve components of white supremacy.

In this way, an official antiracism also served as a developmental discourse. The camaraderie between Lieutenant Michael Grayson and the Nisei soldiers reflected a newfound prosperity that could be enjoyed with the joint efforts of Japan and the United States. This new coalition of white American and Japanese American men in the film also reflected a new possibility that Japanese American men could work alongside whites.

While Japanese American military sacrifice helped to mend U.S. relations with Japan, therefore facilitating the opening of Asian markets to American businesses, in Hawaiʻi it also assisted both a movement for statehood and Japanese American ascendancy. Matsuo Takabuki—442nd veteran, major player in land development, and a once controversial trustee of the Kamehameha School Bishop Estate—recalls that their celebrated record on the battlefield "pushed" them "to the forefront of the statehood effort."[32] In his memoirs, Takabuki writes that John A. Burns told Japanese American veterans, "Do not be ashamed of who you are. Talk about your war record. . . . You have proven that you are Americans. You earned this honor under fire. Flaunt it."[33] Indeed, the Hawaii Statehood Commission would highlight the military achievements of the Nisei in much of its literature.[34]

Armed with the GI Bill, many Nisei veterans left Hawaiʻi again to attain professional and law degrees, which upon their return bolstered the social, economic, and political power of the Japanese American community. John A. Burns helped to reorganize the Democratic Party by drawing heavily from the popularity of the Japanese American veterans, many of whom became hugely successful in political office. Some notable examples include the aforementioned Daniel Inouye and George Ariyoshi, who would become the first Japanese American governor of the state. With other elected officials like Daniel Aoki, Sakae Takahashi, and Matsuo Takabuki, they worked together with Burns to revitalize the Democratic Party in a concerted effort to unseat the Republican Party and its Big Five power base at the legislature.

With the ideological support of returning veterans and the political support of the ILWU, the Democrats were able to accomplish in 1954 what is often referred to as the "Democratic Revolution," wherein political control of the legislature shifted from the Republicans to the new Democratic Party.[35] Takabuki explains, however, that the liberal Burns Faction, from its inception, was not interested in disrupting the economic power of the Big Five: "We saw the potential growth of tourism as an industry, with new and different players. We realized the Big Five were important players in Hawai'i's economy, and we did not want to destroy them. However, we did not want them to continue to dominate and be the only game in town. Tourism would open all kinds of economic avenues for the future, providing opportunities for the upcoming generation of those outside the existing economic oligarchy."[36] This new political force sought a passive revolution; they were not seeking to fundamentally reorder social relations so much as they sought to be accommodated within the economic system of the Big Five. Takabuki writes that prior to the "Democratic Revolution," returning veterans participated in creating a "financial revolution."[37]

After the attack on Pearl Harbor, many white businessmen left Hawai'i fearing further military attack and martial law.[38] This led to an economic vacuum in which many Japanese American and Chinese American entrepreneurs were able to capitalize on abandoned businesses and wide-open markets. According to Takabuki:

> The Fukunagas of Servco started a small garage in Haleiwa, which grew into a large conglomerate of auto and durable goods dealerships, discount stores, and financial institutions. The Fujieki family started a small family market that grew into the Star Supermarket chain. The Teruyas' small restaurant and market in the 1950s and 1960s eventually became Times Supermarket. Chinn Ho started Capital Investment. K.J. Luke and Clarence Ching created Loyalty Enterprises, while Aloha Airlines began with Ruddy Tongg. As the number of local professionals, lawyers, and doctors grew in postwar Hawai'i, the economic, professional, and political landscape also changed rapidly.[39]

Takabuki explains further that the major banks in Hawai'i—the Bank of Hawai'i and Bishop Bank (now First Hawaiian Bank)—would not regularly offer business loans to anyone outside of the white economic circle. This led veterans Daniel Inouye and Sakae Takahashi to open two banks: Central Pacific Bank (CPB) and, later, the City Bank of Honolulu.[40] With financial and administrative support from major banking institutions in Japan, many in the Democratic Party ventured into major residential and tourist-related real estate development projects, as tourism displaced agriculture as the dominant industry in the 1950s and 1960s.

Major land development projects, particularly in hotels and shopping centers, were slowed down, however, because of the aforementioned fear or lack of confidence by stateside lenders and investors in Hawaiʻi's territorial economy. This motivated many Japanese in Hawaiʻi to push for statehood, alongside those on the other end of the political spectrum who were a part of or associated with the Big Five. This emerging historical bloc would not go unnoticed or unchallenged by others. During the war and after it, Kamokila Campbell emerged as a leading opponent of statehood, publicly opposing this new historical bloc while fighting for other forms of self-governance for Kānaka ʻŌiwi.

"SOMETHING INDEFINABLE WOULD BE LOST . . ."

During the period of martial law, after being elected as territorial senator, Kamokila immediately sought out other subjects of U.S. empire, peoples whose American citizenship was forced upon them by the United States, namely Native Americans and other Pacific Islanders. For instance, Kamokila traveled to Washington, DC, in 1943 to attain information on the potential of turning the Hawaiian Homes Commission Act into a kind of Native American reservation to be administered through the Bureau of Indian Affairs. Kamokila's Hawaiian constituents asked her to investigate the Native American reservation system as an "alternative proposal to the present set up," arguing that the government had been negligent in placing Hawaiians on the land.[41] While in Washington, DC, Kamokila was able to hold meetings with powerful and influential elected officials such as President Franklin D. Roosevelt, Secretary of the Interior Harold L. Ickes, and several senators to discuss the possibility of federalizing the Hawaiian Homes Commission. In her meeting with Roosevelt, she gifted him a royal calabash that once belonged to King David Kalākaua. The calabash was "inlaid with a silver rim engraved with mangoes and grapefruit and displays the coat of arms of the Hawaiian Kingdom."[42] Such symbols of Hawaiʻi's independent status undoubtedly placed her minimal request for due consideration into the Bureau of Indian Affairs (BIA) in proper context. Although the Termination Act was officially passed in 1953, aiming at terminating "as rapidly as possible" their treaty-based relationship with the United States as federally recognized nations, some states had already experimented with the juridical aims of termination in the 1940s. Thus, the possibility for the Hawaiian Homes Commission to practice some form of self-determination as a domestic dependent nation became implausible. Kamokila explained that it was her discussions with the BIA, which Congress determined to be extremely mismanaging Native resources, that drew her "more and more away" from the proposal to seek alternative means of "correcting faults" in the commission.[43]

In October 1944, weighing the impact of military occupation against settler colonialism fueled by rampant capitalist development, Kamokila committed what many considered to be political suicide. She asked Congressman Sterling Cole of New York to sponsor a federal bill that aimed to transfer control of United States territories and possessions from the secretary of the interior to the Naval Department. Kamokila argued that the navy would be a better protector of the Pacific Islands than big business. Transferring power from white settlers in Hawai'i to white settlers tied to the federal government and the military is what territorial leaders had feared most since the Massie case in the 1930s. After visiting Guåhan in 1935 and conversing with a Samoan chief, K. Su'a,[44] Kamokila reasoned that because Hawaiians were unable to control immigration into Hawai'i, naval control could actually limit the flow of immigration (as it had in Guåhan) and prohibit non-Natives from owning land (as it did in American Samoa).[45] Kamokila argued, "I sincerely believe the prestige of America would be greatly enhanced if Pacific Island natives, incapable as the old Hawaiians of coping with ruthless business methods, are folded under the care and guidance of our great naval leaders."[46] Contending with the impact of settler colonialism regarding both land dispossession and Native replacement via immigration, Kamokila's actions help us to understand that she was aware that the particular form of settler-colonial power impacting Hawai'i was not synonymous with the interests animating the military occupation. The editor of the *Honolulu Advertiser*, most likely Lorrin P. Thurston, responded, "It is unfortunate that a national committeewoman and territorial senator, whose great wealth was derived from the industrial development of Hawaii, should become so befuddled with an idealistic illusion of a primitive past, whose rigors she herself has never known, that she advocates the permanent surrender of civilian government in Hawaii."[47]

In January 1946, the first congressional hearings on statehood since 1937 were held at 'Iolani Palace. Aware that Kamokila's testimony would be one of the few in opposition to statehood, the Hawaii Equal Rights Commission attempted to squeeze her into an afternoon with other witnesses. Stating that she needed more time for her graphs and charts to be prepared, she skillfully maneuvered the committee to allow her to speak on the last day, specifically January 17, 1946.[48] Aware that this date was the fifty-third anniversary of the 1893 U.S. military–backed overthrow of the Hawaiian Kingdom, Kamokila used this historic date to articulate the national dispossession of the Hawaiian people with the state-led drive for statehood.

While historians have highlighted her 1946 testimony to point out the existence of Hawaiian opposition to statehood, Kamokila's testimony was more tactical and historically precise. She charged the Big Five with orchestrating the statehood movement to expand their economic inter-ests in tourism by attracting "outside capital and independent financial giants." Striking at the heart of the avaricious desires sustaining a move-ment for statehood, Kamokila declared: "I do not feel . . . that we should forfeit the traditional rights and privileges of the natives of our islands for a mere thimbleful of votes in Congress, that we, the lovers of Hawaii from long association with it, should sacrifice our birthright for the greed of alien desires to remain on our shores, that we should satisfy the thirst for power and control of some inflated industrialists and politicians."[49] As a member of the political and economic elite, Kamokila knew that the Big Five desired statehood to gain access to investment money for tour-ism, and thus had been controlling public funds to finance a protracted opinion campaign for such private purposes. Kamokila also called at-tention to the links between Big Five economic domination and the fear and silence that many harbored in opposing statehood. She shared an example of one such sentiment, sent to her in private, that implored her to speak on behalf of those who could not: "We can't, Kamokila. My hus-band would lose his job." Those present at the hearings, however, were able express their sentiments collectively in the thunderous cheers and applause following Kamokila's comments in a packed throne room with over six hundred people in attendance. In one instance, large applause broke out after Kamokila's response to Representative Angell's question of why statehood would not be able to address the problems she cited in the territorial structure. Kamokila responded with a thinly veiled reference to the 1893 overthrow: "Who is it that has put us in the position we are in today but the people who are asking you for statehood?" When asked by the congressmen what kind of government she would want instead of

Honolulu Star-Bulletin

20 PAGES—HONOLULU, T. H., U. S. A., THURSDAY, JANUARY 17, 1946—20 PAGES

Evening Bulletin, Est. 1882, No. 12365
Hawaiian Star, Volume LII. No. 16644

★★★★ AIRPLANE DELIVERY ON ISLANDS OTHER THAN OAHU 7¢ PRICE ON OAHU 5¢

Kamokila Opposes Island Statehood

LATE NEWS FINAL

Japanese, Big Five Are Main Reasons

Victor S. K. Houston, former delegate to congress, appeared before the congressional subcommittee investigating Hawaii's case for statehood, shortly after noon today.

He took the stand, he said, especially to rebut some of the testimony given by Senator Alice Kamokila Campbell, first witness today.

He pointed out that the total Caucasian population here now exceeds the total Japanese population.

Senator Alice Kamokila Campbell today backed her campaign against statehood for Hawaii with a charge that on the "Big Five" and a charge that Hawaii's Japanese population represents "a serious menace to good American government."

Testifying before the house territories subcommittee at its closing hearing on statehood for Hawaii, Mrs. Campbell said:

"All over these islands the influence of the 'Big Five' is felt through some channel or another, sometimes kindly, other times to the point of Hitlerism."

"The Japanese situation in the territory," she said, "is a serious

L. A. To S. F. Air Record Cut To Only 44 Minutes!

LOS ANGELES, Jan. 17. (U.P)—A jet powered fighter plane manufactured by Lockheed today blazed new record of 44 minutes between here and San Francisco, averaging more eighth miles a minute for the 361-mile flight.

Passage Is Now Available To Mainland

Steamship passages to the mainland, for the first time since the beginning of the war, are now available to all applicants, it was announced today.

Senator Alice Kamokila Campbell
She testified before the statehood committee this morning.

Figure 3.1 Kamokila Campbell testifying against U.S. statehood on January 17, 1946. Courtesy of *Honolulu-Star Bulletin*.

statehood, Kamokila responded, "an independent form of government," explaining that if others wanted to live in a U.S. state, they could simply move to any of the forty-eight states in the U.S. nation.

It is within this shifting political landscape of being squeezed between haole conservatives and Japanese American liberals that Kamokila found herself leveraging what political will she could against statehood. In her 1946 testimony, in just one example, Kamokila criticized the numerical dominance of Japanese Americans in racist terms, implying that Japanese Americans aided the attack on Pearl Harbor. She further argued that Japanese Americans moving from the plantations to small businesses could cause the Japanese to "get a hold on the islands." Kamokila's statements played to congressmen who viewed Hawai'i as unworthy of statehood because its population was largely "Asiatic." She thus reinforced the racist exclusion that Japanese in Hawai'i had long sought to counter. Kamokila had been arguing all along that statehood, especially as it was backed by a push for Japanese American ascendancy, was a continuation of Big Five hegemony. Her anti-Japanese statements can be read against the backdrop of the widespread circulation of heroic narratives about Japanese American loyalty during and soon after World War II. In combating the notion that Kānaka 'Ōiwi were destined to disappear and thus be replaced, she heightened fears that Japanese Americans were foreign threats "ineligible to citizenship." In hoping to prevent the latest elaboration of U.S. occupation through the vehicle of statehood, however, Kamokila appealed to a well-established fear among many white Americans that Japanese Americans were perpetual foreign threats; such appeals would work against her aims. In both instances, combating one's form of oppression by appealing to structures of white supremacy, either aiming to stall statehood by reinforcing the Japanese as ineligible to citizenship or fighting for statehood while casting Hawaiians as unfit for self-government, pits both marginalized groups against each other.

Speaking against both the moneyed interests of the Big Five and the ability of the numerical dominance of the Japanese in Hawai'i to politically marginalize Kānaka 'Ōiwi, her testimony received media coverage and editorial responses, mostly negative, for more than a month. Kamokila's testimony was printed in the *Honolulu Advertiser* the next morning and criticism of her was published in both the *Advertiser* and the *Star-Bulletin*.[50] Lorrin P. Thurston was among the first to launch a public critique, desperately relying on sexist and racist portrayals of Kamokila's mind to prevent her arguments from gaining momentum. He wrote in his newspaper that while her testimony was "undoubtedly the high spot of the entire hearings," her logics were confused. Thurston portrayed her as lacking consistency in her loyalty to a political party or stances on statehood and said that what she lacked logically was "made up for by her utter sincerity."[51] Thurston reduced Kamokila's views to little more than emotion and sentiment, figuring her as someone who lacked the white masculine rationale to be logical and discerning. Most responses, however, criticized her for challenging Japanese American loyalty. One editorial asked: "So she thinks the AJAS [Americans of Japanese Ancestry] have received too much publicity? Well, I think they rate it. They paid for it with blood—how does she pay for her publicity? Sooner or later it should dawn on her that people are getting fed up with her line."[52] Another argued that her comments set race relations back fifty years.[53] One day after Kamokila's testimony, the *Hawaii Herald*, previously *Hawaii Hochi*, responded with an editorial titled "Kamokila Is Right!" arguing that "for the very reason that Senator Campbell deplores this undue publicity given to what she terms the AJAS, so, we believe, Japanese-Americans deplore it." Stating that this publicity was initiated by army generals, not the Japanese themselves, the *Hawaii Herald* aimed to point out that the publicity was an attempt to protect Japanese Americans who had been interned in concentration camps on the U.S. continent as they reentered violently racist areas of the United States.[54]

A few days after her 1946 testimony, Kamokila told the press that she had been asked to launch an island-wide petition to oppose statehood. This was similar to what her mother, Abigail Kuaihelani Maipinepine Campbell, had helped accomplish with the 1897 Kūʻē petitions to oppose U.S. annexation. In response, the *Maui News* published an editorial titled "Kamokila in Die Hard Fight against Hawaii," and a few days later warned readers to "Beware of What You Sign."[55] This petition, however, did not circulate because of the risk that it could provide the Big Five with a list of names that could be immediately used to "blacklist" signers. On September of 1947, however, Kamokila continued her opposition to statehood by opening an "Anti-Statehood Clearing House."[56] Designed to be a counter to the Hawaii Statehood Commission, the clearinghouse was used to collect testimony in opposition to statehood and to lobby congressional senators against statehood. Using her contacts in Washington, DC, she would send "anti-statehood information, reports and arguments to congress."[57]

After the congressional hearings in January of 1946, proponents of statehood launched a national publicity campaign that would make it seem as though it were grassroots, not state-led. After consulting with congressional leaders in Washington, DC, Governor Ingram Stainback established the Citizens' Statehood Committee. But that official title was, in fact, a misnomer insofar as the committee was established and managed by top territorial governmental officials with oversight by the federal government in the form of the Pacific Branch of the Secretary of the Interior and Hawaiʻi's business elite. In this way, state projects seeking to shape ideology seem to be most effective when they appear to have resulted freely and spontaneously from the popular sentiment of a free public.[58] In other words, the territory's attempts to shape public opinion would be more effective if they created the impression that everyday people and community groups, rather than government agents or economic interests, initiated the movement for statehood. This tactic of making a state-led movement seem grassroots became the cornerstone of the statehood opinion campaign.

Keeping in line with the perception that statehood was initiated by everyday citizens, attempts at winning public opinion through the media needed to be seen not as government-paid advertisements for statehood, but rather as natural topics of conversation that occurred spontaneously and frequently in major media outlets. In a discussion on "Public Relations," Joseph Farrington, future U.S. congressional delegate who led the statehood movement throughout the 1940s and early 1950s, and son of former Governor Wallace R. Farrington, wrote: "It should be clearly understood that no advertising of any kind is even remotely suggested in behalf of the statehood movement. It needs none and might suffer more than it gains. . . . Public opinion can be mobilized in behalf of statehood by an entirely non-commercial use of such media as newspapers, magazines, radio, public meetings, personal campaigning, the distribution of literature—all appropriate publicity outlets.[59] Farrington also owned the *Honolulu Star-Bulletin*, one of the island's two major dailies, and in fact used his newspaper to front the statehood movement. The Citizens' Statehood Committee's own executive committee, in fact, called for an "article a day in daily newspapers" to reinforce and normalize public opinion in support of statehood.[60] Under the leadership of the Farrington family, their newspaper played a considerable role in doing so.[61] Alfred Pratte, former *Honolulu Star-Bulletin* employee, acknowledged that in regard to statehood, the Farrington family was responsible for "decades of preparing and organizing public opinion in Hawai'i and Washington, D.C."[62]

Skilled at using the media to shape public opinion, Farrington also headed the national publicity campaign for statehood and conceived of the movement as a "dual attack."[63] He argued that Honolulu should serve as the "headquarters" to disseminate information on statehood, targeting populations both locally and nationally, while an office in Washington, DC, should be responsible for lobbying Congress. The committee hired the public relations firm Holst, Cummings, Co. and consulted with the Chamber of Commerce of Honolulu to shape the master document, "Some Essentials of a Program to Secure Statehood for Hawaii."[64] The group estimated the total cost of the campaign to be $50,000, an amount that was funded privately and reimbursed later by the legislature, with support from the Chamber of Commerce of Honolulu.

This organizing and strategizing laid the foundation for a more aggressive and better-financed campaign for statehood. Territorial Senator Eugene Capellas, a member of the Citizens' Statehood Committee Executive Board, introduced Act 115 in July of 1947, which abolished the Hawaii Equal Rights Commission and created the Hawaii Statehood Commission in its place. Composed of nine members who, by law, were required to be known supporters of statehood, the commission was authorized in 1947 to take over the national campaign for statehood. All records and personnel of the Hawaii Equal Rights Commission were transferred to the Statehood Commission. The new commission was also given a budget of $200,000 "to assemble, compile, and disseminate information, conduct national or sectional advertising and publicity campaigns, appear as the representative of the Territory before Congress or any federal department in regard to statehood; and cooperate with any citizens' organization formed to accomplish the objects of the Act."[65]

Indeed, the Honolulu office remained in contact with more than seventeen hundred daily newspaper editors and in the first decade the number of editorials that favored statehood grew from five hundred to about three thousand *annually*.[66] The commission aggressively controlled how statehood was written about and portrayed in the media. It regularly coached witnesses who testified before the different congressional hearings and distributed large numbers of pamphlets, photographs, and letters to different newspapers, government offices, magazines, businesses, community organizations, libraries, schools, and universities, in support of the benefits of statehood. Indeed, Lorrin P. Thurston, the owner of the other major daily newspaper, came to chair the Hawaii Statehood Commission. Like his father, Lorrin P. Thurston was initially opposed to statehood, fearing that "haoles from the mainland" who had more capital than those in Hawai'i would soon displace the white settler elite. As manager of the the *Honolulu Advertiser*, Thurston came to support statehood and, like Farrington, also used his newspaper to campaign for statehood.[67] In response to the formation of the Hawaii Statehood Commission, however, Kamokila struck a major blow when she revealed the statehood campaign to be undemocratic and predetermined.

On January 17, 1948, Kamokila Campbell filed a lawsuit in *Campbell v. Stainback et al.* that challenged the legality of the financing of the Hawaii Statehood Commission. This lawsuit was timed to coincide with both the fifty-fifth anniversary of the overthrow of the Hawaiian nation and Oregon Senator Guy Cordon's impromptu visit to investigate statehood.[68] In the lawsuit, Kamokila charged that the $200,000 (provided by Act 115, which established the Statehood Commission) used by the territorial government to campaign for statehood nationally and locally was "to the exclusion and detriment of citizens and taxpayers opposed to statehood."[69] Her suit targeted especially the commission's publicity campaign on three main points: "(1) A national or sectional advertising and publicity campaign is not a valid public purpose for which public funds may be expended; (2) lobbying in Washington, D.C., is not a valid public purpose for which public funds may be expended; (3) the grant of unlimited discretion to an administrative agency in the expenditure of public funds constitutes an invalid delegation of power by the legislature."[70]

In seeking to place a temporary restraining order on the governor, members of the Statehood Commission, and territorial officials before the court hearing, Kamokila hoped to stop them from spending any more taxpayer money on gaining public opinion for statehood. Circuit Court Judge Wilson C. Moore denied her request, choosing instead to withhold any action until he decided whether the financing of the Statehood Commission was unconstitutional.[71] Attorney General Walter D. Ackerman Jr. would file a demurrer against Kamokila's case. One month later, Kamokila's lawsuit was thrown out of Circuit Court by Judge Moore, who declared, "Regardless of what we think as individuals, we must bow to the will of the majority. The last plebiscite showed more than two to one in favor of statehood and the territory, as an integral part of the United States, is in its democratic realm. The basis on which we operate this government is on the will of the people."[72] But, as indicated in the previous chapter, the 1940 plebiscite was "deliberately imprecise," and even the Hawaii Equal Rights Commission determined that statehood was still a debatable issue.

Kamokila appealed this ruling, and the Hawai'i Supreme Court returned a unanimous decision in her favor. In March of 1949, Justice E. C.

Peters ordered an injunction against the Statehood Commission that prohibited the use of public monies for said purposes. Justice Peters wrote: "The appellees justify the expenditure of public moneys for publicity purposes . . . upon the ground that the purposes thereof subserve the public welfare, are for a 'public purpose' and hence a rightful subject of legislation. With this we cannot agree. To accord validity to expenditures for an indiscriminate publicity campaign upon the ground that it is for a public purpose would do violence to that term as juridically defined and dignify as 'public' what obviously is purely 'political.'"[73] In essence, the High Court rejected the Statehood Commission's arguments, ruling instead that using taxpayer money to sway public opinion did not serve the "public" good, but instead constituted actions "purely political" in nature.

Though it could no longer spend public monies on national and sectional advertising, the Statehood Commission stepped up its indirect, if not underhanded, practice of using media outlets, supposedly autonomous from the government, to continue to sway public opinion. It did this in spite of the High Court's explicit ruling against the government's alleged "right to petition the public for its favorable opinion" on political matters such as statehood in particular: "To conduct a national or sectional advertising campaign on behalf of statehood for Hawaii, and for such other purposes as might be included in the right to petition, is calculated merely to influence the reading public generally. Favorable public opinion upon the subject of statehood undoubtedly may exert a profound psychological effect upon those in whom repose the legislative authority to grant or refuse statehood. . . . [T]he creation of favorable public opinion is foreign to the definition and concepts of the citizen's right to petition."[74] Though the court found that the territory could not "petition the public" to shape public opinion in favor of statehood, it did not, more fundamentally, go so far as to declare the commission invalid, and in fact left room for "reasonable" expenditures for the Statehood Commission to promote statehood. In this regard, the court too was prejudiced against any status other than statehood (or the status quo). This prejudicial view is best captured in the court's opinion that Hawai'i's territorial status was temporary and transitional, with the inevitable end goal being statehood. According to the Supreme Court, the territorial government was created specifically to promote "welfare, peace, happiness and prosperity," and thus opined that to "accelerate the evolutionary process of the political transition from a Territory to a State abstractly accomplishes the same result. Reasonable men cannot differ upon the political advantages resulting from statehood over and above those inherent in a Territory of the United States."[75] Yet, even back then, Kamokila and others were pointing to other forms of self-governance, other forms of international rights, and other ways of understanding Hawai'i's political history. Indeed, Kamokila and others had an international right to other forms of self-governance that were being blocked by U.S. governmental and legal maneuverings.

While condemned by the majority of the residents in Hawai'i, many of Kamokila's views and actions were supported, even mandated, by international law. After World War II, when the United Nations addressed the issue of self-determination, Hawai'i, Alaska, Guåhan, American Samoa, Puerto Rico, and the Virgin Islands were placed on the United Nations' list of Non-Self-Governing Territories under chapter XI. As such, the United Nations declared that the occupying countries had "sacred trust obligations" to foster self-determination and self-governance over the interests of the administering power; it also required these nations to do an annual report on the progress being made toward these aims. Legal scholar Maivân Clech Lâm points out that Italy, Germany, and Japan, the losing nations of World War II, were made to give up their colonial possessions. These possessions were listed under chapter XII, and unlike those Non-Self-Governing Territories listed under chapter XI, these occupied territories were tracked for independence and their occupying powers were forbidden from interfering with this process.[76]

It seems highly probable that Kamokila and others were unaware of the United States' obligations to Hawai'i under the United Nations (UN). Joseph Farrington, however, knew that the United States itself placed Hawai'i on the UN list of Non-Self-Governing Territories, just as he was also probably aware that the requirements for proper decolonization stipulated that the "administering" power make a genuine effort to educate the non-self-governing peoples about their political rights and options. In a letter written by Acting Secretary of the U.S. State Department James E. Webb to Hawai'i Congressional Delegate Joseph R. Farrington on May 24, 1949, Webb responds to Farrington's questions regarding the relationship between the movement for statehood and the United States' responsibilities to the United Nations Charter. Farrington asked whether the congressional "Enabling Act" legislation that would have allowed Hawai'i, per the Northwest Ordinance, to form a state constitution and achieve statehood was in violation of the Charter. Webb wrote that Hawai'i had "repeatedly demonstrated their desire for statehood" and from the standpoint of foreign policy and the international obligations of the United States under chapter XI of the Charter, the Department of State believed "such action by the Congress would be in conformity with the traditional policy of the United States toward those peoples who have not yet become fully self-governing."[77] Webb further explained that in the State Department's view, Hawai'i statehood would actually "serve to support American foreign policy and strengthen the position of the United States in international affairs."[78] Yet, Farrington and others did not make this information available to the general public, even with all the media at their disposal. If, in fact, a democracy relies on an educated populace, by 1959, Hawai'i residents were deliberately only educated on the benefits of statehood. This deliberate containment of Hawai'i's options for political status, combined with a highly partial opinion campaign to secure support for statehood, speaks volumes about the lack of democracy in Hawai'i.

In 1953, Kamokila wrote a letter to Congress, arguing that of the $475,000 that had been appropriated for a government-led statehood campaign since 1947, no money had been apportioned to opponents of statehood. Kamokila argued, "So much has been said and published favoring Statehood for Hawaii that it is only fair that the opposition be heard. Unfortunately, equal treatment under law is denied the opponents of Statehood."[79] By then, Kamokila had begun to campaign for commonwealth status and admitted that while the majority of people in Hawai'i were in favor of statehood, it was the only option being discussed and the general public "never had the opportunity of studying its merits to demerits." She argued that if those in Hawai'i were given a choice between commonwealth status and statehood, she was confident the majority would choose the former, "provided a reasonable time were given for them to receive adequate information concerning Commonwealth Status which thus far has been suppressed."[80] Her letter to Congress in 1953 also shows how her strategies to oppose statehood had changed. Now, instead of arguing against the Japanese, she had begun to highlight two different threats: one, that statehood for Hawai'i would set a precedent for other territories (namely, Guåhan, Puerto Rico, American Samoa, the

Virgin Islands, and the Panama Canal Zone) to gain it as well, and two, that communism in the form of the International Longshore and Warehouse Union (ILWU)—which by the mid-1930s was supporting statehood and was allied with the Democratic Party—had "crippled industry" and would pose a serious threat to the U.S. continent. By the 1950s, then, Kamokila was playing to new congressional fears of communism and the Red Scare to defeat statehood.

Lorrin P. Thurston received copies of Kamokila Campbell's letter, after she asked that it be published in the *Honolulu Advertiser*. Thurston refused to publish it, but sent it nonetheless to the Hawaii Statehood Commission, suggesting that it be "circulated where it will do the most good."[81] In 1954, Kamokila, Harold Hughes, and former Governor Ingram Stainback formed the organization Commonwealth for Hawaii.[82] The Democratic Party, having just taken majority control of the legislature and sensing that statehood was around the corner, roundly condemned the new organization and upstart movement for commonwealth status. Using the same linear logic employed by the Hawai'i Supreme Court in its *Campbell* decision, Arthur Trask, John A. Burns, and William S. Richardson—leaders of the Democratic Party—prepared a "Resolution Denouncing Commonwealth for Hawaii." They declared: "The history of the people of the Hawaiian Islands, ancient and modern, is a positive chronicle of the progressive advancement of man from tribal leadership, absolute kingship, constitutional monarchy, and republic, to the status of an organized territory of the United States of America. . . . [T]he devotion of the people of Hawaii is rooted in the high objective of receiving full political rights as a state in the union of states of America and . . . any other political status is an abomination to the loyal and patriotic citizens of Hawaii." The resolution described commonwealth proponents as "sinister" and labeled their movement "illegal." It was through such tactics of demonization and criminalization that proponents of statehood can be said to have subjugated and obstructed any political alternative to it.

OFFICIAL ANTIRACISM FACILITATES SETTLER COLONIALISM

While many Kānaka 'Ōiwi did in fact support Hawai'i statehood, many others did not, and their voices were purposefully silenced and contained. In fact, the suppression of Hawaiian voices opposed to statehood heads a litany of repressive and unjust actions undertaken by agents of the state in the campaign to gain statehood. These include the monopolization of taxpayer money for private groups and individuals aiming to capitalize on tourism by achieving statehood, limiting political choices for decolonization to statehood or territorial government, and instances of state repression against Hawaiians opposed to statehood. With repeated efforts by leaders like Kamokila to oppose statehood, particularly on dates commemorating the 1893 overthrow of the Hawaiian Kingdom, it becomes impossible to view statehood as not having been resisted by Kānaka ʻŌiwi. Neither can statehood be seen as a form of decolonization in accordance with internationally agreed-upon United Nations standards.

Japanese Americans and Kānaka ʻŌiwi were contending with very different histories and political possibilities shaped by both U.S. foreign policy and the desires of a rapidly growing tourism industry. In combating primitivist notions that Hawaiians are destined to disappear and thus be replaced, Kamokila resisted statehood by playing to an Orientalist fear that Japanese Americans were foreign threats. While racism against Japanese Americans is immediately recognizable in Hawaiʻi, the violent forms of settler colonialism are often naturalized as a necessary yet unfortunate outcome of progress. Although Hawaiʻi's political climate became more inclusive of Japanese Americans, it still maintained a violent colonial rationale, historically created and politically mediated to respond to this new form of liberal inclusion organized around fraternal forms of settler-colonial power sharing. Kanaka ʻŌiwi national claims were dismissed, and as a people they were regarded as primitive, relegated to an anachronistic space, and deemed replaceable, even as tourism promulgated popular images that centered around certain formulations of the "Native."

The state, animated by profit motives, created the conditions for an official antiracism to facilitate forms of settler colonialism under the name of statehood. Japanese Americans and their supporters challenged the view that they were perpetual foreign threats through cultural narratives of civil rights that anchored the Hawaiʻi statehood campaign. This campaign was forged deeply by the histories of Japanese American persecution and later desires to capitalize on land developments in the postwar period. These cultural narratives, however, render invisible their role in maintaining and renewing hegemonic forms of settler colonialism and occupation. At the same time, Kamokila's racist remarks should be neither justified nor taken as an invalidation of her aims to seek justice for Kānaka ʻŌiwi for the overthrow of the Hawaiian nation.

CHAPTER 4

THE PROPAGANDA OF OCCUPATION

Statehood and the Cold War

> Real issues were decided by force and violence, and the men who
> decided them belonged to the little haole oligarchy determined
> to take over Hawaii completely and tie it to an imperialistic
> America.
>
> —"Force and Violence in Hawaii," *Honolulu Record*, 1952

In December of 1949, the president of the University of Hawaiʻi, Gregg M.
Sinclair, sent an official invitation to the nationally renowned publicist Edward L. Bernays. One of New York City's most notorious "mad
men"—a name for the advertising agents who worked along Madison
Avenue—Bernays would be a visiting professor of public relations for the
summer session of 1950.[1] Sinclair offered Bernays a hotel room at the
posh Halekulani Hotel and invited him to teach five seminars to juniors
and seniors. By the time his seminars began, however, the twenty-person
enrollment had expanded to fifty and the students had been replaced by
executives of the Big Five, Hawaiian Sugar Planters' Association (HSPA),
Hawaiian Electric Company, and Bishop Estate Trust Company, as well
as a wide array of military officers, University of Hawaiʻi administrators,
government officials, and civic leaders.[2] Given that the Cold War, with all
of its complex machinations, was in full swing, what Bernays had to teach
was of incredible value to Hawaiʻi elites. In Walter Lippmann's famous
phrasing, the "manufacture of consent" was determined to be critical
in shaping a general public, especially an increasingly defiant nonwhite

population in Hawai'i. Consent needed to be manufactured not just for statehood but also to recruit a general population into believing that a militant labor movement led by the ILWU and an emerging Democratic Party had been infiltrated by Soviet communists.[3]

While Bernays claimed to have invented the term *public relations* himself, he long believed that the most accurate term to describe his profession was "propaganda."[4] Significantly, Bernays's uncle was Sigmund Freud. Bernays, in fact, helped his uncle Freud to reach an audience in the United States, just as Freud, the "father of psychoanalytic theory," helped to shape the public relations work of Bernays. For instance, working for Lucky Strike Cigarettes, Bernays expanded the market for his employer by increasing the sale of cigarettes to women by first consulting Dr. A. A. Brill, an Austrian-born psychoanalyst and Freud devotee. Bernays was told, in sexist terms, that as women begin to do the same work as men, cigarettes became symbolic of the male penis and thus smoking for women was akin to what Brill called "torches of freedom."[5] Taking Brill's analysis, Bernays staged an action at the Easter Sunday parade down Fifth Avenue. Bernays recruited female models to light up their cigarettes in an act of defiance and arranged for a photographer to capture photos that the media circulated nationally. Bernays called such strategies of articulation "hitching private interests to public ones."[6] This spectacle made Bernays famous in the advertising world, and for weeks newspapers from cities across the United States reported on and debated ending "all discriminations." But this story, oft-repeated by Bernays, relied on deception. His biographer, Larry Tye, argues that Bernays never once mentioned that American Tobacco was behind these acts, and he went so far as to include notes in specific instances instructing that "under no circumstances is the name or telephone number of Edward L. Bernays to be given to anyone who calls."[7] Writing of Bernays's decision to leave more than eight hundred boxes of his personal and professional papers to the Library of Congress, Tye writes, "in so doing, he let us see just how policies were made and how, in many cases, they were founded on deception."[8]

Bernays, however, believed that such deception was necessary in a democracy. He long argued that if the general public was left to its own decision making, it would ultimately lead to chaos. In his book titled *Propaganda*, Bernays writes, "The conscious and intelligent manipulation of the organized habits and opinions of the masses is an important element in democratic society. Those who manipulate this unseen mechanism of society constitute an invisible government which is the true ruling power of our country."[9] Bernays's clients included major U.S. corporations such as General Motors, General Electric, Time Inc., American Tobacco, and the United Fruit Company. Just prior to his position as visiting professor at the University of Hawai'i, an article succinctly described the method that made Bernays so popular: If one wishes to tell which way the wind is blowing, one might hold their finger up. But Bernays was argued to have a more modern method—"He blows the wind the way he wants it to go."[10]

After leaving Hawai'i, Bernays orchestrated the CIA overthrow of the democratically elected Jacobo Arbenz administration in Guatemala which had been seeking land reform at the expense of Bernays's clients at the United Fruit Company. The overthrow of Arbenz relied on Bernays painting him as a communist leader under the control of the Soviet Union. Through the Middle American Information Bureau that Bernays created, he issued press releases to media outlets claiming that Soviet communists planned to use Guatemala as a military outpost very close to U.S. soil. Joining U.S. President Dwight D. Eisenhower, CIA agents and the United Fruit Company ousted Arbenz and replaced him with a puppet regime under the control of Colonel Castillo Armas.[11]

The specific role of propaganda campaigns in the Cold War allows for a more expansive view of Hawai'i statehood. In order to make Hawai'i's nonwhite peoples less foreign in the eyes of Congress and a white American public, local proponents of statehood used Hawai'i's alterity to their favor. A diverse range of communities formed a historical bloc, including some Kānaka 'Ōiwi who consented to U.S. nationality, to demonstrate their merit through alternative versions of American modernity. Many argued that Hawai'i's citizenry—theorized as racially diverse but culturally American—should be showcased above all other American achievements for the world to see what only American democracy could accomplish. This was especially key, as criticisms by communist nations perpetuated two arguments: that Hawai'i statehood was a product of U.S. imperialism and its insatiable desire for more colonies, and that the United States was driven by white supremacy and practiced segregation against Black communities. Statehood proponents asserted that this latter argument, which had implications for U.S. global hegemony, could be challenged only if

Hawai'i became a state. Scholars such as Derrick A. Bell Jr., Thomas Borstelman, Penny M. Von Eschen, Nikhil Pal Singh, Christina Klein, Mary Dudziak, and Jodi Melamed have each shown differently how the idea of the United States as a racially diverse nation based on harmonious race relations was mobilized during the Cold War for the purposes of U.S. global hegemony.[12]

The admission of Hawai'i as a U.S. state thus facilitated a larger geopolitical U.S. strategy that Christina Klein terms a "global imaginary of integration," the counterpart to the containment of communism. Truman's Cold War consensus combined the international integration of the liberal Left with the Far Right's fierce opposition to communism. Klein argues that, in this way, a "global imaginary of integration" sought to educate Americans at all levels of society about "how the world worked," making it easier for them to endorse an increasingly militarized foreign policy and the simultaneous development of a national security state.[13] Tracing the ideological role of Hawai'i's admission as a U.S. state within this "global imaginary of integration" is to simultaneously trace the genealogy of Hawai'i's liberal multiculturalism within global imperial politics. Given that U.S. imperialism, however, is constituted by formations of settler colonialism, we must expand such framings to contend with Native peoples under occupation. In other words, such global imaginaries of integration facilitated at once global militarism and a domestic national security state that aimed to secure both settler and imperial futures.

The grand strategy of Edward L. Bernays was taken up by the Pulitzer Prize–winning novelist James Michener and, most effectively, by a lesser-known World War II veteran from New Orleans named George Lehleitner. Lehleitner was a self-made appliance distributor from the South who was a longtime admirer of the work of University of Hawai'i eugenicist Stanley D. Porteus. Lehleitner's work contributed successfully to convincing enough Southern congressmen, who were initially opposed to Hawai'i statehood for racial and partisan reasons, to support Hawai'i's admission as a U.S. state. Publicly, such free-world propaganda argued that denying the admission of U.S. territories amounted to being "un-American," as territorial possessions were equated with colonization, and thus worked against the Cold War project of signifying the United States as a leader of the free world. The fact that they were centrally focused on Hawai'i's admission as a U.S. state, and not on Guåhan, American Samoa, the U.S. Virgin Islands, Puerto Rico, or Native American nations (and only strategically on Alaska), however, is very telling; their position had more to do with geopolitical value of a territory than with processes of self-determination. Nor did they entertain the possibility that Hawaiʻi, like other territories, was entitled to independence or free association, as determined by United Nations resolutions in 1953 and 1960.[14]

Such ideological formations, however, were fiercely resisted by groups in Hawaiʻi who were trained and/or effective at shaping public opinion. I focus on two mutually informed but distinct political groups on the left; both invoked the 1893 U.S. overthrow, yet they fell on different sides on the question of statehood for Hawaiʻi. The first are the communists and labor activists out of Hawaiʻi—specifically Koji Ariyoshi and John Reinecke—two of the Hawaiʻi Seven who were charged in 1951 with violating the Smith Act, or encouraging the use of "force and violence" to overthrow the United States. They drew on the history of the 1893 overthrow not only to make a point that the charges against them were a Red Scare tactic meant to contain a militant labor movement, but also to show how the political order that the Big Five established was itself based on "force and violence."

The second group is more closely informed by Kanaka ʻŌiwi resistance to U.S. occupation and settler colonialism. Local historian Kathleen Dickenson Mellen and Hawaiian genealogist Sammy Amalu each drew on the history of the 1893 overthrow at the same moment as Ariyoshi and Reinecke did, but in radically different ways. Specifically, Mellen and Amalu opposed the violation of Hawaiian national sovereignty via statehood, as well as the underlying aims to fast-track numerous developments that continued to desecrate ʻŌiwi place-based relations. Kathleen Dickenson Mellen, who hailed from Richmond, Virginia, was a locally celebrated and prolific writer in Hawaiʻi during the 1940s and 1950s. Mellen spent twenty years doing archival research and having conversations with Kanaka ʻŌiwi individuals and descendants of those who were intimately involved in resisting the 1893 overthrow and annexation. The histories she wrote received national attention. Mellen narrated the late nineteenth-century historical events leading to the overthrow and alleged annexation in her arguments opposing statehood in the 1940s and 1950s. As a prolific writer, Mellen publicly debated with the popular American writer James Michener regarding his racist and sexist representations of Kanaka ʻŌiwi in his 1959 book *Hawaii*.

Sammy Amalu performed a multimillion-dollar public prank on the tourism and real estate industries in 1962, three years after Hawaiʻi was declared a U.S. state. Posing as an investment company while living destitute in a low-rise apartment in Waikīkī, Amalu's prank drew on Hawaiian history to undermine the notions of property and profit that animated settler elite motivations for statehood. His performance also received national attention. Amalu was eventually sentenced to serve one year in federal prison, where he wrote columns in the *Honolulu Advertiser* about sexuality, incarceration, and Hawaiian history and culture.[15] Kathleen Dickenson Mellen served as the president of the Sammy Amalu Fan Club. Amalu joked that Mellen was the only member. Mellen and Amalu went beyond critiquing statehood to queer it, showing the violence, desecrations, and conformity to subordination that the epistemic normativity of statehood required. While settler and imperial propaganda in the form of liberal multiculturalism moves along the axis of seeming racial equality, it simultaneously demands conformity to heteropatriarchal and capitalist logics that are oppositional to nonwhite, specifically Kanaka ʻŌiwi ways of knowing around sexuality, nongender binarisms, kinship, and relations to land. Amalu, in particular, challenged such notions in a moment when gendered constructions were normalized to facilitate rampant capitalist development over places of significance for Kānaka ʻŌiwi.

THE WHITE SUPREMACY OF LIBERAL MULTICULTURALISM

While at the University of Hawaiʻi, Bernays described Hawaiʻi as a "dynamic field," a laboratory for the study of public relations, because it had "become a 'real melting pot' of the different ethnic groups that make up the human race."[16] Bernays made use of his time in Hawaiʻi accomplishing substantive work not only in teaching but also researching, giving public talks, and publishing articles in national magazines and local Hawaiʻi newspapers. As part of a summer lecture series, Bernays presented a paper titled "The Importance of Public Opinion in Economic Mobilization," speaking about the role of public relations in regard to military rearmament, economic mobilization, and national defense during the Korean War. Using the language of the Cold War, Bernays argued for not only a military arms race but also an ideological one: "I believe it is as possible to stockpile public opinion for economic mobilization and for victory as it is to stockpile things if we go at it the right way and on a planned basis."[17] During his stay, Bernays came to see Hawai'i's admission as a U.S. state as a critical weapon in the ideological arms race with the Soviet Union.

As the Cold War between the United States and the Soviet Union intensified, Hawai'i became a site of ideological battle. In the bifurcated view of communism versus capitalism, Hawai'i was evidence either that the United States was an imperialist nation, as propagated by the Soviet Union and China, or that it benevolently extended its system of capitalism and democracy to territories abroad. For instance, on July 25, 1947, an article in the Soviet newspaper *Vechernyaya Moskva* (*Evening Moscow*) described the House of Representatives' vote that month in favor of admitting Hawai'i as a U.S. state not as an act of decolonization but as another stride in U.S. imperial expansion:

> Half a century lies between the day when the American flag was raised in the Hawaiian Islands for the first time and the recent decision of the House of Representatives of the United States on the transformation of the Hawaiian archipelago into the 49th state. It is not an accident that this step, directed toward perpetuation of the domination of the United States of these islands, which were seized by force, was taken just now when American imperialism is engaged in its expansionistic policies everywhere, when American reaction is forcing the foreign policy of the country into the path of unbridled militarism and is seeking bases and backing reactionary regimes in all corners of the globe.[18]

As the author of the article argued, the U.S. project in Hawai'i was a colonial one accomplished by "force," and admission of Hawai'i as a U.S. state did not resolve occupation; rather, it obscured it. The article's reference to Hawai'i's independence reveals international memory of the Hawaiian Kingdom and its overthrow by the United States, a fact that made claims by the United States to be the "leader of the free world" suspect. Indeed, Russia had diplomatic ties to the Hawaiian Kingdom and had engaged in an 1869 treaty on commerce and navigation with the independent Hawaiian nation.[19]

On November 20, 1950, Edward L. Bernays connected the strategy of utilizing civil rights issues in the service of the Cold War to the movement for statehood in Hawai'i. In an article printed in the *New Leader* titled "HAWAII—The Almost Perfect State?," Bernays argued for Hawai'i's specific role in combating the portrayal of the United States as a white supremacist, imperialist nation. In order to make U.S. statehood for Hawai'i more attractive in the eyes of Congress and the American public, Bernays positioned Hawai'i's exotic nonwhite population in the service of Cold War politics: "Particularly at this time, with the United States so deeply concerned with problems in the Orient, Hawaii has a fourfold significance for us. First, she is our island bastion in the Pacific. Second, she disproves Soviet accusations that imperialism and racism are our national policy. Third, she dramatizes to the mainland that Americans of most diverse backgrounds can live together in harmony. And fourth, she demonstrates that 500,000 Americans, 2,500 miles distant in the Pacific, can successfully work out their destiny democratically."[20] Bernays strategically positioned Hawai'i not as a colonial backwater of the modern "mainland" United States, but as an alternative U.S. modernity that represented a future solution to the racial tensions on the U.S. continent, which were obstacles to U.S. projects for global hegemony. Hawai'i was thus offered as a "future wish," a possible glimpse into an already existent site of racial democracy that simultaneously teaches the United States and the world that racial harmony is possible. This plays off of the University of Hawai'i sociologists who had championed Hawai'i's racial diversity for years, but strategically articulates this "melting pot" discourse of liberal multiculturalism with U.S. ambitions for global hegemony. Hawai'i's congressional delegate, Joseph R. Farrington, wrote a letter to the editor of the *New Leader* saying that Bernays "has caught the spirit and real significance of our fight to win statehood. He has skillfully shown its importance to this country's future in the Pacific."[21]

In the postwar moment when decolonization throughout Asia, Oceania, Africa, and Latin America was transforming a world order, and criticism of Western imperialism was the dominant international sentiment, Bernays argued that Hawai'i statehood was beneficial to the United States both nationally and internationally. Hawai'i's majority nonwhite population could thus front as the new multicultural face of a militarily powerful and economically dominant United States—one that would ideologically assist the maintenance and establishment of U.S. military bases and se-cure access to resources and markets throughout Asia and the Pacific.

What is notable about Bernays's racial strategy was that he based such arguments about Hawai'i's racial harmony on the numerically small population of African Americans in Hawai'i. Based on this, Bernays pre-sumed Hawai'i to be the ideal site from which to enunciate a plan for civil rights: "The fact that a majority of Hawaiians is of Oriental extraction dis-proves allegations of racism made against us by Communists, and proves that intergroup relations here on the mainland could be much better. No Jim Crow laws or race riots or lynchings mar her democracy."[22] Although Hawai'i and the U.S. South are tied by a plantation economy whose va-grancy laws emerge partly from the penal codes of Louisiana, Bernays stated the value of Hawai'i as being that "no Jim Crow laws or race riots or lynchings mar her democracy."[23] As such, the civil rights movement in the continental United States was argued to be the result of the existence of Black communities, not historically produced systems of power mani-fest in structures of white supremacy.

Speaking on one level about the ideological value of Hawai'i's seeming racial harmony to U.S. global politics, Bernays also argued in ways that resonated with a local audience in Hawai'i. His article in the *New Leader* was based on a talk that he gave to the Rotary Club of Honolulu earlier that year, which was also printed in the *Hawaii Chinese Journal*.[24] Speak-ing to labor unrest, Bernays stated that if there existed any disharmony in Hawai'i it was due to what he called the "'Big Five's white supremacy."[25] Bernays argued, "Such disharmony as exists can be blamed for the most part on the little group of myopic men who constitute an expanded Big Five, who are outmoded and outdated in their attitudes and policies, and who are still trying to run the islands." Where many in Hawai'i had viewed statehood as the goal and desire of the Big Five elite, Bernays recruited "Americans of Oriental background" to the cause of statehood by arguing that the Big Five were in fact obstacles to a future utopia that might be achieved if statehood came to pass. In this way, Bernays rear-ticulated the terms by which statehood was often understood, inviting those dissatisfied with the Big Five to mount a campaign on behalf of it.

These strategies transformed Hawai'i's racial diversity from a hindrance to an incredible boon for the U.S. statehood movement. While previously, statehood proponents downplayed Hawai'i's "Oriental" population, Cold

War politics allowed Hawai'i statehood proponents to build on the publicity work of the Japanese Americans in the 442nd and 100th Battalion and further argue for statehood by working through racial difference, not extinguishing it. Christina Klein argues that middlebrow Americans at this time began to produce and consume large amounts of cultural productions with representations of Asia and the Pacific that facilitated integration: "Because U.S. expansion into Asia was predicated on the principle of international integration rather than on territorial imperialism, it demanded an ideology of global interdependence rather than one of racial difference. The Cold War Orientalism generated by middlebrow intellectuals articulated precisely such an ideology. . . . [C]ultural producers imaginatively mapped a network of sentimental pathways between the United States and Asia that paralleled and reinforced the more material pathways along which America's economic, political, and military power flowed."[26] Klein highlights James Michener as one such proponent who championed Hawai'i statehood, highlighting at once Hawai'i's racial diversity and its geopolitical value. In the immediate years prior to statehood, 1958 and 1959, Michener argued that Hawai'i had become a symbol in Asia of the "fair and just manner in which we [white Americans] treat Orientals."[27] For this reason, Michener argued that to deny statehood to Hawai'i was a slap in the face that would reverberate throughout Asia.[28] A 1959 article in Newsweek spoke of the ideological value of Hawai'i statehood: "Hawaii will be the first state with roots not in Europe but in Asia," and no longer would America be known as a "land of the white man" and "tarred with the brush of 'colonialism.'"[29]

GEORGE LEHLEITNER: PRIVATE CITIZEN?

While Michener may be responsible for exposing most middlebrow Americans to a particular view of Hawai'i, the individual who carried out the public relations campaign that led to the admission of Hawai'i as a U.S. state was a man repeatedly described as a "private citizen" from New Orleans named George Lehleitner. John A. Burns stated soon before his own death in 1975 that the role Lehleitner played in passing the Admissions Act for U.S. statehood was critical: "George Lehleitner must have spent upwards of a half million dollars on Statehood and was most effective in his work. . . . [I]n a very real way if it hadn't been for him I don't know how we would have got Statehood to begin with. . . . George had gone to every southern senator. He had gone back to a lot of them. He did everything under the sun that I know a man could do. . . . Nobody really, nobody in Hawaii and nobody else spent as much time and effort and as much money on Statehood as George Lehleitner."[30] Arriving in Hawai'i for the first time in 1944, Lehleitner was the commander of a navy transport ship taking Japanese prisoners of war from Okinawa to concentration camps in Hawai'i. Lehleitner returned to Hawai'i in 1947 aboard a tour cruise inspired to fight for statehood. Lehleitner wrote to Stanley D. Porteus, whose work he had long admired, about his travel plans. Porteus consequently gave Lehleitner a tour of O'ahu and introduced him to Governor Samuel Wilder King, Joseph Farrington, and members of the territorial legislature. Lehleitner also wished to "test the political spectrum" and asked to be introduced to the "young Democrats" such as John Burns and the, in his words, "aggressive young Nisei," Matsuo Takabuki, Daniel Inouye, Spark Matsunaga, and Sakae Takahashi.[31]

Lehleitner's ties to Porteus, who was a known white supremacist and adamant eugenicist, seemingly conflict with the antiracist spirit of Hawai'i's campaign for statehood. Lehleitner's devotion to statehood, however, was inspired by Clarence K. Streit's 1939 book *Union Now*, which argued that the way to defeat Marxism and totalitarianism was through the expansion of the "free world." Lehleitner's commitment to statehood was based on a notion that white settler responsibilities included turning primitive space into U.S. states. That Porteus, who was not supportive of statehood at the time, went out of his way to introduce someone he had just met to some of the highest elected officials in government might also strike some as odd.

As a businessperson from the South who ingratiated himself to the U.S. statehood movements in Hawai'i and Alaska, Lehleitner is exactly the kind of person that both statehood movements needed. It is primarily through Lehleitner's political and media contacts and outreach in the South that the U.S. statehood movements for Hawai'i and Alaska were able to gain traction in Washington, DC. For both racial and partisan reasons, Southern Democrats opposed the admission of Hawai'i and Alaska. In 1956, Lehleitner spoke to this, arguing that contrary to what most believe, antistatehood Southern Democrats were becoming more successful at making both Alaska's and Hawai'i's bids for statehood impossible. Stating that Southern Democrats were in control of eleven out of sixteen committees in the House and seven out of twelve in the Senate, Lehleitner argued that the admission of new U.S. states would ultimately come at the expense of the current House of Representatives since the number of members of the House of Representatives was limited by public law to 435. If Hawai'i and Alaska were admitted, Lehleitner argued, such seats would be "carved from the hides of existing state delegations on the next reapportionment date!"[32] Furthermore, as the populations in Alaska and Hawai'i continued to grow, they became entitled to more seats in the House. But partisan politics was not Lehleitner's major concern, as he argued that Southern Democrats, or more specifically the Dixiecrats, were most obsessed with these new congressmen passing civil rights legislation.

Lehleitner is often descibed as a "private citizen," a consummate salesman who was moved to this work because of the inequality he witnessed in Hawai'i. For a number of reasons—the large-scale nature of the statehood public relations campaigns, the fact that politically both Hawai'i and Alaska needed someone specifically from the South to lobby their case, and that the state- and business-led statehood campaign often strategically attempted to seem grassroots—it is difficult to determine whether Lehleitner did, indeed, work "privately" or whether others might have had an interest in supporting Lehleitner's work.[33] It is worth noting that when George H. Lehleitner is mentioned by others in Hawai'i, he is often tied to Hebden Porteus, the son of Stanley Porteus and the husband of the heiress to Dole Pineapple, Elizabeth Dole. Through complex buyouts, Dole Pineapple links Hawai'i closely to New Orleans, Lehleitner's hometown, in the immediate years after statehood is achieved. In 1964, the Big Five corporation Castle and Cooke extended its power when it bought half the shares of Standard Fruit Company, whose headquarters were in New Orleans, and then the remaining shares in 1968. Castle and Cooke, under the control of Malcolm MacNaughton, pursued statehood to capitalize on tourism (as the previous chapter recounts), but then expanded operations outside of Hawai'i to become one of the largest multinational distributors of fruits and vegetables in the world. Standard Fruit Company was the major competitor of Bernays's clients at the United Fruit Company, and similar to Castle and Cooke, they all manipulated governments, used violence against laborers, and dominated these tropical sites through shipping, propaganda, and agriculture.[34] At this same time, however, Castle and Cooke, which already owned part of the Hawaiian Pineapple Company (better known as Dole Pineapple), eventually bought the remaining shares and renamed their agricultural section Dole Food Company, expanding throughout the world to take advantage of low agricultural labor costs in Southeast Asia and Central America.[35] Castle and Cooke, Inc. both owned Dole Food Company and functioned as a real estate company whose largest land holdings were in Hawai'i. The value of their properties in Hawai'i appreciated after statehood, which enabled their industrial agricultural ventures to expand globally.[36]

Upon returning from Hawai'i to New Orleans in 1947, Lehleitner says that he placed his business under the care of a manager and dedicated his time to campaigning for Hawai'i and Alaska statehood. He began by convincing George Chaplin, who at the time was working in New Orleans as an editor of the *New Orleans Item-Tribune*, to write favorably about Hawai'i's statehood. Chaplin wrote numerous editorials for the admission of Hawai'i as a U.S. state while in New Orleans. George Chaplin was well known in Hawai'i for becoming the editor of the *Honolulu Advertiser* in 1958 and working closely with Thurston Twigg-Smith, the grandson of Lorrin A. Thurston, turning the paper from what one critic described as a "reactionary pro-haole (pro-Caucasian) moth-eaten sheet" into a metropolitan newspaper no longer in bankruptcy.[37] Lehleitner continued to use his connections throughout the South, targeting friends who were editors and writers. Hodding Carter had written a Pulitzer Prize–winning editorial in 1945 about the 442nd Regimental Combat Team and is said to have begun writing in earnest about Hawai'i statehood after conversations with Lehleitner.[38]

But it was Lehleitner's advocating of a specific political and media strategy, what he called the "Tennessee Plan," that is hailed as capturing statehood for both Alaska and Hawai'i. The strategy was first uncovered by two professors at the University of Hawai'i named Daniel W. Tuttle and Robert M. Kamins.[39] Tuttle and Kamins pointed out that previous territories were admitted as states only after following the strategy of Tennessee, which not only created and ratified a state constitution, as Hawai'i did, but also elected congressional senators and representatives, sending them to Washington, DC, to advocate for admission. Lehleitner stated that the admission of the state of Tennessee—a process that led to the forced removal of the Cherokee—led to other territories following the same strategy: "[the] calling of a constitutional convention and the writing by the delegates to the constitutional convention into their constitutions a proviso that gave them, without a single exception, statehood within less than two years after the action had been taken."[40]

When it became clear to Lehleitner that statehood proponents in Hawai'i were not willing to follow this strategy, Lehleitner pursued the "Tennessee Plan" in Alaska. The relationship between both movements for statehood is described in a conversation Lehleitner had with Texas House Representative James Wright in 1988. Wright stated of their strategy, "It was initially the appeal of Hawaii, which led us to consider Alaska, but in reality it was Alaska statehood which preceded and opened the way for Hawaiian statehood."[41] Speaking to constitutional delegates of the Alaska Constitutional Convention on January 23, 1956, Lehleitner stated: "In addition to the fact that you would have three able lobbyists presenting your case in the form of your elected senators and representatives, you would get the benefit, it seems to me, that would come from our modern methods of communication. It would be news, big news, and the justness of Alaska's case would, it seems to me, move from the editorial page to the front page, and your story is going to become known to the vast majority of men and women in American homes."[42] Lehleitner argues that the strategy is useful in creating political power through media spectacle. To bolster the confidence of Alaskan delegates that it would work, Lehleitner read from letters that he received from congressmen who sat on the Interior and Insular Affairs Committee of the House and Senate; each stated that he would not be offended if Alaskan delegates decided to adopt the Tennessee Plan. When the Alaska delegates pursued this strategy, Lehleitner helped to organize their media campaign throughout 1957.

Lehleitner is said to have contacted every media outlet and public library in the nation, in addition to each congressman, about the Alaskan delegates' use of the Tennessee Plan. Central to his strategy was to alert government officials and the general public to prior territories' success with the plan. Lehleitner argued that he contacted every individual who expressed an interest in statehood, sending them a "typed, signed and addressed" copy of a booklet written and printed by himself titled *The Tennessee Plan: How the Bold Became States*. Through such public relations work, he stated, when the Alaska delegation arrived in Washington, DC, they were met with a crowd of reporters.[43] Three days prior to the start of the eighty-fifth congressional session, Tennessee Governor Frank G. Clement arranged for the Alaskan delegates—Senators Elect Ernest Gruening and William Egan, and Representative Elect Ralph Rivers—to be his honored guests at a state dinner in the governor's Nashville mansion. The Alaskan delegates were continually interviewed for radio and television. George Lehleitner and his "Tennessee Plan" were the subjects of a supportive editorial in Henry Luce's *Life* magazine.[44] Lehleitner wrote even to known segregationists such as James J. Kilpatrick, most known for debating Martin Luther King Jr. on national television in 1960.[45] After such thorough and far-reaching work, Lehleitner then asked random representatives and senators, "Has your Congressional mail favoring Alaska's admission increased . . . ?" The usual response was: "Hell, yes!" Louisiana Senator Russel Long helped Lehleitner gain access to researchers in the Library of Congress and saw both the Alaska and Hawai'i bills in both the 85th and 86th Congresses.

In a 1984 interview, Lehleitner explained his views on why he dedicated his own money and time to the admission of Hawai'i as a U.S. state: "I felt Hawaii not only deserved statehood, but if they [Congress] wanted to retain credibility with the other nations of the world, they better get this potential monkey off their back and stop treating American citizens and American taxpayers like second-class citizens."[46] At the same time, Lehleitner understood that the major reason why U.S. statehood was stalled in both Hawai'i and Alaska had less to do with Washington, DC, than with these territories' ambivalence about statehood. Lehleitner wrote privately, "Perhaps you are wondering why the quest by Alaska and Hawaii was so prolonged? One of the reasons—though not the only one—was that public sentiment in Alaska and Hawaii on this subject was quite divided."[47]

THE HAWAI'I SEVEN AND THE 1893 OVERTHROW

Despite statehood expanding business power in Hawai'i, for many of Hawai'i's nonwhite working class, statehood had come to symbolize a rejection of haole hegemony by limiting haole privilege and racism. Hawai'i's territorial structure had been based on an amended Northwest Ordinance that declared that the U.S. president would appoint Hawai'i's territorial governor while its citizenry would vote for a nonvoting delegate to Congress and its legislature. Many of Hawai'i's appointed governors, judges, and politicians were part of the exclusive Big Five power structure and condoned an arrangement of power that was exploitative and often violent toward the numerous labor movements in the 1930s and 1940s that called for better living and work conditions. Hawai'i's sugar planters purposefully kept their labor forces racially divided by using the discourse of scientific racism to determine and justify segregated and hierarchical plantation housing and pay positions.[48] Labor historians Ronald Takaki, Gary Okihiro, Edward D. Beechert, Sanford Zalburg, and Moon-Kie Jung write that paternalism and "divide and conquer" were systematic strategies used to "offset" any one nationality from accumulating power as well as to keep racial groups from effectively uniting to challenge the Big Five.[49]

The International Longshore and Warehouse Union (ILWU), while credited with the successful organizing of Hawai'i's labor force solely around class interests, actually did so through what Moon-Kie Jung argues was a process of "reworking race."[50] Under the slogan "An injury to one is an injury to all," the ILWU coordinated a massive strike in 1946 where twenty-one thousand workers shut down thirty-three of the thirty-four sugar plantations in Hawai'i. When pineapple workers went on strike the following year and dockworkers went on strike two years later in 1949, shutting down Hawai'i's entire island community for 157 days, the Big Five accused the ILWU leadership of being communist infiltrators with connections to the Soviet Union.

While Hawai'i statehood helped to give American race relations a multicultural face before an international community, an emerging discourse of statehood in Hawai'i that was articulated as vehemently anticommunist furnished the Hawai'i elite with a way to reconsolidate their hegemony, which had come under threat. Accusations of Russian-inspired conspiracy in Hawai'i, while a desperate response to the growing power of the labor movement, could attach themselves to the national policies of the federal government in ways that gave them legitimacy. After U.S. President Harry Truman's 1947 Executive Order 9835 set up loyalty procedures for federal workers, Hawai'i, under the direction of Truman appointee Territorial Governor Ingram Stainback, followed suit by screening twenty-six thousand civilian employees of the navy and army. Stainback became weary of the ILWU's power after he himself lost his candidate's bid for congressional delegate due to what he believed was the increasing power of the Political Action Committee of the ILWU. At this time, Lorrin P. Thurston clumsily wrote a series of "Dear Joe" editorials titled "What Are Your Next Orders, Joe?"—accusing the ILWU of working for Joseph Stalin. The editorials were confusing, as many believed the Joe they were referring to was Joseph Farrington, which the *Honolulu Advertiser* had to correct. The Big Five also organized an antilabor group composed of the wives of the Big Five employers to counterpicket striking workers, whom they labeled "communists." Calling themselves IMUA, Hawaiian for "moving forward," they were nicknamed the "Million-Dollar Broom Brigade" by the ILWU. Often IMUA made appeals to the wives of striking workers, visiting their homes and delivering cans of milk while urging striking workers to return to the job.[51]

Communism was made illegal through a specific interpretation of the 1940 Smith Act. In 1948, the Justice Department sought to deport ILWU leader and founder Harry Bridges by highlighting a section of the Smith Act that made "teaching and advocating the overthrow of the United States government by force and violence" illegal. This interpretation was validated by U.S. courts in 1951, when the convictions of twelve members of the Communist Party of the United States of America (CPUSA) were upheld by the U.S. Supreme Court of Appeals in *Dennis v. United States*. This ruling created a doctrine of "clear and present danger," allowing the government to go after any communist as a potential violator of the Smith Act.

Through such "domestic containment programs" by both the federal and territorial governments, these actions targeted the unity of the Left and, in particular, a sentiment that had persisted since the Popular Front of the 1930s. Such reactionary sentiment and policy led to the suspension of two Hawai'i public school teachers on November 25, 1947—Dr. John E. Reinecke, who had been at Farrington High School for seventeen years, and Aiko Reinecke, who had been at Waialae Elementary for twenty years. Both teachers were suspended without pay. This was the first of many instances of government attacks on the civil liberties of Aiko and John Reinecke.[52] The charges against them, of teaching and advocating the overthrow of the U.S. government by "force and violence," were countered by Dr. John Reinecke during his public hearing.

When pushed about the use of "force and violence," Reinecke referenced Marxist theory arguing that socialism was an inevitable future that would come about peacefully, unless the reactionary elements sought to retain capitalism, which would then lead to violence. Reinecke argued, "If the will of the people can be applied through normal democratic channels, there is certainly no need for the use of force and violence to preserve the democratic rights of the people or to extend them."[53] As evidence, Reinecke referenced the use of "force and violence" by the white oligarchy in the 1893 overthrow of the Hawaiian Kingdom. He then argued that the use of violence in the 1895 counterrevolution was justified, as Kanaka ʻŌiwi and non-Native supporters aimed to restore Hawaiʻi to democracy.

> In 1893 the business centers, by *coup d'etat* overthrew the established government. . . . They not only overthrew the established government but they set up what was openly an oligarchy of a small section of the Caucasian population. . . . A number of native Hawaiians, abetted by some of the Whites, rose in rebellion against the oligarchy in 1895 and did their best to overthrow the government by force and violence. It seems to be that this was a futile and anachronistic movement but I certainly could not blame them. If I had been living in Hawaii at that time and had been of an age to join them, I think I would have. . . . However, looking at it from the vantage point of history now, I should say that they would have done better to have waited for annexation.[54]

Reinecke points out that he would have joined what he termed an "anachronistic movement" to restore the monarchy. John Reinecke pointed out the hypocrisy, that the authority of the territorial government was the result of treasonous acts, condemned in the Smith Act. At the same time, Reinecke demonstrated from his historical moment a teleological mode of thinking that determines "annexation" to have been to the benefit of Hawaiʻi. This history continued to play out when Reinecke was among the Hawaiʻi Seven charged with violating the Smith Act.

Four years later, in 1951, labor leaders John Reinecke, Koji Ariyoshi, Jack Hall, Art Rutledge, John McElrath, Eileen Fujimoto, and Warren Fujimoto, like others in different cities of the United States, were charged with violating the Smith Act. Together, they became known as the Hawaiʻi Seven. Soon after being charged, Koji Ariyoshi's *Honolulu Record*, a weekly paper financed partly by the ILWU, published a weekly column titled "Force and Violence in Hawaii" that contained articles about the 1893 U.S. overthrow. The unidentified author(s) tied that history to the very charges brought against the Hawai'i Seven.

The editor of the *Honolulu Record*, Koji Ariyoshi, had received official military training in propaganda by the United States when he was stationed in Yenan, China, working for the Office of War Information (OWI). As the Center for Biographical Research at the University of Hawai'i has uncovered, Ariyoshi's life was informed by a global understanding of political economy that helped him situate Hawai'i within an international context. Exposed to the labor movement as a longshoreman in both Hawai'i and the West Coast, besides growing up in Kona's coffee plantations, Ariyoshi eventually studied at the University of Georgia. There he became close friends with the parents of Erskin Caldwell, author of *Tobacco Road*. While he was in San Francisco working as a stevedore, World War II broke out, leading to Ariyoshi's internment at Manzanar Relocation Center. Enlisting in the U.S. Army specifically for intelligence service, Ariyoshi was assigned to the "Dixie Mission," whose aim was to observe Chinese communists and aid their fight against Japanese imperialism. As such, Ariyoshi was trained in not only propaganda, but interrogation, special investigations, and intelligence evaluations.

In Yenan, Ariyoshi became close friends with Soong Ching-ling, who was married to Sun Yat-sen. Sun Yat-sen had led the Chinese Revolution after first being educated about notions of democracy while living in the Hawaiian Kingdom and partly attending 'Iolani High School. Ariyoshi shared what he knew with the Chinese communists about the troubles of capitalism in Hawai'i. Also befriending Chou En-lai and meeting Mao Tse-tung, historical individuals responsible for establishing the Communist Party in China and the People's Republic of China, Ariyoshi began to write reports that the United States should back the communists, who he believed could not be defeated by an unpopular and corrupt regime led by Chiang Kai-shek. Ariyoshi was consequently accused of being brainwashed by communist propaganda, an accusation repeatedly made against him throughout his life. At the end of his military service, Ariyoshi traveled to New York City and became part of a group called the Democratic Far East. He attempted to publish a book about Yenan, but it was canceled because of growing anticommunist sentiment. After labor organizing began in the postwar moment in Hawai'i, Ariyoshi returned and started the *Honolulu Record*—a much-needed alternative newspaper that would correct and challenge the mainstream *Honolulu Advertiser* and *Honolulu Star-Bulletin*. The *Honolulu Record* was described by the federal government as the mouthpiece of the Communist Party in Hawaiʻi.

The historical column, "Force and Violence in Hawaii," ran for twenty-one weeks, from January until July of 1952. It began with the rule of Kalākaua and the 1887 Bayonet Constitution, leading to the tensions between the numerically dominant Hawaiian votes and haole-dominant property holders. The column ends by speaking to the events of the 1893 overthrow leading to the Blount Report and concludes after the 1895 rebellion. The Hawaiian mayor John H. Wilson wrote in to share his views of the column, which had been written about his father, Marshall C. B. Wilson, who was argued in the column to be "the only man on the Queen's side with guts" during the 1893 overthrow. Arguing that his uncle was a member of those who sought to restore the Hawaiian nation in 1895, Wilson wrote that the rebellion would have been successful if they had only landed the rifles on the island of Maui, where there were fewer individuals tied to the Provisional Government than on Oʻahu.[55] The column's comment that C. B. Wilson was the only man "with guts," while written with a critical eye of white supremacy and U.S. imperialism, simultaneously reproduces dominant tropes that describe Kanaka ʻŌiwi political agency and creative resistance as further evidence of being "unfit for self-government." Kalākaua, for instance, is similarly described as corrupt and shortsighted: "It's easy in 1952 to laugh at muddle-headed Kalakaua's antics: his gingerbread Iolani Palace, his grand coronation and his birthday celebrations, his trip around the world, his plan for an 'Empire of the Pacific' with himself as emperor. But even if Kalakaua had been the most sensible ruler who ever wore a crown, he would still have been behind the eightball. A sugar colony can't be run forever as a native kingdom."[56] In the eyes of the writer, Kānaka are victims of white supremacy but also unable to organize a masculine resistance or create a nation of any substance. In this way, the Hawaiian nation is imagined as laughable and cartoonish, constrained within the heteropatriarchal logics of settler colonialism as destined for replacement. Indeed, while critical of white supremacists and the process by which the Big Five gain control over Hawaiʻi, the column, much like Reinecke's 1947 testimony, simultaneously recruits the audience to join in a kind of settler common sense that mocks Kānaka ʻŌiwi. For instance, failure is often the end result of Kānaka ʻŌiwi imagining themselves as capable of outsmarting haole. The column quotes Sam Damon, who was a banker at the time, as arguing that "Hawaiian thinking" was based on an assumption that because they had a majority of the votes, it gave them real power; they "didn't realize that the intelligence and strong will of the Anglo-Saxon would beat him every-time."[57] Such statements are not challenged in the column but worded as historical facts surrounding the overthrow. These dismissals of Hawaiian political agency reoccur in ways that place the blame of the overthrow of the Hawaiian nation on Hawaiians themselves. Ty Kāwika Tengan argues that during the territorial period, despite the gains Hawaiians made at this time, a prevailing trope of the "lazy kanaka" pivoted around the emasculation of Kanaka ʻŌiwi men who were imagined as incapable of competing with "either the haole elite or the 'hard-working' Chinese and Japanese men."[58] Citing the arrival of U.S. Foreign Minister Albert Willis, who seemingly aimed to restore the Hawaiian Kingdom after the Blount Report, the col-umn quotes Liliʻuokalani as arguing, "There are certain laws of my Gov-ernment by which I shall abide. My decision would be, as the law directs, that such persons should be beheaded and their property confiscated to the Government."[59] These are the same falsehoods that had been brought against Liliʻuokalani in the move for U.S. annexation in the late nineteenth century, and they would also be repeated in James A. Michener's *Hawaii*.[60]

While the ILWU had publicly supported Hawaiʻi's admission as a U.S. state since the 1930s, the hysteria created by McCarthyism and the de-monization of the labor movement provided a political opportunity for the Big Five to write a conservative state constitution that limited the voting power of the general public. Seeking to form a constitution that facilitated statehood, in April of 1950 Hawaiʻi's State Constitutional Con-vention took place. In the same exact month, the House Un-American Activities Committee (HUAC) was called to investigate communism in Hawaiʻi.[61] Under the surveillance of a rising security state, Hawaiʻi's ILWU labor leaders were eventually found in violation of the Smith Act, and the general fear garnered from the sensationalism of the HUAC hearings helped to pass a conservative state constitution. This state constitution is distinct from most other U.S. state constitutions in that it maintains many of the territorial structures of governance through governor appointments, which had allowed the Big Five to monopolize political power.[62] Although the labor leaders of the ILWU and other radicals of the Hawai'i Seven were fined and sentenced to prison, the verdict was met by a general strike of twenty thousand ILWU members who refused to load military cargo headed for the Korean War. Further appeals kept the convicted seven out of jail until they were exonerated in 1958. The ILWU and Democratic Party, however, distanced themselves from radical organizers including Koji Ariyoshi, arguing that his brand of labor activism was too far left and that he never made it out of the caves of Yenan.

HAOLE IN UNEXPECTED PLACES: KATHLEEN DICKENSON MELLEN

In 1922, Kathleen Dickenson Mellen arrived in Hawai'i from Richmond, Virginia, and began asking, "How and why did the Islands become American?"[63] Mellen traveled to Hawai'i after U.S. President Warren Harding asked her to assist in the Republican campaign to elect Harry Baldwin as congressional delegate to succeed the late Prince Jonah Kuhio. Mellen campaigned throughout the islands alongside Princess Abigail Kawānanakoa. Mellen was raised in a political household, where her father, State Senator Robert Walter of Virginia, trained her to espouse a critical view of both history and politics. In her oft-repeated explanation for her interest in Hawaiian history, Mellen recounted, "I found discrepancies between what was recorded in books about Hawaiian history, and what my Hawaiian friends told me. So, I followed up on the subject. A great help was my close friend Princess Abigail Kawānanakoa. I used to go to her house, and there I met the old Hawaiians who had taken an active part in the monarchy."[64] Publishing primarily in the post–World War II period, in the decades when the state-led movement for Hawai'i statehood was most public and visible, Mellen's writings defamiliarized the familiar narrations of Hawai'i's linear history toward statehood.

Through twenty years of archival research and conversations with Abigail Kawānanakoa, Mary Kawena Pukui, Kamokila Campbell, Hawaiian homesteaders at Papakōlea, and those whom she described as "older Hawaiians, active participants in the revolutionary events of 1893 when the monarchy was overthrown," Mellen authored numerous writings, including a series of four books that spanned the time from Kamehameha to the U.S.-backed overthrow of Queen Lili'uokalani. Mellen's prolific writings help maintain memories of historical events that ran contrary to the settler state's narration of itself, especially in the campaign for U.S. statehood. When Kathleen Dickenson Mellen passed away in 1969, her front-page obituary in the *Honolulu Advertiser* labeled her a "controversial Isle historian," since "several of Mrs. Mellen's books expressed the view that Hawaii illegally had been taken over by haole interests in the revolution which overthrew Queen Liliuokalani in 1893."[65]

In a writing style that often blurred the lines between legitimate and disqualified forms of knowledge, the rational present and the "superstitious" past, Mellen's recording of unexpected histories often targeted the very regimes of truth that produced smooth, linear notions of American progress. Dominant historical narrations functioned to both normalize and moralize the U.S. occupation of Hawai'i by mythologizing the colonial practices of haole settlers. In her 1956 book *The Gods Depart*, for instance, Mellen writes that "histories of the Hawaiian Kingdom written by non-Hawaiians customarily present the picture from the viewpoint of the foreigner only.... [M]any of the changes imposed by outsiders and praised by them as 'civilized reforms' proved, in reality, to be destructive of native health, morale, and initiative, leading inevitably to alienation of their sovereignty."[66] Mellen was one of the few in Hawai'i who unsettled the epistemic privileging of sight and seeming objectivity, inserting 'Ōiwi ways of knowing into a presumed natural order of things. It is here that the settler state can be seen going beyond simply providing an alibi for colonial violence, and, similarly to Bernays and the Hawai'i communists, also making Hawaiian modes of life and self-governance seem logically impossible and irrelevant to the present. Mellen's work often countered the epistemic privileging of U.S. settler colonialism and occupation, stating the centrality of occupation to the movement for U.S. statehood.

Following conversations with different Kānaka 'Ōiwi, she began what she called "serious writing" after World War II. Mellen published prolifically in numerous newspapers and magazines: *Paradise of the Pacific, Honolulu Star-Bulletin, Honolulu Advertiser, Polynesian Magazine, Sunday Magazine Digest* of Chicago, and *The Diplomat* of Washington, DC, often targeting both visitors and other haole who had recently moved to the islands. She published on a wide array of topics, including the history of Washington Place (the former private residence of Queen Lili'uokalani that now serves as the residence of U.S. governors); biographies of Jennie "Kini" Wilson, who was chosen by King David Kalākaua as a part of his hula troupe to tour throughout the U.S. continent and Europe (she also performed hula at the 1893 Columbian Exposition); Liliʻuokalani Kawānanakoa, the daughter of Abigail Kawānanakoa; and numerous homesteaders from Papakōlea. Mellen demonstrated how Hawaiian national memory of the 1893 overthrow continued through the turn of the twentieth century into their present, as opposed to being memorialized events of the past. For instance, in a 1948 article in the *Paradise of the Pacific*, "Na Pua o Hawaii," Mellen writes about key figures in the events surrounding the 1893 overthrow and links this generation with the children who lived through its effects. Writing about John Nalani Wilson, the aforementioned mayor of Honolulu, she also speaks about his father, C. B. Wilson, and his mother, Eveline Townsend, who was the lady-in-waiting to Liliʻuokalani and the queen's companion while she was imprisoned after the counterrevolution.

Of the Irish Hawaiian Lane brothers, she writes that these two, along with their four other brothers, were imprisoned after each took part in the "counter-revolution which was staged in an effort to restore the monarchy."[67] Their Irish father, William Carey Lane, who was displaced from Ireland after losing his family lands for refusing to abide by Protestant English rule, told them, "Go my sons, and fight for your mother's land. Fight with all you have in you. And never forget that there flows in your veins the blood of the Careys and Lanes of County Cork."[68] County Cork is also nicknamed the "Rebel County" after its prominent role in the fight for Irish independence and its position as an antitreaty stronghold during the Irish Civil War. Writing of William Carey Lane, Mellen says, "To him, the people who manipulated the overthrow of the Hawaiian monarchy are still 'Those damn rascals.'"[69]

Challenging what colonial authorities deemed inconceivable, Mellen often denaturalized the natural presence of the United States in Hawaiʻi. The cultural work required to transform ideas that are perceived as logically impossible often necessitated a form of narrative that could penetrate and disrupt notions of the seemingly logical and objective. In the December 1945 issue of the *Paradise of the Pacific*, Mellen wrote of the 1928 haunting of the territorial legislators, their family, and the staff at ʻIolani Palace. Using both local and national newspapers that reported on what was considered a national event at that time, Mellen explained that the territorial legislators attempted to mark themselves as the new and rightful leaders of Hawai'i by decorating the room where the House of Representatives met with kāhili, the plumed staff of state used to mark Hawaiian royalty. Three kāhili in total were created, two that were made of dyed goose feathers and a third that used the black feathers of a kāhili belonging to the late Queen Lili'uokalani.

The use of the feathers from Queen Lili'uokalani's kāhili, according to Mellen, was a desecration that led to a "long list of ominous events that were to wreak havoc in the lives of many people during the months to come."[70] In a ceremony that was imagined as demonstrating reverence for Hawaiian traditions, the kāhili with Lili'uokalani's feathers led the procession into 'Iolani Palace. But when the kāhili was a foot away from the steps of the palace it slipped from the hands of the holder and fell onto the stairway. Mellen quotes the *Honolulu Advertiser*, which reported that its black feathers were "ruffled in the fall." The very next day, after another ceremony where the three kāhili were presented to Territorial Governor Wallace Farrington, the man carrying the kāhili was said to be "stricken with paralysis" later that night. Mellen writes that after the opening of the fifteenth territorial legislature in 1929, when the House of Representatives began holding sessions in the throne room, "death began to stalk the homes of the members." As she reports, "First, the wife of a member died; then the mother of another, the child of a third, until by the end of thirty-three days, six people, all close relatives of legislative members, had been taken in death. Then a Hawaiian member of the House broke two ribs in a fall, a Portuguese member was severely injured in an automobile accident, another was taken seriously ill. Next, death invaded the Senate chambers across the hallway."[71]

The supposedly rational territorial legislators, who governed through a seemingly objective white masculinity, found themselves thoroughly spooked. Government officials convened and agreed that the queen's kāhili should not be displayed in the throne room where the House of Representatives met. Mellen writes that Washington, DC, took notice of the legislature's decision, when the *Washington Star* reported, "Uneasiness over deaths of persons closely connected with the Hawaiian Territorial Legislature has led to [an order for] the removal from the hall where the House of Representatives meets, of three 'kahilis,' or tall feather standards, picturesque relics of monarchial days. . . . due to deaths [which] have occurred. The black kahili had once belonged to the late Queen Liliʻuokalani."[72] In conversation with both Mokumaia, the captain of the guards who played a hand in the construction of the kāhili, and Speaker of the House Frederick J. Lowrey, the "black kahili" was taken out at exactly midnight, when the "royal dead may be moved," and placed reverently on the top floor of the palace, above the heads of commoners. Mellen again cites the *Honolulu Advertiser*: "For it was believed by a few that the black kahili, whose feathers were once the property of the late Queen Liliuokalani, was responsible for the deaths close to legislative membership that have occurred since the session opened. So it was decreed that the black kahili would have to be removed from the House."[73]

Mellen's retelling of the haunting of the territorial legislators at ʻIolani Palace queered the "regimes of truth" claimed by white settlers, troubling the normative logics underpinning such injustices. While Hawaiian self-governance, an alternative governance to that of the settler state, was made impossible as a result of linear notions of U.S. history, and the criminal history of this overthrow that made such authority possible was systemically hidden by dominant forms of rational thinking, "hauntings" imported new possibilities for understanding or narrating the present moment. Indeed, it is only after the queen's kāhili is returned to the rightful place at the head of ʻIolani Palace, above the heads of settlers, that the haunting ends.

It was her books, however, that received the most attention. The first one, *In a Hawaiian Valley*, was a collection of essays about individuals she met at Papakōlea while helping to pass legislation that placed Papakōlea on the Hawaiian Homestead Act in 1934. This collection of essays, which blends both historical and fictional narration, was reviewed favorably by the *New York Times*: "It is not of Honolulu and Waikiki Beach but of the real Hawaii of which Mrs. Mellen writes ... the Hawaii the tourist seldom sees." Mellen's next four books spanned the time of Kamehameha to the overthrow of Queen Liliʻuokalani. *The Lonely Warrior* (1949) retold the life of Kamehameha through conversations with "Hawaiians whose grandparents had personal contact with the great king himself." Mary Kawena Pukui is noted as a major resource in writing this book. Her second was *The Magnificent Matriarch*, published in 1952, which told of Kaʻahumanu. In 1958, this book was to be made into a full-color motion picture film by Panavision, and $2 million had been set aside to produce it. However, Panavision canceled the project due to what were described as budgeting problems.[74] Her third book, *The Gods Depart* (1956), discusses the middle years of the Hawaiian Kingdom and was immediately criticized for having "anti-missionary leanings."[75] Her final book, *An Island Kingdom Passes* (1958), narrated the events of 1893 not as a revolution but as an illegal overthrow. Her research is done specifically within English-language sources. But because they are contextualized and cross-referenced within the oral histories of those who were alive during the 1890s, she is able to narrate Hawaiian resistance to occupation. For instance, citing a graphic report in the *Kentucky Post* by Anna Berry, described as the daughter of a congressman from Kentucky, Mellen references the gathering of signatures to the Kū'ē petitions in 1897:

> Suddenly there was silence. The crowd parted and a woman entered—Mrs. Kauihelani Campbell [*sic*], president of the Hawaiian Patriotic League. She wore a flower boa around her neck. She was absolutely queenly in her dignity and repose. She said: "Stand firm, my friends. Love of country means more to you and me than anything else. Have courage and patience; our time will come. Sign this petition to the President of the Great Republic and tell the American people who love their liberty what we are feeling here. How many will sign?" Every man and woman held a hand on high.[76]

In August of 1958, only a few months after *An Island Kingdom Passes* was in print, Mellen received an angry criticism by an anonymous critic calling himself Pro Bono Publico. The criticism, printed in the *Honolulu Advertiser*, held that Mellen's book was overly biased in favor of Kānaka 'Ōiwi who supported Queen Lili'uokalani and that it had too many "misspellings and canards" to be taken seriously. Mellen responded with a challenge to a public debate at a bookstore. Numerous people gathered and waited, but the anonymous critic failed to show. Mellen then responded in the *Honolulu Advertiser*: "In recent years innumerable histories of Hawaii have been written each containing shocking and incredible falsehoods. . . . Do you honestly believe that their [Hawaiians'] side of the story should remain forever buried under an avalanche of lies? The history of Hawaii is far from being a simple and uncomplicated story with all righteousness on one side, all villains on the other. But that, apparently, is the picture you want preserved."[77]

Mellen's private wealth afforded her the ability to publish many criticisms of prominent haole families in the islands, criticisms that were difficult to make for others who were dependent on the Big Five or territorial government for work. And while being white afforded her the space to make historical claims and criticisms that most nonwhites could not make at the time, her gender often led to criticism that reduced her writings to little more than emotion and sentiment. Highlighting her "misspellings and canards" or her identification with those Hawaiians whose government was overthrown, the anonymous critic dismissed her as someone who lacked the capacity to be logical and discerning. Mellen further writes in her response, "In attacking my book you followed the method used over the years to keep the truth suppressed. But you are out of step with the times. Reprisals against those who dared to speak out and give the other side of the story are not so easily carried out as formerly and the future will find more and more fearless writers who will refuse to utilize handouts written by subsidized writers or those who wrote in self defense."[78]

Mellen knew firsthand the "reprisals" with which Hawaiian opposition to the Americanization of Hawai'i was silenced, especially in regard to Hawai'i statehood. The Hawaii Statehood Commission intimidated Papakōlea homesteaders and Mellen herself. In 1948, Mellen and homesteaders met with Senator Hugh Butler of Nebraska during his congressional visit to investigate statehood in Hawai'i. At the meeting, this group agreed to set their opposing viewpoints on paper and send the document to Butler, then chair of the Senate Committee on Interior and Insular Affairs. Butler later wrote to Mellen asking for the letter that the Hawaiian homesteaders had promised him. Mellen responded to Butler saying that the Statehood Commission had discovered their plans and held an "indignation meeting," at which Mellen was "roundly denounced." Mellen wrote, "It was agreed that they [the Statehood Commission] would send a member to talk to the homesteaders. Someone who was present notified me, and I promptly phoned the member who had led the talk and told him that if they tried to intimidate the Hawaiians, or to injure them in any manner, I would notify you [Senator Butler] at once. So they [the Statehood Commission] dropped the matter." According to Mellen, the homesteaders at Papakōlea consequently became "afraid to make the written statement. And I agreed with them—knowing only too well what has happened in the past to those who dared oppose statehood openly."[79] The Hawaii Statehood Commission in 1957 also came up with ways to silence taxi drivers and tour guides who were telling tourists that Hawaiians did not want statehood.[80]

Mellen continued to use her own archival research to challenge congressmen not to view statehood as an inevitable outcome of history. In a January 1957 editorial printed in the *Honolulu Advertiser* titled "Hawaii's Statehood Pledge Challenged," Mellen began by stating that she had been listening to a radio commentator make the charge that Congress had for "six decades violated its pledge to make Hawaii a state."[81] The fact that Hawai'i was an incorporated territory was often given as reason for why Hawai'i did not need to entertain the idea of independence. Mellen writes, "That no such pledge was made at the time of annexation is easily proven by even a casual study of the records of that period. . . . [S]uch an indictment of Congress is totally false." Arguing that only a handful of Hawai'i's total population wanted the annexation of Hawai'i, which was approved by an even smaller proportion of American citizens, Mellen went on to cite prominent leaders in the Republic of Hawai'i who sought annexation but not statehood. She quoted Samuel Mills Damon, who told Washington newsmen, "Hawaii will never ask to become a state because some day we might hold the balance of power in the American Senate and that would not be desirable. . . . If we can come into the Union as a Territory . . . that would suit us just fine." Chief Justice Albert Judd is cited as having told the *Boston Herald*: "As to the question of statehood, I do not think that any sensible man in the Islands expects or wants it. A Territorial government as a permanency is what is desired." Sanford Dole is described as having "agreed to not fight for statehood."[82] Also in January of 1957, Kathleen Dickenson Mellen and her husband George Mellen wrote a letter to U.S. Senator George Smathers, a Democrat of Florida, praising his unwillingness to support statehood. Together they argued that many Hawaiians are "thoroughly angry" and are organizing against the Statehood Plebiscite. The Mellens recommended that instead of statehood, the senators should support "an independent monarchy in Hawaii as an American protectorate."[83] Smathers forwarded the letter to Chairman of the Senate Interior Committee James Murray, who commented to the *Honolulu Star-Bulletin* that such a request to restore the monarchy was "utterly inconceivable."[84]

In June of 1957, however, U.S. House Representative John Pillion of New York, a member of the House Territorial Subcommittee, cited the editorial and introduced it into the Congressional Record. Pillion argued that this editorial reveals the "true story" that "the people of Hawaii had pledged themselves not to seek statehood at the time of annexation."[85] Hawaiʻi's congressional delegate, John Burns, responded that Mellen's arguments required "objective consideration." Victor Houston, former congressional delegate and naval officer, who was also Kānaka ʻŌiwi, was seen as just the person to provide the kind of objectivity necessary to discredit Mellen's arguments. Houston argued that it was true that in 1893, when annexation was being sought, it was desired by only a handful of Hawaiʻi's total population who were "racially non-Hawaiians" and "one fourth of the voters and owners of nine tenths of the private property of the Kingdom." He further stated that annexation was consented to by a Senate in Hawaiʻi that contained but "two native Hawaiian members, and was approved by the President of the Republic and his Council, in which there was but one native Hawaiian member."[86] Houston's disagreement, however, was with Mellen's statement that annexation was approved by an even smaller proportion of American citizens on the continent. Such statements "disregard the status of the American Congress, which through its elected representatives passed the Newlands Resolution in both Houses."[87] Yet, the alleged annexation of Hawaiʻi through a joint resolution was not only illegal as previously mentioned, but the direct result of the failure to find enough numbers in the senate to gain a two-thirds vote.

Mellen's criticisms of the historical arguments underpinning the statehood movement also extended to the accompanying racial narratives coming from writers such as James Michener. This played out in her public criticisms and arguments with Michener's first epic novel titled *Hawaii*, written as a manifesto of the statehood movement and published in 1959 only a few months after statehood was achieved. Michener's arguments gained legitimacy by tying themselves to the scholarship of the University of Hawaiʻi Department of Sociology. By 1978, Michener's *Hawaii* had sold five million copies.

The novel made use of such scientific "racial frontier" logics and sought to redeem U.S. occupation through multicultural forms of settler colonialism. Michener created stories surrounding four families—Hawaiian, haole, Japanese, and Chinese—where each is open to embracing the culture of others, thus culminating into a glorious new type of person, what Michener dubbed the "Golden Man." Yet, the temporal and cultural framings of "primitives" as in the past and "Orientals" as measures of progress can be seen in the differences between his Kanaka ʻŌiwi and Japanese characters. The Japanese Golden Men are the best of both the East and West: "A group of sociologists in Hawaii were perfecting a concept whose vague outlines had occupied them for some years, and quietly among themselves they suggested that in Hawaii a new type of man was being developed. He was a man influenced by both the west and the east, a man at home in either the business councils of New York or the philosophical retreats of Kyoto, a man wholly modern and American yet in tune with the ancient and the Oriental."[88] Yet his Kanaka ʻŌiwi characters led one *New York Times* reviewer to conclude, "Their extinction as a race marks the final tragedy of the novel."[89]

In a writing contest organized by Bob Krauss at the Halekulani Hotel, Kathleen Dickenson Mellen and James Michener were both invited to be guest judges. Before the event began, however, Mellen and Michener argued about Kamehameha Schools. Kamehameha School is a private charitable educational trust created by the will of Princess Bernice Pauahi Bishop (1831–84), who left her lands to be used to educate Kanaka ʻŌiwi children. Michener argued that the schools should be opened to students of all races in "open competition" and that it was a mistake to educate Hawaiian children in what he described as a protective, paternalistic atmosphere that only perpetuated Hawaiian feelings of inferiority.[90] Mellen responded by saying that the Kamehameha Schools are one of the last strongholds of Hawaiian culture and that it would be a mistake to admit children who were not Hawaiian and that after all that had been taken from Hawaiians, they deserved their own schools. Mary Kawena Pukui also expressed concern in 1959 that Hawaiʻi statehood might lead to the further elimination of what few Hawaiian rights remained. Pukui observed: "The question that stands up is what is to be done for my mother's people? . . . Hawaiian people. Will it mean the dissolving of Kamehameha School?"[91]

Mellen argued publicly that Michener's desire to see Hawaiian-specific rights and resources dissolved and made open to the general public was facilitated by the description in his novel of Hawaiians as a people destined for extinction. She argued that he "reconstructed 'history' to fit his own theories and purposes, hence the many historical inaccuracies."[92] In an interview printed in the *Honolulu Star-Bulletin*, Mellen argued that Michener's novel was centered around Hawaiians relinquishing and passively surrendering after the 1893 overthrow: "When writing of modern Hawaii the author becomes 'hortatory,' exhorting the reader at length on his pet subjects, chief of which are the breaking up of all large Hawaiian estates, remolding Island life according to his personal preferences, opening of Kamehameha Schools to all races (for the good of the Hawaiians, he insists!) and a 'brotherhood of man' presented, so it seems to the reader, in the form of bitter hatreds, tensions, and ugly racial conflicts."[93] In this way, one can see how Michener's cultural plurality could not fathom Hawaiians as capable of offering the world something beneficial, and instead only as contributing a laid-back, hedonistic lifestyle that offered comic reprieve from the hard work of modernity. Mellen argues that Michener's global racial framing produced Native peoples as failures: "To none is the author so unkind as to the native Hawaiians from King Kalakaua, whom he portrays (by name, not fiction) as an ignorant boor, to the fictitious beachboy presented as the last of the Hawaiian royal family and, presumably, typical of all present-day Hawaiians."[94]

Hawaiian opposition to statehood and the counterhistories of those like Kathleen Dickenson Mellen were similarly designated for disappearance. Mellen is said to have consoled her friends after the passing of statehood by saying, "Shed your tears, take your moment of meditation. Then get up and build for the future."[95] Mellen was a haole settler, who chose to fight alongside those her nation had helped to dispossess. Although the encroachment of "greed and commercialism" manifested through statehood was insurmountable in her historical moment, her writings helped to clear space for the impossible to one day become achievable. Such forms of slow resistance by archiving the histories, actions, and opinions of those who were opposed to statehood thus created the conditions of possibility and hope for a Hawaiian nation to reemerge in the future.

THE MILLION-DOLLAR HOAX: TAKING ON THE GREED OF STATEHOOD

A 1959 public service announcement starring then Governor William Quinn declared, "Hawaiian paradise is a business, an investment for every citizen which does and must continue to return multimillion dollar profits in paradise. These profits in turn create a better way of life for our people."[96] Three years after Hawai'i's admission as a U.S. state, on May 7, 1962, the headline of the *Honolulu Advertiser* reported that the Sheraton Corporation was being offered $34 million for four of its properties in Waikīkī. Having just purchased these hotels three years earlier, Sheraton would have doubled its investments with this sale. George Murphy was then offered $5 million for his ranch on the island of Moloka'i; that was seventeen times more than he had paid for it seven years earlier. The very next day, the morning paper reported that $9 million had been offered for the entire valley of Makaha and $1.2 million for the ownership of the Waianae Development Company owned by Chinn Ho, who stated, "If they put the money on the line Tuesday, we will sell. . . . [E]verything has its price and we're in business to please our stockholders."[97] Within five days there were seven offers totaling $62 million, and all who received these offers were in negotiations to accept. The economic miracle promised by Hawai'i's twenty-five-year, state-led movement for admission as a U.S. state was seemingly coming to fruition.

Receiving local, national, and international media coverage, the press conferences featured local realtors Ann Felzer and Milton Beamer, who explained, "An American corporation acting as fiscal administrators and investment comptrollers for a number of estates and trusts, both foreign and domestic, wishes to invest in Hawaii. This is primarily because Hawaii seems to be a safe ground for investment."[98] The realtors spoke on behalf of D. Franklin Carson, who himself supposedly represented the Switzerland-based International Trade Exchange Central. Questions about Carson's identity increased, and the media often referred to him as "the little man who wasn't there."[99] Frank Pick, New York financial insider, stated that he had never heard of the International Trade Exchange Central or of Carson: "This, of course, didn't mean he doesn't exist—some of the wealthiest operators in the field of international finance carried on for years without ever getting in the limelight."[100]

While many were in the dark about the identity of the investors, after the papers cited Amalu's possible involvement, those who knew of Sammy Amalu concluded that the whole thing was a prank. Carson told the press that Amalu had no connections to the deal and that the "wealth joined with that of his son, left to them both by the late Princess Maria, is sufficient for him to have accomplished this entire transaction without need of recourse to any of my principals."[101] This statement, printed on the front pages of the newspapers, delivered the punch line for many. Amalu was never married to a Princess Maria nor did he have a son, but was known by many in the Hawaiian community as māhū, or not conforming to Western heteropatriarchal standards. Moreover, Amalu's occupation as a Hawaiian genealogical columnist for the *Honolulu Advertiser* meant he was not of the class background to afford these properties.

As a final deal approached, the press conferences became increasingly odd. Carson, who eventually revealed the punch line, stated that they were ready to exchange money for land, but there were four hundred cows and twenty-seven horses on the Moloka'i Ranch that were missing. D. Franklin Carson was, in fact, a nineteen-year-old surfer from California who had been visiting Hawai'i and hitchhiking with two friends when a Hawaiian man named Sammy Amalu—who spoke with a British accent—picked them up, drove them around, fed them, and then offered them a place to stay in exchange for Carson's help.

Amalu was, indeed, known for pulling off elaborate performance pranks. To name a few, in San Francisco, he posed as an Indian Maharajah, wearing a turban and sitting atop a throne that was carried by four men. He then demanded a room in the Mark Hopkins Hotel and received one. After enlisting in the U.S. Army as a private during World War II, he was soon found wearing an officer's uniform. Amalu was eventually dismissed from the army through a medical discharge of homosexuality, which he denied. A radio personality named Hal Lewis, popularly known as "Aku," said, "Take the Sheraton deal in 1962—I knew almost immediately what was happening. . . . I knew about Sammy and I loved it!"[102]

The multimillion-dollar hoax playfully orchestrated by Sammy Amalu, who had been living modestly on the outskirts of Waikīkī, captured headlines for more than two weeks. Labeled "Sam the Sham," Amalu has been written off historically as simply a "con man" who "failed" at achieving his goals to be wealthy. For instance, historian Gavan Daws writes, "He was possessed by the idea of the dispossessed Hawaiian chief . . . a twentieth-century victim of the nineteenth-century cultural rape and pillage that wrenched land away from Hawaiian chiefs and lodged power in the hands of grasping American haoles . . . He was, in fact, a confidence man, whose life project was to take revenge on the world for what it had done to him."[103] Lewis Hyde, however, writes that "confidence men" are the closest to the rebirth of "tricksters" in the twentieth century; they embody "things that are actually true about America but cannot be openly declared (as, for example, the degree to which capitalism lets us steal from our neighbors, or the degree to which institutions like the stock market require the same kind of confidence that criminal con men need)."[104] Living by his wits, and affirming while displacing the language and logics of capital to serve his own ends, Amalu performed his hoax in order to expose the greedy operations of various individuals and industries in the poststatehood moment.

Vine Deloria Jr. argues that tricksters are capable of bringing order out of chaos, particularly a chaos that has disrupted a previously ordered creation, and can "serve to explain why a certain landscape is *now* the way it is."[105] Deloria, however, also warns that the term *trickster* can potentially obscure more than it reveals. Drawing on Native studies and queer theory, Stephanie Nohelani Teves argues that moʻolelo (history/story) is as much about "survival as a lāhui, as a nation," as it is about refusing the heteropatriarchal, colonial, and commercialized expectations for how Hawaiians can be in the world.[106] This is particularly so in a moment where American writers such as James Michener dominated notions of who Hawaiians were, allowing for the commercialization of Hawaiian culture to run hand-in-hand with U.S. expectations who Hawaiian disappearance.[107] Furthermore, because Amalu was kolohe (the Hawaiian word for "mischievous," "naughty," "rascal," or "criminal"), he is able to comment humorously on the everyday violences caused by encroaching development. Lilikalā Kameʻeleihiwa writes that kolohe is one of "the more valuable aspects of ancient Hawaiian culture that has survived to modern times" and is often associated with Hawaiian moʻolelo.[108] Amalu's public performance, which played out in the media, can be seen as a profound narration and remembering of a Hawaiian nation in the immediate years after U.S. statehood.

Much of the criticism of Amalu also refers to him as a kind of failure. For instance, Gavan Daws uses Amalu's hoax as an example of a *failed* real estate venture and juxtaposes him with Henry Kaiser's *successful* large-scale real estate development of the islands. Daws writes, "What Sammy Amalu only dreams of, Henry J. Kaiser does. His Hawaii Kai development, with the first houses built in 1961, is on a scale never seen before in Hawaii."[109] And yet, it is through such failing that Amalu opens possibilities for alternative worlds to be imagined. Failure is a dominant trope of capitalism, where to accumulate money is to be a success, and to not accumulate it is to fail. Within a system that is itself reliant on various forms of dispossession and exploitation, failing might also be a refusal to succeed at another person's expense. In *The Queer Art of Failure*, Jack Halberstam argues: "In losing it imagines other goals for life, for love, for art, and for being. . . . [W]e can also recognize failure as a way of refusing to acquiesce to dominant logics of power and discipline and as a form of critique."[110] Undoubtedly, Amalu's hoax is what Halberstam describes as an "anti-capitalist and queer tale," one that rejects the values of a heteronormative settler common sense that determined success via capitalist accumulation.[111] Indeed, this accumulation is accomplished through dispossession, specifically of Amalu's own people and the Hawaiian worlds he refused to allow to pass into extinction. Amalu instead worked through a Hawaiian value system, one that defined wealth by a capacity to share as opposed to accumulate at the expense of others.

During the height of the Cold War and Hawai'i's militant labor movement, critiques of U.S. colonialism and capitalism could not be made openly, particularly not without the speaker being disqualified as Soviet inspired or un-American. Kanaka 'Ōiwi issues regarding national sovereignty similarly could not be expressed openly, but were in the form of Amalu's satire. In this way, Daws gets it wrong. To see Sammy Amalu as only a con man is to misunderstand that Amalu lied and stole not so much to get rich but rather to "disturb the established categories of truth and property and by so doing open the road to possible new worlds."[112]

Amalu disrupts, indeed he queers, a developmental and totalizing discourse that normalizes Hawai'i as being completely constituted by U.S. territoriality immediately following statehood. His kolohe ability to shift between different social classes, a millionaire investor and then a destitute Kanaka 'Ōiwi ali'i, served to reveal just whom statehood actually benefited. When we pay close attention to the particular sites of Amalu's performed purchase, and his imagined use of these lands, we are compelled to consider how these lands were made available and radically transformed by a form of capitalism that required the violent break of a Kanaka 'Ōiwi mode of life. Amalu thus drew from the *longue durée* of Hawaiian histories as a genealogical expert, who possessed knowledge of how these places served as sacred sites and/or as resources for food production for specific Hawaiian families, including his own.

The childhood friend and attorney for Amalu's investment group, Harold C. Schnack, stated that he supported Amalu because he spoke of the need to assist "Hawaiian people attaining their rightful place in our community. . . . The selection of lands of particular significance to persons of Hawaiian ancestry, the benevolent plans of caring for and employing Hawaiians and providing scholarships for their children, together with the apparent availability of Swiss funds, made this a project worth encouraging, even if it should fail to materialize."[113] As opposed to Chinn Ho, Amalu planned to keep Makaha Valley "undeveloped as sacred ground."[114] The Moloka'i ranch properties owned by George Murphy are where Amalu stated his ancestors were buried. Murphy, who bought his ranch—an area originally promised to Kānaka 'Ōiwi on the island of Moloka'i—from Bishop Estates in 1955, was notorious for building roads and subdivisions along sacred hillsides, and inserting galvanized lead pipes into the sacred pools above Moa'ula Falls. While many on Moloka'i fought Murphy, believing that he was out to develop the sacred valley and "commercially cover its ancient roots," he began leasing the land and replacing Native families with settler tenants. Furthermore, the Sheraton properties that were to be purchased by Amalu all referred to Hawaiian royalty. Indeed, Carson spoke about Amalu hoping "to make the Makaha ranch one of the biggest in the world—all poultry and dairy products for Hawaii would come from the ranch instead of being imported."[115] In this way, Amalu conveyed other possibilities for the use of land, not as property from which to accumulate profit, but as 'āina—as that which feeds—an alternative future that has profound resonance with current, ongoing land and water struggles for food sovereignty in Hawai'i and other parts of the world.

Amalu's hoax ended when he was arrested in Seattle at the airport en route to New York to apparently close the deal, on a warrant for writing two bad checks in San Francisco. When Amalu was arrested he had been traveling under the name *Albert Wilcox*—a close resemblance to the name of Hawaiian nationalist Robert Wilcox, who led two failed armed rebellions in an attempt to restore the Hawaiian nation in the latter part of the nineteenth century. Extradited to California, Amalu was unable to make the $6,500 bail. He was held on felony charges for a $200 check and another $600 check for the Mark Hopkins Hotel, where he had dressed as an Indian Maharajah. Amalu pleaded guilty and was sentenced to one year in jail.

Soon after his arrest, Amalu stated in an interview from Folsom Prison that he was "thinking of challenging the United States' right to Hawaii— the 50th state—and taking all the land back again."[116] Indeed, Amalu was part of a cultural front, as his friends were some of the most vocal opponents against statehood. Besides Kathleen Dickenson Mellen, Amalu was close to Alice Kamokila Campbell. Long after he was released from prison, on the day after Kamokila Campbell passed on October 23, 1971, Amalu offered her words at the Volcano House at Kīlauea, which overlooks the home of Pele: "Last night, a great lady died. A great Hawaiian. I ask you now to stand to drink a toast to her memory for she represented all that was lovely and beautiful in Hawaii. I pledge a toast to Alice Kamokila Campbell."[117]

It was, in fact, Kamokila Campbell's sister, Abigail Kawānanakoa, who sponsored Amalu's education at the elite private school Punahou. Amalu stated that it was while attending Punahou that he put on a mask and never took it off. This statement gives us some insight into Amalu's ability to slip in and out of different social classes, operating from a space of colonial dispossession. Although a descendant of ali'i, Amalu grew up working class. His father was a beach boy at Waikīkī and his mother a schoolteacher. Seeking to take advantage of the popularity of Amalu's hoax, Thurston Twigg-Smith, a Punahou classmate, offered him a daily column while in prison. In his columns Amalu critiqued the logic of incarceration and debated Hawaiian notions of sexuality. Twigg-Smith and Amalu were an odd coupling, as Twigg-Smith was the grandson of Lorrin A. Thurston, the architect of the 1893 U.S. military–backed overthrow.

In a rare moment a decade after being released from federal prison, Amalu revisited his million-dollar hoax in his column: "I somehow became associated with the likes of the Sheraton people, with Chinn Ho, and with a chap from the wilds of Molokai named George Murphy. Tycoons all and absolutely filthy with lucre. And if there be any among you who cannot recall this particular association, read no further. . . . Nor chance the thought for one single moment that I am going to explain anything. . . . Only twice in my life did I ever try to explain anything and each time

I landed in jail."[118] Instead of challenging the violent structures of economic and settler development head on, Amalu appropriated the language of capital to expose how the economic benefits that statehood and tourism seemingly promised the working class actually helped Hawai'i's elite insulate and expand their economic power. Amalu stated, "With authority, you can prick, you can needle, but you must never bludgeon, and this most people don't understand."[119] In its public response the Sheraton Corporation admitted, "This hasn't cost us any money, but it looks like we're going to have to live with the laughs for some time to come."[120]

"SILENT FEARS"

The day after the statehood bill was passed, on March 13, 1959, Reverend Abraham Akaka delivered a sermon at Kawaiaha'o Church. While the sermon did celebrate statehood as an achievement, Reverend Akaka also acknowledged the existence of Hawaiian opposition to statehood, an antagonism premised on America's desecration of Native sacred sites and a government "motivated by economic greed": "There are some of us to whom statehood brings great hopes, and there are those to whom statehood brings *silent fears*.... There are fears that Hawai'i as a state will be motivated by economic greed; that statehood will turn Hawai'i (as someone has said) into a great big spiritual junkyard filled with smashed dreams, worn out illusions; that will make the Hawaiian people lonely, confused, insecure, empty, anxious, restless, disillusioned—a wistful people."[121] Reverend Akaka's description of Hawaiians' "silent fears" regarding the possible negative effects of statehood resonates with the sentiments expressed by John Ho'opale, Alice Kamokila Campbell, Kathleen Dickenson Mellen, and Sammy Amalu, who had each described Hawaiians who were opposed to statehood as operating within a climate of fear. Reverend Akaka's statement in 1959, that many Hawaiians feared that Hawai'i as a state would be motivated by "economic greed," seemed prophetic in the years after statehood.

In 1971, for instance, Matsuo Takabuki (see chapter 3), who was described as a "skilled operator in the politics of land and power," was appointed by Governor John Burns to serve Kamehameha Schools as Bishop Estate trustee.[122] This was a controversial appointment as Takabuki was Burns's closest political associate. After Takabuki's appointment,

Reverend Akaka thought differently about statehood. He rang the bells of Kawaiahaʻo Church for nearly an hour, arguing, "We are now a nobody as far as the government is concerned."[123]

Sammy Amalu, Kathleen Dickenson Mellen, John Reinecke, and Koji Ariyoshi all articulate the history of the 1893 overthrow in different ways, utilizing their own forms of propaganda and talents to push back against representations of Hawaiʻi that facilitate various forms of violence. Instead, they express a range of anticapitalist, anticolonial, and antiwar politics that illuminate different vulnerabilities to both a U.S. imperialist and settler state. When analyzed together, they fill in the gaps of knowledge among each other, and demonstrate resistance to the public relations work of figures like Edward Bernays, James Michener, and George Lehleitner. Through an analysis of the intersections of U.S. empire—specifically the formation of a national security state, a capitalist system reliant on economic development tied to both Hawaiian dispossession and imperialist wars—from our contemporary standpoint, we can think through how a U.S. nation that emerges from war on the frontiers reproduces itself through the same relations of warfare in civil society. Turning the silent fears of statehood into a joke, Amalu offered new epistemological possibilities by remaining kolohe and performing moʻolelo that was internationally covered, exposing his contempt for the conditions of occupation and capitalism at the same time that he masterfully reconstituted Hawaiʻi as a particularly Kanaka ʻŌiwi place.

CHAPTER 5
ALTERNATIVE FUTURES
BEYOND THE SETTLER STATE

Public signs in the parking lot at the ʻĪao State Park on the island of Maui warn tourists not to leave their valuables in their rental cars and risk having them stolen as they venture into the park. One such sign, however, was defaced by adding "LOCALS WILL," boldly stating just *who* will remove their valuables. While the sign's defacement reveals, in a teasing manner, the underlying animosity that many in Hawaiʻi feel toward tourists, the sign's very location in ʻĪao Valley also reveals an inconsistency in just which kinds of thefts are criminalized and which are otherwise normalized as a natural part of history. Property crimes against tourists are often taken most seriously; as one reporter stated, they tarnish "Hawaiʻi's reputation as a place with gentle people where tourists can relax and unwind."[1] Yet, historic and ongoing crimes in this same valley, such as the desecration of sacred burials, the historic diversion of water that consequently leads to the death of rivers and a way of life, or the theft of government from a nation, are normalized forms of violence only indexed outside of official histories.

Located just beneath the state park, the Kepaniwai Park Heritage Gardens are a popular tourist attraction that narrates poststatehood Hawaiʻi as a liberal multicultural democracy with racial harmony. Started in 1968, the Kepaniwai Heritage Gardens (as they are more commonly known) now comprise eight diverse architectural structures in six gardens that are culturally representative of different groups in Hawaiʻi: a Japanese Tea House, a Filipino nipa hut, a Chinese pavilion with moon gate, a New

Figure 5.1 State sign at the 'Īao State Park parking lot, 2009. Photograph taken by the author.

England saltbox house (missionary house), a Portuguese home with cement oven, a Puerto Rican monument, a Korean pavilion replete with pots for kimchi, and different Kanaka 'Ōiwi structures. One Kanaka 'Ōiwi structure, built of stones made to look like the 1897 Kū'ē Petitions opposing U.S. annexation, was completed on January 16, 2013, the anniversary of the U.S. military–backed overthrow of Hawai'i. This structure importantly disrupts the overall narrative of the park.

Spread across six acres, the racial diversity represented at the park is seen as a material expression of "modern Hawai'i." The diverse architectural structures and gardens together represent a new multicultural order based on liberal equality, defined in opposition to the deep racism of the territorial period, and symbolic of a kind of cultural diversity with global implications as a model for world peace. Made with previous world's fairs in mind, with its capacity to be at once representative of the domestic and global, the impressive natural beauty of 'Īao Valley serves as a backdrop that lends itself to naturalizing the politics of scientific display, educating tourists about the supposedly pluralist harmony in the islands—a presumed historical outcome of the U.S. control of Hawai'i.

When the area for the Kepaniwai Heritage Gardens was first being cleared, a Kanaka 'Ōiwi bulldozer operator came across a giant pōhaku (boulder) that he was unable to move. Believing the boulder could not be moved because it had mana (spiritual or divine power) he asked a Kanaka

Figure 5.2 Chinese Pavilion at the Kepaniwai Heritage Gardens, 2009. Photograph taken by the author.

'Ōiwi family living in the valley about the boulder. The family is said to have told him that the boulder's name was Kapiliokaka'e, the companion of Kaka'e who governed Maui in the fifteenth century. The next day the man approached the boulder and prayed to it. He called Kapiliokaka'e by name, and asked it to move to safety or others would use dynamite. Only then was he able to use the bulldozer to move the pōhaku into the middle of Kapela stream. Soon after this, however, a flash flood destroyed the park grounds and washed out Kinihapai Bridge, and the boulder is said to have disappeared.[2] Today, only a few residents know the location of Kapiliokaka'e. That such instances of the "supernatural," for lack of a better word, are commonly linked to this valley is well known to most Maui residents.

Where a boulder having the agency to leave on its own terms may be dismissed as exotic folklore, such "inconceivable" moments might also have the potential to trouble certain commonsense logics that gatekeep the thinkable. Avery Gordon has notably argued that such occurrences are capable of unsettling pristine zones of knowledge and space, forcing us to confront the haunting presence of past injustices and future possibilities: "It gives notice not only to itself but also to what it represents. What it represents is usually a loss, sometimes of life, sometimes of a path not taken. From a certain vantage point . . . [it] also simultaneously represents a future possibility, a hope. We are in relation to it and it has designs on us such that we must reckon with it graciously, attempting to offer it a hospitable memory *out of a concern for justice*."[3] Just as Kapiliokakaʻe refused to move for the construction of the multicultural park, not to mention its very ability to withstand the bulldozer (and there are other boulders in Hawaiʻi who have similarly refused to move),[4] the pōhaku places ʻĪao Valley within a broader history, forcing us to consider other present and future possibilities produced by other ways of knowing. Representative of a "path not taken," perhaps the "loss" or disruption of a Hawaiian way of life, the pōhaku opens the Kepaniwai Heritage Gardens to a wider range of interpretation set by different epistemological and historical contexts.

Besides the heritage gardens, ʻĪao Valley is perhaps more noted for its Wailuku River, one of four rivers and streams that run through separate valleys and are together referred to as Nā Wai ʻEhā (the Four Great Waters). "Kaulana Nā Wai ʻEhā" (Famous Are the Four Great Waters) is made up of four streams—Waikapū (Water of the Conch), Wailuku (Water of Destruction), Waiʻehu (Water Spray), and Waiheʻe (Squid Liquid)—that irrigated the largest continuous area of loʻi kalo (wetland taro farms) in all of Hawaiʻi, considered the pinnacle of Hawaiian agriculture. Loʻi kalo is a renewable and sustainable mode of Hawaiian farming that makes use of intricate ʻauwai (irrigation canals) to irrigate a diversity of kalo and an array of other plants and animals but then returns this water back to the stream or river. This fresh water, rich with nutrients from having traveled through the loʻi, then flows to the shoreline, mixing with saltwater to create brackish water essential to the health of fisheries and reefs. Centuries of creative practices have shaped knowledge of the specific environmental features of Nā Wai ʻEhā, with positive implications for the overall ecology of the island from mountain to ocean. For more than ten centuries, the vast cultivation of different varieties of taro—the food staple and elder sibling of Kānaka ʻŌiwi—nourished one of the largest and densest populations on the island.[5]

In the latter half of the nineteenth century and the early twentieth century, however, sugar planters claimed ownership of these rivers. White settler planters, seeking infrastructure for a burgeoning sugar and water industry, diverted water away from Kanaka ʻŌiwi communities to arid areas of the island in order to expand the industrial production of sugar sold on the U.S. market.[6] Cutting off access to the required amount of water necessary for loʻi kalo, these water diversions had devastating genocidal effects on Kānaka ʻŌiwi, preventing Hawaiian foodways from continuing. Yet, this original sin of primitive accumulation, the historical robbing of a way of life via water diversion, did not succeed in eliminating local residents' continued knowledge and memory of another way of organizing Nā Wai ʻEhā. In 2004, taro farmers calling themselves the Hui o Nā Wai ʻEhā and environmentalists of Maui Tomorrow, supported by a nonprofit public-interest environmental law firm, Earth Justice, petitioned for the restoration of these four streams and rivers to counter environmental degradation, recharge rapidly depleting groundwater sources, and support Hawaiian modes of life in the area. Despite a long fight, in 2014, these water protectors were successful in restoring twenty-five million gallons per day of water back to these four rivers and streams. This was the first time water had flowed from mountain to ocean in 150 years.

Although the water struggle at Nā Wai ʻEhā and the Kepaniwai Heritage Gardens seem to have nothing to do with each other, the overall story told at the heritage gardens justifies the diversion of water by representing Kanaka ʻŌiwi knowledges and ways of life as primitive and dead in the past. As a museum, garden, and park, the heritage gardens offer visitors a totalizing view of global sites within a six-acre stretch, yet it also obscures the visitor's view of the largest water diversion from ʻĪao Valley. Materially and symbolically, the visitor is limited from viewing the park's obstruction of a Hawaiian *way of life*, one that has historically and currently been hindered by the expropriation of water just behind the Kepaniwai Heritage Gardens. This chapter argues that the heritage gardens should be seen as a kind of "poetics of primitive accumulation." Similar to the way landscape paintings functioned ideologically during the enclosure movements in Europe, the heritage gardens are a form of material culture whose purpose is to legitimate a transition from an Indigenous land-based economy to a settler capitalist one.[7] By portraying Kanaka ʻŌiwi ways of life as irrelevant to the present and dead in the past, while preventing visitors from seeing the environmental and social impact of the water diversions, the Kepaniwai Heritage Gardens exhibit the same Hawaiian ways of life that it itself makes impossible.

In this way, the gardens facilitate settler and imperial violence; they foreclose any alternative Hawaiian futures besides those determined and constrained by the settler state. The work of restoring Kanaka ʻŌiwi place-based economies and foodways, as opposed to the Kepaniwai Heritage Gardens representing Hawaiian ways of life as dead in the past, offers land-based economies as viable futures for Hawaiʻi. There is significant grassroots interest in sustaining memory and a commitment to another way of life and knowing. Much like Kapiliokakaʻe, those fighting for the complete return of water to Nā Wai ʻEhā trouble the common-sense logics of an unsustainable, increasingly war-obsessed, capitalist system.

MULTICULTURAL SETTLER COLONIALISM AND THE KEPANIWAI HERITAGE GARDENS

The settler state theatrics of the Kepaniwai Heritage Gardens sits at the crossroads of U.S. empire, where settler state formation and U.S. imperialism convene. Within this context, we can examine the role liberal multiculturalism plays as a moral regime that facilitates settler colonialism and global imperial structures.[8] The gardens are thus a means of analyzing liberal multiculturalism in connection with the industries—tourism and militarism—that utilized Hawaiʻi's racial diversity to their ideological advantage.

The history of the Kepaniwai Heritage Gardens—including the planning, construction, and cultural politics of them—is cultural evidence of hegemony in its active and formative process, the seeming poststatehood success of liberal antiracist movements opposed to the forms of white supremacy more prevalent during the territorial period.[9] Although I offer a critique of liberal multiculturalism, exposing its local relations to Kanaka ʻŌiwi dispossession and its global maintenance of imperial formations, this liberalism was formed through an important antiracist political struggle against white supremacy. Primarily, however, I contend with the complex ways in which enunciations of Kanaka ʻŌiwi histories are interrupted or rearranged by another marginalized liberal Asian American historical narration. Examining their projects and aims in complex relation helps us to be mindful of the different ways these variegated groups relate to settler state formation and projects of empire without losing sight of the ideological collisions and moments of solidarity. In fact, it was a moment of solidarity that kept Kepaniwai from being paved over as a real estate development in the prewar period.

In 1940, developer John Duarte planned to divide Kepaniwai into sub-divisions for luxury homes including "small Hawaiian style cottages for weekenders." Such plans led to community protest. The Maui Hawaiian Women's Club opposed Duarte's plan, advocating instead to turn the valley into a public park—a Native strategy that residents were using to block the encroachment of real estate development. The Maui Hawaiian Women's Club wrote letters to other community groups asking for support to designate Kepaniwai a public park.[10] Many supported them, including the Maui Rotary Club, Chamber of Commerce, Young Buddhist Association, Junior Chamber of Commerce, and Maui Lions Club, who together through a dime campaign raised nearly $2,000. My mother recalls that my grandmother, Masako Inouye, participated in collecting money for the campaign. Petitions opposing the subdivisions received thousands of signatures, and through a combination of property exchanges and selling county lands, Kepaniwai was eventually turned into a public park owned by Maui County.[11]

A different historical moment, however, shaped by new arrangements of race and capitalism, turned Kepaniwai into a tourist destination. On Maui, Alexander and Baldwin together with Amfac, two of the Big Five, began converting sugarcane and pineapple fields into large-scale resorts. In *Land and Power in Hawaii: The Democratic Years*, George Cooper and Gavan Daws explain that after the "Democratic Revolution," Japanese Americans and Chinese Americans in the Democratic Party gained political power but had no land and limited amounts of capital, while the Big Five had large tracts of land and capital but were limited politically. These groups thus created numerous partnerships, or huis, in Hawai'i. Individuals imagined by a general public to be on opposite ends of the political spectrum collaborated on a variety of tourism development projects and a substantial portion of these partnerships targeted Maui for profit.[12] This new historical bloc worked with the county, state, and federal governments to build large-scale infrastructure to support the new and lucrative (for some) tourism industry, much of which included the creation of tourist attractions to lure tourists and get them to stay longer. With the admission of Hawai'i as a U.S. state, the annual number of tourists to Hawai'i increased by an average of 20 percent per year between the years 1958 and 1973 (from 171,000 to 2,631,000).[13] Statehood, indeed, made it possible for Hawai'i's tourism industry to grow exponentially.

By the 1960s, Maui's notoriety as a tourist destination increased. Richard Tongg, award-winning landscape architect, designed the Kepaniwai Heritage Gardens with an eye toward increasing travel to Maui while supplying "international cultural interest to entice tourists to spend an extra day on the Valley Isle, adding to Maui's economy."[14] Although overall travel to the neighbor islands (other than Oʻahu) decreased by 8 percent, overall travel to Maui rose 16 percent by 1961.[15] Significantly, Richard Tongg is the brother of Rudy Tongg, an entrepreneur who helped found Aloha Airlines, increasing interisland air travel to the neighbor islands by competing with the Hawaiian Airlines monopoly.[16] Through such familial and economic relations, during the construction of the heritage gardens, Aloha Airlines added a third jet plane to its fleet. Heritage and tourism, indeed, are interconnected industries. The heritage industry lures tourists by creating exhibits that can transform places into tourist destinations that, in turn, increase the profit potential of the overall tourism industry.[17]

Transforming Kepaniwai into a tourist destination required making the site visually appealing to tourists. Built with federal, state, and county funding, the Kepaniwai Heritage Gardens' exotic diversity of non-European populations makes them unique. Richard Tongg determined that ʻĪao Valley was "vast enough to compare with Yosemite in California," a site worthy enough to memorialize the "large number of immigrants who came to Hawaii."[18] The heritage gardens use the "vast" valley as a backdrop to tell a story about immigration to Hawaiʻi. Yet, they do all of this at a memorial site for Kanaka ʻŌiwi dead.

Placing the valley within a broader Hawaiian temporal scope, many Kānaka ʻŌiwi view it as a storied landscape with deep historical significance and spiritual meaning, as opposed to the triumphant multicultural landscape narrative. ʻĪao Valley has long been revered as a sacred site where twenty-four generations of aliʻi were buried alongside those deemed to possess mana.[19] Kapiliokakaʻe, the boulder who refused to move for the bulldozer, was part of the preparation for those entombed in ʻĪao Valley. Through interviews in the ʻĪao area in 1924, anthropologist J. F. G. Stokes learned, "Flesh was stripped from the bones, burned to ashes which were placed in a deep pool in the upper stream. The pool was called Kapela. The bones were dried on a large rock called Kapili-o-Kakae, and then wrapped in tapa and encased with braid."[20] The bones were then placed in burial caves that remain hidden in ʻĪao.

Furthermore, the Kepaniwai Heritage Gardens were built on the exact site of a 1790 battle between Kamehameha and Kalanikupule, during which Kamehameha from the island of Hawai'i, armed with cannons and muskets, slaughtered Maui warriors who, in previous battles, had outmatched the Hawai'i island forces. Named after this battle, Kepaniwai translates as the "damming of the waters," caused by the bodies of the thousands who died in the stream. Thus, at a site of Kanaka 'Ōiwi death now lies a heritage garden teeming with settler life. It is here that one can identify a moment where settler subjects are attempting to work through their anxieties and obsessions in material cultural form.[21] By placing the heritage gardens at Kepaniwai, settlers occupied it with an outwardly clear conscience for producing gardens that espouse liberal multicultural tolerance and preserve Indigenous culture through the Kanaka 'Ōiwi exhibit.

It is for some of these reasons that in 1960 the Central Maui Hawaiian Civic Club opposed the construction of a Japanese Tea Garden, arguing that it would be more appropriate for a Hawaiian garden to exist there. In letters to the newspaper, the Hawaiian Civic Club explained that "back in the 1400's Iao Valley was designated as the burial place of kings," further stating that the name 'Īao means "of the dawn" and that the interpretation of the word is closely associated with Kanaka 'Ōiwi sacred beliefs. Inez Ashdown, a member of the Hawaiian Civic Club who also was a part of one of the last families who lived Kaho'olawe before being removed by the navy, pointed out, "Everything in the ['Īao] valley and all of the names are sacred to the people who know its history."[22] The Central Maui Hawaiian Civic Club appealed to the general public, via the *Maui News*, to reconsider the building of the Japanese Tea Garden. The Japanese Tea Garden was the first garden created at the park, laying the precedent for the creation of the other gardens: "We were amazed to learn that the reclamation of forestland now in progress is to build a Japanese Tea Garden. We appreciate Japanese art, and are glad to assemble the art of the entire world BUT . . . the tombs of the greatest Ali'i (royalty) are still hidden in Sacred 'Īao Valley. It is a sacred valley hallowed by deification ceremonies and burial of Hawaiian Kings. . . . We do not feel that anything but a Hawaiian Garden would be appropriate in a Hawaiian Temple of the Dead!"[23] Given the burials in the valley and other sacred sites, the group argued that it would be more appropriate to create a Kanaka 'Ōiwi garden to project cultural and spiritual meanings into the future, as opposed to building over them. Maintaining Kanaka ʻŌiwi historical and cultural continuity with this valley was denied, however, as these aims collided with the county's ostensible celebration of the heritage of all groups.

After the park's construction, Ashdown wrote in the *Honolulu Star-Bulletin* that while the park serves as a "playground" for tourists, to many Kānaka ʻŌiwi it remains "the Sacred Valley of Worthy Kings whose consecrated bones are hidden in the Burial Caves of ʻIao."[24] In April of 1966, as plans for the Japanese Tea Garden were finalized, Hymie Meyer, a member of the Central Maui Hawaiian Civic Club, stated to the group, "Nalowale na mea a pau loa" (Everything is lost, or gone). Meyer added, "Let them have it! We shall join our aoʻao [family gods/ancestors] soon. It is all right."[25] In July of 1967, an announcement in the *Maui News* read, "Hawaiian Group Meets Tuesday on Garden Plan," explaining further that "suggestions for the Hawaiian garden and pavilion of the Kepaniwai Heritage Gardens in Iao Valley will be *so heated* at a meeting scheduled Tuesday night in the Iao School cafetorium."[26]

Arguments for the construction of a Kanaka ʻŌiwi garden, as opposed to a Japanese Tea Garden, were made in a moment when liberal multiculturalism framed the rules of discourse for civil society. A "moral sensibility" demanded that good citizen-subjects commit to multicultural diversity, which was often defined in binary opposition to "monocultural" demands in the form of white racist assimilation or seemingly anachronistic Kanaka ʻŌiwi cultural and political claims.[27] The limits of this commitment to a liberal moral sensibility are exposed when the question of economic profit versus maintaining the cultural integrity of Hawaiian cultural and spiritual sites is posed. Jodi Melamed argues that liberal multiculturalism is a marker of legitimate privilege and universality; it has an uncanny ability to define those whom it dispossesses as "monocultural," a cultural stigma that can be used to justify different forms of violence.[28] Japanese American and Chinese American political ascendancy in the postwar period, coupled with a new need for tourist destinations, added up, in complicated ways, to the relegation of Kānaka ʻŌiwi to anachronistic ideological spaces, even as the tourism industry promulgated a popular image that embraced certain constrained formulations of the "native."

In the planning of the heritage gardens, each exhibit was imagined as showing these groups' "manner of farming and transportation and a natural landscape."[29] As such, the exhibits, not unlike ethnographic museums, signify ways of life or modes of production as objects that can be juxtaposed in hierarchical relation. This is to say that the initial plan for the heritage gardens was, much like world's fairs, to create a hierarchy of the world by juxtaposing different racial groups' modes of life, the different ways that these cultures provided for the basic necessities of life, in order to reduce race to culture, and tie the displays to "signifier[s] of the mind" with the natural supremacy of whiteness and capitalism.[30] The cultural politics of the heritage gardens not only aims to reflect an authentic example of these cultures but, further, to exhibit the power relationship between those who are silenced as objects of knowledge and those who are the producers of knowledge.[31] For instance, the New England saltbox house, complete with a white picket fence and American flagpole, represents the first American Calvinist missionaries who traveled from Boston to proselytize in the islands in 1820. The missionaries, vis-à-vis the house, are celebrated in the following ethnological description on a plaque in front: "Within fifteen years of their arrival, the ABCFM [American Board of Commissioners for Foreign Missions] missionaries had put the Hawaiian language into writing, established hundreds of schools, trained native Hawaiian teachers in Western ways, and printed textbooks, newspapers and government documents in Hawaiian." The purposeful juxtaposition of the New England missionary house with the Kanaka ʻŌiwi house in the background, combined with the description of missionaries as responsible for progress, portrays Kānaka ʻŌiwi as an affectable race, subject to the superior intellect of the more enlightened missionaries.[32]

Liberal multicultural forms of settler colonialism, however, had global implications in their articulation with U.S. imperialist ambitions for global hegemony during the Cold War. In this way, one can see how narrations of Hawaiʻi as a racially harmonious fiftieth state aided the projection of an image of the United States as distinct from the "monoculturalism" of other Western powers. This set Hawaiʻi's exotic characterizations to international memory through global circulation and publicity, while Kanaka ʻŌiwi political and cultural associations with Hawaiʻi were contained or misrepresented.

An outcropping rock profile of Cold Warrior President John F. Kennedy was dedicated in 1970 and was a popular tourist attraction located just above the Kepaniwai Heritage Gardens.[33] This rock profile, however, was previously hailed as that of a kahuna (priest) named Kauka'iwai who lived in the fifteenth century and is said to protect the ali'i burials in the valley. In June of 1963, Kennedy spoke from Hawai'i, as he viewed the islands as an appropriate "intra-racial backdrop" for his civil rights message challenging Alabama Governor George Wallace's refusal to desegregate the University of Alabama.[34] Only two days before his national presidential address calling for civil rights legislation, Kennedy spoke about "Negro-white relations" at a national conference in Honolulu, calling upon mayors of cities and counties to consider the economic value of racial harmony. Kennedy often made mention of Hawai'i's racial diversity, going so far as to state, "Hawai'i is what the United States is striving to be."[35] His "New Frontier" administration maintained a similar pronouncement for global diversity, wherein Kennedy argued that the goal of liberalism was to "help make the world safe for diversity."[36] With transnational support from foreign dignitaries including Imelda Marcos and Prince and Princess Hitachi of Japan, the Japanese Tea House was constructed in Kyoto, Japan, and the Chinese Pavilion was assembled in Taiwan before being shipped to Maui. Indeed, Kennedy is present in the heritage gardens, not only through the literal and figurative resignifying of sacred sites such as the profile of Kauka'iwai, but through the fact that the heritage gardens can be read simultaneously as a mosaic of races, a domestic expression of liberal multiculturalism via a "nation of immigrants" narration, and an international garden framed by U.S. global hegemony.[37]

Kennedy's pronouncement about future U.S. race relations using Hawai'i as a model constructs Hawai'i as both a "primitive" space against which to define U.S. modernity and an alternative modernity toward which the United States was striving. Such conflicting views of Hawai'i speak not to different but rather to concomitant representational strategies of settler colonialism and empire formation. That is to say, modern Hawai'i is no longer temporally behind the U.S. continent, but instead is made into a glorious future model for the United States *only after* liberal

Figure 5.3 Long determined to be the outcrop rock profile of Kaukaʻiwai, in 1970, it became known as the profile of John F. Kennedy, 2009. Photograph taken by the author.

multicultural settler state formation. For instance, in the book *Maui Remembers* the authors write: "As in ancient times, Wailuku retains much of its status as a population and government center and upholds its reputation as a combat site. The only difference is that, today, legal battles in Wailuku's courthouse replace the bloodshed of old."[38] The "peaceful multiculturalism" represented in the heritage gardens is thus defined against a portrayal of precontact Hawaiʻi as savage, reducing Kānaka ʻŌiwi to a caricatured people who solved their differences through bloodshed. As such, Kānaka ʻŌiwi are seen to lack, unlike the United States, the capacity to create harmonious and peaceful relations. In this way, settler colonialism and American exceptionalism are made evident in the heritage gardens' location—where once was war now exists peace—and the "bloodshed of old" is replaced by a seemingly nonviolent approach to resolving conflict through mutual understanding. Hawai'i becomes an object of knowledge that serves as evidence of the United States' ability to foster the cultural diversity of non-Europeans that previous colonial projects sought to extinguish. The United States is thus poised with the seeming democratic power and intelligence to arrange this multiplicity in peaceful harmony, globally.

While such liberal Cold War representations portray U.S. expansion as merely the spreading of democracy, U.S. influence in this region is structured instead by imperial domination and war, often made ideologically invisible by Cold War epistemes. Penny Von Eschen has argued that U.S. cultural hegemony is accompanied by a coercive force, specifically through a violent geopolitics of U.S. military power: "The view that culture was decisive in winning the Cold War assumes an illusory separation of the categories 'culture' and 'militarism.'"[39] While both the Kepaniwai Heritage Gardens and the Kennedy rock profile narrate the United States' ability to create a peaceful world based on reciprocal exchange and interdependence, this liberal multiculturalism is in fact a part of a developmentalist discourse propagated by liberal proponents, who belligerently asserted their military prowess to achieve U.S. global hegemony in the postwar period. With roots in the American progressive tradition, modernization theory was a social science discourse foundational to Cold War liberalism that sought to transport American ideas and institutions to "primitive" societies who needed guidance in development. The aim to espouse global liberalism was twofold: first, to integrate recently decolonized nation-states into capitalist market relations, and second, to prevent nations targeted for development from becoming communist.[40] Kennedy's aim to "make the world safe for diversity," was palatable so long as notions of diversity did not extend into economies outside of U.S. capitalism. In other words, what this particular form of liberal multiculturalism does is divorce modes of life from culture. Anything that disobeys U.S. global capitalism is perceived as a threat, what Ngugi wa Thiong'o succinctly formulates as: "accept theft, or death."[41]

Arguing that the Cold War is more than a historical event but also a knowledge project that determined the possibilities and impossibilities for "telling, querying and knowing," Jodi Kim further shows that the logics of the Cold War obfuscated the extreme violence of U.S. global hegemony. Using an Asian American critique as an "unsettling hermeneutic," a transnational analytic productive of both exposing the atrocities of the Cold War and locating Asian Americans within this violent genealogy of U.S. imperialism, this critical edge can help us think "against the grain of American exceptionalism and nationalist ontology." Kim argues, "While the master narratives of Asian migration to the United States chart a putatively desirable and desired teleology troped as the American Dream— an escape from an unstable, economically devastated, and politically repressive homeland to safe haven in an America full of freedom and opportunity—the home that one leaves often needs to be left precisely because of the havoc wreaked by U.S. imperialist intervention there."[42] Framing Asian American cultural politics as a site for "staging, imagining, and remembering differently" offers a critical lens through which to examine how the Kepaniwai Heritage Gardens are shaped not by peace but by a global landscape torn by U.S. militarism. In other words, by reading the heritage gardens against the grain, each national/ethnic structure also represents imperial relations established through the military violence of U.S. empire.

Through such an "unsettling hermeneutic," the Filipino nipa hut might symbolize the Philippine-American War and the genocidal U.S. military occupation of the Philippines. Such an occupation made Filipinos U.S. nationals of a war-torn country, thus available as exploitable labor for Hawaiʻi's sugar plantations.[43] The Japanese Tea Garden might highlight the forced opening of Japan in 1854 by U.S. Commodore Matthew Perry, which set in motion the Meiji restoration that displaced many Japanese to Hawaiʻi. And we cannot forget the firebombing of major cities and the atomic bombs that targeted Japanese civilians in World War II. The Korean pavilion is reminiscent of the Korean War, often referred to as the "Forgotten War," which resulted in over three million Korean civilian casualties, two million missing or wounded, and almost ten million Koreans separated from friends and relatives, with fewer than ten thousand subsequently reunited.[44]

The most recent addition to the heritage gardens speaks directly to a desire to intervene in a settler narrative. On January 16, 2013, the eve of the anniversary of the 1893 U.S. military–backed overthrow of the Hawaiian Kingdom, a group called Puʻuhonua o Iao created an altar in the Kepaniwai Heritage Gardens using an uncut stone that was strategically placed to represent the 1897 Kūʻē Petitions. The newest addition to the heritage gardens offers an unsettling reference point from which to uncover a critical history of settler colonialism and U.S. military occupation.

While the heritage gardens represent the U.S. presence in Hawaiʻi as bringing peace to both Hawaiʻi and the world, in opposition to Hawaiians' "bloodshed of old," many of Maui's multicultural residents have lost their lives in the service of the United States. Along Kaʻahumanu Avenue, the road that leads to the Kepaniwai Heritage Gardens, lies the War Memorial Stadium and Gym, with the names of the hundreds of Maui residents who died in World War I, World War II, the Korean War, the Vietnam War, and the Gulf War. At the time of writing, the names of soldiers who have been killed in the recent wars in the Middle East had yet to be engraved. Down the road from this memorial, at the Kaʻahumanu Shopping Center in the "Plantation Section," are the recruitment stations for the army, marines, navy, and air force. What is more, the recruitment stations are in aesthetic continuity with the heritage gardens, completed with *totan* roof and plantation-style design.

Not only have Maui residents lost their lives in U.S. wars, the U.S. military presence in the islands has made it a target of other imperialist nations. In U.S. national public memory, Pearl Harbor is defined as the only site in Hawaiʻi attacked by the Japanese military; but the fact that Maui was the site of three other attacks is not forgotten by most Maui residents. On December 15, 1941, and again on December 31, Japanese military submarines fired torpedoes onto the island, missing their primary targets, one of which was the town of Puʻunēnē. In 1942, however, a Japanese submarine successfully sank an army transport off of Maui, killing twenty-four men.[45]

Such attacks justified the U.S. military occupying the island with more than 200,000 soldiers from the marines, navy, army, and air force. The militarized landscape of Maui was interconnected to other militarized sites throughout the Pacific. With more than fifty military training sites on the island, Maui residents were eventually outnumbered four to one by military personnel. In preparation for fighting in the sugar fields of Saipan and Tinian, Maui plantation workers were used to teach marines how to maneuver through dense and sharp sugarcane as well as how to set cane fires. The key training site, however, was at the nearby island of Kahoʻolawe. Controlled by the navy, Kahoʻolawe was used for live-fire training exercises through which seamen rehearsed taking over islands in the Pacific from the Japanese. In fact, marines in the Fourth Division who fought in Iwo Jima named the first street rebuilt after U.S. occupation "Maui Boulevard."[46] Kahoʻolawe continued, after World War II, to be used for live-fire training exercises until Kanaka ʻŌiwi activists in the Protect Kahoʻolawe ʻOhana (PKO) occupied the island to stop the bombing and filed a successful lawsuit, halting the use of the island as a weapons range in 1990.

"THE DAMMING OF THE WATER": KEPANIWAI AND NĀ WAI ʻEHĀ

Kahoʻolawe is an island just eight miles to the south of Maui, and the hydrology between both islands are interdependent. In the last half of the nineteenth century, the island of Kahoʻolawe was used as a sheep pasture. By World War II, the U.S. Armed Forces were using it as a training ground and missile range. Each contributed to the elimination of once dense forests on both islands.[47] In 1909, an unnamed Kanaka ʻŌiwi woman from ʻUlupalakua on Maui explained that forests on the island of Kahoʻolawe previously attracted clouds to the island in the morning. By the afternoon, these clouds, laden with moisture, would travel across the channel to rain over ʻUlupalakua, an area on the leeward slopes of Maui. When both ranchers and the U.S. military eliminated the forests on Kahoʻolawe, the clouds no longer gathered over the island and the ecology at South Maui also went from wet to dry. These factors, combined with earlier deforestation of sandalwood, have left just 5 percent of the native forests in South Maui remaining.[48]

In a 1959 master plan for the economic development of Maui, a lack of water sources in South Maui was considered an obstacle for development. Planners stated that "the expansion of the water system for the Kīhei, Mākena, and Wailea areas must be considered," because the region was "served by a water system unable to take care of any material expansion of residential or agricultural activity."[49] As South Maui was targeted for the development of luxury resorts, the demand for water increased, but no adequate water sources could be found. In 1975, development companies building large-scale resorts struck a deal with Maui County's Board of Water Supply. Four companies—the Wailea Development Company; Seibu, a Japanese development company; and two Big Five corporations owned by C. Brewer and Alexander and Baldwin—were permitted to jointly finance a multimillion-dollar project drilling new wells into the 'Īao aquifer, for the benefit of South Maui, which is twenty-five miles away from 'Īao. The 'Īao aquifer was intended to support a renewable withdrawal of 36 million gallons per day (mgd) and consequently the county of Maui offered to build the infrastructure necessary to transport 19 mgd of water away from Nā Wai 'Ehā to South Maui luxury resorts. The estimate of 36 mgd was much higher than the actual 20 mgd that the aquifer could sustainably yield. This did not sway further development, however, and as tourism slumped, future developments were deemed necessary. Water extraction from the 'Īao aquifer rose to 20.5 mgd, and by 1985 salinity levels had increased, jeopardizing the entire aquifer; the State Water Commission threatened to seize control of the aquifer away from the county by designating it a water management area. That finally happened in 2008, when the state of Hawai'i determined that the water resources remained in jeopardy.

The diversion of water away from Native communities to arid areas for the purposes of development has a long role in settler state formation dating back to the expansion of the American West. The doctrine of prior appropriation, a frontier logic that developed in the mining camps there, not only discounted a Native American presence on and relationship to land and resources prior to settler encroachment but deemed Native peoples without rights as part of the wildlife itself. Donald Worster explains that the doctrine of prior appropriation meant a vested right to the water as a form of property: "Under the doctrine, it mattered not at all how far from the river he lived or how far he diverted the water from its natural course, mattered not at all if he drained the river bone-dry. There was only one rule in that appropriation: 'Qui prior est in tempore, potior est in jure'—he who is first in time is first in right."[50] The control of rivers for economic development was a colonial obsession that signified a mastering of nature and an assertion that settlers were more deserving of disputed space. Aiming to make the desert bloom, settlers claimed that it was wasteful to allow rivers to travel their natural path to the sea. President Theodore Roosevelt argued, "If we could save the waters running now to waste, the western part of the country could sustain a population greater than even the legendary Major Powell dreamed."[51] Major Wesley Powell, director of the United States Geological Survey from 1881 to 1899, believed that development in areas without adequate water sources set a dangerous precedent: "It would be almost a criminal act to go on as we are doing now and allow thousands and hundreds of thousands of people to establish homes where they cannot maintain themselves."[52]

While the doctrine of prior appropriation has never been instituted as law in Hawai'i, settler practices have enacted its logics.[53] Unlike water diversion projects on the U.S. continent, however, it was private groups that funded the transportation of water to arid areas for the purposes of agriculture, not the government. Sugarcane is considered a water-thirsty crop; one pound of sugar requires four thousand pounds of water, roughly five hundred gallons.[54] As a result, by 1866, only four years after the Wailuku Sugar Company was established, the production of taro in Nā Wai 'Ehā had been radically limited and the landscape drastically altered. Ty Kāwika Tengan, in his cultural report on these changes, notes an article in the *Nupepa Kuokoa* written in 1866: "DESPAIR! WAILUKU IS BEING DESTROYED BY THE SUGAR PLANTATION—A letter by S.D. Hakuole, of Kula, Maui arrived at our office, he was declaring that the land of Wailuku is being lost due to the cultivation of sugarcane. Furthermore, he states the current condition of once cultivated taro patches being dried up by the foreigners, where they are now planting sugarcane."[55]

At the turn of the twentieth century, water was seen as a vital new industry, and plantations employed gravel miners from California to mine 'Īao Valley for further groundwater sources.[56] Carol Wilcox notes that by 1920, the sugar industry was utilizing 1,200 mgd of surface and groundwater, compared with the entire city of Boston, which used 80 mgd in 1929.[57] Kapu'ala Sproat, attorney for Earth Justice, a nonprofit law firm that has fought steadily for the acknowledgment of water as a public trust asset, states that after statehood in 1959, judges were appointed who understood Hawaiian custom and tradition. In the landmark 1973 *McBryde Sugar Company v. Robinson* case, Chief Justice Kazuhisa Abe wrote the majority decision: Although both sugar companies could gain access to water, this did not translate into ownership of the water.[58] Instead, the state of Hawai'i held these waters as a public trust asset for the benefit of the entire community. In 1978, the Hawai'i Constitutional Convention created amendments that protected Hawai'i's natural resources, including water. In 1987, the state legislature enacted Hawai'i's Water

Figure 5.4 An empty Wailuku River in Paukūkalo near the shoreline, 2009. Photograph by the author.

Code, establishing a framework for water resource management based on protection and reasonable use.[59]

The seemingly pristine Wailuku River that flows through ʻĪao Valley does not entirely continue out of the valley. Huge grates that extend the width of the river, despite favorable rulings at the Hawaiʻi Supreme Court, continues to divert this water for golf courses, resorts, and new real estate subdivisions. Tourists who visit ʻĪao will most likely marvel at the natural beauty of both the valley and Wailuku River. At the opposite end of Wailuku River, however, they would find it filled in with concrete, where life cannot exist and very little water reaches the ocean. Kaleikoa Kaʻeo, interviewed in the award-winning documentary *Noho Hewa*, calls this an "environmental crime."

> Life actually comes from that mix of that fresh and salt water. And you have of course the production of seaweed. And from the small seaweed of course then you have smaller fish that's eaten by the big fish that's eaten by the Kanaka. . . . "Hahai no ka ua i ka ululaʻau." Rain follows the trees. If the trees are gone, that means the rain is gone. If

you got no rain in the uplands then you got no rain in the lowlands. And having no rain in the lowlands of course has a direct effect on the amount of life that's being produced.

While the amount of water returned to Nā Wai 'Ehā continues to be negotiated over, there are a total of nineteen rivers and streams on the east side of Maui where ditches prevent water from traveling mauka to makai, mountain to sea. Many of the fish, shrimp, and snails in Maui's streams and rivers are diadromous, which means they use both fresh- and saltwater in their life cycles; but they often die because they are unable to make their way back upstream. After storms hit, however, Skippy Hau, a member of the Hui o Nā Wai 'Ehā, scoops up these otherwise doomed species and drives them five miles upstream to release them into the fresh water.

Many residents of Nā Wai 'Ehā have long been at the forefront of contentious debates over the political and ecological transformations and limits of the island. The original sin of water expropriation and competing claims for water tied to opposing modes of life continue to haunt Maui's present. In 2009, for example, a series of conversations and standstills took place that led to the landmark Hawai'i Supreme Court 2012 decision. Hawaiian Commercial and Sugar Company (HC&S) and Wailuku Water Distribution Company (formerly Wailuku Sugar Company), the two companies responsible for the original water diversions from Nā Wai 'Ehā, argued that without continued access of up to seventy million gallons of water a day, their already declining industry would be in jeopardy and eight hundred HC&S workers would be at risk of losing their jobs. The HC&S workers thus organized themselves into a group called Hui o Ka 'Ike, arguing desperately, "Our jobs are at stake, our very livelihood and the ability to support our families."[60] In June of 2010, the Water Commission ruled to return only a third of the stream flow for which the groups had petitioned, and to only two of the four streams—Waihe'e and Waiehu. Hōkūao Pellegrino, whose family lo'i (taro farm) sits along Waikapū stream, which did not receive any of the petitioned water, responded: "I may not be able to employ 800 people, but I can feed 800 people—if I was able to grow on all of my land."[61] Pellegrino's statement illuminates how the diversion of water alienates Native planters from the productivity of their land, thus maintaining an economy of scarcity requiring wage laborers buy their food at the market.

Hōkūao Pellegrino's response allows one to consider a preceding moment in time, an economy of abundance produced by a radically different notion of value, and a way of life that predates the settler state. Pellegrino's response and community work show that lo'i kalo in Nā Wai 'Ehā are viable foundations for Maui's future. Such knowledges are, in fact, grounded in both centuries-old wisdom and ongoing creative practices that do not seek to conquer, but rather work with nature. Not so much a process of "going back," this work is an articulation of Maui's present environmental, social, and economic problems in conjunction with ongoing Indigenous technologies and knowledge, particularly a deep and historical knowledge of the specific environmental features and making of Nā Wai 'Ehā. Kanaka 'Ōiwi ways of life illuminate other paths that are distinct from an overreliance on imported food—nearly 80–90 percent—and an economy sustainable only through militarism and environmental degradation. Viewing Indigenous ways of knowing as irrelevant to present problems replicates the initial logics of colonialism that subjugated these knowledges by deeming Kanaka 'Ōiwi culture a giant "wasteland of non-achievement."[62]

Together Hōkūao Pellegrino and his father, Victor Pellegrino, reopened their taro farm on their family property. Despite the fact that it had lain dormant since the 1930s, the original stones of the lo'i were still in place. With help from the community and from Charlie and Paul Reppun, farmer activists from the island of O'ahu who are well known for gaining water rights through an earlier Hawai'i Supreme Court case at Waiāhole, the lo'i was functioning within two days. Through research, Hōkūao Pellegrino learned that the lo'i was named Noho'ana, which translates as "a way of life." The two have used the farm since 2004 as a community resource to teach traditional subsistence, organic, and sustainable farming techniques to students from preschool to university level. Although the farm has twelve terraced patches that are up to 450 years old, Noho'ana was only able to restore and maintain three with the amount of water the plantation allows to flow into the stream. Victor Pellegrino has since written of the restoration of the lo'i in a children's book called Uncle Kawaiola's Dream. He writes that restoring the lo'i on Maui "is a dream shared by a small but growing number of passionate, dedicated, and hard-working people." Because 'āina (land) translates as that which feeds, Pellegrino's aim is to "return the 'aina for its intended use—agriculture."[63]

Unlike the Pellegrinos' Nohoʻana Farm, a living community resource that feeds and educates the community about a possible "history of the future," the Kepaniwai Heritage Gardens educate the public to see Kanaka ʻŌiwi ways of life as a thing of the past. Barbara Kirshenblatt-Gimblett makes the important point that heritage "depends on display to give dying economies and dead sites a second life as exhibition of themselves."[64] Celebrating the people of Hawaiʻi through *heritage* commemorates these ways of life as forever in the past, as archives of discredited and disregarded ways of living. Like earlier world's fairs, the ethnological structures that make up the heritage gardens are animated by a body of knowledge that categorizes so-called primitive and civilized peoples deploying cultural difference to reinforce a pyramidal view of the world.

Completely returning water to Nā Wai ʻEhā and implementing Hawaiian foodways can allow for the conditions that sustain life to flourish. The colonial trope of an island as a place untouched by time and replete with abundant resources, where life is easy, elides the fact that the Hawaiian Islands possess delicate ecosystems. On Maui, climate change has contributed to an increasing number of brush fires, floods, and droughts, as well as landslides on the neighboring island of Lānaʻi. Dipesh Chakrabarty argues that the distinction between human and nature is no longer tenable as humans become geological agents capable of enormous environmental change—"Humans now wield a geological force."[65] Histories that not only construct nature as the passive backdrop for human narratives but consider the environment's changes slow and subsequently inconsequential now need to contend with the human populations' potentially catastrophic impact on the environment. Since centuries of violent moments of contact with settlers have led to dramatic environmental shifts in their societies, such environmental transformations are nothing new to most Indigenous peoples.

In December of 2016, HC&S, the last-standing sugar plantation in Hawaiʻi, harvested its final crop of sugarcane, ending an industry that has radically altered the political, economic, and social landscape of Hawaiʻi for over a century. In what direction agriculture for the island of Maui and Hawaiʻi generally will take is still yet to be determined. Besides being one of the most militarized places in the world, Hawaiʻi is also the GMO capital of the world, and the two are absolutely intertwined and buttressed by the settler state. Mark Phillipson, an executive of Syngenta, states that:

"Almost any corn seed sold in the U.S. touches Hawaii somewhere."[66] Pesticides and GMO crops are themselves produced by a militarized food industry in which war and agriculture come together, after chemicals produced for war lost their markets and thus the industry reorganized itself to sell those chemicals as agrochemicals.[67] As such, mass-based resistance seeking to rein in an industrial GMO food industry has been taking place with varying results at different levels of government. In November of 2013, on the island of Kaua'i, residents called at the very least for the creation of buffer zones and a disclosure of GMO and pesticide testing, and won by a vote of 6–1 at the county level. Kaua'i's then mayor, Bernard Carvalho, however, vetoed this bill. Despite political maneuverings to prevent the possibility of the council overriding the bill, a successful override of the mayor's veto took place. Hawai'i County soon after set a ban on all GMO foods except papayas. Biotech corporations have promised to take these counties to court. The concern now is that if the counties lose their case, this could set a precedent that will prevent any counties from regulating biotech industries. Carvalho's veto took place despite the fact that students, teachers, and staff from Waimea Canyon Middle School complained of noxious odors between 2006 and 2008 coming from a Syngenta test field, leading at one point to the evacuation of their school and the hospitalization of students. A *New York Times* article reported this and also noted that doctors describe this area as having high rates of asthma, cancer, and birth defects. At the same time that this was occurring, in 2007, the state of Hawai'i leased roughly three thousand more acres of the previously mentioned seized crown lands to Syngenta at an average of fifty dollars per acre, per year, for the next twenty years.

The residents of Maui led a successful grassroots movement defeating a powerful bloc of biotech industry giants—Monstanto, Dow Agro Sciences, and the Council for Biotechnology. In November of 2014 a moratorium law was passed halting the growth, testing, and cultivation of genetically modified or engineered crops until an environmental and public health study finds these practices to be safe and harmless. The county of Maui, however, refused to enact the moratorium voted on by its county residents. A federal ruling eventually argued that the moratorium law passed by voters was beyond the county's authority. Industrial agriculture in the form of genetically engineered crops and the pesticides that accompany them stands to take the place of industrial sugar production.

By taking Indigenous knowledges seriously, however—expanding on a concern with the governance of human bodies to include bodies of land, water, delicate ecosystems, and nonhuman life forms necessary to the very conditions that sustain life—the project of returning water back to all streams and rivers poses the very real possibility that these farmers will be able to create a more viable mode of production that compliments, or perhaps exceeds, the relations of capitalism. Such possibilities serve as the foundation for materialization of a Kanaka ʻŌiwi way of life alternative to the settler state that would radically heal and restore the conditions of life. As is often noted, "water" in the Hawaiian language is *wai* and "wealth" in Hawaiian translates as waiwai. In a period when water wells on the island of Maui are drying up at the same time that residential areas and need for water are increasing, this shift in Hawaiian notions of value tells us that the environment, not profit, needs to determine the conditions of possibility for Hawaiʻi.

SCENES OF RESURGENCE

Slow Violence and Slow Resistance

In the political cartoon, "School Begins," drawn in January 1899 by Louis Dalrymple in the nationally popular magazine *Puck*, we are given a loaded illustration of the racial and gendered ideas that link U.S. settler-state formation to an emerging U.S. empire at the turn of the twentieth century. Drawing connections between various forms of colonial violence and dispossession—slavery, genocide, Manifest Destiny, immigrant exclusion, and war—the cartoon offers a rich and deliberate visual arrangement of differently racialized, gendered, and infantilized groups whose distorted images are used as evidence of white supremacy. The image illustrates the point that the transition from Native territories to U.S. territories and then to statehood is underpinned by a developmental discourse of race and gender—the linear evolution of containing primitive nonwhite peoples and replacing them through white settlement under the guise of future progress, order, and democracy. The cartoon was first printed on the eve of the Philippine-American War to sway public opinion and influence Congress to fund the genocidal conquest of the Philippines. Though the historical moment that produced this political cartoon at the turn of the twentieth century and our current moment should not be equated, we remain literate to the constellation of signs and symbols drawn in this cartoon over a hundred years later.

The lesson for 1899 viewers, bolstered by the assemblage of imperial images and histories, is captured in the writing on the blackboard at the back of the classroom: "The consent of the governed is a good thing in

Figure 6.1 "School Begins," *Puck*, 1899. Cartoon by Louis Dalrymple.

theory but very rare in fact. England has governed her colonies whether they consented or not. By not waiting for their consent she has greatly advanced the Worlds civilization. The U.S. must govern its new territories with or without their consent until they can govern themselves." Along the periphery, yet central to the overall white-supremacist ideology of the illustration, are "distinct yet densely interconnected political geographies" of racial and imperial power.[1] A Native American caricature who reads a book upside down is figured as unassimilable and tied to a history of land dispossession and genocide. A Black caricature washing a window invokes a history of chattel slavery and/or exploitable labor. The Chinese caricature is figured as studious yet excluded from the classroom, referencing general anti-immigrant sentiment but specifically the 1882 Chinese Exclusion Act, a federal law that barred Chinese laborers from entering the United States. Taken together, these images nurture, in the citizenry's imagination, a genocidal project of white supremacy that justifies the continuity of settler colonialism in the continental United States with the occupation of island nations in 1898 and 1899.

Within the spatial arrangement and developmental logics of a school, depicting Uncle Sam as a benevolent teacher gives him the colonial authority to categorize, instruct, and discipline his students. Central to the illustration is Uncle Sam's "new class in Civilization"—the Philippines, Hawai'i, Puerto Rico, and Cuba—who appear unruly, infantilized, and dark. The masculine military represented through Uncle Sam's stick looms over them, ready to discipline his students with corporal punishment. The orderly, mostly white and female students figured as U.S. territories and states—Arizona, California, Texas, New Mexico, and Alaska—serve as a backdrop from which to amplify the unruliness of the newer territories. Such juxtapositions are exemplary of what Amy Kaplan has called manifest domesticity, "the stable haven or feminine counterbalance to the male activity of territorial conquest."[2] In the move from masculine conquest to feminine domesticity there is the elision of the Native lands and sovereignties invaded by settler states. This settler colonial discourse of U.S. territories and states continues to erase or infantalize other political powers, despite the fact that they have the radical possibilities to address many of the fail-forward problems of the settler state. These possibilities persist in spite of genocidal formations because Native peoples have refused various colonial impositions in favor of another form of governance. As Audra Simpson (Kanawà:ke Mohawk) argues, "There is more than one *political* show in town."[3]

In 1960, on the opening day of the legislative session of the newly minted state of Hawai'i, Kamokila Campbell submitted to the state senate a vision and message she had received from the goddess Pele. Her statement was inserted into the public record by Senate President William H. Hill and read to the Senate by clerk Walter G. Chuck. Kamokila wrote that she had never previously received a visit from Pele, but had always been surrounded by "queer and incredible incidents." She explained that in the face of such supernatural occurrences, "with the assistance of the old sages and knowledge given me by my mother and grandmother, I have been able to work out miraculous results." Kamokila explained that she first received a vision of Pele in 1959 on the morning of November 9, and recalled her mother's instruction to, at times like these, call aloud the names of those she thought were appearing to her. Kuaihelani Campbell was said to have explained, "When you mention the correct name the vision will suddenly disappear."[4] After calling different names, she called the name *Pele*, and the vision disappeared. Taking this as a sign, Kamokila traveled to Kīlauea Crater on the island of Hawai'i, where Pele instructed her to transmit this message to Kānaka 'Ōiwi: "My people, my beloved people of Hawaii nei, I am here with you in all the attributes of womanhood, to alert, guide and protect you, the present and future generation against the many pitfalls that could engulf you in hasty decisions and spectacular progress." Stating that the "affairs of state are in such a tangled mess," Pele warned of a hidden agency "being drawn toward us led by a strong desire for possession." Pele closed with a challenge: "Now that we are at the crisis of our destiny, are we to fall into oblivion?"[5] Pele's visit to Kamokila took place a week prior to one of the most dramatic eruptions at Kīlauea crater. Indeed, Kamokila's message to the state legislature considers the volcanic eruption as Pele's own protest against statehood. Kamokila is not seeking multicultural inclusion of a Hawaiian voice into the settler state; rather, an effect of her statement is to subvert the self-imaginings of the seemingly mature settler state of Hawai'i on its very first day. She instead appeals to a feminine power whose expanse of time can be measured in the partial creation of land itself. Far from Lorrin A. Thurston's 1893 depictions of Pele in his "Kilauea Cyclorama," used to narrate the 1893 U.S. military–backed overthrow and campaign for annexation, Kamokila's invocation of Pele—as numerous mana wahine scholars have shown—refuses the "strong desire for possession" underwriting alternatives to heteropatriarchal forms of settler colonialism and occupation.[6]

Throughout 1960, legislators determined that the year was to be spent celebrating U.S. statehood. On the Fourth of July in 1960, the state of Hawai'i held a flag ceremony where they replaced the recently changed U.S. flag that had forty-nine stars, marking Alaska's statehood in 1958, with the new flag that had fifty stars. This flag ceremony was a reenactment of the program held on August 12, 1898, when the Hawaiian national flag was lowered and the U.S. flag was raised. In a press release for the 1960 event, organizers of the flag ceremony refer to 'Iolani Palace as a "scene of both great happiness and sorrow throughout the history of Hawaii."[7] The "sorrow" mentioned includes the 1898 flag ceremony, which is widely remembered as a moment when Kānaka 'Ōiwi who were present publicly grieved over the occupation of their nation. Noenoe K. Silva shows that the three hui who protested annexation—Hui Kālai'āina, Hui Aloha 'Āina, and the Hui Aloha 'Āina o Nā Wāhine—boycotted this ceremony, and still the flag ceremony made U.S. officials nervous enough that they called for U.S. troops to flank the palace.[8] Kathleen Dickenson Mellen quotes one American reporter as describing the 1898 flag ceremony as having the "tension of an execution."[9] In 1960, 'Iolani Palace served as the backdrop for the settler state, welcoming statehood by reenacting the alleged annexation of Hawai'i in 1898. Such theatrics would seemingly settle the wrongs that had been committed by the United States. Prior to the event, Hawaiian Lieutenant Governor James Kealoha put out a call asking for those who were in attendance at the first flag ceremony on August 12, 1898, to participate as special guests of the new state. One of the three sailors who raised the U.S. flag at the 1898 ceremony was eager to attend, as were many of the children of legislators of the Provisional Government. How Fo Chong, however, expressed a desire to attend but was less celebratory of the actual day in 1898. She explained that she "witnessed the lowering of the Hawaiian flag slowly during which . . . the middle-aged and the elderly Hawaiian women wept with their heads bowed."[10]

Lieutenant Governor James Kealoha welcomed the over ten thousand attendees in both English and Hawaiian and wore a bright red and yellow feathered cape, a symbol of Hawaiian ali'i. Also in attendance and given prominent space to be seen by all were members of Hawaiian civic clubs. When the forty-nine-star flag was brought down, it was given to the Hawaiian civic clubs. While Kānaka 'Ōiwi were visually centered on stage, this was done only to simultaneously marginalize them to the past. That is, the legitimacy of the state of Hawai'i via settler state theatrics rested on showing Kānaka 'Ōiwi as at once no longer having claims to Hawai'i and yet central to welcoming and thus legitimizing U.S. control of Hawai'i. In this way, their constrained participation portrayed U.S. statehood as emblematic of the expansion of democracy, rather than the continuance of occupation.

In Governor William F. Quinn's speech he talked about the relationship between Hawai'i statehood and anticolonial movements for independence. Quinn argued that the admission of Hawai'i as a U.S. state should serve as inspiration for nationalist movements aiming for decolonization.

> The nations which have thrown off the yoke of colonialism in the past fifteen years have an inevitable pattern which they must follow if they would have the success with their independence that we have had with ours. . . . Free men should be working men . . . building men . . . creating men . . . men who are raising their standard of living and shaping the economic stability of their country. . . . [The fiftieth star] stands for

a place where peoples of every nationality and culture have learned to live in harmony with each other. We are proud that we have not found this difficult to do. Now it is our task to show the rest of the world that any community, or country can prosper regardless of the racial ancestry of the people who comprise it.[11]

Hawai'i's admission as a U.S. state played a key role in expanding empire; the Cold War liberal multiculturalism that Hawai'i became an example of allowed for such acts of imperialism to be recoded in the language of decolonization. Arguing Hawai'i's admission as a U.S. state to be a "success" with "independence," Quinn referenced Cold War hotspots such as the Republic of Congo and the Philippines, saying that the industrial revolution, capitalism, and democracy all bring economic stability and are a "must" for newly decolonized nations. Quinn made these statements despite the fact that U.S. statehood occurred in Hawai'i not because of stability, but because of numerous rounds of economic depressions strung together through a fail-forward logic that viewed incorporation as a resolution to economic crisis or expansion.

Quinn concluded by stating that Hawai'i would play a leadership role in global politics by serving as the location for the East-West Center, which broke ground in 1961 at the University of Hawai'i at Mānoa. According to Lyndon B. Johnson, the East-West Center served as the "meeting place for the intellectuals of the East and West," where newly decolonized countries could learn about the benefits of U.S. capitalism and democracy. Quinn's speech making special note of the newly formed Republic of Congo is of strange relevance to the East-West Center. In defiant response to the building of the East-West Center, the Soviet Union built the Peoples' Friendship University in 1960, which was renamed the Patrice Lumumba University in 1961. The Soviet Union chose to rename their university after the Congolese independence leader and first prime minister who, after aiming to use the country's resources to benefit his own people, was assassinated in 1961. It is believed that the United States, Belgium, and England played a role in Lumumba's death. The renaming of the Soviet university after Patrice Lumumba sought to memorialize this fact. The flag ceremony on the Fourth of July in 1960, like other Fourth of July celebrations wherever the United States has extended its imperial reach, obscures both the settler-colonial and imperial makeup of the United States. Much of the stability that Quinn urged other nations to emulate, the prosperity that statehood was expected to accomplish, remains a future wish in this contemporary moment.

When the fiftieth anniversary of U.S. statehood was celebrated in 2009, the United States was in another major economic crisis.[12] The global financial crisis or Great Recession in 2008 led then Governor Linda Lingle and Attorney General Mark Bennett to successfully appeal to the U.S. Supreme Court to gain the ability to sell or transfer 1.2 million acres of so-called ceded lands. Such forms of settler accumulation by Native dispossession—the state of Hawai'i attempting to "sell or transfer" these contested lands to make up for a governmental deficit—took place alongside a kind of military Keynesianism and an ongoing War on Terror. In 2008, a newly elected Barack Obama, born and raised in Honolulu, offered a softer liberal form of U.S. imperial aggression.[13] The historical evolution of the settler state in Hawai'i remains tied to a series of contradictions and crises; rather than slowing down and deliberately resolving themselves, they split these contradictions by belittling and often criminalizing Kānaka 'Ōiwi for standing up to this dispossession. Because this dispossession is profitable for some, settler state theatrics interweave futurity into itself, whereby settlers justify a future wish to develop Native lands by arguing that they, themselves, are a more deserving power. It is thus difficult to come to terms with historical and present failures in terms of illegitimate sovereignty, economic crises, growing gaps between the rich and poor, and ecological crises.

An example of Kānaka 'Ōiwi being made to suffer the present consequences of the future wishes of settler elites is best exemplified in the desire to construct a massive Thirty Meter Telescope (TMT) atop sacred Mauna a Wākea. In 2014, a billion-dollar project to build a massive telescope on Mauna a Wākea, a mountain of major cultural and ecological significance, was blocked by hundreds and then thousands of protectors, who would not allow the construction of the TMT to desecrate this sacred place. A Final Environmental Impact Statement (FEIS) had already determined that, after thirty years of astronomy development atop Mauna a Wākea, "substantial, adverse and significant"[14] impacts had resulted. The new Thirty Meter Telescope was estimated to be the size of a football stadium. Under pressure, as many viewed it as economically necessary for Hawai'i, Governor David Ige proceeded with the TMT construction despite being in legal violation of the settler state's own rules that govern conservation districts like Mauna a Wākea.

Such a growing Kanaka ʻŌiwi movement to protect sacred places and fortified with genuine claims to independence and sustainability is often the target of settler state co-optation. The future wish of settler colonialism animated by a fail-forward pattern of capitalism still seeks to contain Hawaiian sovereignty through propaganda commissions. In 2011, Act 195—the First Nation Government Bill—was passed by the state of Hawaiʻi aiming to create a "Native Hawaiian governing entity." J. Kēhaulani Kauanui succinctly describes Act 195 as "legislation with a long genealogy stemming from efforts to undercut the restoration of the Hawaiian nation under international law."[15] This state legislation giving financial support to an opinion campaign for federal recognition is eerily similar to Act 115 of 1947, which financed the propaganda commissions for statehood. This is the same Act 115 that Kamokila challenged by filing a successful lawsuit against the territory (*Campbell v. Stainback et al.*) on January 17, 1948—the anniversary of the 1893 overthrow—seeking to stop taxpayer monies from being used to propagandize for statehood. Such attempts to limit Hawaiian self-determination to federal recognition are forms of colonial domination, as proven during the 2014 Department of the Interior (DOI) testimony regarding the "advanced notice of proposed rulemaking," a step in the process of federal recognition. The overwhelming majority of Hawaiians who testified stated clearly that they did not desire federal recognition.

SLOW RESISTANCE

As we reach a critical point in this planet's history, global systems of U.S. empire, militarism, and capitalism reveal themselves as accountable to abstract notions of profit and power, yet increasingly materialize in their capacity to destroy the resources and relations sustaining various forms of life. Indeed, there are few places in the world where the adverse effects of rising sea levels caused by capitalist development and climate crisis are felt so dramatically as they are in the island archipelagoes of Oceania. Such forms of ecological crises—climate change, rising sea levels, deforestation, species extinction—are attritional and often go unnoticed. Rob Nixon terms such forms of environmental violence "slow violence," which are not spectacle driven and thus do not capture the media or public's attention.

How might the environmental degradation described by "slow vio-lence" be addressed in the slow and deliberate work of rebuilding differ-ent economies and modes of life? By a kind of slow resistance, the Native resurgence of loko iʻa (fish ponds) and loʻi kalo (taro farms) sets up future generations to succeed by addressing environmental crises in a manner that is mindful of capitalism's destruction of the very conditions neces-sary for life. In a system that is not sustainable either economically or environmentally, how might we create space for Kanaka ʻŌiwi and other forms of Indigenous resurgence to chart new sustainable ways of living for the twenty-first century? How do we begin to replace unsustainable ways of living with alternative ways that are sustainable?

By taking into account Native epistemes, histories, and knowledges, we can transform ways of knowing with implications for ways of observing and dismantling the material force of settler colonialism, particularly in-justices that are often obfuscated or ideologically invisible to non-Natives, the very groups who seemingly stand to benefit. As Native Pacific cul-tural studies scholar Vicente M. Diaz has long argued and practiced, in geopolitical regions as diverse as Oceania and the Great Lakes, the survival and revival of traditional seafaring practices tied to the routes and roots of Indigenous peoples furnish an analytic to advance political and cultural struggles for "indigenous peoples in lands heavily settler-colonized."[16] Diaz argues that seafaring practices "provide an indige-nously ordered, anti-colonial praxis that can simultaneously furnish what we might identify as an indigenous oceanic critique of political programs that are centered firmly on nation-state based claims of sovereignty."[17] Although in a different context, Dene scholar Glen Sean Coulthard calls such place-based practices that can lead to radical alternatives to settler colonialism "grounded normativity": "Indigenous struggles against cap-italist imperialism are best understood as struggles oriented around the question of land—struggles not only for land, but also deeply informed by what the land as a mode of reciprocal relationship (which is itself in-formed by place-based practices and associated forms of knowledge) ought to teach us about living our lives in relation to one another and our surroundings in a respectful, nondominating and nonexploitative way."[18] Michi Saagig Nishnaabeg storyteller, scholar, and activist Leanne Simp-son argues that "Indigenous resurgence, in its most radical form, is na-tion building, not nation-state building, but nation building, again, in the context of grounded normativity by centring, amplifying, animating, and actualizing the processes of grounded normativity as flight paths or fugitive escapes from the violences of settler colonialism."[19] Indigenous resurgence within diverse contexts for grounded normativity shows how the routes and roots of diaspora and indigeneity can be thought through in "reciprocal relationship." Diaz argues that Native and non-Native relationships should be theorized in a manner similar to the fluid and relational dynamics of the ocean. Such possible forms of kinship can be articulated not in opposition, but rather in mutual interdependence. Indeed, Indigenous resurgence may serve as "flight paths or fugitive escapes" from the fail-forward violence of settler colonialism, as the search for alternatives to the current unsustainable system may bring us together.

Naomi Klein, for example, recounts in *This Changes Everything: Capitalism vs. the Climate* that in talking with climate activists in Bolivia, she began to consider that climate change could be a "galvanizing force for humanity, leaving us all not just safer from extreme weather, but with societies that are safer and fairer in all kinds of other ways as well."[20] Many scholars examining the Anthropocene—which is the idea that we live in an epoch where humans produce enough carbon emissions to be considered a geological force on the planet capable of producing climate change—together argue that we are in a historical moment where the environment cannot be treated as simply a backdrop to human events. And yet, it is also important to be aware that contrary to representations of the land in theorizations of the Anthropocene or even autonomous Marxist perspectives that pivot around the commons, the land that the settler state claims sovereignty and territoriality over is often under dispute and has a longer Native history of what Mishuana Goeman calls "spatial epistemologies," which remain ongoing and ever changing despite settler colonialism.[21] Goeman recalls the multidirectional and fluid spatial practices of her own Seneca family: "Unlike the maps that designate Indian land as existing only in certain places, wherever we went there were Natives and Native spaces, and if there weren't, we carved them out."[22] This is to say that U.S. colonialism is not an extension of the United States beyond its shore, but rather that everywhere that is seemingly determined by U.S. settler sovereignty has a longer history of Indigenous economies and knowledges that may serve as "histories of the future."[23]

This human-centric way of living productive of climate change is explained by Robert Warrior, who importantly notes: "The difference between the Osage way of living with the land and that of the invading Euro-Americans was a difference not so much between primitive people and advanced people, but between people who channeled their ornamentation urge toward balance with nature and those who, disastrously, considered the freedom of ornamentation to be a release from natural processes."[24] In this way, freedom and other supposed American virtues, whereby settlers liberate themselves from "nature" by conquering nature, is more accurately understood as a structure of feelings that disastrously accompany war and environmental degradation.

While speaking about the resurgence of place-based economies is considered unthinkable, if not romantic and idealistic, I want to end by turning briefly to my own family's genealogy and the alternative histories of Hawaiʻi's plantations, particularly those set on the margins of the state. Here, I aim to illuminate that alternative land-based economies were, in fact, central to many of the victories in Hawaiʻi's labor movement. In 1951, on the island of Lānaʻi, primarily Filipino laborers organized a strike. The pineapple industry refused a raise for their workers, and all Hawaiian Pine ILWU units, except those from the island of Lānaʻi, ratified the contract. Deciding to go out on strike alone, Lānaʻi strikers were openly mocked by ILWU leaders and were said to be as uncontrollable as "wildcats." Lou Goldblatt, the ILWU International Secretary-Treasurer, pointed out that the 1947 strike had the entire support of the ILWU and failed after lasting for only five days: "If you guys are thinking about a 30-day strike, or something like that is gonna win, forget it!"[25] The 1951 Lānaʻi pineapple strike was, according to Jack Hall—a key labor organizer and political insider—doomed to failure because it went against the major strategy of the ILWU, forming unified strikes across plantations that could then pressure planters to negotiate. Ninety days into the Lānaʻi strike, Hall attempted to speak on the strikers' behalf and negotiate a deal, which the workers later rejected. The strike, in total, lasted far beyond what was imaginable to ILWU leaders, totaling not five days, but 201 days. People say that you could smell the unharvested and rotting pineapple from the west side of Maui.

Indeed, the Lānaʻi workers were deliberately quiet about their strategy for waiting out the plantation. At the first meeting after voting to go out on strike, the chairman of the Strike Strategizing Committee, Pedro de la Cruz, whom ILWU leaders described as a man "who couldn't talk," began by asking those in attendance to divide themselves according to those who knew how to fish, hunt, and plant, and these three committees were charged with feeding the strikers. Furthermore, according to Noboru Oyama, a Hawaiian Pineapple Company manager at the time, Filipino laborers by the 1930s had already established the Federation Camp, a fishing village with homes made entirely out of driftwood and scrapped lumber, but more importantly, capable of subsisting entirely through fishing and planting. Indeed, much of the marine life in Hawai'i was already familiar to them from the Philippines. My great-grandparents, Sabas and Crispine Bibilone, were part of this camp; I believe this is similar to the maroon societies talked about in the Black radical tradition.

The Strike Strategizing Committee, with the support of the Federation Camp, had already anticipated the tactics of management and utilized a wholly different strategy from that of the ILWU leaders, one that allowed their resistance to be literally fed from the land, and, in this way, allowed the land to set the conditions of possibility. Thus, because Filipino laborers were able to anticipate the tactics of management and create a land-based economy—what the Zapatistas refer to as the "material conditions of resistance"[26]—they were not vulnerable to plantation managers who alienated them from their wages. The strategy of the Lāna'i workers was considered so "brilliant" that plantation managers believed it was developed by the ILWU union leaders, not the Lāna'i laborers themselves. Ultimately, the Lāna'i strike managed to gain a fifteen-cent increase, three cents higher than their original demand, and secured industry-wide bargaining, with all pineapple workers receiving the same benefits as the Lāna'i strikers. This strike is sometimes referred to as a "happy strike." While some of this might be attributed to a kind of nostalgic "memory without pain," workers were not living according to capitalist time and had, in fact, built a large bamboo structure where more than three hundred were able to communally share their meals. Such alternative histories not only articulate Indigenous and labor aims together, but build on past struggles in ways that allow non-Native peoples to be accountable to present Kanaka 'Ōiwi movements that engage in the alternative worlds that are often disqualified as nonsensical. This is an example of what might be possible in place-based struggles that take a capacious non-human-centric and nonstatist view of a politics of affinity. Ways of seeing are often guided intimately by ways of knowing, which are themselves shaped by a pedagogy of history, culture, and one's position within the cultural politics of the everyday.

In the summer of 2015, there was a string of media articles reporting the "unthinkable and unprecedented" three Category 4 hurricanes swirling simultaneously in the Pacific Ocean. It is ironic that the size and strength of extreme weather patterns are described as "unthinkable and unprecedented," at the same time that moves to create land-based economies to counter climate crisis are also disqualified as "unthinkable and unprecedented." Is it any wonder, then, at a time when alternatives to global capitalism are most needed, and Kānaka ʻŌiwi and other Native peoples possess such alternatives, that Native knowledges are often disqualified from being seen as such? These challenges and demands for more robust forms of affinity use an analysis of settler colonialism not for a politics of blame and accusation but to open our worlds to a plurality of possibilities outside of the dimming futures set in motion by the settler state. By taking seriously a Kānaka ʻŌiwi movement for deoccupation, we can create another future, and in the creation of an alternative future, I believe we can bring to fruition worlds that are not yet thinkable.

NOTES

PREFACE: "STATEHOOD SUCKS"

1. Jodi A. Byrd, *The Transit of Empire: Indigenous Critiques of Colonialism* (Minneapolis: University of Minnesota Press, 2011), xxxvi.

2. Vine Deloria Jr. and Clifford M. Lytle, *The Nations Within: The Past and Future of American Indian Sovereignty* (New York: Pantheon Books, 1984).

3. Chalmers Johnson, *The Sorrows of Empire: Militarism, Secrecy, and the End of the Republic* (New York: Metropolitan Books, 2005), 4; David Vine, "The United States Probably Has More Foreign Military Bases Than Any Other People, Nation, or Empire in History," *The Nation*, September 14, 2015.

4. Stephen Kinzer, *Overthrow: America's Century of Regime Change from Hawaii to Iraq* (New York: Henry Holt, 2006).

5. Jokay Dowell, "Hundreds Oppose Centennial Celebration at Capitol," *Cherokee Phoenix*, November 19, 2007; see also Jeffrey Burton, *Indian Territory and the United States, 1866–1905: Courts, Government, and the Movement for Oklahoma Statehood* (Norman: University of Oklahoma Press, 1995).

6. "Capitol Events Mark 150 Years of Minnesota Statehood," *Twin Cities Pioneer Press*, May 11, 2008; "Waziyatawin: Take Down Fort Snelling," Minnesota Public Radio Interview, June 28, 2016.

7. Waziyatawin, *What Does Justice Look Like?: The Struggle for Liberation of Dakota Homeland* (St. Paul, MN: Living Justice Press, 2008), 3–4.

8. Suzan Shown Harjo, "American Indian Land and American Empire: An Interview with Philip J. Deloria," in *Nation to Nation: Treaties between the United States and American Indian Nations*, ed. Suzan Shown Harjo, 12–13 (New York: National Museum of the American Indian, 2014).

9. Bill Ashcroft, Gareth Griffiths, and Hellen Tiffin, "Settler Colony," in *Post-Colonial Studies: The Key Concepts* (New York: Routledge Taylor and Francis Group, 1998), 210–12.

10. See Manu Vimalassery, "The Wealth of Natives: Towards a Critique of Settler-Colonial Political Economy," in *The Settler Complex: Recuperating Binarism in Colonial Studies*, ed. Patrick Wolfe, 173–92 (Los Angeles: UCLA American Indian Studies Center, 2016).

11. John Patrick Leary, *A Cultural History of Underdevelopment: Latin America in the U.S. Imagination* (Charlottesville: University of Virginia Press, 2016), 27.

12. See Sarah Vowell, *Unfamiliar Fishes* (New York: Riverhead Books, 2011), 219.

13. Mark Niesse, "Hawaii Celebrates 50 Years of Statehood: Celebrates Anniversary of Bill Making It the 50th State, Though Protestors Not Cheerful," *Associated Press*, March 19, 2009.

14. Niesse, "Hawaii Celebrates 50 Years of Statehood."

15. Wayne Kaumualii Westlake, "Poems from Down on the Sidewalk in Waikiki," in *Westlake: Poems by Wayne Kaumualii Westlake*, ed. Mei-Li M. Siy and Richard Hamasaki (Honolulu: University of Hawaiʻi Press, 2009), 138; various artists in *Down on the Sidewalk in Waikiki: Songs From Wayne Kaumualii Westlake's Poems*, 2014, CD.

16. Joan Conrow, "Another Side of Statehood: A Native Son Comes Home to Fill a Void During Statehood Celebrations," *Honolulu Weekly*, August 12, 2009.

17. Noelani Goodyear-Kaʻōpua, "Introduction," in *A Nation Rising: Hawaiian Movements for Life, Land, and Sovereignty* (Durham, NC: Duke University Press, 2014), 4–5; see also Leilani Basham, "Ka Lāhui Hawaiʻi: He Moʻolelo, He ʻĀina, He Loina, a He Ea Kākou," *Hūlili: Multidisciplinary Research on Hawaiian Well-Being* 6 (2010): 54.

18. As quoted in Manulani Aluli-Meyer, *Hoʻoulu: Our Time of Becoming* (Honolulu: ʻAi Pōhaku Press, 2014).

INTRODUCTION

Epigraph: *Campbell v. Stainback et al.*, 38 Haw. 310 (1949): 311; "Public Funds Misused, Says Kamokila," *Honolulu Star-Bulletin*, January 17, 1948.

1. Diana Leone, "Statehood Celebration at Palace Gets Heated," *Honolulu Star-Bulletin*, August 19, 2006.

2. Peter Sur, "Group to Protest Strykers," *Hawaii Tribune-Herald*, November 9, 2009; "Uranium Revelation Upsets Isle Activists," *Honolulu Star-Bulletin*, January 6, 2006.

3. Winona LaDuke and Sean Aaron Cruz, *The Militarization of Indian Country* (East Lansing: Makwa Enewed, 2012).

4. Mark Niesse, "Peaceful Protests Greet Admissions Day," *Honolulu Star-Bulletin*, August 21, 2009.

5. *Hawaii et al. v. Office of Hawaiian Affairs et al.*, 556 U.S. (2009).

6. Newlands Resolution of 1898, 55th Cong. (1898).

7. Some Hawaiians argue that they are not "homeless" but rather "houseless" since Hawai'i is their home.

8. Kenneth R. Conklin, "Hawaii Statehood—A Brief History of the Struggle to Achieve Statehood, and Current Challenges," *Hawaiian Sovereignty*, accessed August 29, 2010, www.angelfire.com/hi2/hawaiiansovereignty/statehoodhistandcurr .html; Andrew Walden, "Hawaii Statehood Day 2006," *Hawaiian Sovereignty*, accessed September 29, 2017, www.angelfire.com/planet/bigfiles40 /statehoodday2006.html.

9. Robert McElrath, interview, June 1986, transcript, "Perspectives on Hawai'i's Statehood" Oral History Project, Social Science Research Institute, University of Hawai'i at Mānoa, 117.

10. Secretary of Hawaii, "Results of Votes Cast (Three Propositions) Held 27 June 1959," Hawaii State Archives, Honolulu.

11. Mililani Trask, "Hawai'i and the United Nations," in *Asian Settler Colonialism in Hawai'i: From Local Governance to the Habits of Everyday Life in Hawai'i*, ed. Candace Fujikane and Jonathan Okamura (Honolulu: University of Hawai'i Press, 2008), 68–70.

12. Miguel Alfonso Martinez, *Study on Treaties, Agreements and Other Constructive Arrangements between Indigenous Peoples and Nation States* (Working Group on Indigenous Peoples, July 1997).

13. Homi K. Bhabha, "Introduction: Narrating the Nation," in *Nation and Narration*, ed. Homi K. Bhabha, 1–7 (New York: Routledge, 1990).

14. Pat Gee, "Hawaii Diversity Applauded at Statehood Celebration," *Honolulu Star-Bulletin*, March 19, 2009.

15. "Hawaii—A Bridge to Asia," *Businessweek*, May 13, 1950; "Hawaii: The New Breed," *Time*, March 23, 1959; James A. Michener, "Hawaii's Statehood Urged," letter to the editor, *New York Times*, January 1, 1959.

16. For nonstatist forms of decolonization see Judith Butler, "Palestine, State Politics and the Anarchist Impasse," in *The Anarchist Turn*, ed. Jacob Blumenfeld, Chiara Bottici, and Simon Critchley, 203–23 (London: Pluto Press, 2013); Noelani Goodyear-Ka'ōpua, "Kuleana Lāhui: Collective Responsibility for Hawaiian Nationhood in Activists' Praxis," *Affinities: A Journal of Radical Theory, Culture and Action* (July 2009): 1–28; Leanne Betasamosake Simpson, "Indigenous Resurgence and Co-resistance," *Critical Ethnic Studies* 2, no. 2 (fall 2016): 19–34.

17. Michel Foucault, "Politics and the Study of Discourse," in *The Foucault Effect: Studies in Governmentality*, ed. Graham Burchell, Colin Gordon, and Peter Miller, 59–60 (Chicago: University of Chicago Press, 1991).

18. Philip J. Deloria, *Indians in Unexpected Places* (Lawrence: University Press of Kansas, 2004), 14.

19. Willy Daniel Kaipo Kauai, "The Color of Nationality: Continuity and Discontinuities of Citizenship in Hawai'i" (PhD diss., University of Hawai'i, 2014); Keanu

Sai, "The American Occupation of the Hawaiian Kingdom: Beginning the Transition from Occupied to Restored State" (PhD diss., University of Hawai'i, 2008); Sai, "A Slippery Path towards Hawaiian Indigeneity: An Analysis and Comparison between Hawaiian State Sovereignty and Hawaiian Indigeneity and Its Use and Practice in Hawai'i Today," *Journal of Law and Social Challenges* 10 (fall 2008): 68–133; Kūhiō Vogeler, "Outside Shangri La: Colonization and the U.S. Occupation of Hawai'i," in *A Nation Rising: Hawaiian Movements for Life, Land, and Sovereignty*, ed. Noelani Goodyear-Ka'ōpua, Ikaika Hussey, and Erin Kahunawaika'ala Wright, 252–66 (Durham, NC: Duke University Press, 2014).

20. See Rosa Luxemburg, *The Accumulation of Capital*, trans. Agnes Schwarzschild (New York: Routledge, 2003), xxxv, 328–65; Jamie Peck, *Constructions of Neoliberal Reason* (Oxford: Oxford University Press, 2010).

21. Gabriel Paquette, "Colonies and Empire in the Political Thought of Hegel and Marx," in *Empire and Modern Political Thought*, ed. Sankar Muthu, 292–323 (New York: Cambridge University Press, 2014); Georg Wilhelm Friedrich Hegel, *Elements of the Philosophy of Right*, ed. Allen W. Wood (Cambridge: Cambridge University Press, 1991); Edward Gibbon Wakefield, *England and America: A Comparison of the Social and Political State of Both Nations* (London: W. Nicol, 1833); Wakefield, *A Letter from Sydney: The Principal Town of Australasia, Together with the Outline of a System of Colonization* (London: Joseph Cross, 1829); Wakefield, *A View of the Art of Colonization: In Letters between a Statesman and a Colonist* (Oxford: Clarendon Press, 1849).

22. See Karl Marx, *Capital: A Critique of Political Economy*, vol. 1, trans. Ben Fowkes and David Fernbach (Harmondsworth, UK: Penguin, 1976), 915–40; Marx, "Revolution in China and in Europe," *New York Daily Tribune* 14 (June 1853). See also David Harvey, interview by Neil Smith, "Reading Marx's *Capital* Vol 1—Chapters 26–33," 2012, podcast audio, http://davidharvey.org/2008/09/capital-class-12/.

23. Walter LaFeber, *The New Empire: An Interpretation of American Expansion, 1860–1898*, 35th anniversary ed. (Ithaca, NY: Cornell University Press, [1963] 1993), 19.

24. Michel Foucault, *Security, Territory, Population: Lectures at the Collège de France, 1977–78* (New York: Palgrave Macmillan, 2007), 264–65, 272.

25. Ann Laura Stoler, "Affective States," in *A Companion to Anthropology of Politics*, ed. David Nugent and Joan Vincent, 4–20 (Malden, MA: Blackwell, 2004).

26. Edward W. Said, *The Question of Palestine* (New York: Vintage, 1972), 9.

27. Marita Sturken and Lisa Cartwright, *Practices of Looking: An Introduction to Visual Culture* (Oxford: Oxford University Press, 2003), 189.

28. Kathleen Dickenson Mellen, MS 19, Bishop Museum Archives, Honolulu.

29. Malcolm MacNaughton, interview, June 1986, transcript, "Perspectives on Hawai'i's Statehood" Oral History Project, Social Science Research Institute, University of Hawai'i at Mānoa, 52–53.

30. I thank Nikhil Pal Singh for engaging with early versions of this manuscript and helping to illuminate these tensions.

31. Edward L. Bernays, "HAWAII—The Almost Perfect State?," *New Leader*, November 20, 1950; "Bernays Gives Analysis of Hawaii Community," *Hawaii Chinese Journal*, August 17, 1950; Dean Itsuji Saranillio, "Colliding Histories: Hawai'i Statehood at the Intersection of Asians 'Ineligible to Citizenship' and Hawaiians 'Unfit for Self-Government,'" *Journal of Asian American Studies* 13, no. 3 (October 2010): 283–309.

32. Christina Klein, *Cold War Orientalism: Asia in the Middlebrow Imagination, 1944–1961* (Berkeley: University of California Press, 2003), 250–51.

33. Joseph Garner Anthony, *Hawaii under Army Rule* (Stanford, CA: Stanford University Press, 1955).

34. Romanzo C. Adams, *The Peoples of Hawaii* (Honolulu: American Council Institute of Pacific Relations, 1935).

35. Roger Bell, *Last among Equals: Hawaiian Statehood and American Politics* (Honolulu: University of Hawai'i Press, 1984), 3.

36. Ronald T. Takaki, *Strangers from a Different Shore: A History of Asian Americans* (New York: Back Bay Books, 1998), 171.

37. Takaki, *Strangers from a Different Shore*, 10.

38. Takaki, *Strangers from a Different Shore*, 176.

39. Emphasis my own. R. Bell, *Last among Equals*, 293.

40. Haunani-Kay Trask makes this argument earlier than the extended article "Settlers of Color," which is based on her keynote at the 1997 Multi-Ethnic Literature of the United States (MELUS) Conference. Haunani-Kay Trask, "Settlers of Color and 'Immigrant' Hegemony: 'Locals' in Hawai'i," in *Asian Settler Colonialism: From Local Governance to the Habits of Everyday Life in Hawai'i*, ed. Candace Fujikane and Jonathan Okamura (Honolulu: University of Hawai'i Press, 2008); H.-K. Trask, "Writing in Captivity: Poetry in a Time of De-Colonization," in "Navigating Islands and Continents: Conversations and Contestations in and around the Pacific," ed. Cynthia Franklin, Ruth Hsu, and Suzanne Kosanke, special issue, *Literary Studies East and West* 17 (Honolulu: University of Hawai'i, 2000).

41. See J. Kēhaulani Kauanui, "'A Structure, Not an Event': Settler Colonialism and Enduring Indigeneity," in "Forum: Emergent Critical Analytics for Alternative Humanities," special issue, *Lateral: Journal of the Cultural Studies Association* 5, no. 1 (spring 2016): accessed March 18, 2018, http://www.doi.org/10.25158/L5.1.7. Studies that narrate the critique of settler colonialism without acknowledging Haunani-Kay Trask not only decenter a Native feminist scholar but actively erase her numerous contributions. Examples of such work include Judy Rohrer, *Staking Claim: Settler Colonialism and Racialization in Hawai'i* (Tucson: University of Arizona Press, 2016); Corey Snelgrove, Rita Dhamoon, and Jeff Corntassel, "Unsettling Settler Colonialism: The Discourse and Politics of Settlers, and Solidarity

with Indigenous Nations," *Decolonization: Indigeneity, Education and Society* 3, no. 2 (2014): 8, 11–12.

42. H.-K. Trask, "Settlers of Color," 46.

43. For a particularly strong critique of such arguments see Aiko Yamashiro, "Vigilant and Vulnerable Collaboration: Writing Decolonial Poetry in Hawai'i" (paper presented at the annual meeting for the Native American and Indigenous Studies Association, Mānoa, HI, May 18, 2016).

44. Eve Tuck and Wayne Yang argue that "settler moves to innocence are those strategies or positionings that attempt to relieve the settler of feelings of guilt or responsibility without giving up land or power or privilege, without having to change much at all." Eve Tuck and Wayne Yang, "Decolonization Is Not a Metaphor," *Decolonization: Indigeneity, Education and Society* 1, no. 1 (2012): 10.

45. Jodi A. Byrd, *The Transit of Empire: Indigenous Critiques of Colonialism* (Minneapolis: University of Minnesota Press, 2011), xxxviii–xxxix.

46. Benjamin J. Cayetano, *Ben: A Memoir, From Street Kid to Governor* (Honolulu: Watermark Publishing, 2009), 445; see Dean Itsuji Saranillio, "Why Asian Settler Colonialism Matters: A Thought Piece on Critiques, Debates, and Indigenous Difference," ed. Patrick Wolfe, special issue, "Settler Colonialism and Indigenous Alternatives in Global Context (2)," *Settler Colonial Studies* 3, no. 304 (2013): 280–94.

47. Haunani-Kay Trask, "The Color of Violence." *The Color of Violence: The INCITE! Anthology* (Boston: South End Press, 2006), 67.

48. Some argue that Asians in Hawai'i are not settlers, and do so by equating a history of Asian labor exploitation on Hawai'i's plantations with African histories of enslavement. Such analyses can unintentionally erase the specificities of *chattel slavery*. An example of such flattening of distinctions can be found in Nadine Ortega, "Settler Colonialism Still Defines Power in Hawaii: Who Benefits from Our Continued Disunity in Hawaii? A Handful of Mostly White Men," *Honolulu Civil Beat*, November 20, 2017.

49. H.-K. Trask, "Settlers of Color," 47–48.

50. Grace Lee Boggs, *Living for Change: An Autobiography* (Minneapolis: University of Minnesota Press, 1998), 152, 149.

51. Here I am informed by the conversations taking place in critical disability studies around the use of the term *crip*. See Alison Kafer, *Feminist, Queer, Crip* (Bloomington: Indiana University Press, 2013), 14.

52. This is not to be mistaken as an argument that "settler" is itself a personal choice. Rather, I hold no readymade answers for the correct political subjectivity that will facilitate non-Native peoples to examine structures of settler colonialism. See Dean Itsuji Saranillio, "Why Asian Settler Colonialism Matters: A Thought Piece on Critiques, Debates, and Indigenous Difference," ed. Patrick Wolfe special issue, "Settler Colonialism and Indigenous Alternatives in Global Context (2)," *Settler Colonial Studies* 3, no. 304 (2013): 282.

53. H.-K. Trask, "Settlers of Color," 50.

54. Tuck and Yang, "Decolonization Is Not a Metaphor," 1–40.

55. Fujikane, "Cartography and Moʻoʻāina as Method at the Intersection of Indigenous and Settler Colonial Studies" (paper presented at the American Studies Association Conference, Denver, CO, November 17–20, 2016).

56. See Walden Bello, Herbert Docena, Marissa de Guzman, and Marylou Malig, *The Anti-Development State: The Political Economy of Permanent Crisis in the Philippines* (London: Zed Books, 2006).

57. Dipesh Chakrabarty warns against thinking of ourselves, as the Anthropocene argument goes, as merely a geophysical force with no deliberate agency and urges us all to refuse the invitation of the Anthropocene. This refusal of the conditions of anthropogenic climate change can be understood in relation to Audra Simpson's theorizing around a politics of refusal. In her book *Mohawk Interruptus: Political Life across the Borders of Settler States*, Simpson argues: "They refuse the 'gifts' of American citizenship; they insist upon the integrity of Haudenosaunee governance" (Durham, NC: Duke University Press, 2014). And thus in this moment of the Anthropocene, perhaps, a deep engagement with abolishing a political economy of settler colonialism actually opens political possibilities via a range of human and nonhuman relations that are often foreclosed by the anthropocentric view of settler governance.

58. Tasha Hubbard, "Buffalo Genocide in Nineteenth-Century North America: 'Kill, Skin, and Sell,'" in *Colonial Genocide in Indigenous North America*, ed. Alexander Laban Hinton, Andrew Woolford, and Jeff Benvenuto, 292–305 (Durham, NC: Duke University Press, 2014).

59. Goodyear-Kaʻōpua, *Seeds We Planted*, 127.

60. See Noelani Goodyear-Kaʻōpua, Kenneth Gofigan Kuper, and Joakim "Joejo" Peter, "Together We Are Stronger: Hawaiian and Micronesian Solidarity for Climate Justice," forthcoming.

61. Candace Fujikane, Facebook page, accessed October 29, 2017, www.facebook .com/candace.fujikane; see also Candace Fujikane, "Mapping Wonder in the Māui Moʻolelo on the Moʻoʻāina: Growing Aloha ʻĀina through Indigenous and Settler Affinity Activism," *Marvels and Tales* 30, no. 1 (2016): 45–69.

62. Labrador, *Building Filipino Hawaiʻi*, 135.

63. Stuart Hall, "Gramsci's Relevance for the Study of Race and Ethnicity," *Journal of Communication Inquiry* 10, no. 2 (1986): 5–27; Hall, "On Postmodernism and Articulation: An Interview with Stuart Hall," *Journal of Communication Inquiry* 10, no. 2 (1986): 45–60.

64. Fujikane, "Asian American Critique and Moana Nui 2011," 4.

65. Patricio N. Abinales, *Making Mindanao: Cotabato and Davao in the Formation of the Philippine Nation-State* (Manila: Ateneo de Manila University Press, 2000); Rene G. Ontal, "Fagen and Other Ghosts: African-Americans and the Philippine-American War," in *Vestiges of War: The Philippine-American War*

and the Aftermath of an Imperial Dream, 1899–1999, 118–33 (New York: New York University Press, 2002).

66. Nerissa S. Balce, "Filipino Bodies, Lynching and the Language of Empire," in *Positively No Filipinos Allowed: Building Communities and Discourse*, ed. Antonio Tiongson, Ed Gutierrez, and Rick Gutierrez, 43–60 (Philadelphia: Temple University Press, 2006).

67. Dylan Rodríguez, "Inhabiting the Impasse: Racial/Racial-Colonial Power, Genocide Poetics, and the Logic of Evisceration," *Social Text* 33, no. 3(124) (2015): 33.

68. Manu Vimalassery, "Fugitive Decolonization," *Theory and Event* 19, no. 4 (2016), accessed March 13, 2018, https://muse.jhu.edu/article/633284.

69. John S. Whitehead, *Completing the Union: Alaska, Hawai'i, and the Battle for Statehood* (Albuquerque: University of New Mexico Press, 2004).

70. Saranillio, "Colliding Histories."

CHAPTER 1: A FUTURE WISH

1. Anne McClintock, *Imperial Leather: Race, Gender and Sexuality in the Colonial Contest* (New York: Routledge, 1995), 207–31.

2. Long before Hawai'i was imagined as a U.S. frontier after the 1893 overthrow, the larger Pacific, particularly Samoa, had been a site for the intersection of various empires, what Damon Salesa refers to as an "international frontier." See Damon Salesa, "Samoa's Half-Castes and Some Frontiers of Comparison," in *Haunted by Empire: Geographies of Intimacy in North American History*, ed. Ann Laura Stoler, 71–93 (Durham, NC: Duke University Press, 2006).

3. Ralph S. Kuykendall, *The Hawaiian Kingdom, Volume III: The Kalakua Dynasty, 1874–1893* (Honolulu: University of Hawai'i Press, 1967), 634; see also Andrew Farrel, "Preface," in Lorrin A. Thurston, *Writings of Lorrin A. Thurston*, ed. Andrew Farrel (Honolulu: Advertising Publishing Co., 1936), v.

4. "Cyclorama of Kilauea, What Mr. Thurston Is Doing in Chicago—The Effects of Advertising," *Daily Pacific Commercial Advertiser*, June 3, 1893; Hawaiian Bureau of Information, *Hawaii: The Paradise and Inferno of the Pacific* (Honolulu: Hawaiian Bureau of Information, 1892); Kuykendall, *Hawaiian Kingdom*, 634; Lorrin A. Thurston, *Writings of Lorrin A. Thurston*, ed. Andrew Farrel, 81–83 (Honolulu: Advertising Publishing Co., Ltd., 1936).

5. William Adam Russ Jr., *The Hawaiian Republic, 1894–98, and Its Struggle to Win Annexation* (Selinsgrove, PA: Susquehanna University Press, 1961), 220.

6. Frederick Jackson Turner, "The Significance of the Frontier in American History" (paper presented at the American Historical Association, Chicago, July 12, 1893).

7. Jeffrey Ostler, *The Plains Sioux and U.S. Colonialism from Lewis and Clark to Wounded Knee* (Cambridge: Cambridge University Press, 2004), 345.

8. Philip J. Deloria, *Indians in Unexpected Places* (Lawrence: University Press of Kansas, 2004), 62.

9. William Appleman Williams, *The Tragedy of American Diplomacy* (New York: W. W. Norton, [1959] 1972), 29. For a list of business periodicals and messages from the Harrison administration regarding the state of the economy, see Walter LaFeber, *The New Empire: An Interpretation of American Expansion, 1860–1898* (Ithaca, NY: Cornell University Press, [1963] 1998), 29, 151.

10. LaFeber, *New Empire*, 29.

11. LaFeber, *New Empire*, 15.

12. As cited in LaFeber, *New Empire*, 200.

13. LaFeber, *New Empire*, 19.

14. Theodore Roosevelt, *The Winning of the West, Volume 2: From the Alleghenies to the Mississippi, 1777–1783* (Lincoln: University of Nebraska Press, 1995); "Theodore Roosevelt's New Volume: The Winning of the West," *New York Times*, December 30, 1894; L. A. Thurston, *Writings of Lorrin A. Thurston*, 57.

15. Frederick Douglass, Irvine Garland Penn, Ferdinand Lee Barnett, and Ida B. Wells, *The Reason Why the Colored American Is Not in the World's Columbian Exposition* (Chicago: University of Illinois Press, 1999).

16. The response of the Provisional Government is not archived at the Hawai'i State Archive, but tensions existed between the Executive Advisory Council and the *Chicago Tribune* because of some editorials that criticized the Provisional Government's control of Hawai'i. Claude H. Wetmore to Executive and Advisory Councils of the Provisional Government of the Hawaiian Islands, March 30, 1893, "1893 Executive Advisory Councils: Petitions," Folder 6, Hawai'i State Archives; Claude H. Wetmore to Executive and Advisory Councils of the Provisional Government of the Hawaiian Islands, April 6, 1893, Folder 6, Hawai'i State Archives. Emphasis added.

17. Richard Halpern, *The Poetics of Primitive Accumulation: English Renaissance Culture and the Genealogy of Capital* (Ithaca, NY: Cornell University Press, 1991).

18. Haunani-Kay Trask, *From a Native Daughter: Colonialism and Sovereignty in Hawai'i*, rev. ed. (Honolulu: University of Hawai'i Press, 1999), 7.

19. Jonathan Kay Kamakawiwo'ole Osorio, *Dismembering Lāhui: A History of the Hawaiian Nation to 1887* (Honolulu: University of Hawai'i Press, 2002), 168.

20. Russ, *The Hawaiian Revolution, 1893–1894* (Selinsgrove, PA: Susquehanna University Press, 1992), 12.

21. Noel J. Kent, *Hawaii: Islands under the Influence* (Honolulu: University of Hawai'i Press, 1993), 47.

22. Kuykendall, *Hawaiian Kingdom*, 452–53.

23. Noenoe K. Silva, *Aloha Betrayed: Native Hawaiian Resistance to American Colonialism* (Durham, NC: Duke University Press, 2004), 123–63.

24. Silva, *Aloha Betrayed*, 128–29.

25. Kathleen Dickenson Mellen, *An Island Kingdom Passes: Hawaii Becomes American* (New York: Hastings House, 1958), 239.

26. Seats in the House of Nobles had a property requirement of $3,000 or annual income of $600 to either run for these offices or vote for them.

27. Kuykendall, *Hawaiian Kingdom*, 637. Emphasis added.

28. Russ, *Hawaiian Republic*, 131.

29. Eiichiro Azuma, *Between Two Empires: Race, History, and Transnationalism in Japanese America* (Oxford: Oxford University Press, 2005), 10–11.

30. Azuma, *Between Two Empires*, 20.

31. Russ, *Hawaiian Republic*, 130–77.

32. Azuma, *Between Two Empires*, 20.

33. Kathleen Dickenson Mellen, MS 19, Box 3.4, Bishop Museum Archives, Honolulu.

34. "A Petition Signed by Several Hundred Chinese Will Be Presented to the Councils Today, Asking That the Chinese in Hawaii Be Given the Voting Franchise," *Pacific Commercial Advertiser*, May 17, 1894.

35. Kuykendall, *Hawaiian Kingdom*, 534.

36. Kuykendall, *Hawaiian Kingdom*, 536.

37. James G. Blaine to James M. Comly, Department of State, December 1, 1881, in Lorrin A. Thurston, Miscellaneous Papers, M-144, Hawaii State Archives, Honolulu.

38. Patrick Wolfe, "Settler Colonialism and the Elimination of the Native," *Journal of Genocide Research* 8, no. 4 (2006): 388.

39. LaFeber, *New Empire*, 203.

40. LaFeber, *New Empire*, 205.

41. Mellen, *Island Kingdom Passes*, 288.

42. Robert W. Rydell, *All the World's a Fair: Visions of Empire at American International Expositions, 1876–1916* (Chicago: University of Chicago Press, 1984), 65.

43. Rydell, *All the World's a Fair*, 65.

44. Rydell, *All the World's a Fair*, 64.

45. Rydell, *All the World's a Fair*, 67.

46. Rydell, *All the World's a Fair*, 4.

47. Rydell, *All the World's a Fair*, 43–46.

48. Susan Buck-Morss, *The Dialectics of Seeing: Walter Benjamin and the Arcades Project* (Cambridge, MA: MIT Press, 1991), 58–59.

49. Rydell, *All the World's a Fair*, 59–60.

50. Maile Arvin points out that referring to Polynesians as Caucasians was actually used to justify white possession. See Maile Arvin, "The Polynesian Problem and Its Genomic Solutions," *Native American and Indigenous Studies* 2, no. 2 (2015): 27–56; figure 1.5 in Anne McClintock, *Imperial Leather*, 38.

51. Michael Adas, "From Settler Colony to Global Hegemon: Integrating the Exceptionalist Narrative of the American Experience into World History," *American Historical Review* 106, no. 5 (December 2001): 1692–720.

52. Ngũgĩ wa Thiong'o, *Decolonising the Mind: The Politics of Language in African Literature* (Oxford: Heinemann, 1981), 3.

53. Mellen, *Island Kingdom Passes*, 322.

54. Ernest Andrade Jr., *Unconquerable Rebel: Robert W. Wilcox and Hawaiian Politics, 1880–1903* (Niwot: University Press of Colorado, 1996), 219.

55. Rydell, *All the World's a Fair*, 4.

56. Buck-Morss, *Dialectics of Seeing*, 95.

57. Rydell, *All the World's a Fair*, 44.

58. William Cronon, *Nature's Metropolis: Chicago and the Great West* (New York: W. W. Norton, 1991), 343.

59. Turner, "Significance of the Frontier."

60. Michael Perelman, *The Invention of Capitalism: Classical Political Economy and the Secret History of Primitive Accumulation* (Durham, NC: Duke University Press, 2000), 13–91.

61. Joanna Brooks, *Why We Left: Untold Stories and Songs of America's First Immigrants* (Minneapolis: University of Minnesota Press, 2013), 19.

62. Wolfe, "Settler Colonialism and the Elimination of the Native," 392.

63. H.-K. Trask, "The Color of Violence," in *Color of Violence: The INCITE! Anthology* (Boston: South End Press, 2006), 82; see also Brendan C. Lindsay, *Murder State: California's Native American Genocide, 1846–1873* (Lincoln: University of Nebraska Press, 2012); David E. Stannard, *American Holocaust: Columbus and the Conquest of the New World* (New York: Oxford University Press, 1992), 144.

64. Jack N. Rakove, "Ambiguous Achievement: The Northwest Ordinance," in *Northwest Ordinance: Essays on Its Formulation, Provisions and Legacy* (Ann Arbor: Michigan State University Press, 1989). See Philip Schuyler to the President of Congress, July 29, 1783, Papers of the Continental Congress, item 153, vol. 3, f. 601–8, National Archives; George Washington to James Duane, September 7, 1783, in *The Writings of George Washington*, ed. John C. Fitzpatrick (Washington, DC: U.S. Government Printing Office, 1931), 27, 133–40.

65. Frederick Douglass, "Introduction," in *The Reason Why the Colored American Is Not in the World's Columbian Exposition*, ed. Frederick Douglass, Irvine Garland Penn, Ferdinand Lee Barnett, and Ida B. Wells (Chicago: Privately published, 1893), 9.

66. Jacqueline Goldsby, *A Spectacular Secret: Lynching in American Life and Literature* (Chicago: University of Chicago Press, 2006), 17.

67. Ida B. Wells, "Lynch Law," in *The Reason Why the Colored American Is Not in the World's Columbian Exposition*, ed. Frederick Douglass, Irvine Garland Penn, Ferdinand Lee Barnett, and Ida B. Wells (Chicago: Privately published, 1893), 29.

68. Wells, "Lynch Law," 29.

69. Goldsby, *Spectacular Secret*, 24.

70. John N. Low, *Imprints: The Pokagon Band of Potawatomi Indians and the City of Chicago* (East Lansing: Michigan State University Press, 2016); see also Matthew L. M. Fletcher, "Avoiding Removal: The Pokagon Band of Potawatomi Indians," in *Nation to Nation: Treaties between the United States and American*

Indian Nations, ed. Suzan Shown Harjo (New York: Smithsonian Books, 2014), 86–87.

71. Low, *Imprints*, 104.

72. Low, *Imprints*, 69–70.

73. Low, *Imprints*, 168–69.

74. Henry Yu, *Thinking Orientals: Migration, Contact, and Exoticism in Modern America* (New York: Oxford University Press, 2001).

75. Rydell, *All the World's a Fair*, 51.

76. Rydell, *All the World's a Fair*, 48–49.

77. Rydell, *All the World's a Fair*, 51.

78. Azuma, *Between Two Empires*, 18.

79. See Danika Medak-Saltzman, "Transnational Indigenous Exchange: Rethinking Global Interactions of Indigenous Peoples at the 1904 St. Louis Exposition," ed. Paul Lai and Lindsay Claire Smith, *American Quarterly* 62, no. 3 (September 2010): 593, 613.

80. Rydell, *All the World's a Fair*, 50–51.

81. Tom Coffman, *The Island Edge of America: A Political History of Hawai'i* (Honolulu: University of Hawai'i Press, 2003), 22.

82. Kuykendall, *Hawaiian Kingdom*, 110.

83. "Friends Abroad a Tribute to the Provisional Government," *Daily Pacific Commercial Advertiser*, April 10, 1893.

84. See Kuykendall, *Hawaiian Kingdom*, 536–37.

85. Years later, the Hawai'i territorial legislature would act on this same sentiment when it passed a bill urging Congress to pay the fares of "[C]aucasian farmers and farm laborers" to "diversify agriculture," but also to provide a "stronger local militia" for the "military defense of the United States." Senate Concurrent Resolution No. 9, offered on April 17, 1911, by A. F. Judd, adopted in the Senate, April 19, 1911, and House April 22, 1911.

86. L. A. Thurston, *Writings of Lorrin A. Thurston*, 81.

87. Cristina Bacchilega, *Legendary Hawai'i and the Politics of Place: Tradition, Translation, and Tourism* (Philadelphia: University of Pennsylvania Press, 2007), 93.

88. Bacchilega, *Legendary Hawai'i and the Politics of Place*, 93.

89. Marita Sturken and Lisa Cartwright, *Practices of Looking: An Introduction to Visual Culture* (Oxford: Oxford University Press, 2003), 195–96.

90. Frank H. Smith, *Art, History, Midway Plaisance and World's Columbian Exposition* (Chicago: Foster Press, 1893).

91. For an examination of Hawaiian performers at world's fairs, see Adria L. Imada, *Aloha America: Hula Circuits through the U.S. Empire* (Durham, NC: Duke University Press, 2012), 104–51.

92. F. Smith, *Art, History, Midway Plaisance*.

93. Imada, *Aloha America*, 130–31.

94. Kealani R. Cook, "Kahiki: Native Hawaiian Relationships with Other Pacific Islanders, 1850–1915" (PhD diss., University of Michigan, 2011), 182–83.

95. kuʻualoha hoʻomanawanui, *Voices of Fire: Reweaving the Literary Lei of Pele and Hiʻiaka* (Minneapolis: University of Minnesota Press, 2014), 132–33, 166; see also hoʻomanawanui, "Mana Wahine: Feminism and Nationalism in Hawaiian Literature," *Anglistica* 14, no. 2 (2010): 27–43.

96. Silva, *Aloha Betrayed*, 84.

97. Liliʻuokalani, *Hawaii's Story by Hawaii's Queen* (Honolulu: Mutual Publishing, 1990), 246–49.

98. Liliʻuokalani, *Hawaii's Story by Hawaii's Queen*, 291.

99. Lucy G. Thurston, *Life and Times of Mrs. Lucy G. Thurston, Wife of Rev. Asa Thurston, Pioneer Missionary to the Sandwich Islands, Gathered from Letters and Journals Extending over a Period of More than Fifty Years Selected and Arranged by Herself* (Ann Arbor, MI: S. C. Andrews, 1882), 218–19.

100. Silvia Federici, *Caliban and the Witch: Women, the Body and Primitive Accumulation* (New York: Autonomedia, 2004), 63.

101. Thomas Jaggar, *Volcanoes Declare War: Logistics and Strategy of Pacific Volcano Science* (Honolulu: Paradise of the Pacific, 1945).

102. Mellen, *Hawaiian Scrapbook* (Honolulu: Paradise of the Pacific, 1945), 32.

103. Vicente M. Diaz, *Repositioning the Missionary: Rewriting the Histories of Colonialism, Native Catholicism, and Indigeneity in Guam* (Honolulu: University of Hawaiʻi Press, 2010), 127.

104. F. Smith, *Art, History, Midway Plaisance*.

105. Silva, *Aloha Betrayed*, 173–76.

106. L. A. Thurston, *Writings of Lorrin A. Thurston*, 83.

107. Russ, *The Hawaiian Revolution*, 220.

108. *Aloha Magazine*, March/April 1979.

109. Meiric K. Dutton, *Hawaii's Great Seal and Coat of Arms* (Honolulu: Loomis House Press, 1960), 14.

110. Silva, *Aloha Betrayed*, 123–63.

111. L. A. Thurston, *A Hand-book on the Annexation of Hawaii* (Michigan: A. B. Morse Company, 1897), 5; Kent, *Hawaii*, 61.

112. Russ, *Hawaiian Republic*, 132.

113. Russ, *Hawaiian Republic*, 135.

114. Russ, *Hawaiian Republic*, 332.

115. Russ, *Hawaiian Republic*, 332.

116. L. Frank Baum, "The Wounded Knee Editorial," *Saturday Pioneer*, January 3, 1891; "'Oz' Family Apologizes for Racist Editorials," National Public Radio, August 17, 2006.

117. Roger Bell, *Last among Equals: Hawaiian Statehood and American Politics* (Honolulu: University of Hawaiʻi Press, 1984), 55.

CHAPTER 2: THE COURAGE TO SPEAK

1. Lorrin P. Thurston, "About Statehood," *Honolulu Advertiser*, November 16, 1940.

2. Lili'uokalani, *Hawaii's Story by Hawaii's Queen* (Honolulu: Mutual Publishing, 1999), 231.

3. Noel J. Kent, *Hawaii: Islands under the Influence* (Honolulu: University of Hawai'i Press, 1993), 69.

4. Ka Ho'okolokolonui Kānaka Maoli—Peoples' Tribunal Hawai'i, *The Tribunal*, Honolulu, Nā Maka o ka 'Āina, 1994, DVD.

5. Moon-Kie Jung, *Reworking Race: The Making of Hawaii's Interracial Labor Movement* (New York: Columbia University Press, 2006), 16.

6. Howard Zinn, *The Twentieth Century: A People's History* (New York: Perennial, 1980), 111.

7. Sumner J. La Croix, "The Economic History of Hawai'i: A Short Introduction," working paper, Department of Economics, University of Hawai'i, East-West Center, January 9, 2002.

8. The Jones-Costigan Act reduced the quota of sugar that Hawai'i planters were allowed to send to the United States and limited Hawai'i sugar planters to refining only 3 percent of their raw sugar locally. Unincorporated territories such as Cuba were allowed to refine 22 percent of their crop, and the Philippines and Puerto Rico were able to refine nearly 10 percent. See Roger J. Bell, *Last among Equals: Hawaiian Statehood and American Politics* (Honolulu: University of Hawai'i Press, 1984), 60.

9. Act 212 (S.L.H. 1935).

10. See Dean Spade, *Normal Life: Administrative Violence, Critical Trans Politics, and the Limits of Law* (Brooklyn, NY: South End Press, 2011), 102–15.

11. Piya Chatterjee and Sunaina Maira, "The Imperial University: Race, War and the Nation-State," in *The Imperial University: Academic Repression and Scholarly Dissent*, ed. Piya Chatterjee and Sunaina Maira (Minneapolis: University of Minnesota, 2014), 6–7.

12. Victor Bascara, "New Empire, Same Old University?: Education in the American Tropics after 1898," in *The Imperial University: Academic Repression and Scholarly Dissent*, ed. Piya Chatterjee and Sunaina Maira (Minneapolis: University of Minnesota Press, 2014), 60; see also Lauren Parnaby, "The Possessive Investment in Haoleness: The Performances of Haole on the University of Hawai'i, Mānoa and the Administration's Relationship with Haole Students as a Colonial University" (undergraduate honor's thesis, Department of Social and Cultural Analysis, New York University, 2016).

13. Michel Foucault, *The Courage of Truth: The Government of Self and Others II* (New York: Palgrave Macmillan, 2011), 12–13.

14. Ralph S. Kuykendall and A. Grove Day, *Hawaii: A History from Polynesian Kingdom to American Statehood* (Englewood Cliffs, NJ: Prentice-Hall, 1961), 289.

15. Brian McAllister Linn, *Guardians of Empire: The U.S. Army and the Pacific, 1902–1940* (Chapel Hill: University of North Carolina, 1997), 87–88.

16. Linn, *Guardians of Empire*, 87–88.

17. David E. Stannard, *Honor Killing: How the Infamous "Massie Affair" Transformed Hawai'i* (New York: Viking, 2005), 61.

18. John P. Rosa, "Local Story: The Massie Case Narrative and the Cultural Production of Local Identity in Hawai'i," *Amerasia Journal* 26, no. 2 (2000): 102.

19. Stannard, *Honor Killing*, 224.

20. Stannard, *Honor Killing*, 387.

21. "Sex in Hawaii," *Times Magazine*, April 18, 1932.

22. Caroline Elkins and Susan Pederson, "Introduction," in *Settler Colonialism in the Twentieth Century: Projects, Practices, Legacies*, ed. Caroline Elkins and Susan Pedersen (New York: Routledge, 2005), 4. Emphasis added.

23. Rosa, *Local Story: The Massie-Kahahawai Case and the Culture of History* (Honolulu: University of Hawai'i Press, 2014), 103.

24. As cited in Rosa, *Local Story*, 12.

25. Ruth Wilson Gilmore offers this definition of racism: "Racism, specifically, is the state-sanctioned or extralegal production and exploitation of group-differentiated vulnerabilty to premature death." See Gilmore, *Golden Gulag: Prisons, Surplus, Crisis, and Opposition in Globalizing California* (Berkeley: University of California Press, 2007), 28.

26. As cited in Roland Kotani, *The Japanese in Hawaii: A Century of Struggle* (Honolulu: Hawaii Hochi, 1985), 68.

27. Teresia Teaiwa, "The Ancestors We Get to Choose: White Influences I Won't Deny," in *Theorizing Native Studies*, ed. Audra Simpson and Andrea Smith (Durham, NC: Duke University Press, 2014), 44.

28. Robert Neal, "Hawaii's Land and Labor Problem," *Current History* 13 (October 1920–March 1921), 391.

29. J. Kēhaulani Kauanui, *Hawaiian Blood: Colonialism and the Politics of Sovereignty and Indigeneity* (Durham, NC: Duke University Press, 2008), 19.

30. Edward D. Beechert, *Working in Hawaii: A Labor History* (Honolulu: University of Hawai'i Press, 1985), 220–21.

31. Stanley D. Porteus and Marjorie E. Babcock, *Temperament and Race* (Boston: R. G. Badger, 1926).

32. For more of his construction of Australian aboriginals as "primitives," see Stanley D. Porteus, *Primitive Intelligence and Environment* (New York: Macmillan, 1937).

33. Stannard, "Honoring Racism: The Professional Life and Reputation of Stanley D. Porteus," *Social Process in Hawai'i* 39 (1999): 100.

34. Stannard, "Honoring Racism," 308.

35. Stannard, "Honoring Racism," 308.

36. Stannard, "Honoring Racism," 307.

37. Stannard, "Honoring Racism," 29, 49.

38. Stannard, "Honoring Racism," 49.

39. Stannard, "Honoring Racism," 308.

40. Stannard, "Honoring Racism," 49.

41. Stannard, "Honoring Racism," 101.

42. Elizabeth Dole Porteus, *Let's Go Exploring: The Life of Stanley D. Porteus, Hawaii's Pioneer Psychologist* (Honolulu: Ku Pa'a, 1991), 68.

43. Mary Cawte, "Craniometry and Eugenics in Australia: R. J. A. Berry and the Quest for Social Efficiency," *Historical Studies* 22 (1986): 49.

44. Cawte, "Craniometry and Eugenics in Australia," 49.

45. S. Porteus, "Possible Effects of Rate of Global Spin," *Perceptual and Motor Skills* 30 (1966): 503–9; see also E. Porteus, *Let's Go Exploring*, 170–71; Stannard, "Honoring Racism," 114.

46. Aileen Moreton-Robinson, *The White Possessive: Property, Power, and Indigenous Sovereignty* (Minneapolis: University of Minnesota Press, 2015), 126; see also Maile Arvin, "The Polynesian Problem and Its Genomic Solutions," *Native American and Indigenous Studies* 2, no. 2 (2015): 27–56.

47. "Thurston admitted that the island population was not homogenous and that a large proportion of it was unfit either for self-government or American citizenship" (Ralph S. Kuykendall, *The Hawaiian Kingdom, Volume III: The Kalakaua Dynasty, 1874–1893* [Honolulu: University of Hawai'i Press, 1967], 634).

48. See Siobhan Senier and Clare Barker, eds., *Journal of Literary and Cultural Disability Studies* 7, no. 2, special issue (2013).

49. Alison Kafer, *Feminist, Queer, Crip* (Bloomington: Indiana University Press, 2013), 30.

50. Noelani Goodyear-Ka'ōpua, "Protectors of the Future, Not Protestors of the Past: Indigenous Pacific Activism and Mauna a Wākea," *South Atlantic Quarterly* 116, no. 1 (January 2017); Kafer, *Feminist, Queer, Crip*, 1–46; Eve Tuck and Rubén A. Gaztambide-Fernández, "Curriculum, Replacement, and Settler Futurity," *Journal of Curriculum Theorizing* 29, no. 1 (2013): 80.

51. E. Porteus, *Let's Go Exploring*, ix.

52. Denise Ferreira da Silva, *Toward a Global Idea of Race* (Minneapolis: University of Minnesota Press, 2007), 1.

53. da Silva, *Toward a Global Idea of Race*, 117.

54. da Silva, *Toward a Global Idea of Race*, 117.

55. Jonathan Y. Okamura, "The Illusion of Paradise: Privileging Multiculturalism in Hawai'i," in *Making Majorities: Constituting the Nation in Japan, Korea, China, Malaysia, Fiji, Turkey, and the United States*, ed. Dru C. Gladney (Stanford, CA: Stanford University Press, 1998), 267.

56. Okamura, "The Illusion of Paradise," 269.

57. Christine Manganaro, "Assimilating Hawai'i: Racial Science in a Colonial 'Laboratory,' 1919–1939" (PhD diss., University of Minnesota, 2012), 286.

58. Thomas Wakefield Goodspeed, *A History of the University of Chicago, Founded by John D. Rockefeller: The First Quarter-Century* (Chicago: University of Chicago Press, 1916), 438.

59. Henry Yu, *Thinking Orientals: Migration, Contact, and Exoticism in Modern America* (New York: Oxford University Press, 2001), 80–83.

60. Yu, *Thinking Orientals*, 81.

61. Eduardo Bonilla-Silva and Gianpaolo Baiocchi, "Anything but Racism: How Sociologists Limit the Significance of Racism," in *Handbook of the Sociology of Racial and Ethnic Relations*, ed. Hernan Vera and Joe R. Feagin, 117–31 (New York: Springer U.S., 2007); Robert Ezra Park, "Our Racial Frontier on the Pacific," *Survey Graphic* 56 (May 1926): 192–96.

62. Yu, *Thinking Orientals*, 35; da Silva, *Toward a Global Idea of Race* (Minneapolis: University of Minnesota Press, 2007), 154–55, 157.

63. Yu, *Thinking Orientals*, 87.

64. Yu, *Thinking Orientals*, 80.

65. Yu, *Thinking Orientals*, 87–88.

66. R. Bell, *Last among Equals*, 115.

67. Manganaro, "Assimilating Hawai'i," 186.

68. Manganaro, "Assimilating Hawai'i," 164.

69. da Silva, *Toward a Global Idea of Race*, 158.

70. Manganaro, "Assimilating Hawai'i," 288.

71. George Wright, "The Statehood Issue," *Hawaii Hochi*, October 9, 1937.

72. Wright, "Statehood Issue."

73. Wright, "Statehood Issue."

74. "8th Hawaiian Products Show," *Honolulu Advertiser*, September 28, 1937.

75. *Voice of Labor*, October 7, 1937.

76. George Wright, "The Lid Comes Off," *Hawaii Hochi*, October 27, 1937.

77. Jung, *Reworking Race*, 108–10.

78. Jung, *Reworking Race*, 111.

79. "Hawaii Asks to Be Treated as Part of the United States and Not as a Foreign Country," Pacific Collection, University of Hawai'i Library; "Hawaii Outgrows the 'Political' Suit Given Her by Uncle Sam."

80. Wright, "He Doesn't Know Half of It!," *Hawaii Hochi*, October 10, 1937.

81. George Wright, *Hawaii Hochi*, October 19, 1937.

82. As quoted in Tom Coffman, *The Island Edge of America: A Political History of Hawai'i* (Honolulu: University of Hawai'i Press, 2003), 38.

83. U.S. Congress, Joint Committee on Hawaii, *Statehood for Hawaii: Hearings before the United States Joint Committee on Hawaii, Seventy Fifth Congress, Second Session, on Oct. 6, 8, 9, 12, 13, 15, 17–22* (Washington, DC: U.S. Congress, 1937), 59–60; see also *Voice of Labor*, October 7, 1937, 11.

84. U.S. Congress, *Statehood for Hawaii*, 79.

85. U.S. Congress, *Statehood for Hawaii*, 95–97.

86. U.S. Congress, *Statehood for Hawaii*, 95–97.

87. U.S. Congress, *Statehood for Hawaii*, 95–97.

88. U.S. Congress, *Statehood for Hawaii*, 60.

89. U.S. Congress, *Statehood for Hawaii*, 12, 13.

90. U.S. Congress, *Statehood for Hawaii*, 242.

91. U.S. Congress, *Statehood for Hawaii*, 242.

92. U.S. Congress, *Statehood for Hawaii*, 426.

93. U.S. Congress, *Statehood for Hawaii*, 579.

94. U.S. Congress, *Statehood for Hawaii*, 579.

95. U.S. Congress, *Statehood for Hawaii*, 431.

96. U.S. Congress, *Statehood for Hawaii*, 431.

97. U.S. Congress, *Statehood for Hawaii*, 431.

98. U.S. Congress, *Statehood for Hawaii*, 579.

99. Patrick Wolfe, "Nation and MiscegeNation: Discursive Continuity in the Post-Mabo Era," *Social Analysis* 36 (October 1994): 93–152.

100. U.S. Congress, *Statehood for Hawaii*, 173.

101. U.S. Congress, *Statehood for Hawaii*, 174.

102. Ty Kāwika Tengan, *Native Men Remade: Gender and Nation in Contemporary Hawai'i* (Durham, NC: Duke University Press, 2008), 45.

103. U.S. Congress, *Statehood for Hawaii*, 174.

104. U.S. Congress, *Statehood for Hawaii*, 284.

105. As cited in Jon M. Van Dyke, *Who Owns the Crown Lands of Hawai'i?* (Honolulu: University of Hawai'i Press, 2008), 256.

106. "'Statehood for Hawaii,' Letter from the Chairman of the Joint Committee on Hawaii, Transmitting Pursuant to Senate Concurrent Resolution No. 18: A Report of an Investigation and Study of the Subject of Statehood and Other Subjects Relating to the Welfare of the Territory of Hawaii, January 5, 1938" (Washington, DC: U.S. Government Printing Office, 1938), 33.

107. Stannard, *Honor Killing*, 78.

108. R. Bell, *Last among Equals*, 65.

109. "'Statehood for Hawaii,'" 94.

110. "'Statehood for Hawaii,'" 33.

111. Wright, "Lid Comes Off."

112. Wright, "Lid Comes Off."

113. By 1940 hostility against the territorial government had remained high. In August 1938 tensions between labor and the Big Five erupted into state violence in the "Hilo Massacre," in which fifty people, including many union members and even a child, had been gunned down by the police under orders from Sheriff Henry K. Martin. The territorial government did not take responsibility for the violence, and even beat a lawsuit filed by Kai Urutani against the police officers. The territorial government did not enjoy widespread popular support. R. Bell, *Last among Equals*, 73.

114. R. Bell, *Last among Equals*, 73–74.

CHAPTER 3: "SOMETHING INDEFINABLE WOULD BE LOST"

Epigraph: Jack de Mello and Kamokila Campbell, "Legend of Pele, the Fire Goddess," in *Legends of Hawai'i*, 1994, CD.

1. I refer to Alice Kamokilaikawai Campbell as Kamokila, as this was the name with which she was referred to by Hawaiians alive at this time. For instance, Sammy Amalu referred to her as "Alice Campbell, the Chiefess Kamokila." See Kaupiikauinamoku, "Song of Eternity: Kane Creates Hina, Who Became Mother of Gods," *Honolulu Advertiser*, January 2, 1956.

2. "New Theater to Feature Old Arts," *P. G. and E. Progress* 10, no. 8 (July 1933).

3. Anna Sommer, "Kamokila's Dream of Art Temple Turns Church into Little Theater," San Francisco Public Library, History Center, Biography Files (print collections), Vertical Files; "New Theater to Feature Old Arts."

4. Noelani Goodyear-Ka'ōpua, "Introduction," in *A Nation Rising: Hawaiian Movements for Life, Land, and Sovereignty*, ed. Noelani Goodyear-Ka'ōpua, Ikaika Hussey, and Erin Kahunawaika'ala Wright (Durham, NC: Duke University Press, 2014), 4.

5. Noenoe K. Silva, *Aloha Betrayed: Native Hawaiian Resistance to American Colonialism* (Durham, NC: Duke University Press, 2004), 130, 133, 148, 150, 161, 194.

6. Kathleen Dickenson Mellen, "The Incomparable Kamokila: Kathleen Mellen Recalls Mrs. Campbell's Greatest Coup d'Etat: She Blitzed the Election on Maui," *Paradise of the Pacific*, July 1962, 12.

7. Kaupiikauinamoku, "Song of Eternity: Kane Creates Hina, Who Became Mother of Gods," *Honolulu Advertiser*.

8. Roger J. Bell, *Last among Equals: Hawaiian Statehood and American Politics* (Honolulu: University of Hawai'i Press, 1984), 116.

9. See Ruth Wilson Gilmore, *Golden Gulag: Prisons, Surplus, Crisis, and Opposition in Globalizing California* (Berkeley: University of California Press, 2007), 24, 37–39, 78–86; Jodi Kim, *Ends of Empire: Asian American Critique and the Cold War* (Minneapolis: University of Minnesota Press, 2010), 24, 25.

10. Malcolm MacNaughton, interview, June 1986, transcript, "Perspectives on Hawai'i's Statehood" Oral History Project, Social Science Research Institute, University of Hawai'i at Mānoa, 52–53.

11. Noel J. Kent, "The Rules of Hawaii," *Hawaii Pono*, July 1971, 30.

12. Candace Fujikane, "Mapping Wonder in the Maui Mo'olelo on the Mo'o'āina: Growing Aloha 'Āina through Indigenous and Settler Affinity Activism," *Marvels and Tales* 30, no. 1 (2016): 57.

13. As cited in John S. Whitehead, "The Anti-Statehood Movement and the Legacy of Alice Kamokila Campbell," *Hawaiian Journal of History* 27 (1993): 43–63. Whitehead writes very differently on statehood in this article than in his book *Completing the Union: Alaska, Hawai'i, and the Battle for Statehood* (Albuquerque: University of New Mexico Press, 2004).

14. "Senator Campbell Is Not a Candidate for Delegate, She Says," *Honolulu Star-Bulletin*, September 4, 1944.

15. Moon-Kie Jung, *Reworking Race: The Making of Hawaii's Interracial Labor Movement* (New York: Columbia University Press, 2006), 98–105.

16. Jung, *Reworking Race*, 82.

17. Roland Kotani, *The Japanese in Hawaii: A Century of Struggle* (Honolulu: Hawaii Hochi, 1985), 115.

18. As cited in Tom Coffman, *The Island Edge of America: A Political History of Hawai'i* (Honolulu: University of Hawai'i Press, 2003), 84–87.

19. Bosley Crowther, "The Screen in Review; 'Go for Broke!,' Tribute to War Record of Nisei Regiment, Opens at the Capitol," *New York Times*, May 25, 1951.

20. Metro-Goldwyn-Mayer Publicity Department, *Facts for Editorial Reference about the Filming of M-G-M's "Go for Broke!,"* University of Hawai'i Hamilton Library, 1.

21. Robert Pirosh, *Go for Broke! Script*, University of Hawai'i Hamilton Library, 2.

22. Pirosh, *Go for Broke! Script*, 6.

23. Pirosh, *Go for Broke! Script*, 7.

24. Pirosh, *Go for Broke! Script*, 7.

25. Pirosh, *Go for Broke! Script*, 13.

26. Jodi Kim, *Ends of Empire*, 101.

27. For a discussion on the "theological dimension of political sovereignty," see Wendy Brown, *Walled States, Waning Sovereignty* (New York: Zone Books, 2010), 132.

28. Kotani, *Japanese in Hawaii*, 115.

29. Kotani, *Japanese in Hawaii*, 115.

30. Pirosh, *Go for Broke! Script*, 11.

31. Takashi Fujitani, "Go for Broke, the Movie: Japanese American Soldiers in U.S. National, Military, and Racial Discourses," in *Perilous Memories: The Asia-Pacific War(s)*, ed. Takashi Fujitani, Geoffrey M. White, and Lisa Yoneyama (Durham, NC: Duke University Press, 2001), 252.

32. Hawaii Statehood Commission, *Hawaii, U.S.A., and Statehood: History, Premises and Essential Facts of the Statehood Movement* (Honolulu: Hawaii Statehood Commission, 1948), 58–59; see also Hawaii Statehood Commission, *Hawaii and Statehood* (Honolulu: Hawaii Statehood Commission, 1951).

33. Matsuo Takabuki, *An Unlikely Revolutionary: Matsuo Takabuki and the Making of Modern Hawai'i* (Honolulu: University of Hawai'i Press, 1998), 70.

34. Hawaii Statehood Commission, *Hawaii, U.S.A., and Statehood*, 58–59; Hawaii Statehood Commission, *Hawaii and Statehood*.

35. Coffman, *Island Edge of America*, 148–53.

36. Takabuki, *Unlikely Revolutionary*, 64.

37. Takabuki, *Unlikely Revolutionary*, 79.

38. Takabuki, *Unlikely Revolutionary*, 64–65.

39. Takabuki, *Unlikely Revolutionary*, 65.

40. Takabuki, *Unlikely Revolutionary*, 81.

41. "Kamokila Back in Washington," *Honolulu Advertiser*, June 15, 1943.

42. "For the President," *Honolulu Star-Bulletin*, May 21, 1943.

43. "Kamokila Back in Washington"; see also "Hawaii Woman Discusses Homes Act with Ickes," *Honolulu Star-Bulletin*, July 28, 1944; "Homes Commission Frowns on New Story Opened by Kamokila for Homesteaders," *Honolulu Advertiser*, June 27, 1944; "FDR, Wife Plan Visit Here—Mrs. Campbell," *Honolulu Star-Bulletin*, July 19, 1943; "FR Receives Calabash Molokai Mothers' Gift," *Honolulu Star-Bulletin*, June 23, 1943; "Kamokila in DC on Isle Matters," *Honolulu Advertiser*, July 25, 1944; "Kamokila Meets with Women of US Congress," *Honolulu Star-Bulletin*, June 22, 1944; "Kamokila Talks with Tydings on Molokai Project," *Honolulu Star-Bulletin*, June 19, 1943; "Maui Woman Senator, at Washington, Sees Flaws in 'Reservation System,'" *Honolulu Star-Bulletin*, June 17, 1943.

44. The authority of Chief K. Su'a seems to have been challenged, as was his authority to speak on behalf of American Samoa regarding a desire to be governed under a navy commission. See American Samoan Commission, *American Samoa: Hearings before the Commission Appointed by the President of the United States* (Washington, DC: U.S. Government Printing Office, 1930), 20–30.

45. Dorothy Benyas, "Kamokila Favors Navy Control of Territory, Envisions Greater Safety from Future Attacks," *Honolulu Advertiser*, October 1, 1944, 15.

46. Benyas, "Kamokila Favors Navy Control," 15.

47. "Not Representative of Hawaii Opinion," *Honolulu Advertiser*, October 6, 1944, editorial page.

48. Whitehead, "Anti-Statehood Movement," 49–50.

49. "Text of Kamokila's Testimony: Senator Discusses Objections in Detail; Cites Racial Issues," *Honolulu Advertiser*, January 17, 1946.

50. "Text of Kamokila's Testimony"; the last editorial was "Hawaii Soldiers Resent Kamokila's Statement," *Honolulu Star-Bulletin*, February 19, 1946.

51. "Kamokila's Statements before the Subcommittee Statehood Committee," *Honolulu Advertiser*, January 19, 1946.

52. George Rogers, "His Comment on Kamokila Campbell's Attitude," *Honolulu Star-Bulletin*, January 22, 1946.

53. Esther Mitchell, "Editorial: Senator Campbell and Race Relations," *Honolulu Advertiser*, January 23, 1946.

54. "Kamokila Is Right!," *Hawaii Herald*, January 18, 1946.

55. "Kamokila in Die Hard Fight against Hawaii," *Maui News*, January 23, 1946; "Editorial: Beware of What You Sign," *Maui News*, January 26, 1946.

56. "Anti-Statehood 'Clearing House,'" *Honolulu Star-Bulletin*, September 18, 1947.

57. "Anti-Statehood 'Clearing House,'" *Honolulu Star-Bulletin*, September 18, 1947.

58. Stuart Hall, "The Toad in the Garden: Thatcherism among the Theorists," in *Marxism and the Interpretation of Culture*, ed. Cary Nelson and Lawrence Grossberg (Chicago: University of Illinois Press, 1988), 47.

59. Citizens' Statehood Committee, *Summary Report of Public Relations Activities*, August 1, 1946, Hawaii State Archives.

60. Citizens' Statehood Committee, *Summary Report of Public Relations Activities*.

61. Helen Geracimos Chapin, *Shaping History: The Role of Newspapers in Hawai'i* (Honolulu: University of Hawai'i Press, 1996), 230.

62. Citizens' Statehood Committee, *Summary Report of Public Relations Activities*.

63. Citizens' Statehood Committee, *Summary Report of Public Relations Activities*.

64. Hawaii Equal Rights Commission, Citizens' Statehood Committee, CSC-Sub-Committee on National Campaign, 1946–47, Hawaii State Archives.

65. Hawaii Equal Rights Commission, Citizens' Statehood Committee.

66. R. Bell, *Last among Equals*, 124.

67. Lorrin P. Thurston was often critical of Joseph Farrington's support of labor unions. Thurston argued that it fomented a Soviet-inspired communist plot to take over Hawai'i.

68. "Decision on Statehood Case Fund Reversed," *Honolulu Advertiser*, March 29, 1948.

69. "Public Funds Misused, Says Kamokila," *Honolulu Star-Bulletin*, January 17, 1948.

70. Supreme Court of Hawaii, "Opinion of the Court," 311–12.

71. "Court Denies Campbell Plea on 'State' Fund," *Honolulu Advertiser*, January 24, 1948.

72. "Campbell Suit against Statehood Fund Dismissed," *Honolulu Advertiser*, February 4, 1948.

73. *Campbell v. Stainback et al.*, 38 Haw. 310 (1949): 315.

74. *Campbell v. Stainback*, 320–21.

75. *Campbell v. Stainback*, 321.

76. http://statehoodhawaii.org/vid_mavian.html.

77. James E. Webb to Joseph R. Farrington, Department of State, May 24, 1949, Hawaii State Archives.

78. James E. Webb to Joseph R. Farrington, Department of State, May 24, 1949, Hawaii State Archives.

79. Hawaii Statehood Commission, Honolulu Office General Records, Tavares, NC—Campbell, Kamokila, 1953, Hawaii State Archives.

80. Hawaii Statehood Commission, Honolulu Office General Records, Tavares, NC—Campbell, Kamokila, 1953, Hawaii State Archives.

81. Lorrin P. Thurston to Nils Tavares, Hawaii State Archives.

82. R. Bell, *Last among Equals*, 158.

CHAPTER 4: THE PROPAGANDA OF OCCUPATION

Epigraph: "Force and Violence in Hawaii," *Honolulu Record*, January 24, 1952, 2.

1. Letter from Gregg M. Sinclair to Edward L. Bernays, December 12, 1949, Part I: General Correspondence, 1913–1963, Box I: 20 1949 Miscellaneous, Manuscript Division, Library of Congress, Washington, DC.

2. These included James W. Carey, HSPA; Leslie A. Hicks, president of the Hawaiian Electric Company; Herbert R. Loomis, Bishop Trust Company; Yukata Nakahata, University of Hawaiʻi; K. C. Lebrick, vice president of the University of Hawaiʻi; Ruth D. Ackland, Department of Health; Grace C. Hamman, Bureau of Sight Conservation and Work with the Blind; Christina Lam, Department of Public Welfare; and Sister Grace Mary, Catholic Social Service. In *Space and Time*, July 17, 1950; "Public Relations Seminar," *Alumni News* 4, no. 1, August 25, 1950; "Public Relations Seminar in Hawaii," *Editor and Publisher*, July 22, 1950.

3. See T. Michael Holmes, *The Specter of Communism in Hawaii* (Honolulu: University of Hawaiʻi Press, 1994); Ichiro Izuka, *The Truth about Communism in Hawaii* (Honolulu: I. Izuka, 1947); Tom Lawrence O'Brien, *The Plot to Sovietize Hawaii* (Hilo: Hawaii News Printshop, 1948).

4. Edward Bernays, *Propaganda* (Brooklyn, NY: IG Publishing, 1926), 10–15.

5. Larry Tye, *The Father of Spin: Edward L. Bernays and the Birth of Public Relations* (New York: Henry Holt, 1998), 28.

6. As cited in Tye, *Father of Spin*, 10.

7. Tye, *Father of Spin*, 32–33.

8. Tye, *Father of Spin*, ix.

9. Bernays, *Propaganda*, 37.

10. Text McCrary and Jinx Falkenburg, "Press Agent de Luxe Even Changes Their Direction," *Detroit Michigan News*, January 12, 1950.

11. Christian C. Appy, "Eisenhower's Guatemalan Doodle, or: How to Draw, Deny, and Take Credit for a Third World Coup," in *Cold War Constructions: The Political Culture of United States Imperialism, 1945–1966*, ed. Christian G. Appy, 183–213 (Amherst: University of Massachusetts Press, 2000).

12. Derrick A. Bell Jr., *Silent Covenants: Brown v. Board of Education and the Unfulfilled Hopes for Racial Reform* (New York: Oxford University Press, 2004); Thomas Borstelmann, *The Cold War and the Color Line: American Race Relations in the Global Arena* (Cambridge, MA: Harvard University Press, 2001); Mary L. Dudziak, *Cold War Civil Rights: Race and the Image of American Democracy* (Princeton, NJ: Princeton University Press, 2000); Nikhil Pal Singh, "Culture/ Wars: Recoding Empire in an Age of Democracy," *American Quarterly* 50 (1998): 471–522; Penny M. Von Eschen, *Race against Empire: Black Americans and Anticolonialism, 1937–1957* (Ithaca, NY: Cornell University Press, 1997); Von Eschen, *Satchmo Blows Up the World: Jazz Ambassadors Play the Cold War* (Cambridge, MA: Harvard University Press, 2004).

13. Christina Klein, *Cold War Orientalism: Asia in the Middlebrow Imagination, 1945–1961* (Los Angeles: University of California Press, 2003), 37.

14. Mililani Trask, "Hawai'i and the United Nations," in *Asian Settler Colonialism: From Local Governance to the Habits of Everyday Life in Hawai'i*, ed. Candace Fujikane and Jonathan Okamura (Honolulu: University of Hawai'i Press, 2008), 69; United Nations, "Declaration on the Granting of Independence to Colonial Countries and Peoples," adopted by the United Nations General Assembly on December 14, 1960, Resolution 1514.

15. See Doris Jividen, *Sammy Amalu: Prince, Pauper or Phony?* (Honolulu: Erin Enterprises, 1972).

16. "Hawaii Dynamic Public Relations Field: Bernays," *Honolulu Advertiser*, July 5, 1950.

17. Bernays, "The Importance of Public Opinion in Economic Mobilization," in *Summer Lectures, 1950*, occasional paper no. 54, University of Hawai'i, Honolulu, 1951.

18. "49th State of the Dollar Empire," *Evening Moscow*, July 25, 1947; see also *Aloha Hawaii: Islanders Celebrate Long-Sought Statehood*, Universal-International News, August 1959, video.

19. www.hawaiiankingdom.org/treaty_russia.shtml, accessed August 16, 2016.

20. Edward Bernays, "HAWAII—The Almost Perfect State?" *New Leader*, November 20, 1950.

21. "Hawaiian Delegate in Congress Appreciates Bernays Article," Part I: Speech and Article File, 1919–67, n.d. Box 1: 719 1950 Personal Newsclippings, Library of Congress.

22. Bernays, "HAWAII—The Almost Perfect State?" *New Leader*, November 20, 1950.

23. Marion Kelly, "Testimony at the Hearing on the Name Change for the Social Science Building," *Social Process in Hawai'i* 39 (1999): 307–13.

24. "Bernays Gives Analysis of Hawaii Community," *Hawaii Chinese Journal*, August 17, 1950.

25. Edward Bernays also wrote in his memoirs that "Hawaii was not perfect. The white descendants over a hundred years ago missed the great movements toward equalitarianism on the mainland. Their actions toward fellow men smacked more of the 1830s than the post 1930s" (Bernays, *Biography of an Idea: Memoirs of Public Relations Counsel Edward L. Bernays* [New York: Simon and Schuster, 1965], 799).

26. C. Klein, *Cold War Orientalism*, 16–17.

27. As cited in C. Klein, *Cold War Orientalism*, 250.

28. C. Klein, *Cold War Orientalism*, 251.

29. "Enchanting 'State,'" *Newsweek*, February 23, 1959.

30. Letter from Edward Burns to George Lehleitner, March 19, 1984, Box 7, Folder 2, George H. Lehleitner Papers, New Orleans Historical Society.

31. Lois Taylor, "One Man's Campaign for Hawaii Statehood," *Honolulu Star-Bulletin*, August 21, 1984, newspaper clipping, Box 7, Folder 3, New Orleans Historical Society.

32. Letter from George Lehleitner to John Whitehead, June 27, 1986, Folder 3, Papers of George Lehleitner, New Orleans Historical Society.

33. Larry Tye argues about public relations campaigns that "discerning readers might have suspected a commercial interest had prompted the campaign, but it would have taken a detective to pinpoint the company" (Tye, *The Father of Spin*, 31).

34. Dan Koeppel, *Banana: The Fate of the Fruit That Changed the World* (New York: Hudson Street Press, 2008).

35. Laura E. Lyons, "Dole, Hawai'i, and the Question of Land under Globalization," in *Cultural Critique and the Global Corporation*, ed. Purnima Bose and Laura E. Lyons (Indianapolis: Indiana University Press, 2010), 88.

36. As has been argued regarding the opinion campaigns of Bernays, it is virtually impossible to know how specific campaigns are run or who is actually involved.

37. Daniel W. Tuttle Jr., "George Chaplin: Journalist and Community Leader," in George Chaplin, *Presstime in Paradise* (Honolulu: University of Hawai'i Press, 1998), 391.

38. John S. Whitehead, *Completing the Union: Alaska, Hawai'i, and the Battle for Statehood* (Albuquerque: University of New Mexico Press, 2004), 251.

39. George Lehleitner, *The Tennessee Plan: How the Bold Became States* (pamphlet), Papers of George H. Lehleitner, New Orleans Historical Society, 3.

40. Lehleitner, "An Address by George H. Lehleitner, a Private Citizen of New Orleans, Louisiana, Delivered to the Delegates of the Alaska Constitutional Convention," University of Alaska, January 23, 1956.

41. James C. Wright, interview by John Whitehead and George Lehleitner, March 15, 1988, Washington, DC, transcript, Box 8, Folder 2, Papers of George H. Lehleitner, New Orleans Historical Society.

42. Lehleitner, "Address by George H. Lehleitner."

43. Letter from George Lehleitner to R. Thurston Green, "Vercolline," 1957, Folder 4, Papers of George Lehleitner, New Orleans Historical Society.

44. "Step toward State of Alaska," *Life*, May 14, 1956.

45. Letter from George H. Lehleitner to James J. Kilpatrick, September 21, 1956, James Kilpatrick Papers, Box 31, Albert and Shirley Small Special Collections Library, University of Virginia.

46. George Lehleitner, interview by Chris Conybeare and Warren Nishimoto, "A Statehood Hero," March 5, 1984, Folder 3, Proceedings and Debates of the 85th Congress Second Session Volume 104, Part 7, May 12, 1958, to May 18, 1958, New Orleans Historical Society.

47. Letter from George Lehleitner to Honorable Luis Davils Colon, Esquire, Office of the Governor, La Fortaleza, San Juan Puerto Rico, Folder 4, Papers of George H. Lehleitner, New Orleans Historical Society.

48. Stanley D. Porteus and Marjorie E. Babcock, *Temperament and Race* (Boston: R. G. Badger, 1926).

49. Ronald Takaki, *Pau Hana: Plantation Life and Labor in Hawaii, 1835–1920* (Honolulu: University of Hawai'i Press, 1984), 24; see also Edward D. Beechert, *Working in Hawaii: A Labor History* (Honolulu: University of Hawai'i Press, 1985); Moon-Kie Jung, *Reworking Race: The Making of Hawaii's Interracial Labor Movement* (New York: Columbia University, 2006); Gary Y. Okihiro, *Cane Fires: The Anti-Japanese Movement in Hawaii, 1865–1945* (Philadelphia: Temple University Press, 1991).

50. Jung, *Reworking Race*, 108–10.

51. Frank Marshall Davis and John Edgar Tidwell, *Livin' the Blues: Memoirs of a Black Journalist and Poet* (Madison: University of Wisconsin Press, 1992), 367–68.

52. The state of Hawai'i acknowledged such in 1978, offering monetary compensation for lost pay and retirement benefits.

53. As cited in Holmes, *Specter of Communism in Hawai'i*, 105.

54. Holmes, *Specter of Communism in Hawai'i*, 105.

55. "Looking Backward," *Honolulu Record*, April 10, 1952.

56. "Looking Backward."

57. "Looking Backward."

58. Ty Kāwika Tengan, *Native Men Remade: Gender and Nation in Contemporary Hawai'i* (Durham, NC: Duke University Press, 2008), 45.

59. "Looking Backward."

60. James A. Michener, *Hawaii* (New York: Random House, 1959), 634–35.

61. Holmes, *Specter of Communism in Hawaii*, 150–77; Sanford Zalburg, *A Spark Is Struck!: Jack Hall and the ILWU in Hawaii* (Honolulu: University of Hawai'i Press, 1979).

62. John Devlin, "Toward a State Constitutional Analysis of Allocation of Powers: Legislators and Legislative Appointees Performing Administrative Functions," *Temple Law Review* 66 (1993): 1205–68.

63. Steve Wilcox, "The Mellens of Makalei: The Magnificent Matriarch and the Lonely Warrior," *Honolulu Beacon*, June 1965, 18–21.

64. Napua Stevens Poiré, "Mellen, Kathleen Dickenson," in *Who's Who?*, edited by Nelson Prather (Honolulu: University of Hawai'i, Office for Women's Research, 1947), 262; Wilcox, "The Mellens of Makalei."

65. "Controversial Isle Historian Kathleen D. Mellen Dies," *Honolulu Advertiser*, August 2, 1969.

66. Kathleen Dickenson Mellen, *The Gods Depart: A Saga of the Hawaiian Kingdom, 1832–1873* (New York: Hastings House, 1956), ix.

67. Mellen, "Na Pua o Hawaii: Descendants of Distinguished Hawaiians," *Paradise of the Pacific* 60, no. 12 (December 1948): 65.

68. Mellen, "Na Pua o Hawaii."

69. Mellen, "Na Pua o Hawaii."

70. Mellen, "The Death Kahili," *Paradise of the Pacific* 61, no. 12 (December 1945): 65–67, 130.

71. Mellen, "Death Kahili."

72. Mellen, "Death Kahili."

73. Mellen, "Death Kahili."

74. "Mellen's 'Matriarch' to Become Major Movie," *Honolulu Star-Bulletin*, January 20, 1958; Eddie Sherman, "In the Spotlight: Filmland Won't Change Mrs. Mellen," *Honolulu Advertiser*, January 21, 1958.

75. "Controversial Isle Historian Kathleen D. Mellen Dies," *Honolulu Advertiser*, August 2, 1969, 1.

76. Mellen, *An Island Kingdom Passes: Hawaii Becomes American* (New York: Hastings House, 1958), 338.

77. Letter from Kathleen Dickenson Mellen to Pro Bono Publico, August 1, 1958, in "Bio. Mellen, Kathleen (Dickenson)," Hawaiian Collection, Gregg M. Sinclair Library, University of Hawai'i.

78. Letter from Kathleen Dickenson Mellen to Pro Bono Publico, August 1, 1958, in "Bio. Mellen, Kathleen (Dickenson)," Hawaiian Collection, Gregg M. Sinclair Library, University of Hawai'i.

79. Letter from Kathleen Dickenson Mellen to Senator Hugh Butler, February 27, 1949, Box 97, "Confidential Letters," Nebraska National Historical Society.

80. Whitehead, "The Anti-Statehood Movement and the Legacy of Alice Kamokila Campbell," *Hawaiian Journal of History* 27 (1993): 43–63.

81. Mellen, "Hawaii's Statehood Pledge Challenged," *Honolulu Advertiser*, January 9, 1957.

82. Mellen, "Hawaii's Statehood Pledge Challenged."

83. Frank Hewlett, "Islander's Plea for Hawaii Monarchy Labeled 'Inconceivable' by Senator," *Honolulu Star-Bulletin*, April 22, 1957.

84. Hewlett, "Islander's Plea for Hawaii Monarchy."

85. "Pillion Charges New Anti-Statehood Evidence," *Honolulu Advertiser*, June 21, 1957.

86. Victor S. K. Houston, "Implied Statehood Promise Given," *Honolulu Advertiser*, August 15, 1957.

87. Houston, "Implied Statehood Promise Given."

88. Michener, *Hawaii*, 891.

89. Barbara Prock, "Let's Talk 'About Michener's Hawaii,'" *Honolulu Star-Bulletin*, December 9, 1959.

90. Bob Krauss, "Kathleen Mellen Dreamed of Isle Palaces and Kings," August 3, 1969.

91. Mary Kawena Pukui, interview by Gabriel Kalama Pea, Andrew Poepoe, and E. Pea Nahale, Birch Street, 1959, Bishop Museum 1959.236 (Haw 40.3).

92. Prock, "Let's Talk 'About Michener's Hawaii.'"

93. Prock, "Let's Talk 'About Michener's Hawaii.'"

94. Prock, "Let's Talk 'About Michener's Hawaii.'"

95. Wilcox, "Mellens of Makalei."

96. As featured in *Taking Waikiki*, directed by Edward Coll and Carol Bain (Kaua'i, HI: Kauai World Wide Communications, 1994), DVD.

97. Jividen, *Sammy Amalu*.

98. Jividen, *Sammy Amalu*, 7.

99. Jividen, *Sammy Amalu*, 11; "Mystery Deepens on Offer to Buy 4 Sheraton Hotels," *Wall Street Journal*, May 16, 1962.

100. Jividen, *Sammy Amalu*, 11.

101. As cited in Jividen, *Sammy Amalu*, 13.

102. "I remember as an April Fool's joke, Aku [Hal Lewis] one time announced that on April Fool's Day that it'd been voted in Congress to declare us a commonwealth and if you'd go down to the offices of the IRS, you could put in a claim for last year's income taxes. About forty minutes later, they called up and asked for help. They were (chuckles) under water with people standing in line" (Malcolm MacNaughton, interview, June 1986, transcript, "Perspectives on Hawai'i's Statehood" Oral History Project, Social Science Research Institute, University of Hawai'i at Mānoa, 53).

103. Gavan Daws, *Hawaii, 1959–1989: The First Thirty Years of the Aloha State with Memorable Photographs from the Honolulu Advertiser* (Honolulu: Mutual Publishing, 1990), 38.

104. Lewis Hyde, *Trickster Makes This World: Mischief, Myth and Art* (New York: Farrar, Straus and Giroux, 1998), 11.

105. Vine Deloria Jr., "The Trickster and the Messiah," in *Spirit and Reason: The Vine Deloria, Jr., Reader*, ed. Barbara Deloria, Kristen Foehner, and Sam Scinta (Golden, CO: Fulcrum Publishing, 1999), 26.

106. See Stephanie Nohelani Teves, *Defiant Indigeneity: The Politics of Hawaiian Performance* (Chapel Hill: University of North Carolina Press, 2018), xiv.

107. Teves, "Aloha State Apparatuses," *American Quarterly* 67, no. 3 (fall 2015): 705–26.

108. Lilikalā Kame'eleihiwa, *Kamapuaa: The Hawaiian Pig God* (Honolulu: Bishop Museum Press, 1996), xvi.

109. Daws, *Hawaii, 1959–1989*, 40.

110. Judith [Jack] Halberstam, *The Queer Art of Failure* (Durham, NC: Duke University Press, 2011), 88–89.

111. Halberstam, *Queer Art of Failure*, 88.

112. Hyde, *Trickster Makes This World*, 13.

113. Jividen, *Sammy Amalu*, 38.

114. Jividen, *Sammy Amalu*, 38–39.

115. Jividen, *Sammy Amalu*, 36.

116. As cited in Jividen, *Sammy Amalu*, 117.

117. Jividen, *Sammy Amalu*, 105.

118. Jividen, *Sammy Amalu*, 43.

119. Jividen, *Sammy Amalu*, 76.

120. Jividen, *Sammy Amalu*, 30.

121. Whitehead, "Anti-Statehood Movement." Emphasis added.

122. Samuel P. King and Randall W. Roth, *Broken Trust: Greed, Mismanagement and Political Manipulation at America's Largest Charitable Trust* (Honolulu: University of Hawai'i Press, 2006), 67.

123. King and Roth, *Broken Trust*, 66–67. See also Amalu's biography of Governor John A. Burns, which is a kind of hagiography that takes compliments too far to be read as only such (Samuel Crowningburg-Amalu, *Jack Burns: A Portrait in Transition* [Honolulu: Mamalahoa Foundation, 1974]).

CHAPTER 5: ALTERNATIVE FUTURES BEYOND THE SETTLER STATE

1. Kelly Yamanouchi, "When Tourists Become Victims," *Honolulu Advertiser*, November 30, 2003.

2. Inez Ashdown, "The Valley Worthy of Kings," *Sunday Star-Bulletin*, July 24, 1960; "Ghost Picture Excites Japanese," *Maui News*, April 18, 1919; "Work Starts on Picnic Grounds in Iao Valley," *Maui News*, November 3, 1951.

3. Avery F. Gordon, *Ghostly Matters: Haunting and the Sociological Imagination* (Minneapolis: University of Minnesota Press, 1997), 63–64.

4. At the Bishop Museum Kāneikokala is the name of a ki'i pōhaku who decided not to leave Hawai'i Hall when decisions were made to move the pōhaku outside. It currently remains in Hawai'i Hall at the Bishop Museum. Or take for instance the quote from Abraham Piianaia about his grandfather: "Kalākaua sent him to England, and still he always said something nice to rocks" (Manulani Aluli-Meyer, *Ho'oulu: Our Time of Becoming* [Honolulu: 'Ai Pōhaku Press, 2004], 141).

5. E. S. Craighill Handy and Elizabeth Green Handy, *Native Planters in Old Hawaii: Their Life, Lore, and Environment* (Honolulu: Bishop Museum Press, 1972), 272.

6. "Tunneling for Water: A New and Important Industry Being Developed on Maui," *Maui News*, February 2, 1901.

7. Ann Bermingham, *Landscape and Ideology: The English Rustic Tradition, 1740–1860* (Los Angeles: University of California Press, 1986); Richard Halperns, *The Poetics of Primitive Accumulation: English Renaissance Culture and the Genealogy of Capital* (Ithaca, NY: Cornell University Press, 1991); Peter Linebaugh, *The Magna Carta Manifesto: Liberties and Commons for All* (Los Angeles: University of California Press, 2008).

8. David Harvey, *The New Imperialism* (Oxford: Oxford University Press, 2003), 137–82.

9. Raymond Williams, *Marxism and Literature* (Oxford: Oxford University Press, 1977), 113–14.

10. "Drive to Establish Park in Iao Valley Opens Here," *Maui News*, November 23, 1940.

11. "County Gets Park Site: Kepaniwai Property Is Conveyed for Public Park," *Maui News*, April 30, 1941; "County to Sell Main-Market St. Lot at Auction," *Maui News*, February 5, 1941; "Iao Valley Park Drive Nears Goal," *Maui News*, November 30, 1940; "Kepaniwai Park Is Dedicated: New County Playground in Iao Valley Now Open to Public," *Maui News*, July 19, 1952; "Land Change on Iao Park Project Okayed by Board: Deal to Raise $6,000," *Maui News*, January 18, 1941; "Main-Market Street Lot to Be Auctioned Today," *Maui News*, March 29, 1941; "Shortage of Funds Halts Iao Project: Final Decision Is Up to Legislature and County," *Maui News*, January 8, 1941; "Thousands Sign Park Petitions: Purchase of Iao Valley Site Sought," *Maui News*, November 27, 1940; "T. Ikeoka Buys County Lot at Main-Market St. Corner with $7,350 Bid," *Maui News*, April 2, 1941.

12. George Cooper and Gavan Daws, *Land and Power in Hawaii: The Democratic Years* (Honolulu: University of Hawai'i Press, 1990).

13. Mansel G. Blackford, *Fragile Paradise: The Impact of Tourism on Maui, 1959–2001* (Lawrence: University Press of Kansas, 2001), 19.

14. "International Gardens in Kepaniwai Park Scheme," *Maui News*, April 11, 1964.

15. Blackford, *Fragile Paradise*, 20.

16. Hawaiian Airlines had previously refused to hire Asian Americans, but changed their policy in 1946 after Tongg established his Trans-Pacific Airlines, which would be renamed Aloha Airlines. See Cooper and Daws, *Land and Power in Hawaii*, 151.

17. Barbara Kirshenblatt-Gimblett, *Destination Culture: Tourism, Museums, and Heritage* (Los Angeles: University of California Press, 1998), 151.

18. Robert Johnson, "Cultural Heritage Park Proposed for Iao Valley," *Honolulu Advertiser*, March 13, 1967.

19. Samuel Kamakau, *Hawaiian Annual* (Honolulu: Thos. G. Thrum, 1932).

20. A special thank you to Ty Kāwika Tengan for sharing with me his research. Ty Kāwika Tengan with collaboration from J. Lahela A. Perry and Nanea Armstrong, *Report on the Archival, Historical and Archaeological Resources of Nā Wai 'Ehā, Wailuku District, Island of Maui* (Honolulu: Office of Hawaiian Affairs, 2007), 12.

21. Anna Johnston and Alan Lawson, "Settler Colonies," in *A Companion to Postcolonial Studies*, ed. Henry Schwarz and Sangeeta Ray (Malden, MA: Blackwell, 2005), 364.

22. "Development of Iao Is Aim of Civic Club," *Maui News*, July 9, 1960.

23. Inez Ashdown, "The Valley of Worthy Kings," *Sunday Star-Bulletin*, July 24, 1960.

24. Ashdown, "The Valley of Worthy Kings," *Sunday Star-Bulletin*.

25. Hymie Meyer's statement is printed by Ashdown, who likely transcribed it. In the printed version, Ashdown writes her statement as: "Nalu wale nua mea pau loa" [*sic*]. I thank Noenoe K. Silva for alerting me to this mistake (Inez Ashdown, Ashdown Papers, Bailey House Museum, H919.68).

26. "Hawaiian Group Meets Tuesday on Garden Plan," *Maui News*, July 7, 1967.

27. For more on a "moral sensibility" in relation to multicultural forms of settler colonialism, see Elizabeth A. Povinelli, *The Cunning of Recognition: Indigenous Alterities and the Making of Australian Multiculturalism* (Durham, NC: Duke University Press, 2002), 9.

28. Jodi Melamed, "The Spirit of Neoliberalism: From Racial Liberalism to Neoliberal Multiculturalism," *Social Text* 24, no. 4(89) (winter 2006): 16.

29. "'Heritage Pavilion' in Kepaniwai Park Plans," *Maui News*, May 17, 1967; Robert Johnson, "Cultural Heritage Park Proposed for Iao Valley," *Honolulu Advertiser*, March 13, 1967.

30. Denise Ferreira da Silva, *Toward a Global Idea of Race* (Minneapolis: University of Minnesota Press, 2007), 116.

31. Henrietta Lidchi, "The Poetics and the Politics of Exhibiting Other Cultures," in *Representation: Cultural Representations and Signifying Practices*, ed. Stuart Hall (Thousand Oaks, CA: SAGE, 1997), 191.

32. Such moves to define Western modernity against Indigenous primitivism are characteristic of social scientific colonial discourse; but as contemporary Kanaka 'Ōiwi scholars, armed with language and cultural knowledge, have pointed out, Kānaka 'Ōiwi asserted a long and commanding intellectual tradition throughout the nineteenth century (and beyond). Utilizing newspapers to express anticolonial sentiments, many Kānaka 'Ōiwi responded to the 1893 U.S. military–backed overthrow, led by descendants of missionaries, in the Hawaiian language as a means to "make it harder for the oppressor to decipher," as Noenoe Silva has asserted (Noenoe K. Silva, *Aloha Betrayed: Native Hawaiian Resistance to American Colonialism* [Durham, NC: Duke University Press, 2004], 5; Silva, "Nā Hulu Kupuna: To Honor Our Intellectual Ancestors," *Biography* 32, no. 1 [winter 2009]: 43).

33. One Maui County councilman attempted to turn this rock profile into a national monument for John F. Kennedy. Signage for this profile was changed back to Kauka'iwai ("Kennedy Studying Iao Memorial to Brother," *Maui News*, August 19, 1971; "Monument for JFK Profile in Iao Valley," *Maui News*, July 22, 1970).

34. Chuck Frankel, "Isles Called Appropriate for Kennedy Rights Talk," *Honolulu Star Bulletin*, June 6, 1963; "Text of Kennedy's Speech to Mayors," *Honolulu Star-Bulletin*, June 10, 1963.

35. As cited in Tom Coffman, *The Island Edge of America: A Political History of Hawai'i* (Honolulu: University of Hawai'i Press, 2003), 2.

36. James T. Fisher, "'A World Made Safe for Diversity': The Vietnam Lobby and the Politics of Pluralism, 1945–1963," in *Cold War Constructions: The Political Culture of United States Imperialism, 1945–1966*, ed. Christian G. Appy (Amherst: University of Massachusetts, 2000), 218.

37. Kennedy's posthumously released book, *A Nation of Immigrants*, popularized the term in the national lexicon. John F. Kennedy, *A Nation of Immigrants* (New York: Harper Perennial, 2008).

38. Gail Bartholomew and Bren Bailey, *Maui Remembers: A Local History* (Taiwan: Mutual Publishing, 1994), 128.

39. Penny M. Von Eschen, *Satchmo Blows Up the World: Jazz Ambassadors Play the Cold War* (Cambridge, MA: Harvard University Press, 2004), 254.

40. Jonathan Nashel, "The Road to Vietnam: Modernization Theory in Fact and Fiction," in *Cold War Constructions: The Political Culture of United States Imperialism, 1945–1966*, ed. Christian G. Appy (Amherst: University of Massachusetts, 2000), 132–54.

41. Ngũgĩ wa Thiong'o, *Decolonising the Mind: The Politics of Language in African Literature* (Portsmouth, NH: Heinemann, 1986), 3.

42. Jodi Kim, *Ends of Empire: Asian American Critique and the Cold War* (Minneapolis: University of Minnesota Press, 2010), 12.

43. Dylan Rodríguez, *Suspended Apocalypse: White Supremacy, Genocide, and the Filipino Condition* (Minneapolis, University of Minnesota Press, 2009).

44. Kim, *Ends of Empire*, 276.

45. Bartholomew and Bailey, *Maui Remembers*, 149.

46. Bartholomew and Bailey, *Maui Remembers*, 146–47.

47. Matthew Spriggs, "'Preceded by Forest': Changing Interpretations of Landscape Change on Kaho'olawe," *Asian Perspectives* 30, no. 1 (1991): 71–116.

48. "1909 Article Tells Why Ulupalakua Dried Up," *Maui News*, November 9, 1977; *Noho Hewa: The Wrongful Occupation of Hawai'i*, directed by Anne Keala Kelly (Honolulu: Kuleana Works, 2009), DVD.

49. Blackford, *Fragile Paradise*, 122.

50. Donald Worster, *Rivers of Empire: Water, Aridity, and the Growth of the American West* (New York: Oxford University Press, 1985), 88.

51. As cited in Vandana Shiva, *Water Wars: Privatization, Pollution, and Profit* (Boston: South End Press, 2002), 54.

52. Shiva, *Water Wars*, 54–55.

53. Blackford, *Fragile Paradise*, 116–23.

54. Carol Wilcox, *Sugar Water: Hawaii's Plantation Ditches* (Honolulu: University of Hawai'i Press, 1996), 5.

55. Tengan, Perry, and Armstrong, *Report*, 16.

56. "Tunneling for Water: A New and Important Industry Being Developed on Maui," *Maui News*, February 2, 1901.

57. Wilcox, *Sugar Water*, 1–11, 16.

58. *McBryde Sugar Company v. Robinson* (1973), 175.

59. D. Kapu'ala Sproat, "Water," in *The Value of Hawai'i: Knowing the Past, Shaping the Future*, ed. Craig Howes and Jonathan Kamakawiwo'ole Osorio (Honolulu: University of Hawai'i Press, 2010), 191.

60. Hamilton, "Na Wai Eha: HC&S Speaks Jobs, Fields at Risk in Stream Water Dispute," *Maui News*, October 9, 2009.

61. Hamilton, "Na Wai Eha: Decision in but Dispute Lingers," *Maui News*, June 13, 2010.

62. wa Thiong'o, *Decolonising the Mind*, 3.

63. Victor C. Pellegrino, *Uncle Kawaiola's Dream* (Wailuku, HI: Maui ar-Thoughts, 2010), 4.

64. Kirshenblatt-Gimblett, *Destination Culture*, 7.

65. Dipesh Chakrabarty, "The Climate of History: Four Theses," *Critical Inquiry* 35 (winter 2009): 206.

66. Andrew Pollack, "Unease in Hawaii's Cornfields," *New York Times*, October 7, 2013.

67. Jon Letman, "GM Seeds and the Militarization of Food: An Interview with Vandana Shiva," *Earthfirst Newswire*, March 22, 2013, http://earthfirstnews.wordpress.com/2013/03/22/gm-seeds-and-the-militarization-of-food-an-interview-with-vandana-shiva/, accessed August 31, 2013.

CONCLUSION: SCENES OF RESURGENCE

1. Ruth Wilson Gilmore, "Race and Globalization," in *Geographies of Global Change: Remapping the World*, ed. R. J. Johnston, Peter J. Taylor, and Michael J. Watts (Malden, MA: Blackwell, 2002), 261.

2. Amy Kaplan, *The Anarchy of Empire in the Making of U.S. Culture* (Cambridge, MA: Harvard University Press, 2002), 24–25.

3. Audra Simpson, *Mohawk Interruptus: Political Life across the Borders of Settler States* (Durham, NC: Duke University Press, 2014), 11.

4. Alice Kamokila Campbell to state senate, January 31, 1960, Hawaii State Archives; "Report of Pele Vision Put in Senate Records," *Honolulu Advertiser*, February 2, 1960.

5. Alice Kamokila Campbell to state senate, January 31, 1960, Hawaii State Archives; "Report of Pele Vision Put in Senate Records."

6. ku'ualoha ho'omanawanui, *Voices of Fire: Reweaving the Literary Lei of Pele and Hi'iaka* (Minneapolis: University of Minnesota Press, 2014); Brandy Nālani McDougal, *Finding Meaning: Kaona and Contemporary Hawaiian Literature* (Tucson: University of Arizona Press, 2016); Noenoe K. Silva, "Talking Back to Empire: Hula in Hawaiian-Language Literature in 1861," in *Law and Empire in the Pacific: Fiji and Hawai'i*, ed. Sally Engle Merry and Donald Brenneis, 101–22 (Santa Fe, NM: School of American Research, 2003).

7. Hawaii Statehood Celebration Committee, press release, June 8, 1960.

8. Silva, *Aloha Betrayed*, 161.

9. Kathleen Dickenson Mellen, *An Island Kingdom Passes: Hawaii Becomes American* (New York: Hastings House, 1958), 347.

10. Letter from Vera Chong to James Kealoha, June 23, 1960, Hawaii Statehood Commission, Hawai'i State Archives.

11. "Text of Governor's Flag Speech," *Honolulu Advertiser*, July 5, 1960.

12. Paul Krugman, *The Return of Depression Economics and the Crisis of 2008* (New York: W. W. Norton, 2008).

13. Dylan Rodríguez, "The Dreadful Genius of the Obama Moment: Inaugurating Multiculturalist White Supremacy," *Colorlines*, November 10, 2008.

14. University of Hawai'i at Hilo, "Final Environmental Impact Statement: Thirty Meter Telescope Project," Hilo, Hawai'i, May 8, 2010.

15. J. Kēhaulani Kauanui, "Resisting the Akaka Bill," in *A Nation Rising*, ed. Noelani Goodyear-Ka'ōpua, Ikaika Hussey, and Erin Kahunawaika'ala Wright (Durham, NC: Duke University Press, 2014), 312.

16. Vicente M. Diaz, "Voyaging for Anti-Colonial Recovery: Austronesian Seafaring, Archipelagic Rethinking, and the Re-mapping of Indigeneity," *Pacific Asia Inquiry* 2.1 (2011): 21.

17. Diaz, "Voyaging for Anti-Colonial Recovery," 21.

18. Glen Sean Coulthard, *Red Skin, White Masks: Rejecting the Colonial Politics of Recognition* (Minneapolis: University of Minnesota Press, 2014), 60.

19. Leanne Betasamosake Simpson, "Indigenous Resurgence and Co-resistance," *Critical Ethnic Studies* 2, no. 2 (fall 2016): 22.

20. Naomi Klein, *This Changes Everything: Capitalism vs. the Climate* (New York: Simon and Schuster, 2014), 7.

21. Mishuana Goeman, *Mark My Words: Native Women Mapping Our Nations* (Minneapolis: University of Minnesota Press, 2013), 3.

22. Goeman, *Mark My Words*, 5.

23. Goeman, *Mark My Words*, 3.

24. Robert Allen Warrior, *Tribal Secrets: Recovering American Indian Intellectual Traditions* (Minneapolis: University of Minnesota Press, 1995), 65.

25. As cited in Sanford Zalburg, *A Spark Is Struck!: Jack Hall and the ILWU in Hawaii* (Honolulu: University of Hawai'i Press, 1979), 312–13.

26. Raúl Zibechi, *Territories in Resistance: A Cartography of Latin American Social Movements* (Oakland, CA: AK Press, 2012), 128.

BIBLIOGRAPHY

Abinales, Patricio N. *Making Mindanao: Cotabato and Davao in the Formation of the Philippine Nation-State*. Quezon City: Ateneo de Manila University Press, 2000.

Adams, Romanzo C. *The Peoples of Hawaii*. Honolulu: American Council Institute of Pacific Relations, 1935.

Adas, Michael. "From Settler Colony to Global Hegemon: Integrating the Exceptionalist Narrative of the American Experience into World History." *American Historical Review* 106, no. 5 (December 2001): 1692–720.

Aikau, Hokulani. *Chosen People, a Promised Land: Mormonism and Race in Hawai'i*. Minneapolis: University of Minnesota, 2012.

Aikau, Hokulani. "Indigeneity in the Diaspora: The Case of Native Hawaiians at Iosepa, Utah." *American Quarterly* 62, no. 3 (September 2010): 477–500.

Aloha Hawaii: Islanders Celebrate Long-Sought Statehood. Universal-International News. August 1959. Video.

Aluli-Meyer, Manulani. *Ho'oulu: Our Time of Becoming*. Honolulu: 'Ai Pōhaku Press, 2004.

American Samoan Commission. *American Samoa: Hearings before the Commission Appointed by the President of the United States*. Washington, DC: U.S. Government Printing Office, 1930.

Andrade, Ernest, Jr. *Unconquerable Rebel: Robert W. Wilcox and Hawaiian Politics, 1880–1903*. Niwot: University Press of Colorado, 1996.

Anthony, Joseph Garner. *Hawaii under Army Rule*. Stanford, CA: Stanford University Press, 1955.

Appy, Christian C. "Eisenhower's Guatemalan Doodle, or: How to Draw, Deny, and Take Credit for a Third World Coup." In *Cold War Constructions: The Political Culture of United States Imperialism, 1945–1966*, edited by Christian G. Appy, 183–213. Amherst: University of Massachusetts Press, 2000.

Arvin, Maile. "The Polynesian Problem and Its Genomic Solutions." *Native American and Indigenous Studies* 2, no. 2 (2015): 27–56.

Ashcroft, Bill, Gareth Griffiths, and Hellen Tiffin. "Settler Colony." In *Post-Colonial Studies: The Key Concepts*, edited by Henry Schwarz and Sangeeta Ray, 360–76. New York: Routledge Taylor and Francis Group, 1998.

Azuma, Eiichiro. *Between Two Empires: Race, History, and Transnationalism in Japanese America*. Oxford: Oxford University Press, 2005.

Bacchilega, Cristina. *Legendary Hawai'i and the Politics of Place: Tradition, Translation, and Tourism*. Philadelphia: University of Pennsylvania Press, 2007.

Balce, Nerissa S. "Filipino Bodies, Lynching and the Language of Empire." In *Positively No Filipinos Allowed: Building Communities and Discourse*, edited by Antonio Tiongson, Ed Gutierrez, and Rick Gutierrez, 43–60. Philadelphia: Temple University Press, 2006.

Bartholomew, Gail, and Bren Bailey. *Maui Remembers: A Local History*. Taiwan: Mutual Publishing, 1994.

Bascara, Victor. "New Empire, Same Old University?: Education in the American Tropics after 1898." In *The Imperial University: Academic Repression and Scholarly Dissent*, edited by Piya Chatterjee and Sunaina Maira, 53–77. Minneapolis: University of Minnesota Press, 2014.

Basham, Leilani. "Ka Lāhui Hawai'i: He Mo'olelo, He Āina, He Loina, a He Ea Kākou." *Hūlili: Multidisciplinary Research on Hawaiian Well-Being* 6 (2010): 37–72.

Beechert, Edward D. *Working in Hawaii: A Labor History*. Honolulu: University of Hawai'i Press, 1985.

Bell, Derrick A., Jr. *Silent Covenants: Brown v. Board of Education and the Unfulfilled Hopes for Racial Reform*. New York: Oxford University Press, 2004.

Bell, Roger J. *Last among Equals: Hawaiian Statehood and American Politics*. Honolulu: University of Hawai'i Press, 1984.

Bello, Walden, Herbert Docena, Marissa de Guzman, and Marylou Malig. *The Anti-Development State: The Political Economy of Permanent Crisis in the Philippines*. London: Zed Books, 2006.

Berger, John. *Ways of Seeing*. London: BBC, 1977.

Berger, Martin A. *Sight Unseen: Whiteness and American Visual Culture*. Berkeley: University of California Press, 2005.

Bermingham, Ann. *Landscape and Ideology: The English Rustic Tradition, 1740–1860*. Los Angeles: University of California Press, 1986.

Bernays, Edward L. *Biography of an Idea: Memoirs of Public Relations Counsel Edward L. Bernays*. New York: Simon and Schuster, 1965.

Bernays, Edward L. "The Importance of Public Opinion in Economic Mobilization." In *Summer Lectures, 1950*. Occasional paper no. 54, University of Hawai'i, Honolulu, 1951.

Bernays, Edward L. *Propaganda*. Brooklyn, NY: IG Publishing, 1926.

Bhabha, Homi K. "Introduction: Narrating the Nation." In *Nation and Narration*, edited by Homi K. Bhabha, 1–7. New York: Routledge, 1990.

Blackford, Mansel G. *Fragile Paradise: The Impact of Tourism on Maui, 1959–2001.* Lawrence: University Press of Kansas, 2001.

Boggs, Grace Lee. *Living for Change: An Autobiography.* Minneapolis: University of Minnesota Press, 1998.

Borstelmann, Thomas. *The Cold War and the Color Line: American Race Relations in the Global Arena.* Cambridge, MA: Harvard University Press, 2001.

Brooks, Joanna. *Why We Left: Untold Stories and Songs of America's First Immigrants.* Minneapolis: University of Minnesota Press, 2013.

Brown, Wendy. *Walled States, Waning Sovereignty.* New York: Zone Books, 2010.

Buck-Morss, Susan. *The Dialectics of Seeing: Walter Benjamin and the Arcades Project.* Cambridge, MA: MIT Press, 1991.

Burton, Jeffrey. *Indian Territory and the United States, 1866–1905: Courts, Government, and the Movement for Oklahoma Statehood.* Norman: University of Oklahoma Press, 1995.

Butler, Judith. "Palestine, State Politics and the Anarchist Impasse." In *The Anarchist Turn*, edited by Jacob Blumenfeld, Chiara Bottici, and Simon Critchley, 203–23. London: Pluto Press, 2013.

Byrd, Jodi A. *The Transit of Empire: Indigenous Critiques of Colonialism.* Minneapolis: University of Minnesota Press, 2011.

Camacho, Keith L. *Cultures of Commemoration: The Politics of War, Memory, and History in the Mariana Islands.* Honolulu: University of Hawai'i Press, 2011.

Caronan, Faye. *Legitimizing Empire: Filipino American and U.S. Puerto Rican Cultural Critique.* Urbana: University of Illinois Press, 2015.

Cawte, Mary. "Craniometry and Eugenics in Australia: R. J. A. Berry and the Quest for Social Efficiency." *Historical Studies* 22 (1986): 35–53.

Chakrabarty, Dipesh. "The Climate of History: Four Theses." *Critical Inquiry* 35 (winter 2009): 197–222.

Chang, David A. *The World and All the Things upon It: Native Hawaiian Geographies of Exploration.* Minneapolis: University of Minnesota Press, 2016.

Chapin, Helen Geracimos. *Shaping History: The Role of Newspapers in Hawai'i.* Honolulu: University of Hawai'i Press, 1996.

Chatterjee, Piya, and Sunaina Maira. "The Imperial University: Race, War and the Nation-State." In *The Imperial University: Academic Repression and Scholarly Dissent*, edited by Piya Chatterjee and Sunaina Maira, 1–50. Minneapolis: University of Minnesota, 2014.

Citizens' Statehood Committee. *Summary Report of Public Relations Activities.* August 1, 1946. Hawaii State Archives.

Coffman, Tom. *Catch a Wave: A Case Study of Hawaii's New Politics.* 2nd ed. Honolulu: University Press of Hawai'i, 1973.

Coffman, Tom. *The Island Edge of America: A Political History of Hawai'i*. Honolulu: University of Hawai'i Press, 2003.

Coll, Edward, and Carol Bain, dir. *Taking Waikiki*. Kaua'i, HI: Kauai World Wide Communications, 1994. DVD.

Compoc, Kim. "Emergent Allies: Decolonial Hawai'i from a Filipin@ Perspective." PhD diss., University of Hawai'i, 2017.

Compoc, Kim. "Filipinos and Statehood: Reflections on American Assimilation and Settler Complicity." Master's diss., University of Hawai'i at Mānoa, 2010.

Cook, Kealani R. "Kahiki: Native Hawaiian Relationships with Other Pacific Islanders, 1850–1915." PhD diss., University of Michigan, 2011.

Cook, Kealani R. *Return to Kahiki: Native Hawaiians in Oceania*. New York: Cambridge University Press, 2018.

Cooper, George, and Gavan Daws. *Land and Power in Hawaii: The Democratic Years*. Honolulu: University of Hawai'i Press, 1990.

Coulthard, Glen Sean. *Red Skin, White Masks: Rejecting the Colonial Politics of Recognition*. Minneapolis: University of Minnesota Press, 2014.

Crampton, Jeremy W., and Stuart Elden. *Space, Knowledge and Power: Foucault and Geography*. Aldershot, UK: Ashgate, 2007.

Crenshaw, Kimberlé. *Critical Race Theory: The Key Writings That Formed the Movement*. New York: New Press, 1995.

Cronon, William. *Nature's Metropolis: Chicago and the Great West*. New York: W. W. Norton, 1991.

Crowningburg-Amalu, Samuel. *Jack Burns: A Portrait in Transition*. Honolulu: Mamalahoa Foundation, 1974.

da Silva, Denise Ferreira. *Toward a Global Idea of Race*. Minneapolis: University of Minnesota Press, 2007.

Davis, Frank Marshall, and John Edgar Tidwell. *Livin' the Blues: Memoirs of a Black Journalist and Poet*. Madison: University of Wisconsin Press, 1992.

Daws, Gavan. *Hawaii, 1959–1989: The First Thirty Years of the Aloha State with Memorable Photographs from the Honolulu Advertiser*. Honolulu: Mutual Publishing, 1990.

Daws, Gavan. *Shoal of Time: A History of the Hawaiian Islands*. New York: Macmillan, 1968.

Dean, Mitchell. *Governmentality: Power and Rule in Modern Society*. London: SAGE, 1999.

Deloria, Philip J. *Indians in Unexpected Places*. Lawrence: University Press of Kansas, 2004.

Deloria, Philip J. *Playing Indian*. New Haven, CT: Yale University Press, 1998.

Deloria, Vine. *Custer Died for Your Sins: An Indian Manifesto*. New York: Macmillan, 1969.

Deloria, Vine, Jr. "The Trickster and the Messiah." In *Spirit and Reason: The Vine Deloria, Jr., Reader*, edited by Barbara Deloria, Kristen Foehner, and Sam Scinta, 17–31. Golden, CO: Fulcrum Publishing, 1999.

Devlin, John. "Toward a State Constitutional Analysis of Allocation of Powers: Legislators and Legislative Appointees Performing Administrative Functions." *Temple Law Review* 66 (1993): 1205–68.

Diaz, Vicente M. *Repositioning the Missionary: Rewriting the Histories of Colonialism, Native Catholicism, and Indigeneity in Guam*. Honolulu: University of Hawai'i Press, 2010.

Diaz, Vicente M. "Voyaging for Anti-Colonial Recovery: Austronesian Seafaring, Archipelagic Rethinking, and the Re-mapping of Indigeneity," *Pacific Asia Inquiry* 2, no. 1 (fall 2011): 21–32.

Douglass, Frederick. "Introduction." In *The Reason Why the Colored American Is Not in the World's Columbian Exposition*, edited by Frederick Douglass, Irvine Garland Penn, Ferdinand Lee Barnett, and Ida B. Wells, 7–16. Chicago: Privately published, 1893.

Douglass, Frederick, Irvine Garland Penn, Ferdinand Lee Barnett, and Ida B. Wells. *The Reason Why the Colored American Is Not in the World's Columbian Exposition*. Chicago: University of Illinois Press, 1999.

Dreyfus, Hubert L., Paul Rabinow, and Michel Foucault. *Michel Foucault: Beyond Structuralism and Hermeneutics*. 2nd ed. Chicago: University of Chicago Press, 1983.

Dudziak, Mary L. *Cold War Civil Rights: Race and the Image of American Democracy*. Princeton, NJ: Princeton University Press, 2000.

Dutton, Meiric K. *Hawaii's Great Seal and Coat of Arms*. Honolulu: Loomis House Press, 1960.

Duus, Masayo. *The Japanese Conspiracy: The Oahu Sugar Strike of 1920*. Berkeley: University of California Press, 1999.

Duus, Masayo. *Unlikely Liberators: The Men of the 100th and 442nd*. Honolulu: University of Hawai'i Press, 1987.

Elkins, Caroline, and Susan Pedersen. "Introduction." In *Settler Colonialism in the Twentieth Century: Projects, Practices, Legacies*, edited by Caroline Elkins and Susan Pedersen, 1–20. New York: Routledge, 2005.

Fanon, Frantz. *The Wretched of the Earth*. New York: Grove Press, [1963] 1965.

Farrel, Andrew. "Preface." In Lorrin A. Thurston, *Writings of Lorrin A. Thurston*, edited by Andrew Farrel. Honolulu: Advertising Publishing Co., 1936.

Federici, Silvia. *Caliban and the Witch: Women, the Body and Primitive Accumulation*. New York: Autonomedia, 2004.

Felipe, Virgilio Menor. *Hawai'i, a Pilipino Dream*. Honolulu: Mutual Publishing, 2002.

Ferguson, Kathy E., and Phyllis Turnbull. *Oh, Say, Can You See?: The Semiotics of the Military in Hawai'i*. Vol. 10. Minneapolis: University of Minnesota Press, 1999.

Fisher, James T. "'A World Made Safe for Diversity': The Vietnam Lobby and the Politics of Pluralism, 1945–1963." In *Cold War Constructions: The Political Culture of United States Imperialism, 1945–1966*, edited by Christian G. Appy, 217–37. Amherst: University of Massachusetts, 2000.

Fletcher, Matthew L. M. "Avoiding Removal: The Pokagon Band of Potawatomi Indians." In *Nation to Nation: Treaties between the United States and American Indian Nations*, edited by Suzan Shown Harjo, 86–87. Washington, DC: Smithsonian Books, 2014.

Foucault, Michel. *The Archaeology of Knowledge*. New York: Harper and Row, 1976.

Foucault, Michel. *The Courage of Truth: The Government of Self and Others II*. New York: Palgrave Macmillan, 2011.

Foucault, Michel. "Politics and the Study of Discourse." In *The Foucault Effect: Studies in Governmentality*, edited by Graham Burchell, Colin Gordon, and Peter Miller, 59–60. Chicago: University of Chicago Press, 1991.

Foucault, Michel. *Security, Territory, Population: Lectures at the Collège de France, 1977–78*. New York: Palgrave Macmillan, 2007.

Foucault, Michel, and Colin Gordon. *Power/Knowledge: Selected Interviews and Other Writings, 1972–1977*. Brighton, UK: Harvester Press, 1980.

Foucault, Michel, et al. *The Foucault Effect: Studies in Governmentality with Two Lectures by and an Interview with Michel Foucault*. London: Harvester Wheatsheaf, 1991.

Foucault, Michel, et al. *"Society Must Be Defended": Lectures at the Collège de France, 1975–76*. New York: Picador, 2003.

Fuchs, Lawrence H. *Hawaii Pono: A Social History*. New York: Harcourt, Brace and World, 1961.

Fujikane, Candace. "Asian American Critique and Moana Nui 2011: Securing a Future beyond Empires, Militarized Capitalism and APEC." *Inter-Asia Cultural Studies* 13, no. 2 (March 2012): 1–22.

Fujikane, Candace. "Cartography and Mo'o'āina as Method at the Intersection of Indigenous and Settler Colonial Studies." Paper presented at the American Studies Association Conference, Denver, CO, November 17–20, 2016.

Fujikane, Candace. "Foregrounding Native Nationalisms: A Critique of Anti-nationalist Sentiment in Asian American Studies." In *Asian American Studies after Critical Mass*, edited by Kent A. Ono, 73–96. Malden, MA: Blackwell, 2005.

Fujikane, Candace. "Introduction: Asian Settler Colonialism in the U.S. Colony of Hawai'i." In *Asian Settler Colonialism: From Local Governance to the Habits of Everyday Life in Hawai'i*, edited by Candace Fujikane and Jonathan Y. Okamura, 1–42. Honolulu: University of Hawai'i Press, 2008.

Fujikane, Candace. "Mapping Wonder in the Māui Moʻolelo on the Moʻoʻāina: Growing Aloha ʻĀina through Indigenous and Settler Affinity Activism." *Marvels and Tales* 30, no. 1 (2016): 45–69.

Fujikane, Candace, and Jonathan Y. Okamura. *Asian Settler Colonialism: From Local Governance to the Habits of Everyday Life in Hawaiʻi.* Honolulu: University of Hawaiʻi Press, 2008.

Fujitani, Takashi. "Go for Broke, the Movie: Japanese American Soldiers in U.S. National, Military, and Racial Discourses." In *Perilous Memories: The Asia-Pacific War(s)*, edited by Takashi Fujitani, Geoffrey M. White, and Lisa Yoneyama, 239–66. Durham, NC: Duke University Press, 2001.

Fujitani, Takashi, Geoffrey M. White, and Lisa Yoneyama. *Perilous Memories: The Asia-Pacific War(s).* Durham, NC: Duke University Press, 2001.

Gilmore, Ruth Wilson. *Golden Gulag: Prisons, Surplus, Crisis, and Opposition in Globalizing California.* Berkeley: University of California Press, 2007.

Goeman, Mishuana. *Mark My Words: Native Women Mapping Our Nations.* Minneapolis: University of Minnesota Press, 2013.

Goldsby, Jacqueline. *A Spectacular Secret: Lynching in American Life and Literature.* Chicago: University of Chicago Press, 2006.

Gonzalez, Vernadette Vicuna. *Securing Paradise: Tourism and Militarism in Hawaiʻi and the Philippines.* Durham, NC: Duke University Press, 2013.

Goodspeed, Thomas Wakefield. *A History of the University of Chicago, Founded by John D. Rockefeller: The First Quarter-Century.* Chicago: University of Chicago Press, 1916.

Goodyear-Kaʻōpua, Noelani. "Introduction." In *A Nation Rising: Hawaiian Movements for Life, Land, and Sovereignty*, edited by Noelani Goodyear-Kaʻōpua, Ikaika Hussey, and Erin Kahunawaikaʻala Wright, 1–33. Durham, NC: Duke University Press, 2014.

Goodyear-Kaʻōpua, Noelani. "Kuleana Lāhui: Collective Responsibility for Hawaiian Nationhood in Activists' Praxis." *Affinities: A Journal of Radical Theory, Culture and Action* (July 2009): 1–28.

Goodyear-Kaʻōpua, Noelani. "Protectors of the Future, Not Protestors of the Past: Indigenous Pacific Activism and Mauna a Wākea." *South Atlantic Quarterly* 116, no. 1 (January 2017): 184–94.

Goodyear-Kaʻōpua, Noelani. *The Seeds We Planted: Portraits of a Native Hawaiian Charter School.* Minneapolis: University of Minnesota Press, 2013.

Goodyear-Kaʻōpua, Noelani, Kenneth Gofigan Kuper, and Joakim "Joejo" Peter. "Together We Are Stronger: Hawaiian and Micronesian Solidarity for Climate Justice." Forthcoming.

Gordon, Avery. *Ghostly Matters: Haunting and the Sociological Imagination.* Minneapolis: University of Minnesota Press, 1997.

Greevy, Ed, and Haunani-Kay Trask. *Kuʻe Thirty Years of Land Struggles in Hawaii.* Honolulu: Mutual Publishing, 2004.

Halberstam, Judith [Jack]. *The Queer Art of Failure*. Durham, NC: Duke University Press, 2011.

Hall, Stuart. "Gramsci's Relevance for the Study of Race and Ethnicity." *Journal of Communication Inquiry* 10, no. 2 (1986): 5–27.

Hall, Stuart. "On Postmodernism and Articulation: An Interview with Stuart Hall." *Journal of Communication Inquiry* 10, no. 2 (1986): 45–60.

Hall, Stuart. "The Toad in the Garden: Thatcherism among the Theorists." In *Marxism and the Interpretation of Culture*, edited by Cary Nelson and Lawrence Grossberg, 35–73. Chicago: University of Illinois Press, 1988.

Hall, Stuart, David Morley, and Kuan-Hsing Chen. *Stuart Hall: Critical Dialogues in Cultural Studies*. London: Routledge, 1996.

Halpern, Richard. *The Poetics of Primitive Accumulation: English Renaissance Culture and the Genealogy of Capital*. Ithaca, NY: Cornell University Press, 1991.

Handy, E. S. Craighill, and Elizabeth Green Handy. *Native Planters in Old Hawaii: Their Life, Lore, and Environment*. Honolulu: Bishop Museum Press, 1972.

Haney-López, Ian. *White by Law: The Legal Construction of Race*. New York: New York University Press, 2006.

Hannah, Matthew G. *Governmentality and the Mastery of Territory in Nineteenth-Century America*. Vol. 32. Cambridge: Cambridge University Press, 2000.

Harjo, Suzan Shown. "American Indian Land and American Empire: An Interview with Philip J. Deloria." In *Nation to Nation: Treaties between the United States and American Indian Nations*, edited by Suzan Shown Harjo, 12–13. New York: National Museum of the American Indian, 2014.

Hartman, Saidiya V. *Scenes of Subjection: Terror, Slavery, and Self-Making in Nineteenth-Century America*. New York: Oxford University Press, 1997.

Harvey, David. Interview by Neil Smith. "Reading Marx's *Capital* Vol 1—Chapters 26–33." 2012. Podcast audio. http://davidharvey.org/2008/09/capital -class-12/.

Harvey, David. *The New Imperialism*. Oxford: Oxford University Press, 2003.

Hawaiian Bureau of Information. *Hawaii: The Paradise and Inferno of the Pacific*. Honolulu: Hawaiian Bureau of Information, 1892.

Hawaii Statehood Commission, *Hawaii and Statehood*. Honolulu: Hawaii Statehood Commission, 1951.

Hawaii Statehood Commission. *Hawaii, U.S.A., and Statehood: History, Premises and Essential Facts of the Statehood Movement*. Honolulu: Hawaii Statehood Commission, 1948.

Hegel, Georg Wilhelm Friedrich. *Elements of the Philosophy of Right*, edited by Allen W. Wood. Cambridge: Cambridge University Press, 1991.

Holmes, T. Michael. *The Specter of Communism in Hawaii*. Honolulu: University of Hawai'i Press, 1994.

ho'omanawanui, ku'ualoha. "Mana Wahine: Feminism and Nationalism in Hawaiian Literature." *Anglistica* 14, no. 2 (2010): 27–43.

hoʻomanawanui, kuʻualoha. *Voices of Fire: Reweaving the Literary Lei of Pele and Hiʻiaka*. Minneapolis: University of Minnesota Press, 2014.

Hooper, Paul F. *Elusive Destiny: The Internationalist Movement in Modern Hawaii*. Honolulu: University Press of Hawaiʻi, 1980.

Hubbard, Tasha. "Buffalo Genocide in Nineteenth-Century North America: 'Kill, Skin, and Sell.'" In *Colonial Genocide in Indigenous North America*, edited by Alexander Laban Hinton, Andrew Woolford, and Jeff Benvenuto, 292–305. Durham, NC: Duke University Press, 2014.

Hyde, Lewis. *Trickster Makes This World: Mischief, Myth and Art*. New York: Farrar, Straus and Giroux, 1998.

Ignacio, Abe. *The Forbidden Book: The Philippine-American War in Political Cartoons*. San Francisco: T'Boli, 2004.

Ileto, Reynaldo Clemeña. *Filipinos and Their Revolution: Event, Discourse, and Historiography*. Quezon City: Ateneo de Manila University Press, 1998.

Imada, Adria L. *Aloha America: Hula Circuits through the U.S. Empire*. Durham, NC: Duke University Press, 2012.

Incite! Women of Color against Violence. *Color of Violence: The INCITE! Anthology*. Boston: South End Press, 2006.

Isaki, Bianca. "HB 645, Settler Sexuality, and the Politics of Local Asian Domesticity in Hawaiʻi." *Settler Colonial Studies* 1, no. 2 (2011): 82–102.

Izuka, Ichiro. *The Truth about Communism in Hawaii*. Honolulu: I. Izuka, 1947.

Jaggar, Thomas. *Volcanoes Declare War: Logistics and Strategy of Pacific Volcano Science*. Honolulu: Paradise of the Pacific, 1945.

Jennings, Francis. *The Invasion of America: Indians, Colonialism, and the Cant of Conquest*. Chapel Hill: University of North Carolina Press, 1975.

Jividen, Doris. *Sammy Amalu: Prince, Pauper or Phony?*. Honolulu: Erin Enterprises, 1972.

Johnson, Chalmers. *The Sorrows of Empire: Militarism, Secrecy, and the End of the Republic*. New York: Metropolitan Books, 2005.

Johnston, Anna, and Alan Lawson. "Settler Colonies." In *A Companion to Postcolonial Studies*, edited by Henry Schwarz and Sangeeta Ray, 360–76. Malden, MA: Blackwell, 2005.

Jung, Moon-Kie. *Reworking Race: The Making of Hawaii's Interracial Labor Movement*. New York: Columbia University Press, 2006.

Kafer, Alison. *Feminist, Queer, Crip*. Bloomington: Indiana University Press, 2013.

Kamakau, Samuel. *Hawaiian Annual*. Honolulu: Thomas G. Thrum, 1932.

Kameʻeleihiwa, Lilikalā. *Kamapuaa: The Hawaiian Pig God*. Honolulu: Bishop Museum Press, 1996.

Kaomea, Julie. "Indigenous Studies in the Elementary Curriculum: A Cautionary Hawaiian Example." *Anthropology and Education Quarterly* 36, no. 1 (2005): 24–42.

Kaplan, Amy. *The Anarchy of Empire in the Making of U.S. Culture*. Cambridge, MA: Harvard University Press, 2002.

Kaplan, Amy, and Donald E. Pease. *Cultures of United States Imperialism*. Durham, NC: Duke University Press, 1993.

Kauai, Willy Daniel Kaipo. "The Color of Nationality: Continuity and Discontinuities of Citizenship in Hawai'i." PhD diss., University of Hawai'i, 2014.

Kauanui, J. Kēhaulani. *Hawaiian Blood: Colonialism and the Politics of Sovereignty and Indigeneity*. Durham, NC: Duke University Press, 2008.

Kauanui, J. Kēhaulani. "Resisting the Akaka Bill." In *A Nation Rising: Hawaiian Movements for Life, Land, and Sovereignty*, edited by Noelani Goodyear-Ka'ōpua, Ikaika Hussey, and Erin Kahunawaika'ala Wright, 312–30. Durham, NC: Duke University Press, 2014.

Kauanui, J. Kēhaulani. "'A Structure, Not an Event': Settler Colonialism and Enduring Indigeneity," in "Forum: Emergent Critical Analytics for Alternative Humanities," special issue, *Lateral: Journal of the Cultural Studies Association* 5, no. 1 (spring 2016). Accessed March 18, 2018. http://www.doi.org/10.25158/L5.1.7.

Kazanjian, David. *The Colonizing Trick: National Culture and Imperial Citizenship in Early America*. Minneapolis: University of Minnesota Press, 2003.

Kelly, Anne Keala, dir. *Noho Hewa: The Wrongful Occupation of Hawai'i*. Honolulu: Kuleana Works, 2009. DVD.

Kelly, Marion. "Testimony at the Hearing on the Name Change for the Social Science Building," *Social Process in Hawai'i* 39 (1999): 307–13.

Kennedy, John F. *A Nation of Immigrants*. New York: Harper Perennial, 2008.

Kent, Noel J. *Hawaii: Islands under the Influence*. Honolulu: University of Hawai'i Press, 1993.

Kim, Jodi. *Ends of Empire: Asian American Critique and the Cold War*. Minneapolis: University of Minnesota Press, 2010.

King, Samuel P., and Randall W. Roth. *Broken Trust: Greed, Mismanagement and Political Manipulation at America's Largest Charitable Trust*. Honolulu: University of Hawai'i Press, 2006.

Kinzer, Stephen. *Overthrow: America's Century of Regime Change from Hawaii to Iraq*. New York: Henry Holt, 2006.

Kirshenblatt-Gimblett, Barbara. *Destination Culture: Tourism, Museums, and Heritage*. Los Angeles: University of California Press, 1998.

Klein, Christina. *Cold War Orientalism: Asia in the Middlebrow Imagination, 1945–1961*. Los Angeles: University of California Press, 2003.

Klein, Kerwin Lee. *Frontiers of Historical Imagination: Narrating the European Conquest of Native America, 1890–1990*. Berkeley: University of California Press, 1997.

Klein, Naomi. *This Changes Everything: Capitalism vs. the Climate*. New York: Simon and Schuster, 2014.

Koeppel, Dan. *Banana: The Fate of the Fruit That Changed the World*. New York: Hudson Street Press, 2008.

Kosasa, Eiko. "Ideological Images: U.S. Nationalism in Japanese Settler Photographs." In *Asian Settler Colonialism: From Local Governance to the Habits of Everyday Life in Hawai'i*, edited by Candace Fujikane and Jonathan Okamura, 209–32. Honolulu: University of Hawai'i Press, 2008.

Kosasa, Karen K. "Searching for the 'C' Word: Museums, Art Galleries, and Settler Colonialism in Hawai'i." In *Studies in Settler Colonialism: Politics, Identity and Culture*, edited by Fiona Bateman and Lionel Pilkington, 153–68. New York: Palgrave Macmillan, 2011.

Kotani, Roland. *The Japanese in Hawaii: A Century of Struggle*. Honolulu: Hawaii Hochi, 1985.

Krauss, Bob. *Johnny Wilson: First Hawaiian Democrat*. Honolulu: University of Hawai'i Press, 1994.

Krugman, Paul. *The Return of Depression Economics and the Crisis of 2008*. New York: W. W. Norton, 2008.

Kuykendall, Ralph S. *The Hawaiian Kingdom, Volume III: The Kalakaua Dynasty, 1874–1893*. Honolulu: University of Hawai'i Press, 1967.

Kuykendall, Ralph S., and A. Grove Day. *Hawaii: A History from Polynesian Kingdom to American Statehood*. Englewood Cliffs, NJ: Prentice-Hall, 1961.

Labrador, Roderick N. *Building Filipino Hawai'i*. Chicago: University of Illinois Press, 2015.

La Croix, Sumner J. "The Economic History of Hawai'i: A Short Introduction." Working paper, Department of Economics, University of Hawai'i, East-West Center, January 9, 2002.

LaDuke, Winona, and Sean Aaron Cruz. *The Militarization of Indian Country*. East Lansing, MI: Makwa Enewed, 2012.

LaFeber, Walter. *The New Empire: An Interpretation of American Expansion, 1860–1898*. 35th anniversary ed. Ithaca, NY: Cornell University Press, [1963] 1998.

Lâm, Maivân. *At the Edge of the State: Indigenous Peoples and Self-Determination*. Ardsley, NY: Transnational Publishers, 2000.

Leary, John Patrick. *A Cultural History of Underdevelopment: Latin America in the U.S. Imagination*. Charlottesville: University of Virginia Press, 2016.

Lehleitner, George. "An Address by George H. Lehleitner, a Private Citizen of New Orleans, Louisiana, Delivered to the Delegates of the Alaska Constitutional Convention." University of Alaska, January 23, 1956.

Lehleitner, George. Interview by Chris Conybeare and Warren Nishimoto. "A Statehood Hero." March 5, 1984. Folder 3, Proceedings and Debates of the 85th Congress Second Session Volume 104, Part 7, May 12, 1958, to May 18, 1958, New Orleans Historical Society.

Lehleitner, George. *The Tennessee Plan: How the Bold Became States* (pamphlet). Papers of George H. Lehleitner, New Orleans Historical Society.

Lidchi, Henrietta. "The Poetics and the Politics of Exhibiting Other Cultures." In *Representation: Cultural Representations and Signifying Practices*, edited by Stuart Hall. Thousand Oaks, CA: SAGE, 1997.

Liliʻuokalani. *Hawaii's Story by Hawaii's Queen*. Honolulu: Mutual Publishing, 1990.

Lind, Andrew William. *Hawaii's People*. 4th ed. Honolulu: University Press of Hawaiʻi, 1980.

Lindsay, Brendan C. *Murder State: California's Native American Genocide, 1846–1873*. Lincoln: University of Nebraska Press, 2012.

Linebaugh, Peter. *The Magna Carta Manifesto: Liberties and Commons for All*. Los Angeles: University of California Press, 2008.

Linn, Brian McAllister. *Guardians of Empire: The U.S. Army and the Pacific, 1902–1940*. Chapel Hill: University of North Carolina Press, 1997.

Low, John N. *Imprints: The Pokagon Band of Potawatomi Indians and the City of Chicago*. East Lansing: Michigan State University Press, 2016.

Luxemburg, Rosa. *The Accumulation of Capital*. Translated by Agnes Schwarzschild. New York: Routledge, 2003.

Lyons, Laura E. "Dole, Hawaiʻi, and the Question of Land under Globalization." In *Cultural Critique and the Global Corporation*, edited by Purnima Bose and Laura E. Lyons, 64–101. Indianapolis: Indiana University Press, 2010.

Lyons, Laura E. "From the Indigenous to the Indigent: Homelessness and Settler Colonialism in Hawaiʻi." In *Studies in Settler Colonialism: Politics, Identity and Culture*, edited by Fiona Bateman and Lionel Pilkington, 140–52. New York: Palgrave Macmillan, 2011.

Manganaro, Christine. "Assimilating Hawaiʻi: Racial Science in a Colonial 'Laboratory,' 1919–1939." PhD diss., University of Minnesota, 2012.

Martinez, Miguel Alfonso. *Study on Treaties, Agreements and Other Constructive Arrangements between Indigenous Peoples and Nation States*. Working Group on Indigenous Peoples, July 1997.

Marx, Karl. *Capital: A Critique of Political Economy*, vol. 1, translated by Ben Fowkes and David Fernbach. Harmondsworth, UK: Penguin, 1976.

McClintock, Anne. *Imperial Leather: Race, Gender and Sexuality in the Colonial Conquest*. New York: Routledge, 1995.

McDougal, Brandy Nālani. *Finding Meaning: Kaona and Contemporary Hawaiian Literature*. Tucson: University of Arizona Press, 2016.

McElrath, Robert. Interview. June 1986. Transcript. "Perspectives on Hawaiʻi's Statehood" Oral History Project. Social Science Research Institute, University of Hawaiʻi at Mānoa.

McGregor, Davianna. *Nā Kuaʻāina: Living Hawaiian Culture*. Honolulu: University of Hawaiʻi Press, 2007.

McKee, Ruth Eleanor. *After a Hundred Years*. Garden City, NY: Doubleday, Doran and Co., 1935.

Medak-Saltzman, Danika. "Transnational Indigenous Exchange: Rethinking Global Interactions of Indigenous Peoples at the 1904 St. Louis Exposition." *American Quarterly* 62, no. 3, (September 2010): 591–615.

Mehta, Uday Singh. *Liberalism and Empire: A Study in Nineteenth-Century British Liberal Thought*. Chicago: University of Chicago Press, 1999.

Melamed, Jodi. "The Spirit of Neoliberalism: From Racial Liberalism to Neoliberal Multiculturalism." *Social Text* 24, no. 4 (89) (winter 2006): 1–24.

Mellen, Kathleen Dickenson. *The Gods Depart: A Saga of the Hawaiian Kingdom, 1832–1873*. New York: Hastings House, 1956.

Mellen, Kathleen Dickenson. *Hawaiian Heritage: A Brief Illustrated History*. New York: Hastings House, 1963.

Mellen, Kathleen Dickenson. *Hawaiian Majesty*. New York: Andrew Melrose Limited, 1954.

Mellen, Kathleen Dickenson. *Hawaiian Scrapbook*. Honolulu: Paradise of the Pacific, 1945.

Mellen, Kathleen Dickenson. *In a Hawaiian Valley*. New York: Hastings House, 1947.

Mellen, Kathleen Dickenson. *An Island Kingdom Passes: Hawaii Becomes American*. New York: Hastings House, 1958.

Mellen, Kathleen Dickenson. *The Lonely Warrior: Kamehameha the Great of Hawaii*. New York: Hastings House, 1949.

Mellen, Kathleen Dickenson. *The Magnificent Matriarch: Kaahumani Queen of Hawaii*. New York: Hastings House, 1952.

Merry, Sally Engle. *Colonizing Hawai'i: The Cultural Power of Law*. Princeton, NJ: Princeton University Press, 2000.

Merry, Sally Engle, and Donald Lawrence Brenneis. *Law and Empire in the Pacific: Fiji and Hawaii*. Santa Fe, NM: School of American Research Press, [2003] 2004.

Michener, James A. *Hawaii*. New York: Random House, 1959.

Moreton-Robinson, Aileen. *The White Possessive: Property, Power, and Indigenous Sovereignty*. Minneapolis: University of Minnesota Press, 2015.

Nashel, Jonathan. "The Road to Vietnam: Modernization Theory in Fact and Fiction." In *Cold War Constructions: The Political Culture of United States Imperialism, 1945–1966*, edited by Christian G. Appy, 132–154. Amherst: University of Massachusetts, 2000.

Neal, Robert. "Hawaii's Land and Labor Problem." *Current History* 13 (October 1920–March 1921): 389–97.

Nelson, Cary, and Lawrence Grossberg. *Marxism and the Interpretation of Culture*. Urbana: University of Illinois Press, 1988.

O'Brien, Tom Lawrence. *The Plot to Sovietize Hawaii*. Hilo: Hawaii News Printshop, 1948.

Odo, Franklin. *No Sword to Bury: Japanese Americans in Hawai'i during World War II*. Philadelphia: Temple University Press, 2004.

Okamura, Jonathan Y. *Ethnicity and Inequality in Hawai'i*. Philadelphia: Temple University Press, 2008.

Okamura, Jonathan Y. "The Illusion of Paradise: Privileging Multiculturalism in Hawai'i." In *Making Majorities: Constituting the Nation in Japan, Korea, China, Malaysia, Fiji, Turkey, and the United States*, edited by Dru C. Gladney, 264–84. Stanford, CA: Stanford University Press, 1998.

Okihiro, Gary Y. *Cane Fires: The Anti-Japanese Movement in Hawaii, 1865–1945*. Philadelphia: Temple University Press, 1991.

Omi, Michael, and Howard Winant. *Racial Formation in the United States: From the 1960s to the 1980s*. New York: Routledge and Kegan Paul, 1986.

Onishi, Yuichiro. "Occupied Okinawa on the Edge: On Being Okinawan in Hawai'i and U.S. Colonialism toward Okinawa." *American Quarterly* 64, no. 4 (2012): 741–65.

Ontal, Rene G. "Fagen and Other Ghosts: African-Americans and the Philippine-American War." In *Vestiges of War: The Philippine-American War and the Aftermath of an Imperial Dream, 1899–1999*, edited by Angel Velasco Shaw and Luis H. Francia, 118–33. New York: New York University Press, 2002.

Ortner, Sherry B. *Culture/Power/History: Series Prospectus*. Ann Arbor: University of Michigan, 1989.

Osorio, Jonathan Kay Kamakawiwo'ole. *Dismembering Lāhui: A History of the Hawaiian Nation to 1887*. Honolulu: University of Hawai'i Press, 2002.

Ostler, Jeffrey. *The Plains Sioux and U.S. Colonialism from Lewis and Clark to Wounded Knee*. Cambridge: Cambridge University Press, 2004.

Paquette, Gabriel. "Colonies and Empire in the Political Thought of Hegel and Marx." In *Empire and Modern Political Thought*, edited by Sankar Muthu, 292–323. New York: Cambridge University Press, 2014.

Park, Robert Ezra. "Our Racial Frontier on the Pacific." *Survey Graphic* 56 (May 1926): 192–96.

Park, Robert Ezra. *Society: Collective Behavior, News and Opinion, Sociology and Modern Society*. Vol. 3. Glencoe, IL: Free Press, 1955.

Park, Robert Ezra, and Ralph H. Turner. *On Social Control and Collective Behavior*. Chicago: University of Chicago Press, 1967.

Parnaby, Lauren. "The Possessive Investment in Haoleness: The Performances of Haole on the University of Hawai'i, Mānoa and the Administration's Relationship with Haole Students as a Colonial University." Undergraduate honor's thesis, Department of Social and Cultural Analysis, New York University, 2016.

Peck, Jamie. *Constructions of Neoliberal Reason*. Oxford: Oxford University Press, 2010.

Pellegrino, Victor C. *Uncle Kawaiola's Dream*. Wailuku, HI: Maui arThoughts, 2010.

Perelman, Michael. *The Invention of Capitalism: Classical Political Economy and the Secret History of Primitive Accumulation*. Durham, NC: Duke University Press, 2000.

Poblete, Joanna. *Islanders in the Empire: Filipino and Puerto Rican Laborers in Hawai'i*. Urbana: University of Illinois Press, 2014.

Poiré, Napua Stevens. "Mellen, Kathleen Dickenson." In *Who's Who?*, edited by Nelson Prather, 65–66. Honolulu: University of Hawai'i, Office for Women's Research, 1994.

Porteus, Elizabeth Dole. *Let's Go Exploring: The Life of Stanley D. Porteus, Hawaii's Pioneer Psychologist*. Honolulu: Ku Pa'a, 1991.

Porteus, Stanley D. "Possible Effects of Rate of Global Spin." *Perceptual and Motor Skills* 30 (1966): 503–9.

Porteus, Stanley D. *Primitive Intelligence and Environment*. New York: Macmillan, 1937.

Porteus, Stanley D., and Marjorie E. Babcock. *Temperament and Race*. Boston: R. G. Badger, 1926.

Povinelli, Elizabeth A. *The Cunning of Recognition: Indigenous Alterities and the Making of Australian Multiculturalism*. Durham, NC: Duke University Press, 2002.

Pukui, Mary Kawena. Interview by Gabriel Kalama Pea, Andrew Poepoe, and E. Pea Nahale. Birch Street, 1959. Bishop Museum 1959.236 (Haw 40.3).

Rafael, Vicente L. *White Love and Other Events in Filipino History*. Durham, NC: Duke University Press, 2000.

Raibmon, Paige Sylvia. *Authentic Indians: Episodes of Encounter from the Late Nineteenth-Century Northwest Coast*. Durham, NC: Duke University Press, 2005.

Rakove, Jack N. "Ambiguous Achievement: The Northwest Ordinance." In *Northwest Ordinance: Essays on Its Formulation, Provisions and Legacy*. Ann Arbor: Michigan State University Press, 1989.

Ricoeur, Paul. *Memory, History, Forgetting*. Chicago: University of Chicago Press, 2004.

Robertson, Lindsay Gordon. *Conquest by Law: How the Discovery of America Dispossessed Indigenous Peoples of Their Lands*. Oxford: Oxford University Press, 2005.

Rodríguez, Dylan. "Inhabiting the Impasse: Racial/Racial-Colonial Power, Genocide Poetics, and the Logic of Evisceration." *Social Text* 33, no. 3 (124) (2015): 19–44.

Rodríguez, Dylan. *Suspended Apocalypse: White Supremacy, Genocide, and the Filipino Condition*. Minneapolis: University of Minnesota Press, 2009.

Rohrer, Judy. "Attacking Trust: Hawai'i as a Crossroads and Kamehameha Schools in the Crosshairs." *American Quarterly* (September 2010): 437–55.

Rohrer, Judy. *Staking Claim: Settler Colonialism and Racialization in Hawai'i*. Tucson: University of Arizona Press, 2016.

Roosevelt, Theodore. *The Winning of the West, Volume 2: From the Alleghenies to the Mississippi, 1777–1783*. Lincoln: University of Nebraska Press, 1995.

Rosa, John P. "Local Story: The Massie Case Narrative and the Cultural Production of Local Identity in Hawai'i." *Amerasia Journal* 26, no. 2 (2000): 93–115.

Rosa, John P. *Local Story: The Massie-Kahahawai Case and the Culture of History.* Honolulu: University of Hawai'i Press, 2014.

Russ, William Adam, Jr. *The Hawaiian Republic, 1894–98, and Its Struggle to Win Annexation.* Selinsgrove, PA: Susquehanna University Press, 1961.

Russ, William Adam, Jr. *The Hawaiian Revolution, 1893–94.* Selinsgrove, PA: Susquehanna University Press, 1992.

Rydell, Robert W. *All the World's a Fair: Visions of Empire at American International Expositions, 1876–1916.* Chicago: University of Chicago Press, 1984.

Sai, Keanu. "The American Occupation of the Hawaiian Kingdom: Beginning the Transition from Occupied to Restored State." PhD diss., University of Hawai'i, 2008.

Sai, Keanu. "A Slippery Path towards Hawaiian Indigeneity: An Analysis and Comparison between Hawaiian State Sovereignty and Hawaiian Indigeneity and Its Use and Practice in Hawai'i Today." *Journal of Law and Social Challenges* 10 (fall 2008): 101–66.

Said, Edward W. *Covering Islam: How the Media and the Experts Determine How We See the Rest of the World.* New York: Pantheon, 1981.

Said, Edward W. *Culture and Imperialism.* New York: Knopf, 1993.

Said, Edward W. *Orientalism.* 25th anniversary ed. New York: Vintage, [1994] 2003.

Said, Edward W. *The Question of Palestine.* New York: Vintage, 1979.

Salesa, Damon. "Samoa's Half-Castes and Some Frontiers of Comparison." In *Haunted by Empire: Geographies of Intimacy in North American History*, edited by Ann Laura Stoler, 71–93. Durham, NC: Duke University Press, 2006.

San Juan, E. *After Postcolonialism: Remapping Philippines–United States Confrontations.* Lanham, MD: Rowman and Littlefield Publishers, 2000.

Saranillio, Dean Itsuji. "Colliding Histories: Hawai'i Statehood at the Intersection of Asians 'Ineligible to Citizenship' and Hawaiians 'Unfit for Self-Government.'" *Journal of Asian American Studies* 13, no. 3 (October 2010): 283–309.

Saranillio, Dean Itsuji. "Kēwaikaliko's *Benocide*: Reversing the Imperial Gaze of *Rice v. Cayetano* and Its Legal Progeny." *American Quarterly* 62, no. 3 (September 2010): 457–76.

Scott, James C. *Domination and the Arts of Resistance: Hidden Transcripts.* New Haven, CT: Yale University Press, 1990.

Scott, James C. *Seeing like a State: How Certain Schemes to Improve the Human Condition Have Failed.* New Haven, CT: Yale University Press, 1998.

Senier, Siobhan, and Clare Barker, eds. *Journal of Literary and Cultural Disability Studies* 7, no. 2, special issue (2013).

Shigematsu, Setsu, and Keith L. Camacho. *Militarized Currents: Toward a Decolonized Future in Asia and the Pacific.* Minneapolis: University of Minnesota Press, 2010.

Shiva, Vandana. *Water Wars: Privatization, Pollution, and Profit*. Boston: South End Press, 2002.

Silva, Noenoe K. *Aloha Betrayed: Native Hawaiian Resistance to American Colonialism*. Durham, NC: Duke University Press, 2004.

Silva, Noenoe K. "Talking Back to Empire: Hula in Hawaiian-Language Literature in 1861." In *Law and Empire in the Pacific: Fiji and Hawai'i*, edited by Sally Engle Merry and Donald Brenneis, 101–22. Santa Fe, NM: School of American Research, 2003.

Silva, Noenoe K., and Jonathan Goldberg-Hiller. "Sharks and Pigs: Animating Hawaiian Sovereignty against the Anthropological Machine." *The South Atlantic Quarterly* 110, no. 2 (spring 2011): 429–46.

Simpson, Leanne Betasamosake. *Dancing on Our Turtle's Back: Stories of Nishnaabeg Re-creation, Resurgence and a New Emergence*. Winnipeg: Arbeiter Ring Publishing, 2011.

Simpson, Leanne Betasamosake. "Indigenous Resurgence and Co-resistance." *Critical Ethnic Studies* 2, no. 2 (fall 2016): 19–34.

Singh, Nikhil Pal. "Culture/Wars: Recoding Empire in an Age of Democracy." *American Quarterly* 50 (1998): 471–522.

Singh, Nikhil Pal. *Race and America's Long War*. Oakland: University of California Press, 2018.

Smith, Frank H. *Art, History, Midway Plaisance and World's Columbian Exposition*. Chicago: Foster Press, 1893.

Snelgrove, Corey, Rita Dhamoon, and Jeff Corntassel. "Unsettling Settler Colonialism: The Discourse and Politics of Settlers, and Solidarity with Indigenous Nations." *Decolonization: Indigeneity, Education and Society* 3, no. 2 (2014): 1–32.

Spade, Dean. *Normal Life: Administrative Violence, Critical Trans Politics, and the Limits of Law*. Brooklyn, NY: South End Press, 2011.

Spriggs, Matthew. "'Preceded by Forest': Changing Interpretations of Landscape Change on Kaho'olawe." *Asian Perspectives* 30, no. 1 (1991): 71–116.

Sproat, D. Kapu'ala. "Water." In *The Value of Hawai'i: Knowing the Past, Shaping the Future*, edited by Craig Howes and Jonathan Kamakawiwo'ole Osorio, 187–94. Honolulu: University of Hawai'i Press, 2010.

Spurr, David. *The Rhetoric of Empire: Colonial Discourse in Journalism, Travel Writing, and Imperial Administration*. Durham, NC: Duke University Press, 1993.

Stannard, David E. *American Holocaust: Columbus and the Conquest of the New World*. New York: Oxford University Press, 1992.

Stannard, David E. *Before the Horror: The Population of Hawai'i on the Eve of Western Contact*. Honolulu: Social Science Research Institute, University of Hawai'i, 1989.

Stannard, David E. "Honoring Racism: The Professional Life and Reputation of Stanley D. Porteus," *Social Process in Hawai'i* 39 (1999): 1–22.

Stannard, David E. *Honor Killing: How the Infamous "Massie Affair" Transformed Hawai'i.* New York: Viking, 2005.

"'Statehood for Hawaii,' Letter from the Chairman of the Joint Committee on Hawaii, Transmitting Pursuant to Senate Concurrent Resolution No. 18: A Report of an Investigation and Study of the Subject of Statehood and Other Subjects Relating to the Welfare of the Territory of Hawaii, January 5, 1938." Washington, DC: U.S. Government Printing Office, 1938.

Stoler, Ann Laura. "Affective States." In *A Companion to Anthropology of Politics*, edited by David Nugent and Joan Vincent, 4–20. Malden, MA: Blackwell, 2004.

Sturken, Marita, and Lisa Cartwright. *Practices of Looking: An Introduction to Visual Culture.* Oxford: Oxford University Press, 2003.

Takabuki, Matsuo. *An Unlikely Revolutionary: Matsuo Takabuki and the Making of Modern Hawai'i: A Memoir.* Honolulu: University of Hawai'i Press, 1998.

Takaki, Ronald T. *Pau Hana: Plantation Life and Labor in Hawaii, 1835–1920.* Honolulu: University of Hawai'i Press, 1983.

Takaki, Ronald T. *Strangers from a Different Shore: A History of Asian Americans.* New York: Back Bay Books, 1998.

Teaiwa, Teresia. "The Ancestors We Get to Choose: White Influences I Won't Deny." In *Theorizing Native Studies*, edited by Audra Simpson and Andrea Smith, 43–55. Durham, NC: Duke University Press, 2014.

Tengan, Ty Kāwika. *Native Men Remade: Gender and Nation in Contemporary Hawai'i.* Durham, NC: Duke University Press, 2008.

Tengan, Ty Kāwika, J. L. A. Perry, and N. Armstrong. *Report on the Archival, Historical and Archaeological Resources of Nā Wai 'Ehā, Wailuku District, Island of Maui.* Honolulu: Office of Hawaiian Affairs, 2007.

Teves, Stephanie Nohelani. "Aloha State Apparatuses." *American Quarterly* 67, no. 3 (fall 2015): 705–26.

Teves, Stephanie Nohelani. *Defiant Indigeneity: The Politics of Hawaiian Performance.* Chapel Hill: University of North Carolina Press, 2018.

Teves, Stephanie Nohelani. "We're All Hawaiian Now: Kanaka Maoli Performance and the Politics of Aloha." PhD diss., University of Michigan. Ann Arbor, MI: ProQuest/UMI, 2012.

Thurston, Lorrin A. *A Hand-book on the Annexation of Hawaii.* St. Joseph, MI: A. B. Morse Company, 1897.

Thurston, Lorrin A. *Writings of Lorrin A. Thurston.* Honolulu: Advertising Publishing Co., 1936.

Thurston, Lucy G. *Life and Times of Mrs. Lucy G. Thurston, Wife of Rev. Asa Thurston, Pioneer Missionary to the Sandwich Islands, Gathered from Letters and Journals Extending Over a Period of More than Fifty Years Selected and Arranged by Herself.* Ann Arbor, MI: S. C. Andrews, 1882.

Torgovnick, Marianna. *Gone Primitive: Savage Intellects, Modern Lives.* Chicago: University of Chicago Press, 1990.

Trask, Haunani-Kay. "The Color of Violence." In *Color of Violence: The INCITE! Anthology*. Boston: South End Press, 2006.

Trask, Haunani-Kay. *From a Native Daughter: Colonialism and Sovereignty in Hawai'i*. Rev. ed. Honolulu: University of Hawai'i Press, 1999.

Trask, Haunani-Kay. "Settlers of Color and 'Immigrant' Hegemony: 'Locals' in Hawai'i." In *Asian Settler Colonialism: From Local Governance to the Habits of Everyday Life in Hawai'i*, edited by Candace Fujikane and Jonathan Okamura, 45–65. Honolulu: University of Hawai'i Press, 2008.

Trask, Haunani-Kay. "Writing in Captivity: Poetry in a Time of De-colonization." In "Navigating Islands and Continents: Conversations and Contestations in and around the Pacific," edited by Cynthia Franklin, Ruth Hsu, and Suzanne Kosanke, special issue, *Literary Studies East and West* 17. Honolulu: University of Hawai'i, 2000.

Trask, Mililani. "Hawai'i and the United Nations." In *Asian Settler Colonialism in Hawai'i: From Local Governance to the Habits of Everyday Life in Hawai'i*, edited by Candace Fujikane and Jonathan Okamura, 67–70. Honolulu: University of Hawai'i Press, 2008.

Trouillot, Michel-Rolph. *Silencing the Past: Power and the Production of History*. Boston: Beacon Press, 1995.

Tuck, Eve, and Rubén A. Gaztambide-Fernández. "Curriculum, Replacement, and Settler Futurity." *Journal of Curriculum Theorizing* 29, no. 1 (2013): 72–89.

Tuck, Eve, and Wayne Yang. "Decolonization Is Not a Metaphor." *Decolonization: Indigeneity, Education and Society* 1, no. 1 (2012): 1–40.

Turner, Frederick Jackson. "The Significance of the Frontier in American History." Paper presented at the American Historical Association, Chicago, July 12, 1893.

Tuttle, Daniel W., Jr. "George Chaplin: Journalist and Community Leader." In George Chaplin, *Presstime in Paradise*, ix–x. Honolulu: University of Hawai'i Press, 1998.

Tye, Larry. *The Father of Spin: Edward L. Bernays and the Birth of Public Relations*. New York: Henry Holt, 1998.

University of Hawai'i at Hilo. "Final Environmental Impact Statement: Thirty Meter Telescope Project." Hilo, Hawai'i, May 8, 2010.

U.S. Congress, Joint Committee on Hawaii. *Statehood for Hawaii: Hearings before the United States Joint Committee on Hawaii, Seventy Fifth Congress, Second Session, on Oct. 6, 8, 9, 12, 13, 15, 17–22*. Washington, DC: U.S. Congress, 1937.

Van Dyke, Jon M. *Who Owns the Crown Lands of Hawaii?*. Honolulu: University of Hawai'i Press, 2008.

Vimalassery, Manu. "Fugitive Decolonization." *Theory and Event* 19, no. 4 (2016). Accessed March 13, 2018. https://muse.jhu.edu/article/633284.

Vimalassery, Manu. "The Wealth of Natives: Towards a Critique of Settler-Colonial Political Economy." In *The Settler Complex: Recuperating Binarism in*

Colonial Studies, edited by Patrick Wolfe, 173–92. Los Angeles: UCLA American Indian Studies Center, 2016.

Vimalassery, Manu, Juliana Hu Pegues, and Alyosha Goldstein. "On Colonial Unknowing." *Theory and Event* 19, no. 4 (2016): 1–13.

Vogeler, Kūhiō. "Outside Shangri La: Colonization and the U.S. Occupation of Hawai'i." In *A Nation Rising: Hawaiian Movements for Life, Land, and Sovereignty*, edited by Noelani Goodyear-Ka'ōpua, Ikaika Hussey, and Erin Kahunawaika'ala Wright, 252–66. Durham, NC: Duke University Press, 2014.

Von Eschen, Penny M. *Rage against Empire: Black Americans and Anticolonialism, 1937–1957*. Ithaca, NY: Cornell University Press, 1997.

Von Eschen, Penny M. *Satchmo Blows Up the World: Jazz Ambassadors Play the Cold War*. Cambridge, MA: Harvard University Press, 2004.

Vowell, Sarah. *Unfamiliar Fishes*. New York: Riverhead Books, 2011.

Wakefield, Edward Gibbon. *England and America: A Comparison of the Social and Political State of Both Nations*. London: W. Nicol, 1833.

Wakefield, Edward Gibbon. *A Letter from Sydney: The Principal Town of Australasia, Together with the Outline of a System of Colonization*. London: Joseph Cross, 1829.

Wakefield, Edward Gibbon. *A View of the Art of Colonization: In Letters between a Statesman and a Colonist*. Oxford: Clarendon Press, 1849.

Walden, Andrew. "Hawaii Statehood Day 2006." *Hawaiian Sovereignty*. Accessed September 29, 2017. www.angelfire.com/planet/bigfiles40/statehoodday2006.html.

Washington, George. *The Writings of George Washington*, edited by John C. Fitzpatrick. Washington, DC: U.S. Government Printing Office, 1931.

wa Thiong'o, Ngũgĩ. *Decolonising the Mind: The Politics of Language in African Literature*. Portsmouth, NH: Heinemann, 1986.

Waziyatawin. *What Does Justice Look Like?: The Struggle for Liberation of Dakota Homeland*. St. Paul, MN: Living Justice Press, 2008.

Wells, Ida B. "Lynch Law." In *The Reason Why the Colored American Is Not in the World's Columbian Exposition*, edited by Frederick Douglass, Irvine Garland Penn, Ferdinand Lee Barnett, and Ida B. Wells, 29–43. Chicago: Privately published, 1893.

Westlake, Wayne Kaumualii. *Westlake: Poems by Wayne Kaumualii Westlake (1947–1984)*, edited by Mei-Li M. Siy and Richard Hamasaki. Honolulu: University of Hawai'i Press, 2009.

White, Hayden V. *The Content of the Form: Narrative Discourse and Historical Representation*. Baltimore: Johns Hopkins University Press, 1987.

Whitehead, John S. "The Anti-Statehood Movement and the Legacy of Alice Kamokila Campbell." *Hawaiian Journal of History* 27 (1993): 43–63.

Whitehead, John S. *Completing the Union: Alaska, Hawai'i, and the Battle for Statehood*. Albuquerque: University of New Mexico Press, 2004.

Wilcox, Carol. *Sugar Water: Hawaii's Plantation Ditches.* Honolulu: University of Hawai'i Press, 1996.

Williams, Raymond. *Marxism and Literature.* Oxford: Oxford University Press, 1977.

Williams, Robert A. *The American Indian in Western Legal Thought: The Discourses of Conquest.* New York: Oxford University Press, 1990.

Williams, William Appleman. *The Tragedy of American Diplomacy.* New York: W. W. Norton, [1959] 1972.

Wolfe, Patrick. "Nation and MiscegeNation: Discursive Continuity in the Post-Mabo Era." *Social Analysis* 36 (October 1994): 93–152.

Wolfe, Patrick. "Settler Colonialism and the Elimination of the Native." *Journal of Genocide Research* 8, no. 4 (2006): 387–409.

Wolfe, Patrick. *Settler Colonialism and the Transformation of Anthropology: The Politics and Poetics of an Ethnographic Event.* London: Cassell, 1999.

Wolfe, Patrick. *Traces of History: Elementary Structures of Race.* Brooklyn: Verso, 2016.

Worster, Donald. *Rivers of Empire: Water, Aridity, and the Growth of the American West.* New York: Oxford University Press, 1985.

Wright, James C. Interview by John Whitehead and George Lehleitner. March 15, 1988, Washington, DC. Transcript. Box 8, Folder 2, Papers of George H. Lehleitner, New Orleans Historical Society.

Yamashiro, Aiko. "Vigilant and Vulnerable Collaboration: Writing Decolonial Poetry in Hawai'i." Paper presented at the annual meeting of the Native American and Indigenous Studies Association, Mānoa, HI, May 18, 2016.

Yoshinaga, Ida. "Pacific (War) Time at Punchbowl: A Nebutsu for Unclaiming Nation." *Chain* 11 (summer 2004): 328–43.

Yu, Henry. *Thinking Orientals: Migration, Contact, and Exoticism in Modern America.* New York: Oxford University Press, 2001.

Zalburg, Sanford. *A Spark Is Struck!: Jack Hall and the ILWU in Hawaii.* Honolulu: University Press of Hawai'i, 1979.

Zibechi, Raúl. *Territories in Resistance: A Cartography of Latin American Social Movements.* Oakland, CA: AK Press, 2012.

Zinn, Howard. *The Twentieth Century: A People's History.* New York: Perennial, 1980.

INDEX

Laakapu (Hawaiian deity), 100

labor politics: communism and, 146–47; "Democratic Revolution" and, 113–14; Hawaiian activism and, 36–37, 222n85; Hawai'i Seven and, 146, 151–52; pineapple strike and, 207–8; place-based economics and, 207–9; race relations and, 76–85; statehood campaign and, 14–20, 26, 87, 135–36; sugar industry and, 37–38, 69–70, 146, 228n113; U.S. economic crises and, 33

Laenui, Poka, 2

LaFeber, Walter, 10, 33

Land and Power in Hawaii: The Democratic Years (Cooper and Daws), 177–81

land development and land seizure: Amalu hoax and, 163–69; Chicago-Pokagon land dispute, 49–50; immigration and, 116; Kepaniwai Heritage Gardens and, 172–81; resort development and, 177–81; sovereignty linked to, xviii–xix; statehood and development projects and, 114–15, 203–4; by sugar industry, 68–69, 174–75; white triangulation concerning, 79–80

land run reenactments, Native nations' opposition to, xi

Lane, William Carey, 154

Lane brothers, 154

Last Among Equals (Bell), 26–27

Lee, S. Heijin, xvi, 2

Lehleitner, George H., 27, 134, 140–45

Lewis, Hal, 164, 238n105

liberal multiculturalism: Cold War ideology and, 133–36, 202–3; imperialism and, 182–87; Kepaniwai Heritage Gardens as symbol of, 171–81; "racial melting pot" discourse and, 28; settler colonialism and, 176–87; white supremacy and, 13–21, 81–85, 136–40

Lili'uokalani (Queen): Cleveland's support for, 39–40; incarceration of, 1–2; kāhili staff of state of, 155–56; Kamokila's memories of, 99–100; Mel-

len's discussion of, 156–58; overthrow of, 31–32, 43, 58–61, 151–53; statehood campaign and, 92; Washington Place residence of, 153

Lincoln, Abraham, xi

Lingle, Linda, 3, 203

Lippmann, Walter, 131–32

local identity, race and, 75–76

Local Motion Hawai'i, xvii

Local Story: The Massie-Kahahawai Case and the Culture of History (Rosa), 75

lo'i kalo (wetland taro farms), 174–75, 191–92

The Lonely Warrior (Mellen), 156

Long, Russell, 145

Lono (Hawai'ian deity), xvii

Lord, Edward J., 73

Low, John, 49

Lowrey, Frederick J., 156

Luce, Henry, 110, 145

Lucky Strike Cigarettes, 132

Lumumba, Patrice, 202

lynch laws, 48–49

Mabini, Apolinario, 24

MacNaughton, Malcolm, 101–2, 142, 235n102

The Magnificent Matriarch (Mellen), 156–57

mana wahine (female empowerment), 58

Manganaro, Christine, 82, 84

"manufacture of consent," statehood campaign and, 131–32

Manzanar Relocation Center, 149

Mao Tse-tung, 149

Marcos, Imelda, 182

Martin, Henry K., 228n113

Martinez, Miguel, 5

Marumoto, Barbara, 1

Mason, Otis T., 43

Massacre at Wounded Knee (1890), 32, 66

Massie, Thalia, 72–76

Massie, Thomas, 73

Massie Case, 72–76, 90, 116

White City. *See* Columbian Exposition of 1893 (White City) (Chicago)

white supremacy: Columbian Exposition as expression of, 31–35, 46–52; economic crises and, 26; *Go for Broke!* (film) and, 109–15; liberal multiculturalism and, 13–21, 81–85, 136–40, 176–81; Orientalism and primitivism and, 40–52; statehood campaign and, 71–72, 133–36; triangulation and, 76–85. *See also* haole (white) settlers

Why We Left (Brooks), 47

Wilcox, Carol, 189

Wilcox, Robert W., 43, 64, 167

Willie Vocalite, 85–86

Willis, Albert, 151

Wilson, Jennie "Kini," 154

Wilson, John Nalani, 150, 154

Wilson, Marshall C. B., 150, 154

Wilson-Gorman Tariff, 40

The Winning of the West (Roosevelt), 34

The Wizard of Oz, 66

Wolfe, Patrick, 47

women in, in Kanaka Ōiwi culture, 58–60

world's fairs (1876–1916), 42–43

World War II: Japanese American heroism during, 105–15; Japanese attacks on Hawaii during, 186–87; Pearl Harbor attack and, 95; U.S. bombing of Japan during, 185

Worster, Donald, 188

Wright, George, 8, 85–88, 95

Wright, James, 144

Yang, Wayne, 17

Yellow Peril threat, Hawai'i and, 64–66

Young Buddhist Association, 177

Yu, Henry, 82–83

Zalburg, Sanford, 146